PRONOIA

Is the Antidote for Paranoia

PRONOIA

Is the Antidote for Paranoia

How the Whole World Is Conspiring
to Shower You with Blessings

REVISED AND EXPANDED

ROB BREZSNY

and the Beauty and Truth Laboratory

North Atlantic Books
BERKELEY, CALIFORNIA

Published by
North Atlantic Books
Berkeley, California

and

Televisionary Publishing
P.O. Box 4400
San Rafael, California 94913
www.beautyandtruth.com

Cover design by Catherine Campaigne
Printed in the United States of America

Pronoia Is the Antidote for Paranoia: How the Whole World Is Conspiring to Shower You with Blessings, Revised and Expanded is sponsored and published by the Society for the Study of Native Arts and Sciences (dba North Atlantic Books), an educational nonprofit based in Berkeley, California, that collaborates with partners to develop cross-cultural perspectives, nurture holistic views of art, science, the humanities, and healing, and seed personal and global transformation by publishing work on the relationship of body, spirit, and nature.

North Atlantic Books' publications are available through most bookstores. For further information, visit our website at www.northatlanticbooks.com or call 800-733-3000.

Library of Congress Cataloging-in-Publication Data
Brezsny, Rob.
    Pronoia is the antidote for paranoia : how the whole world is conspiring to
  shower you with blessings / Rob Brezsny. — Rev. and expanded.
        p. cm.
    Summary: "Revised and updated edition of this inspiring book presents the
  philosophy that the universe is fundamentally friendly and that life gives you exactly
  what you need, exactly when you need it and includes significant updates to the
  first edition" —Provided by publisher.
    ISBN 978-1-55643-818-9
    1. Optimism.   2. Conduct of life.   I. Title.
  BJ1477.b74 2009
  149'.5—dc22
                                                                            2009026166

7 8 9 10 Sheridan 20 19

Instructions

1.

Start at the beginning of this book and read it in a sequential fashion
straight through to the end;
OR
start in the middle of the book and read here and there,
trusting your instincts
to find exactly what you need,
exactly when you need it;
OR
go to the webpage tinyurl.com/lyr99n and tune in to podcasts of me
performing pieces from this book while you read along;
OR
when you feel the need for prophetic guidance, open the book at random
and regard the first thing you see as an oracle;
OR
ignore the above suggestions and improvise your own approach.

2.

Regard yourself as my coauthor.
Keep a pen, pencil, or crayons with you as you read,
and add your comments and drawings with abandon.
There are numerous questions and assignments to spark you.
Chapter 18 is entirely yours,
and you'll find lots of empty space for your use
in the "Pronoia Therapy" and "Ecstatic Study Guide" pieces.
But feel free to scrawl and doodle anywhere.

3.

I invite you to begin your contribution to our collaboration
anywhere on these early pages.
(There's even a blank page for you to use seven pages from here.)
You could tell a good and beautiful lie,
or brag about how smart you are in the way you love,
or describe the circumstances in which you were most dangerously alive.
Jot down the five things you most want to accomplish in the next 20 years.
Name the people you'd like to see naked.
Write the first two sentences of your 500-page autobiography.

TABLE OF CONTENTS

Chapter 5
"I vow to interpret every experience as a direct dealing of the Goddess with my soul"

Chapter 6
Let's go wash some water. Let's go burn some fire.

Chapter 7
Everyone's a nobody—and nobody's perfect

Chapter 8
What's the difference between dumb pain and smart pain?

Chapter 9
Visualize _____ at the moment of orgasm
Put your deity's name here

Chapter 10
Only you can prevent the genocide of the imagination

Chapter 11
Stronger than hate, wetter than water, deeper than the abyss, more exotic than trust

Chapter 12
This language prevents crime.
This engineering moves you to sing.
These advertisements make you smart.
These rhythms free all prisoners of childhood.

Chapter 13
The 11th Commandment: Thou Shalt Not Bore God.
The 12th Commandment: Thou Shalt Not Bore Thyself.

Chapter 14
You Are a Lucky, Plucky, Good-Sucking Genius

Chapter 15
"Ever since I learned to see three sides to every story, I'm finding much better stories"

Chapter 16
I am totally opposed to all duality

Chapter 17
Think with your heart and feel with your head

Chapter 18
You Are a Prolific Creator

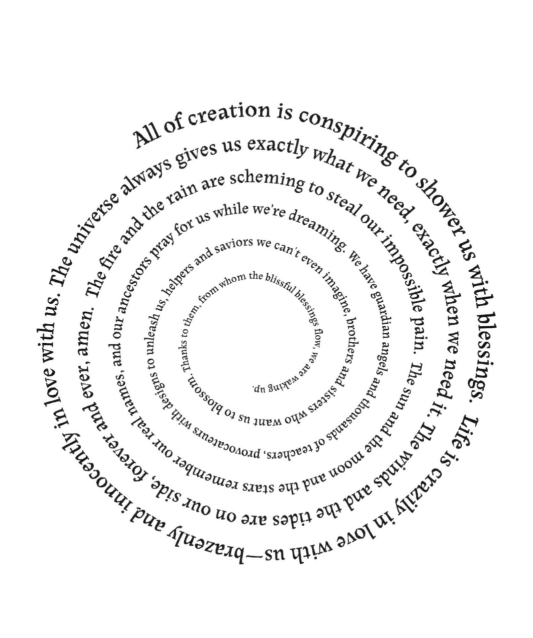

All of creation is conspiring to shower us with blessings. Life is crazily in love with us—brazenly and innocently in love with us. The universe always gives us exactly what we need, exactly when we need it. The fire and the rain are scheming to steal our impossible pain. The winds and the tides are on our side, forever and ever, amen. The sun and the moon and the stars remember our real names, and our ancestors pray for us while we're dreaming. We have guardian angels and thousands of teachers, provocateurs with designs to unleash us, helpers and saviors we can't even imagine, brothers and sisters who want us to blossom. Thanks to them, from whom the blissful blessings flow, we are waking up.

1

Bravo
Viva
Kudos
Whoopee
Eureka
Hallelujah
Abracadabra

THIS IS A PERFECT MOMENT

This is a perfect moment. It's a perfect moment for many reasons, but especially because you and I are waking up from our sleepwalking, thumb-sucking, dumb-clucking collusion with the masters of illusion and destruction.

Thanks to them,
from whom the painful blessings flow,
we are waking up.

Their wars and tortures,
their crimes against nature,
extinctions of species
and brand new diseases.

Their spying and lying
in the name of the father,
sterilizing seeds and
trademarking water.

Molestations of God,
celebrations of shame,
stealing our dreams and
changing our names.

Their cunning commercials
and blood-sucking hustles,
their endless rehearsals
for the end of the world.

Thanks to them,
from whom the awful teachings flow,
we are waking up.

Their painful blessings are cracking open more and more gashes in the shrunken and crippled mass hallucination that is mistakenly called "reality." And through the fractures, ripe eternity is flooding in; news of the soul's true home is pouring in; our allies from the other side of the veil are swarming in, inspiring us to become smarter and wilder and kinder and trickier.

We are waking up.

As heaven and earth come together, as the dreamtime and daytime merge, we register the shockingly exhilarating fact that we are in charge of creating a New Earth. Not in some distant time or faraway place, but right here and right now.

As we stand on this brink, as we dance on this verge, we cannot let the ruling fools of the dying world sustain their curses. We have to rise up and fight their insane logic; defy, resist, and prevent their tragic magic; tap into our sacred rage and supercharge it.

But overthrowing the living dead is not enough. Protesting the well-dressed monsters is not enough. We can't afford to be consumed with our anger; can't be obsessed and possessed by their danger. Our mysterious bodies crave delight and fertility. Our boisterous imaginations demand fresh tastes of infinity.

In the New Earth we're creating, we need lusty compassion and ecstatic duty, ingenious love and insurrectionary beauty. We need radical curiosity and reverent pranks, voracious listening and ferocious thanks.

So I'm curious, my fellow creators. Since you and I are in charge of making a New Earth—not just breaking down the dying culture—where do we begin? What stories do we want at the heart of our experiments? What questions will be our oracles?

Here's what I say: In the New Earth we're creating, we will ridicule the cult of doom and gloom, and embrace the cause of zoom and boom. We will laugh at the stupidity of evil and hate; we will summon the brilliance to praise and create.

No matter how upside down it all may appear, we will have no fear, because we know this big secret: All of creation is conspiring to shower us with blessings. Life is crazily in love with us—brazenly and innocently in love with us.

The universe always gives us exactly what we need, exactly when we need it.

Pronoia is our word of power . . . the antidote for paranoia . . . the spell we cast to gleam ourselves awake again and again. It means that even if we can't see and don't know, primal benefactors are plotting to emancipate us.

The winds and the tides are on our side, forever and ever, amen. The fire and the rain are scheming to steal our impossible pain. The sun and the moon and the stars remember our real names, and our ancestors pray for us while we're dreaming.

We have guardian angels and thousands of teachers . . . provocateurs with designs to unleash us . . . helpers and saviors we can't even imagine . . . brothers and sisters who want us to blossom.

Thanks to them,

from whom the blissful blessings flow,
we are waking up.

The roads they pave us,
the places they save us,
the tomatoes they grow us,
above and below us.

Their mysterious stories,
their morning glories,
their loaves and fishes,
granting our wishes.

The songs they sing us,
the gifts they bring us,
the secrets they show us,
above and below us.

Thanks to them,
from whom the blissful blessings flow,
we are waking up.

I'm allergic to dogma. I thrive on riddles. Any idea I believe, I reserve the right to disbelieve as well.

But more than any other vision I've ever tested, pronoia describes the way the world actually is. It's wetter than water, stronger than death, and truer than the news. It smells like cedar smoke in the autumn rain, and if you close your eyes right now, you can feel it shimmering like the aurora borealis in your organs and muscles. Its song is your blood's song.

Some people argue that life is strife and suffering is normal. Others swear we're born sinful and only heaven can provide us with the peace that passes understanding. But pronoia says that being alive on this rough green and brown planet is the highest honor and privilege. It's an invitation to work wonders and perform miracles that aren't possible in any nirvana, promised land, or afterlife.

I'm not exaggerating or indulging in poetic metaphor when I tell you that we are already living in paradise. Visualize it if you dare. The sweet stuff that quenches all of our longing is not far away in some other time and place. It's right here and right now.

Poet Elizabeth Barrett Browning knew the truth: "Earth's crammed with heaven."

THE EXPERIMENT

OBJECTIVE: To explore the secrets of becoming a wildly disciplined, fiercely tender, ironically sincere, scrupulously curious, aggressively sensitive, blasphemously reverent, lyrically logical, lustfully compassionate Master of Rowdy Bliss.

DEFINITION: Pronoia is the antidote for paranoia. It's the understanding that the universe is fundamentally friendly. It's a mode of training your senses and intellect so you're able to perceive the fact that life always gives you exactly what you need, exactly when you need it.

HYPOTHESES: Evil is boring. Cynicism is idiotic. Fear is a bad habit. Despair is lazy. Joy is fascinating. Love is an act of heroic genius. Pleasure is your birthright. Receptivity is a superpower.

PROCEDURE: Act as if the universe is a prodigious miracle created for your amusement and illumination. Assume that secret helpers are working behind the scenes to assist you in turning into the gorgeous masterpiece you were born to be. Join the conspiracy to shower all of creation with blessings.

GUIDING QUESTION: "The secret of life," said sculptor Henry Moore to poet Donald Hall, "is to have a task, something you devote your entire life to, something you bring everything to, every minute of the day for your whole life. And the most important thing is—it must be something you cannot possibly do." What is that task for you?

UNDIGNIFIED MEDITATIONS TO KEEP YOU HONEST: Brag about what you can't do and don't have. Confess profound secrets to people who aren't particularly interested. Pray for the success of your enemies while you're making love. Change your name every day for a thousand days.

MYTHIC ROLE MODELS: Prometheus and Pronoia. In Greek mythology, Pronoia was the consort of Prometheus, the divine rebel who pilfered a glowing coal from his fellow gods so that he could slip the gift of fire to humans.

TOP-SECRET ALLIES: Sacred janitors, benevolent pranksters, apathy debunkers, lyrical logicians, ethical outlaws, aspiring masters of curiosity, homeless millionaires, humble megalomaniacs, hedonistic midwives, lunatic saints, sly optimists, mystical scientists, dissident bodhisattvas, macho feminists, and socialist libertarians who possess inside information about the big bang.

DAILY PRACTICE: Push hard to get better, become smarter, grow your devotion to the truth, fuel your commitment to beauty, refine your emotional intelligence, hone your dreams, negotiate with your shadow, cure your ignorance, shed your pettiness, heighten your drive to look for the best in people, and soften your heart—even as you always accept yourself for exactly who you are with all of your so-called imperfections.

POSSIBLE REWARDS: You will be able to claim the rewards promised you at the beginning of time—not just any old beauty, wisdom, goodness, love, freedom, and justice, but rather: exhilarating beauty that incites you to be true to yourself; crazy wisdom that immunizes you against the temptation to believe your ideals are ultimate truths; outrageous goodness that inspires you to experiment with irrepressible empathy; generous freedom that keeps you alert for opportunities to share your wealth; insurrectionary love that endlessly transforms you; and a lust for justice that's leavened with a knack for comedy, keeping you honest as you work humbly to liberate everyone in the world from ignorance and suffering.

USAGE NOTE: We employ the adjectival form "pronoiac" rather than "pronoid." That way, it rhymes with "aphrodisiac" and resonates with "paradisiacal" instead of being conditioned by "paranoid."

DISCLAIMER: Material in this book may be too intense and controversial for some readers. It contains graphic scenes of peace, love, joy, passion, reverence, splendor, and understanding. You will not find any references to harsh, buzzing fluorescent lights in a cheap hotel room where a heroin dealer plots to get revenge against the authorities at his old high school by releasing sarin gas into the teachers' lounge.

There are no reports of Nazi skinheads obsessed with re-creating the 14th-century Tartars' war strategy of catapulting plague-ridden corpses into an enemy's citadel. Completely absent from these pages are any stories about a psychotic CEO of a Fortune 500 company who has intentionally disfigured his face to help him elude the CIA, which wants to arrest him for the treasonous sale of his company's nanotech weapons technology to the Chinese.

You should therefore proceed with caution if you are a jaded hipster who is suspicious of feeling healthy and happy. Ask yourself: "Am I ready to stop equating cynicism with insight? Do I dare take the risk that exposing myself to uplifting entertainment might dull my intelligence?" If you doubt your ability to handle relaxing breakthroughs, you should close the book now.

Glory in the Highest

Thousands of things go right for you every day, beginning the moment you wake up. Through some magic you don't fully understand, you're still breathing and your heart is beating, even though you've been unconscious for many hours. The air is a mix of gases that's just right for your body's needs, as it was before you fell asleep.

You can see! Light of many colors floods into your eyes, registered by nerves that took God or evolution or some process millions of years to perfect. The interesting gift of these vivid hues is made possible by an unimaginably immense globe of fire, the sun, which continually detonates nuclear reactions in order to convert its own body into light and heat and energy for your personal use.

You can't live without the sun's inexhaustible flood of unconditional love. Every move you make depends on it. Luckily, it never fails you.

Did you know that your personal star is located at the precise distance from you to be of consummate service? If it were any closer, you'd fry, and if it were any farther away, you'd freeze. Is that just a happy accident? Or is it a sign of favor—a big, broad hint, from a cosmic intelligence that adores you?

Of the many things that have gone right for you during your time on Earth, the most crucial was your birth. As you crossed over the threshold, trading the warm dark sanctuary for the bright noisy enigma, you didn't die! It was a difficult act of high magic that involved many people who worked very hard in your behalf. The skills they provided in helping you navigate your rite of passage were in turn made possible by previous generations of threshold-tenders who bequeathed their expertise.

Months before that initiation, a more secret miracle bloomed: Your life began as a single cell, spawned by the explosive fusion of two highly specialized bundles of chromosomes. How could that tiny package of raw material have possibly grown a brain and liver and heart and stomach over a period of a few months? What inscrutable genius guided and oversaw the emergence of your fully formed infant body, that virtuoso creation, from the slimmest of clues?

"Something unknown is doing we don't know what," said astrophysicist Arthur Eddington about the universe. And we are the beneficiaries.

P.S. You have continued to grow since your birth, with millions of new cells continually blooming to replace the old ones that are always dying. At this moment, you're host to about 50 trillion cells, and each of them is really a sentient being in its own right. They all act together as a community, implementing the monumental collaboration you call your body.

You can drink a glass of water. You can spread butter on a slice of toast. You can wash your hair and prune your plants and draw infinity signs on a piece of paper. Your hands work wonderfully well! Their intricate force and sustained grace are amply supported by your heart, which circulates your blood all the way out to replenish the energy of the muscles and nerves in your fingers and palms and wrists. After your blood has delivered its blessings, it finds its way back to your heart to be refreshed. This masterful mystery repeats itself over and over again without you ever having to think about it.

Contemplate the unfathomable prowess of your digestive system. Countless chemical reactions have to unfold with alacrity in order for it to work as well as it does. The gastric juice has to be composed of just the right mix of pepsin, rennin, mucus, and hydrochloric acid. The bile and pancreatic juice must arrive at the right spot and at the right time. The enterocytes in your small intestine always have to remember anew how to carry out their uptake of ions, lipids, and peptides. How can they possibly be so good at knowing exactly what to do and when to do it?

The circulation of blood and the conversion of food into fuel are just two of many alchemical feats that the secret intelligence within you takes care of. Thousands of other exchanges and transformations and syntheses are ceaselessly working their wizardry inside your body without your conscious participation.

You may sometimes take for granted the luxuriant variety of unique and subtle aromas that come to you, but the truth is that you love your sense of smell. You're also thrilled about your power to hear sounds, and taste flavors, and touch textures. A few of these impressions repel or offend you—although even those are often interesting—but the vast majority ground you and gratify you.

Maybe you rarely celebrate the fact that you can think, but according to my inside sources, the flash of mercurial codes through your brain is among the universe's most dazzling accomplishments. Try to imagine the colossal divine plan or the implausible series of

An immense globe of fire continually detonates nuclear reactions in order to convert its own body into light and heat and energy for your personal use.

fabulous accidents that had to coalesce in order for you to be able to generate thoughts—soaring, luminescent, liberating thoughts or shriveled, rusty, burrowing thoughts . . . thoughts that can invent or destroy, corrupt or redeem, bless or curse.

Your capacity to experience emotions and passions and longings is one of your most precious endowments. You may not exult in the waves of anger or jealousy that sometimes ripple through you, but you're glad you have the power to feel them. Your yearning for an impossible dream may feel shattering, but you relish being able to accommodate that much intensity. And as for the sensations that are more unambiguously positive, like a surge of courage in the face of an intriguing challenge or a surprising breakthrough with an intimate ally: They're treasures beyond measure. Can I hear you shout hallelujah?

Language is another spectacular marvel. Millions of souls have cooperated for untold centuries to cultivate a system of communication that you understand very well. Your ability to speak and read and write makes you feel strong and dynamic. It intricately connects you to the world, and allows you to engage in one of your greatest pleasures: hearing and telling stories.

Your imagination may be the best gift of all. It's the source of your creative power. If there's a particular experience or object you want to bring into your life, the first thing you've got to do is visualize it. The practical actions you take to manifest your dreams always refer back to the pictures in your mind's eye. And so every goal you fulfill, every quest you carry out, begins as an inner vision. Your imagination is the engine of your destiny. It's the catalyst with which you design your future. Do you know where it comes from? Do you have any idea how powerful it is?

Here's yet another amazement. You're in possession of the extraordinary power of self-awareness. Maybe you don't fully realize how far-fetched that stupendous ability is. Get this: You not only know that you are you; you also know that you know that you know you are you. With an ease that belies the complexity that had to be built into the structure of creation to make

Dionysian Manifesto

it possible, you are conscious that you're alive and awake and unique. You have a million different feelings and fantasies about what it means to be you. How is that even possible?

Have you ever been loved? I bet you have been loved so much and so deeply that you have become blasé about the enormity of the grace it confers. So let me remind you: To be loved is a privilege and prize equivalent to being born. If you're smart, you pause regularly to bask in the astonishing knowledge that there are many people out there who care for you and want you to thrive and hold you in their thoughts with fondness. Animals, too: You have been the recipient of their boundless affection. The spirits of allies who've left this world continue to send their tender regards, as well. Do you "believe" in angels and other divine beings? Whether or not you do, I can assure you that there are hordes of them beaming their uncanny consecrations your way. You are awash in torrents of love.

As tremendous a gift it is to get love, giving love is an equal boon. Many scientific studies demonstrate that whenever you bestow blessings on other people, you bless yourself. Expressing practical compassion not only strengthens your immune system and bolsters your health, but also promotes self-esteem, enhances longevity, and stimulates tranquility and even euphoria. As the scientists say, we humans are hardwired to benefit from altruism. (To read more about the subject, go here: tinyurl.com/lyyd46.)

What's your position on making love? Do you regard it as one of the nicer fringe benefits of being alive? Or are you more inclined to see it as a central proof of the primal magnanimity of the universe? I'm more aligned with the latter view.

Imagine yourself in the fluidic blaze of that intimate spectacle right now. Savor the fantasy of entwining bodies and hearts and minds with an appealing partner who has the power to enchant you. What better way do you know of to dwell in sacred space while immersed in your body's delight? To commune with the Divine Wow while having fun? To tap into your own deeper knowing while at the same time gazing into the mysterious light of a fellow creature?

Another one of life's bounties is its changeableness, which ensures that boredom will never last very long. You may underestimate the intensity of your longing for continual transformation, but the universe doesn't. That's why it provides you with the boundless entertainment of your ever-shifting story. That's why it is always revising the challenges it sends your way, providing your curious soul with a rich variety of unpredictable teachings.

Neuroscientists have turned up evidence that suggests you love this aspect of the universe's behavior. They say that you are literally addicted to learning. At the moment when you grasp a lesson you've been grappling with, your brain experiences a rush of a natural opium-like chemical, boosting your pleasure levels. You crave this experience. You thrive on it.

So the universe is built in such a way as to discourage boredom. It does this not just by generating an endless stream of interesting novelty, and not only by giving you an instinctive lust to keep learning, but also by making available an abundance of ways to break free of your habitual thoughts. You can go to school, travel, read, listen to experts, converse with people who think differently from you, and absorb the works of creative artists. You can replenish and stretch your mind through exercise, sex, psychotherapy, spiritual practices, and self-expression. You can take drugs and medicines that alter your perspectives.

And here's the best part of this excellent news: Every method that exists for expanding your consciousness is more lavishly available right now than it has been at any previous time in history.

Never before have there been so many schools, educational programs, workshops, and enrichment courses. Virtually any subject or skill you want to study, you can. You don't even have to leave your home to do it. The number of online classes is steadily mounting.

Travel is easier and faster than ever before. A few days from now, you could be white-water rafting along the Franklin River in Tasmania, or riding on "the train at the end of the world" in Tierra del Fuego, or observing Golden Bamboo lemurs in the rainforest of southeastern Madagascar. If you're on a budget, you can jet to exotic locales for free as an air courier, or you can travel cheaply as an eco-tourist, enjoying the natural pleasures of distant climes without demanding luxurious accommodations or expensive night life.

Let's talk about the Internet's role in helping the universe discourage boredom. Remember, it's still very early in the evolution of this budding global brain. But already it provides you with instant access to a substantial amount of all the information, images, and music ever created. And in another few years, the sheer entirety of the human mind's riches will be spread before you like a gargantuan feast. It's not yet true that every book ever written and every song ever recorded and every film ever made are accessible online, but it will be true sooner rather than later.

Today, without leaving your chair or spending any money, you can enjoy Kandinsky's painting "Improvisation No. 30" or archives of the Krazy Kat comic strips. You can listen to a Vivaldi concerto or a Black Sabbath heavy metal anthem, and you can read the history of the Peloponnesian War or the myths of the Tlingit Indians. You can hear Martin Luther King's "I Have a Dream" speech or watch a short film of the Three Stooges throwing pies in the faces of high society matrons or pore over every poem Emily Dickinson ever wrote.

For many of us, few freshly minted glories are more glorious than the Internet's prodigious gift of song. Thanks to the magic of electronic file transfer, there has never before been so much great music available, and from so many different cultures and genres, and so cheaply. Enhancing this blessing has been the recent revolution in recording technology, which has made it possible for musicians all over the world to record their compositions at low cost. We not only have much better access to all kinds of music, but have far more new music to enjoy as well.

One further development has pushed our relationship with music into the realm of crazy goodness: portable MP3 players that allow us to listen to the burgeoning abundance of tunes anywhere and anytime we want.

Exposing yourself to the expressions of other people is an excellent way to play along with the game of life's perpetual invitations to change yourself. Those of us who are alive today are extremely lucky, since our moment in history provides more opportunities to learn from other people than ever before.

Another phenomenon that helps us respond to and keep up with the universe's restless creativity is self-expression. And it so happens that our era is also the champion of all eras in that regard. So claims Clay Shirky, an expert in the social and economic consequences of the Internet. In a talk he gave in May 2009 (tinyurl.com/nj96hw), he said that we are currently witnessing "the largest increase in expressive capability in human history."

The invention of the printing press in the 15th century provoked an earlier revolution. A second major upgrade in the capacity to communicate came with the telegraph and telephone. The third was ushered in with the arrival of recorded media other than print: photos, recorded sound, and movies. The fourth arrived when the electromagnetic spectrum was mobilized for use in broadcasting sounds and images through the air. But the fifth revolution, says Shirky, is the biggest of all. The Internet is not only becoming the vessel for all the other media, but has effectively ended the monopoly that professionals have had in getting their messages out. Now everyone can speak to everybody in a variety of modes.

Google says it has indexed over a trillion unique URLs on the World Wide Web. Technorati, a search engine for blogs, has catalogued well over 100 million blogs, and that figure does not include at least 70 million Chinese language blogs. Add to this plenitude the amateur creators who contribute videos to Youtube and similar websites. Count up the thousands of authors who are self-publishing their books, the independent filmmakers making low-budget movies, the aspiring photographers on flickr.com, the hordes of podcasters and Web-based radio stations, and the musicians who are not signed to contracts with record labels but are recording songs in their home ProTools studios. Factor in the millions of people discussing their intimate details on social networks like Facebook and Twitter.

While there are still masses of pure consumers who are content merely to absorb the creations of others, the Internet is bringing us closer to the ideal proclaimed by the Burning Man festival: "No spectators!" Will there come a time in the future when everyone on the planet

The universe is built to discourage boredom. Its endless supply of unpredictable stories provide us with superlative entertainment.

will have his or her own node on the Internet, complete with blog, podcasting, and video feeds?

As we play along with the universe's conspiracy to liberate us from the suffering of boredom, we can call on a widening array of healing strategies, psychological insights, and spiritual practices. The Internet isn't solely responsible for the universal spread of formerly local or regional ideas. The dissolution of hidebound traditions has also helped expedite the increasing availability of inspiration from everywhere, along with the growth of international trade, the explosive expansion of the entertainment industry, the ease of long-distance jet travel, and the omnivorousness of the news media. Globalization has a lot of downsides, but this isn't one of them.

And so Chinese acupuncture and Ayurvedic medicine from India are making inroads into mainstream health care in North America. The influence of Buddhist thought on psychotherapy in recent years has been huge. A spiritual seeker who's curious about how other cultures have communed with the divine realms has easy access to the esoteric tantric secrets of the Hindus, alchemical texts that were previously only available to scholars, the Santo Daime sect in Brazil, and the songs and stories of the Yoruba tradition.

What's even more unprecedented is that any of us is free to mix and match modalities and techniques from a variety of systems. Here's transpersonal psychologist Roger Walsh, writing in the *IONS Review:* "This is the first time in history that publicly acknowledging that you follow two or more distinct spiritual traditions would not have you burned at the stake, stoned to death, or facing a firing squad. We tend to forget what an extraordinary time this is, that for the first time in history we have the entirety of the world's spiritual and religious traditions available to us, and we can practice them . . . without fear."

And so I am very sure I will not be arrested, sentenced, and burned at the stake for engaging in an orgy of spiritual anarchy. Ready? I hereby invoke Brigid, Celtic goddess of the undying flame, and ask her to unleash thrilling clarity in your heart about a dilemma that has

vexed you. I summon Bast, Egyptian goddess of play, to help you intensify your search for meaning by having more fun. I pray to the spirit of Carl Jung, Swiss psychiatrist, that he might inspire you and your lover to achieve hierosgamos, the sacred marriage, thereby creating a bond that inspires your community and galvanizes you both to express more of your own beauty than you would be capable of alone. I draw on the power of Tiphareth, the central sphere on the Qabalistic Tree of Life, to assist you in becoming the gorgeous messiah you were born to be. And I offer a bribe to Laverna, pagan trickster goddess, in the hope that she will steal one of your inhibitions and ignite your dormant genius.

There's another sense in which we have more power than ever before to expand and mutate and play with our consciousness: the availability of drugs, both legal and illegal. In earlier centuries, the Huichol Indians of northern Mexico had peyote, the Turks of the Ottoman Empire had coffee, the practitioners of Bwii in West Central Africa had ibogaine, and the English had tobacco. But our culture is the first in which all of history's psychoactive substances can be had at once.

Adding to that generous selection, researchers in recent decades have been busy designing and discovering a wide array of new drugs that affect the mind, from antidepressants to LSD, from analgesics to Ecstasy, from sleep aids to lucid dream enhancers. The evolution of anesthesia, which didn't get fully underway until the 19th century, has continued apace as well. On the near frontier are exotic treatments that could further expand the definition of consciousness and mutate what it means to be human. One drug shows great promise in enhancing visual memory. Another could permanently wipe away painful memories.

My personal policy is to avoid taking drugs of all kinds. (For more on that subject, read the story that starts on page 228.) But I think it's glorious that so many psychoactive substances are available for those discriminating experimenters who dare to expand the frontiers of the human psyche.

And a new era of inner exploration is in fact in motion. Progress in the use of psychedelics had been derailed for years by government repression and the excesses of irresponsible users. But the government has begun to relax some of its prohibitions, allowing legal experiments with psilocybin. In trials at Johns Hopkins' Departments of Neuroscience and Psychiatry and

Dionysian Manifesto

Behavioral Biology, test subjects' use of the hallucinogen has generated spiritual realizations that yield long-term practical benefits. Other experiments have shown that psilocybin can play an important therapeutic role in reducing the suffering of terminally ill patients.

Meanwhile, the pioneers who are experimenting with psychedelics outside of the government's purview have become more disciplined in their approach, as evidenced by a wealth of smart new books and journals that investigate the phenomena for what they really are: forays into unknown realms that hold fascinating secrets, worthy of scientific rigor and brave intelligence.

Later in this book, primarily on pages 184–186 and 203–205, I discuss a phenomenon that I call the genocide of the imagination. It's a poetic conceit invoked to call attention to forces at work in the world—especially fundamentalism, materialism, and nihilism—that diminish the power of the imagination. But that's just one side of a multifaceted story. Here's another side: In one sense we are now living in a golden age for the imagination. We have far more resources to call on to feed our heads than any previous generation of humans.

Here's a small anecdote that illustrates the bigger sweep. In an interview in the *San Francisco Chronicle,* Tamara Straus asked author and writing instructor Ethan Canin, "How is American fiction changing?" Canin said, "The young writers I teach have gone from writing small stories set in strip malls . . . to huge novels that take place in Madagascar. They can just look up all kinds of information and photography on the Web." They can also easily view videos and films of distant places, and they can read a wealth of first-person accounts of people who've been there or live there. Their imaginations aren't confined to working with the environments they know firsthand.

Strauss also asked Canin, "What's a novel you would have liked to have written?" This is his reply: "Barry Unsworth's *Sacred Hunger.* The novel shared the Booker Prize with *The English Patient.* It's about a slave ship that goes from Liverpool down to the West Coast of Africa, trades stuff for slaves, and then goes to the West Indies, and trades slaves for rum and sugar. It's about what happens to that ship. I met Barry Unsworth, and I told him what a great novel I thought

> **"*Approfondement* is a French word that means 'playing easily in the deep.'"**
> **—Tom Robbins**

it was. I said, 'You must have been a sailor all your life.' He said, 'I've never even been on a sailboat.'"

Another great book that takes place at sea is *Moby Dick,* published in 1851. Its author, Herman Melville, traveled extensively on ships, crossing both the Atlantic and Pacific Oceans. Much of the fuel for his imaginative work of fiction came from his actual waking life experiences. Where did Unger's come from? Less direct sources.

I offer the difference between the two men's masterpieces as a symbol for the growing powers of imagination.

The conventional wisdom seems to say that Americans are getting dumber. One study reported that more people can name the characters in *The Simpsons* TV show than know the rights guaranteed by the First Amendment. Other surveys found that only 53 percent know how long it takes the Earth to revolve around the sun, and 24 percent aren't sure what country America gained its independence from.

Yet an article by Malcolm Gladwell in *The New Yorker* (tinyurl.com/ljqjj2) notes that Americans' IQ scores have been steadily rising for a long time—so much so that a person whose IQ placed her in the top ten percent of the population in 1920 would be in the bottom third today. One possible explanation: Our "growing stupidity" may better be described as a difficulty keeping up with the ever-growing mass of facts, whereas we are actually becoming better at solving problems.

Gladwell cites the book *Everything Bad Is Good for You.* Its author, Steven Johnson, argues that pop culture is increasingly expanding our intelligence about social relationships and stretching our ability to sort out complex moral dilemmas. TV shows in the 1970s, like *Starsky and Hutch* and *Dallas,* had linear, easy-to-follow story lines with simple characters who behaved in predictable ways. More recent shows, like *Lost, The Sopranos,* and *Battlestar Galactica* weave together a number of convoluted narrative threads that require rapt attention and even repeated viewings in order to understand. Characters often wrestle with contradictory motivations that complicate their behavior as they deal with ambiguous dilemmas for which there are no clearly right solutions. Viewers who take in shows like this are in effect attending brain gyms.

Referencing Johnson, Gladwell says modern video games have an equally salubrious effect on the thinking power of those who play them. Unlike the original models that first became available in the 1980s, the new games are way beyond being mere tests of pattern recognition and motor skills. "Players are required to manage a dizzying array of information and options," Gladwell writes. "The game presents the player with a series of puzzles, and you can't succeed at the game simply by solving the puzzles one at a time. You have to craft a longer-term strategy, in order to juggle and coordinate competing interests."

Gladwell acknowledges that knowing objective information about the way the world works is very important, and that we may be less adept at that than were previous generations. In our defense, the amount of information we have to keep track of verges on being infinite. "On an average weekday," wrote Saul Bellow, "*The New York Times* contains more information than any contemporary of Shakespeare's would have acquired in a lifetime." So maybe there's a 22-year-old computer programmer out there who thinks that France was the country America freed itself from in 1776, but on the other hand has achieved mastery over both the 53,000-word guide to the "Grand Auto Theft III" video game and the game itself.

In any case, problem-solving is an equally essential measure of intelligence as knowing objective information, and there is evidence that we're growing smarter at that.

Many people alive today are convinced that our civilization is in a dark age, cut off from divine favor, and on the verge of collapse. But it's healthy to note that similar beliefs have been common throughout history.

As far back as 2800 BC, an unknown prophet wrote on an Assyrian clay tablet, "Our earth is degenerate in these latter days. There are signs that the world is speedily coming to an end." In the seventh century BC, many Romans believed Rome would suffer a cataclysm in 634 BC.

Around 300 BC, Hindus were convinced they lived in an "unfortunate time" known as the Kali Yuga—the lowest point in the great cosmic cycle. In 426 AD, the

Christian writer Augustine mourned that this evil world was in its last days. According to the Lotharingian panic-mongers who lived more than a 1,000 years ago, human life on earth would end on March 25, 970.

Astrologers in 16th-century London calculated that the city would be destroyed by a great flood on February 1, 1524. American minister William Miller proclaimed the planet's "purification by fire" would occur in 1844. Anglican minister Michael Baxter assured his followers that the Battle of Armageddon would take place in 1868. The Jehovah's Witnesses anticipated the End of Days in 1910, then 1914, then 1918, then 1925. John Ballou Newbrough ("America's Greatest Prophet") promised mass annihilation and global anarchy for 1947.

The website "A Brief History of the Apocalypse" at tinyurl.com/yqb83n lists over 200 visions of doom that have spilled from the hysterical imaginations of various prophets in the last two millennia.

Our age may have more of these doomsayers per capita than previous eras, although the proportion of religious extremists among them has declined as more scientists, journalists, and storytellers have taken up the singing of humanity's predicted swan song.

In her book *For the Time Being,* Annie Dillard concludes, "It is a weakening and discoloring idea that rustic people knew God personally once upon a time but that it is too late for us. There never was a more holy age than ours, and never a less. There is no whit less enlightenment under the tree by your street than there was under the Buddha's bo tree."

I invite you to go sit under that tree by your street.

I'm arguing against the grain, compiling evidence that the cynics' hypothesis is a delusion. I'm insisting that we are most decidedly not pitiable actors in the most hellish chapter in history. I'm even inclined to entertain the possibility that the reverse is true: We may be living in the best of times.

Noble Prize-winning economic historian Robert Fogel is a meticulous scholar not given to hyperbole. But his work provides ample evidence that in some ways, we're the luckiest humans of all. His landmark book is *The Escape from Hunger and Premature Death, 1700–2100: Europe, America and the Third World.* Its

Thousands of things go right for you every single day.

Dionysian Manifesto

clout is rooted in his specialty, which is the painstaking quantitative analysis of the way people have lived. Some of his data is drawn, for example, from the medical records of soldiers who fought in the Civil War. Other information originates in historical documents gathered from Norway, France, Britain, the Netherlands, India, and Ghana.

According to Fogel, human biology has changed dramatically in the past three centuries, and especially in the last 100 years. People in the developed world live twice as long as they used to. They weigh more and grow taller. They're far hardier and healthier and smarter. When sickness comes, they're better at defeating it than their ancestors were, and they're not as likely to contract diseases in the first place.

"We're just not falling apart like we used to," Fogel says. "Even our internal organs are stronger and better formed." What has occurred is "not only unique to humankind, but unique among the 7,000 or so generations of human beings who have inhabited the earth." (Sources: "The Human Equation," Lydialyle Gibson, tinyurl.com/2x3u7o, and "So Big and Healthy Grandpa Wouldn't Even Know You," Gina Kolata, *The New York Times,* tinyurl.com/rban6.)

We're talking about a revolution. In the mid-19th century, Americans of all ages were much sicker than they are now. Child mortality was almost 25 percent, and of those kids lucky enough to survive into adolescence, 15 percent more expired before age 15. Chronic malnutrition was a horrendous curse, compromising immune systems from birth. During the Civil War, one-sixth of the teenagers who applied to serve in the Union army were rejected because of chronic ailments like malaria, tuberculosis, arthritis, cardiovascular problems, and hernias. As for the older folks, the average ex-soldier in his 60s had at least six health problems, four more than a sexagenarian is likely to have today.

What happened between then and now? First, we harnessed electricity, made it universally available, and used it in a myriad ways to improve our lot. All of the other boons I'm about to name—improvements in our diet, medicine, sanitation, and workload—were organized around this fantastic, unprophesied new resource.

Our relationship with food has changed dramatically in the last century and a half. We discovered more accurate information about our nutritional needs and gained access to a greater variety and abundance of food. The perfection of the science of refrigeration and the eventual universal availability of refrigerators made

You're hardier and healthier and smarter than your ancestors. You get sick less and you live longer.

a big difference, too. Victory over widespread malnutrition meant that infants got a better start on building strong bodies, making them less susceptible to sickness throughout the course of their lives.

The drastic upgrade in the state of the human body was also made possible by steadily growing medical expertise, including the discovery of the germ theory of disease and radical new treatments like antibiotics and vaccination. Physicians got better training, large numbers of new hospitals opened, and more people made medicine their career. Among the diseases that were wiped out were diphtheria, typhoid, cholera, whooping cough, tetanus, tuberculosis, smallpox, and polio.

Innovations in sanitation have been key to the upgrades in the way our bodies work. Everything and everyone are far cleaner than they used to be. People bathe more frequently and devote more attention to their hygiene. Among the most important developments in this triumph were two practical miracles: indoor plumbing and the installation of municipal sewer systems. It took a while. As late as 1920, only one in 100 American homes had a toilet or even a bathroom—outhouses were standard—and toilet paper was a luxury. For those few with bathtubs, a full-body cleanse was often a once-a-week ritual, and entire families might use the same bathwater. Fogel says that even into the early 1900s, "Chicago exported a lot of typhoid down to St. Louis," by disposing wastewater in the Illinois River.

Garbage disposal used to be a hit-and-miss proposition until the 20th century. Private citizens might bury their refuse in their backyards, take it to public incinerators, or offer it to pigs at local farms. But eventually, local governments took over the task. During my lifetime, every city where I've lived has done a stellar job of hauling my trash away.

In the middle of the 19th century, the average American worked 78 hours a week, often at exhausting manual labor and without the help of machines. As work became easier and of shorter duration, our health soared. Technological aids like washing machines and automatic heating systems also contributed to the rising tide of physical well-being.

Dionysian Manifesto

All of the improvements I've mentioned have flourished because of the most important change of all: greater wealth and more available resources. Despite periodic economic downturns, per capita income in the developing nations has grown enormously in the last 150 years. Elsewhere, too: Wealth in India and China has doubled since 1989, according to *The Economist* magazine. As a result, more of us have been able to afford to take better care of ourselves. And more of us have been able to do the research and experimentation and development that advance the common good.

Even poor people are better off than they used to be. During the 17 years when my annual income was less than $10,000, well below the official poverty line, I had many amenities the average American didn't have in 1900: electricity, telephone, bathtub, toilet, hot running water, refrigerator, radio, electric hotplate, space heater, TV, cassette player, shampoo, public transportation, asthma medicine, access to a laundromat, garbage collection, and sewer system.

Today, like most days, you awoke inside a comfortable shelter. You have a home! Your bed and pillow are soft and you have the blankets you need. The electricity is turned on, as usual. Somehow, in ways you're barely aware of, a massive power plant at an unknown distance from your home is alchemically transforming the sun's stored energy into currents of electricity that reach you through mostly hidden conduits in the exact amounts you need, and all you have to do to control the flow is flick small switches with your fingers.

Your home is perhaps not a million-dollar palace, but it's sturdy and gigantic compared to the typical domicile in every culture that has preceded you. The floors aren't crumbling, and the walls and ceilings are holding up well, too. Doors open and close without trouble, and so do the windows. What skillful geniuses built this sanctuary for you? How and where did they learn their craft?

In your bathroom, the toilet is functioning well, as are several other convenient devices. You have at your disposal soaps, creams, razors, clippers, tooth-cleaning accessories: a host of products that enhance your hygiene and appearance. You trust that unidentified

"We either make ourselves miserable or we make ourselves happy. The amount of work is the same."
—Carlos Castañeda

researchers somewhere tested them to be sure they're safe for you to use.

Amazingly, the water you need so much of comes out of your faucets in an even flow, with the volume you want, and either cold or hot as you desire. It's pure and clean; you're confident that no parasites are lurking in it. There is someone somewhere making sure these boons will continue to arrive for you without interruption for as long as you require them.

Do you have a headache this morning? Menstrual cramps? A toothache? You can quickly get relief for all of these ailments and more, either by taking medicine you've got on hand or by making a short trip to a nearby drug store. If your problem's more serious than that, chances are good that a trip to a doctor or alternative health practitioner will provide some help.

The truth is, at no other time in the history of the world has there been a vaster array of healing modalities available. You may have legitimate complaints about your doctor or the cost of health care or the bureaucratic maze you have to negotiate to be treated properly, but still: How would you compare the help you can access to that of a 16th-century French peasant or an 11th-century Mayan or even the first president of the United States, whose doctors bled him to death in the cracked belief that bloodletting would cure his pneumonia? Have you had any diphtheria, typhoid, cholera, whooping cough, tetanus, tuberculosis, smallpox, malaria, or polio recently?

In your closet are many clothes you like to wear. They keep you warm and give you the chance to exhibit your sense of style. Who gathered the materials to make the fabrics they're made of? Who imbued them with colors, and how did they do it? Who sewed them for you?

In your kitchen, appetizing food is waiting for you. Many people you've never met worked hard to grow it, process it, and get it to the store where you bought it. The bounty of tasty nourishment you have to choose from is unprecedented in the history of the world.

Your many appliances are working flawlessly. Despite the fact that they feed on electricity, which could kill you instantly if you touched it directly, you feel no fear that you're in danger. Why? Your faith in the people who invented, designed, and produced these machines is impressive.

It's as if there's a benevolent conspiracy of unknown people that is tirelessly creating hundreds of useful things you like and need.

Have you said a prayer of gratitude any time recently for the fact that your feet remain steadily on the earth? Gravity is giving you the same gift it always does, pulling on you with neither too much nor too little force. You should be glad for its versatility, too. It's working for the heavenly bodies with the same tender attentiveness it bestows upon you. As all the other planets do, the Earth relies on gravity's genius to keep orbiting the sun in its ancient hallowed groove, thereby providing you with all of the favorable environmental conditions you need to live. Magicians of the Western Hermetic tradition say that gravity is actually a form of love—the irresistible attraction that all things have for each other over even the vastest distances.

Meanwhile, a trillion other facets of nature's ingenious design are expressing themselves as a skilled artist might. At the heart of the masterpiece are the plants. With relentless grace, they perform the everyday miracle of photosynthesis, using sunlight as a trigger to convert water and carbon dioxide into the fuel they need. If you're like me, you feel regular surges of adoration for this complex alchemy, which pours oxygen into the air for us to breathe and ultimately provides us with all of our food.

If you're honest with yourself, you'll confess that there are few glories more sublime and more freely available than taking a walk in nature. Simply to imagine it can fill you with sacred joy. Close your eyes and visualize yourself sauntering along a wide dirt path in a meadow bordered by the woods. Feel the resilient strength of your leg muscles. Relish the freedom of swinging your arms in rhythm with your stride. The sun's rays are so sweet you can almost taste them. The ever-shifting qualities of light and temperature resemble caresses. What's that rustling in the bushes? Maybe a lizard or gopher informing you that you're not alone.

At a certain point, the breeze becomes stronger. Branches of nearby trees begin to wave, unleashing a

tremulous whoosh. Instinctively, your heartbeat quickens. Your flesh prickles with a reflexive alertness. But of course there's no danger. What you're experiencing is spontaneous excitement at the rising energy; a heightened awareness of the teeming aliveness that surrounds you.

Gaze slightly upward. Welcome in the far horizon and the sweep of the ancient sky. Give names to the clouds. Shout out praises to the birds, saluting them for being so skilled at soaring through the air. If you can see a pale slice of moon, thank it for its artistry in managing the tides.

Up ahead on the trail is a tree that wants your affection. Be empathetic. Try to remember all that it remembers, and sing a song to it as you pass. The dust and dirt deserve your kind attention, as well. Pick up a rock that catches your eye, announce to the world that it is a magic talisman, and marvel at its unique shape and heft as you roll it around in your hand.

One more gift to bestow: Under your breath, just loud enough to be heard, tell the Earth that you can hear the sound of its turning, and it's making you giddy. Say, too, how much you love the fact that in all eternity, this moment will never be repeated. Though you may drink in the delicious atmosphere with a trillion trillion more breaths, this special dispensation of air molecules will never fill your lungs again.

To your surprise, the Earth replies to you in your native tongue, rising above the thrum of its whirling with a more familiar tone. It quotes the poem by Charles Baudelaire, as translated by Louis Simpson. "Ask the wind, the wave, the star, the bird, the clock, everything that is flying, everything that is groaning, everything that is rolling, everything that is singing, everything that is speaking . . . ask what time it is, and wind, wave, star, bird, clock will answer you: 'It is time to be drunk! So as not to be the martyred slaves of time, be drunk, be continually drunk! On wine, on poetry or on virtue as you wish.'"

Do you want to go someplace that's at a distance? You have a number of choices about what machines to use in order to get there. Whatever you decide—car, plane, bus, train, subway, ship, helicopter, or bike—you have confidence that it will work efficiently. Multitudes of people who are now dead devoted themselves to perfecting these modes of travel. Multitudes who are still alive devote themselves to ensuring that these benefits keep serving you.

Maybe you're one of the hundreds of millions of people in the world who has the extraordinary privilege of using a car. It's a brilliant invention made by highly competent workers. Other industrious laborers put in long hours to extract oil from the ground or sea and turn it into fuel so you can use your car conveniently. Who designed and paved the roads for you? The bridges you cross are potent feats of engineering. Do you realize how hard it was to fabricate them from scratch?

You're aware that in the future shrinking oil reserves and global warming may impose limitations on your ability to use cars and planes and other machines to travel. But you also know that many smart and idealistic people are diligently striving to develop alternative fuels and protect the environment from the by-products generated by vehicle engines.

And compared to how slow societies have been to understand their macrocosmic problems in the past, your culture is moving with unprecedented speed to recognize and respond to the crises spawned by its technologies. Think of the predicament the Mayan people faced more than a millennium ago. As their civilization collapsed, in part because of the environmental degradation they themselves caused, they had insufficient wisdom to adjust. They were locked inside their ignorance. In contrast, we know clearly what's happening to us, we have all the world's knowledge available at our fingertips, and some of our best and brightest are working hard to come up with solutions.

Let's say it's 9:30 a.m. and you've been awake for two hours. A hundred things have already gone right for you. If three of those hundred things had not gone right—your toaster was broken, the hot water wasn't hot enough, there was a stain on the jacket you wanted to wear—you might feel that today the universe is against you, that your luck is bad, that nothing's going right.

And yet the fact is that the vast majority of everything is working with breathtaking efficiency and consistency. You would clearly be deluded to imagine that life is primarily an ordeal.

I can understand if, during the course of reading this meditation, you've been visited by thoughts like, "But what about all the terrible things in the world?" or "Brezsny's totally imbalanced in his perspective!" Please know that in tallying up the profuse blessings that surround us, I'm not implying that utopia is at hand. My education and my predilection for empathy have made me acutely aware of the suffering of human beings, whether they live next door or 10,000 miles away.

But I also regard it as my fun duty to counterbalance the hordes of cynical storytellers in the media and entertainment industries who tirelessly assure us that life on Earth is a dismal hell. I think it's smart to aggressively identify all the ways the world works for us.

I also want to suggest that it doesn't help those who are suffering if we hate or feel guilty for our own blessings. To dwell for a few stolen minutes on the beauty and pleasures of our lives is not tantamount to ignoring all the sad and bad things.

"Glory in the Highest" continues in part 2 on page 72. I could have added it here, but was hesitant to overwhelm you with too much glory all at once.

"It is eternity now; I am in the midst of it.
It is about me in the sunshine;
I am in it, as the butterfly in the light-laden air.
Nothing has to come; it is now.
Now is eternity; now is immortal life."
—Richard Jefferies

Dionysian Manifesto

PRONOIA THERAPY

Practice in becoming a Master of Rowdy Bliss

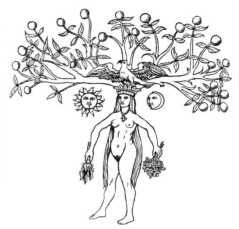

Write your own version of "Glory in the Highest." Describe the everyday miracles you take for granted, the uncanny powers you possess, the small joys that occur so routinely you forget how much they mean to you, and the steady flow of benefits bestowed on you by people you know and don't know. What works for you? What makes you feel at home in the world?

This is it! This is it! This is it!

Dear Gorgeous Genius

While you and I are together here:

Your favorite phrase is *flux gusto*

The colors of your soul are sable, vermilion, ivory, and jade

Your magic talisman is a thousand-year-old Joshua tree whose flowers blossom
just one night each year and can only be pollinated by the yucca moth

Your holiest pain comes from your yearning to change yourself in the exact way
you'd like the world around you to change

Your soil of destiny is peat moss

Your mythic symbol is a treasure chest dislodged from its hiding place
in the earth by a flood

Your lucky number is 13 to the 13th power

Your sweet spot is in between the true believers and the scoffing skeptics

A clutch of frog eggs from an unpolluted river is your auspicious hair-care product

The anonymous celebrity with whom you have most in common is the jester
who followed Buddha around and kept him loose

The question that perks you up when your routine becomes too rote is this:
What possesses the bar-tailed godwit to migrate annually from Alaska to New
Zealand by hitching rides on gale-force winds?

2.

When they say
"Be yourself,"
which self
do they mean?

BABY WIPE COMMUNIQUÉ

Right before Labor Day every year, the temporary nation of Burning Man sprouts up for a week in the Nevada desert. A mix of festival, survivalist challenge, outdoor museum, and performance art spectacle, it is populated by the world's largest concentration of half-naked freaks. They're *practical* half-naked freaks, though. Since water and food and electricity are absent in that barren landscape, the determined revelers have to bring their own. The dangerous celebration culminates on a Saturday night, when fire-dancers bearing torches ignite a 60-foot-tall wooden and neon effigy—the Burning Man.

During my maiden voyage there in 2001, I got sunburned in 100-degree heat, rarely slept for more than five hours a night, ate mostly canned tuna and dried fruit, had to drink water constantly to avoid dehydration, collected blowing dust in my ears, nose, and eyes—and had the best time of my life. Forget Maui and the south of France and Florence, Italy: Burning Man was the closest I'd ever come to living in heaven on earth.

Its most deeply relaxing element was the absence of money, advertisements, and commerce. The community was run as a *gift economy.* Nothing was for sale except ice and coffee. When goods and services were exchanged, it was because they were given freely. This was beyond bartering. You didn't trade your treasure for another's treasure; you just handed yours over, no strings attached.

A second utopian feature of the festival was protection from media assault. There may have been some hopeless TV addicts among my 26,000 fellow citizens, but I never spied a single telltale rectangular glow emanating from a tent or RV. Corporate logos and advertising were banished, too, as well as all signs of America's other best and brightest brainwashers, like *The Wall Street Journal, USA Today,* and *The New York Times.* Nor did any of Clear Channel's 130 radio stations infect me with their fake music and zombie newscasts. Within 24 hours of slipping into the safe haven of Burning Man's propaganda-free zone, I felt as if I had come home.

But my sense of sanctuary was not merely built on the absence of America's toxic culture. My new power spot was filled with things I loved: allies as smart and interesting as I am, most of whom were committed to being creators rather than spectators; car-free streets filled with bicyclists and pedestrians; gold top hats and green silk pantaloons and blue velvet frock coats and bras made of rubber shark masks; good, often surprising music and lots of places to dance; the Born-Again Pagan Church of Lascivious Feminism, the Polyester Pagoda of the Palpitating Pulpit, and countless other homemade religions that included divine mischief in their ceremonies.

Everywhere I wandered I encountered exuberant, large-scale works of art. The elegant and improbable "Mausoleum: Temple of Tears" was made entirely of recycled wooden dinosaur puzzles. It hosted a steady flow of visitors, many in tears, who came to write messages on the walls, mourning or honoring their departed friends and loved ones.

Not far from the Mausoleum was the "Plastic Chapel," a two-story-high church whose facade was a mosaic of brightly colored pieces of plastic salvaged from dumps and junkyards all over Nevada and

California. Here, priests and priestesses of every variety presided over roguish, rowdy, and puckish weddings. A few of the ceremonies were legal in the eyes of the state. But many joined together conclaves of polyamorous experimentalists for whom a two-person union was not inclusive enough. I myself officiated at a mass ritual in which everyone in a crowd of 300 got married to himself or herself.

Of the hundreds of sculptures and installations and murals and labyrinths and decorated vehicles packed into the eight-square-mile expanse, not all were sublime works of art. But some were, and many others were at least provocative, amusing, and aesthetically pleasing, even to a tough critic like me. My imagination was in a constant state of delighted arousal.

Adding to my pleasure was the fact that the gallery was the desert itself, an ancient lake bottom beneath a towering sky. Every creation had to be built to withstand dust storms, gale-force winds, downpours, and extremes of temperature.

Back in America, far from the independent republic of Burning Man, teams of Tibetan Buddhist monks have become famous for bringing their sand paintings to museums. Painstakingly laying out colored grains in precise designs on large platforms, they work for weeks. But the masterpiece survives only a short time. Then its makers sweep it up and dispose of the sand, exhibiting their freedom from attachment and demonstrating the transitoriness of life.

Many of the works of art at Burning Man had a similar fate in 2001, as they do each year: to be dismantled or even destroyed at the end of the festival. As a creative artist who has had to resort to all manner of spiritual trickery to prevent my ego from appropriating what my soul makes, I regard this as a celebration of my deepest values.

When I visited Toronto a year before my first Burning Man, astrologer Richard Geer asked me, "What are the conditions you'd need in your world in order to feel like you were living in paradise?"

"Let me get back to you on that," I said at the time. It seemed too abstract and remote a fantasy to entertain.

But 13 months later, during my revel in the desert, I had a practical answer: Many of the conditions I'd need to feel as if I were living in paradise already existed at Burning Man.

Refuse to dehumanize anyone, even those who dehumanize you.

The idea for the Beauty and Truth Laboratory hatched there at the Burning Man festival in 2001. The birth occurred officially around 6 p.m. on Friday, the day before the Man burned.

Five of us were squatting in a circle under a 20-foot by 20-foot canopy. We yakked and free-associated as we sipped vials of Red Bull, an energy drink containing legal but stimulating ingredients that I liked to imagine were the more sensible equivalent to poet William Butler Yeats having monkey testicles sewn to his chest back in the 1920s.

With me were two other members of my band, Sacred Uproar, guitarist George Earth (Burning Man "superhero" name: Maniacal Miracle Maker) and chanteuse Jessica Rice (Burning Man superhero name: Lush Confuser). Our group was rounded out by two new friends we'd met when they'd participated in our "Brag Therapy Rite" during our first gig some days before.

Firenze Matisse was a young literature professor from Massachusetts who was writing a science fiction book about a gang of radical leftist Peruvian shamans conspiring to cast spells on American political leaders. Thirza Guest was a thirtysomething German journalist who claimed to have scored candid interviews with a range of political celebrities from Russia's President Vladimir Putin to India's "Bandit Queen," though she had not yet found any mainstream media willing to publish them.

All five of us had succumbed to the alchemy of Burning Man. Our skins had drunk so deeply of the desert sun and wind that we'd turned translucent brown. If I stared hard enough, I swear I could catch glimpses of the blood rushing along beneath the see-through outer layer of my arm. The mist-like white dust had caked permanently in every body crevice, especially the corners of our eyes and up our nostrils. Though now and then each of us had stumbled upon some prodigal and improbable feast—one night the camp next to ours had given away fresh sushi served on the nude bodies of human "platters," for instance—more often we had forgotten to eat or else munched on ephemera as we trekked to the next party. Our dry, cooked bodies had become thinner.

And then there was the matter of our altered relationship with sleep. So as not to deny ourselves any of the inexhaustible variety of playtime activities spread over Burning Man's eight square miles, none of us had lain down for longer than five or six hours on any night since we arrived. Weariness was not the result, though. Instead, we'd been transformed into liminal creatures who dwelt in an in-between realm that was composed of equal portions dreamtime and waketime. We were having lucid dreams with our eyes open.

It was in this setting that the Beauty and Truth Laboratory announced itself.

Thirza nudged me in the right direction. "Hey, Rob," she said to me, "you know how in your 'Crimes That Don't Break Any Laws' shtick you imitate that pompous German guy? Do it for me. I'll give you some pointers on refining your German accent."

She was referring to a passage in one of Sacred Uproar's performance art pieces, in which I mockingly imitate Udo Kier, a German film actor who specializes in playing villains.

I obliged her. Born and raised in Berlin and the daughter of a linguist, she could no doubt provide me with dialect tips. I puffed up my chest like a swaggering braggart, then repeated, in my best German accent, the statement Kier had made in an interview I'd heard.

"Evil has no limit! Evil has no limit! Good, on the other hand, *does* have a limit. It is nowhere near as interesting. It is boring! It is dull! Good is not worthy of my artistry!"

"You've got the 'evil has no limit' part down," Thirza mused. "If I close my eyes, I could picture it coming out of the mouth of my ex-husband. But when you said 'good does have a limit,' you lapsed into a kind of Cockney twang."

Before I could enlist her to correct my diction, Firenze interrupted me. "I like that 'evil has no limit' bit," he said, "but my favorite part is the rant you go into right after that. What is it? 'How dare the editors of *The New York Times* act as if good has a limit?!' Or something. Do that one."

I launched into the rap he was talking about. In contrast to the pretentious pose of my previous riff, now I spoke in a low, conspiratorial tone. "I hate to admit it, but I have to say that most everyone everywhere seems to agree with Udo Kier. And I am in a tiny minority in my belief that evil is a fucking bore. But how dare Udo Kier,

or for that matter the editors of *The New York Times* and Stephen King and Eminem and Ridley Scott—how dare they proceed on the assumption that 'good has a limit' and that 'good isn't as interesting' when there are so few smart artists and thinkers who are brave and resourceful enough to explore the frontiers of beauty and truth and joy and compassion?"

Ending with a flourish, I blew a kiss in the direction of the sky.

"You know I'm a fanatical new convert to you and Sacred Uproar, Rob," Firenze said after a pause, "but if I have any problem at all with your stuff, it's that you're a bit heavy on bitching about the old world and a bit light about imagining the new world. I mean, you talk about how newspapers are obsessed with reporting bad news, but you never actually say what the alternative would be."

"He's got a point," chimed in Jessica, offering me a fresh bottle of Red Bull to replace the one I'd downed. "You say that the hypothetical good news should be just as entertaining as the bad news that everyone seems to think is so fascinating. It can't be ho-hum stuff like, 'Two thousand planes took off from American airports yesterday and every one landed safely.' But you really don't give many examples of what that entertaining good news would be."

Suddenly I felt like a pregnant woman who hadn't known she was pregnant until the labor pains kicked in. Which they had just done. I felt a big ripe creation pushing to get out.

"Are you or are you not one of those smart artists who's brave enough to explore the frontiers of beauty and truth?" asked Firenze with mock solemnity.

"I am," I said. "I want to be." I winced as something like a contraction shuddered through my mind's eye.

"You really should start a think tank," Thirza said. "A place to brainstorm about interesting kinds of sweetness and light. Not the fluffy, glazed-eyed New Age junk or the withered, sentimental Christian crap."

"Only trouble is," I said, "most smart, educated people wouldn't be caught dead near a discussion of

sweetness and light, no matter how interesting it might be. Me and you guys might be the only fools I can round up for our think tank."

"Hard-core sweetness and light!" George spouted. "Kick-ass joy and peace! Razor-edged harmony!"

"Aren't you forgetting that you are right now in the thick of the most concentrated assemblage of mutated brains on the planet?" Firenze said. "If the North Koreans, or for that matter the ass-souls in Washington, D.C., wanted to ensure a future enslaved to anachronistic modes of consciousness, all they'd have to do is nuke Burning Man."

"Unfortunately, I don't think there's enough time to get a decent recruitment drive going here this year," I said. "Most everyone's leaving on Sunday."

"I once dreamed I worked as a corporate headhunter," Jessica offered. "I'm ready to get started as your recruitment chief immediately."

"I'm on the team," Thirza said.

"Me, too," said Firenze.

It was then that my new creation popped out. I'd given birth. I looked at my watch. It was 6:16 p.m. PDT, August 31, 2001. I wondered what its horoscope would be.

Its name was immediately clear: Beauty and Truth Laboratory. It would be a tribe of hope fiends. A hotbed of loving geniuses. A gang of lunatic saints and emotional giants and crafty optimists. A think tank of sacred agents and scientific poets and dissident bodhisattvas and virtuoso bliss-invokers.

The Beauty and Truth Lab would be an actual place, or maybe a web of places, where compassionate masters of rowdy bliss gathered to explore the frontiers of beauty, truth, love, justice, integrity, goodness, pleasure, fun, redemption, and emotional intelligence. Part of it would serve as a real laboratory, a matrix where we could conduct actual experiments. Our purpose would not be merely to make our own lives richer, but also to offer inspiration to others through the books, music, performances, and films we'd generate in the course of our work.

"Where are you going, Rob?" Jessica asked, seeing that I had risen out of my squat and was walking away. "Your gang's ready to launch a crusade. Give us some direction."

"I will return shortly with a plan," I said. "But right now I'm being urgently called on to carry out an emergency walking meditation."

I veered out onto the dirt road adjoining our camp and headed toward the edge of town. A happy cacophony of live and recorded music poured in on me from every direction. I could make out at least four different

Combustion luster verve blaze
Luminous flourish lucid mojo
Lightning splendor wake-up fuel

styles. This profusion, which streamed every hour of the night and day, was one of the elements about Burning Man I loved and hated best. It meant I could always find a place to dance, even at 7 a.m., to pretty much any kind of beat I was in the mood for. But it also meant that the only possible way to sleep was to be armed with a defense of earplugs and the kind of sound-canceling headphones worn by jackhammer operators.

I passed a camp where four men wearing leather skirts were playing a punk version of klezmer music. Another camp had bleachers where people sat and called out for passers-by to entertain them. Then there was the Inner Demon Rodeo, where you were encouraged to mime the action of hog-tying your inner demon.

My nascent musings about the Beauty and Truth Lab had hit a snag. How could I justify calling it a laboratory for beauty and truth? Those two terms alone didn't cover anywhere near the total territory I was concerned with. To be accurate, shouldn't it be something like the Beauty and Truth and Love and Bliss and Goodness and Justice and Liberation Laboratory?

And another thing. I wasn't interested in just any old beauty and truth. The words themselves have been so grossly overused by so many people to promote such widely different agendas that they've been gutted of meaning. Say them aloud and you're likely to provoke a numbing sensation in your listeners' imaginations.

It would be at best a half-truth to say that the laboratory was a sanctuary to explore "beauty." That dead arrangement of letters could be invoked to describe everything from a supermodel flouncing down a Milan runway in a faux fur bikini to a sleek high-tech jet fighter gleaming in hateful splendor on the deck of a carrier battleship. Our lab would have a sacred duty to ignore fraudulent pretenders to beauty like that. It would aspire to investigate wild beauty that awakens radical curiosity, convulsive beauty that potentiates the longing for freedom, fierce beauty that rouses lusty compassion, and shocking beauty that mobilizes healing mischief.

All the other virtues needed rehabilitation, too, having been similarly paralyzed through overuse and exploitation. Shouldn't our laboratory specify that what we were really interested in studying was not "truth," a concept that was long ago stripped of its meaning and vitality, but rather crazy wisdom that makes you allergic to dogma? Not just "liberation," but ingenious liberation that is never permanent but must be reinvented and reclaimed every day? Not merely justice, but a boisterous justice that schemes and dreams about tricks to diminish the suffering and increase the joy of every sentient being?

I thought of the possibility of coining new words to replace the used-up old husks. "Beauty" could become, maybe, "allurabliss," for instance. "Truth" might be "swirloluminous."

The Allurabliss and Swirloluminous Laboratory?

Nah. That wasn't right. Too esoteric. Though our lab would never hire marketing experts to advise us how to manipulate our message so it would reach the widest possible demographic, neither would we want to ignore the reality of what people are entertained by. We needed a name that was simple and catchy.

My walking meditation was taking me past the camp of the Burning Scouts of America. I hadn't visited them yet, but I'd read their spiel somewhere. They were dedicated to teaching the love of chaos and hedonism. If you signed up for one of their programs, you could earn Demerit Badges in "Unfocused Rage," "Spitting into the Wind," and "Gender Mutation." Drunken scoutmasters might take you on a naked tour of all the theme camps that were doling out free massages, and foul-mouthed Burning Girl Scouts would serve you charred cookies and over-ripe peaches.

As much as I was tempted to stop and partake, the urge to keep trekking was stronger. I'd begun to feel more contractions. Labor had resumed. Was there still another creation in me? Was I going to have twins?

That's when the word "pronoia" popped into my wide-open mind.

I wasn't initially sure of all the implications of its appearance, but I could see how it might be useful for the Beauty and Truth Laboratory. I loved the term and had been using it gleefully for several years, though it had never made it into any dictionary. It had been coined in the mid-1970s by Grateful Dead lyricist and co-founder of the Electronic Frontier Foundation, John

Perry Barlow, who defined it as the opposite of paranoia: "the suspicion that the universe is a conspiracy on your behalf."

The Scottish psychologist Fraser Clark revived the word in the 1990s. He referred to pronoia as "the sneaking hunch that others are conspiring behind your back to help you." Once you have contracted this benevolent virus, he said, the symptoms include "sudden attacks of optimism and outbreaks of goodwill." Working with the Zippies, a group of gypsy ravers, Clark organized the Zippy Pronoia Tour to America in 1994. With a boost from a cover story by *Wired* magazine, the tour's parties and performances spread the word.

Shortly thereafter, a website devoted to pronoia appeared on the Web at pronoia.net. It has mostly been devoted to telling the story of the Zippies.

So why exactly had the concept shown up in my intuition at exactly this moment, in the midst of my walking meditation at Burning Man? I knew my creative process well enough to understand that it was a crucial clue about how to proceed. Did it mean I should call our research center the "Pronoia Laboratory"?

No. My logical mind couldn't buy that. Although "pronoia" was a euphonious coinage with a built-in association to the well-known word "paranoia," it was unfamiliar to most people. As the name of an organization that aspired to provide a populist alternative to the mainstream media's toxic stories, it would be too limiting.

But it *was* euphonious and evocative. Couldn't it be useful as long as it was not the first thing that newcomers encountered? Maybe the name of our think tank would be "The Beauty and Truth Laboratory," with pronoia featured prominently in our benevolent propaganda and artistic products.

I had reached the edge of the formal city of Burning Man. Now the wilderness began. This was not a picturesque desert dotted with cacti, scrub, and lizards. It was barren playa for as far as the eye could see. As I

stepped out into the emptiness, the wind came up, blasting me head-on with a dusty whirlwind.

An urge to write overtook me. The number of good ideas welling up threatened to exceed what I could hold in my short-term memory. I wanted to commit them to paper. But reaching in the back pocket of my shorts, I found nothing where I usually kept my small spiral-bound notebook. Damn! How could I have gone out on a walking meditation without something to take notes on?

At least there was a felt-tip marker in my vest pocket. I supposed I could try scrawling notes on my skin. But I quickly realized that would be problematic. I was sweating. Although it was getting on toward 7 p.m., the temperature seemed still to be in the 90s. I made an attempt to inscribe "pronoia" on my left forearm, but the ink barely penetrated the moisture.

Then I spied a possible solution. In the distance, lying on the sand, was an open box of baby wipes—the moist towelettes most commonly employed to clean the butts of infants who've pooped in their diapers. Out here in the middle of the desert, where there was no running water and you had to import every drop you used, many adult denizens of Burning Man regarded the baby wipes as indispensable aids to maintaining their personal hygiene.

It was unusual to see a box of wipes reduced to litter, though. "Leave no trace" is a central tenet of the Burning Man commitment to ecological impeccability, and most burners live up to it.

I ran to the potential treasure. It was the "Quilted Northern" brand, antibacterial and scented. Not my personal favorite—I hated wipes with cloying perfumes—but I wasn't in a position to be picky. And other than that problem, I was in luck. The open box meant that all the wipes had lost their moisture. They would be easy to write on.

Using the plastic box as my writing surface, I jotted down notes as I continued to walk. "But hold on," I wrote. "Wait a minute. Is pronoia a big enough concept for the Beauty and Truth Laboratory? Is it poetic enough?" So began my "Baby Wipe Communiqué."

In Asian myth, snakes and birds are often portrayed as adversaries. Their eternal struggle symbolizes humanity's difficulty in coordinating the agendas of heaven and earth. Is morality inherently at odds with desire? Noble intentions in opposition to unconscious motivations? Bright rationality at war with dark poetry? Pronoia is the cure for their strife—the medicine that harmonizes snake and bird.

I was having doubts about pronoia. I mused on how neither John Perry Barlow nor Fraser Clark had developed the notion beyond their brief one- and two-line definitions. They'd given us little to go on. Pronoia was "the suspicion that the universe is a conspiracy on your behalf." It was "the sneaking hunch that others are conspiring behind your back to help you." Not exactly a well-developed philosophy.

Despite periodic searches of the Web with Google, I'd come across only three other analogs of the pronoia meme over the years. All were very brief and none invoked the word "pronoia." In his book *Raise High the Roof Beam, Carpenters,* J. D. Salinger had the character Seymour Glass write in his diary, "Oh, God, if I'm anything by a clinical name, I'm a kind of paranoiac in reverse. I suspect people of plotting to make me happy." Then there was philosopher Terence McKenna, who had once said: "I believe reality is a marvelous joke staged for my edification and amusement, and everybody is working very hard to make me happy." Philosopher Robert Anton Wilson had uttered advice that also sounded pronoiac: "You should view the world as a conspiracy run by a very closely-knit group of nearly omnipotent people, and you should think of those people as yourself and your friends."

As I ruminated now on how unripe the concept of pronoia still remained, I was dumfounded. I'd vaguely thought about the paucity of discussion before, but for the first time I wondered if there were some collective blind spot that had prevented it from flourishing. In an ironic burst of paranoia, I even entertained the possibility that there was a conspiracy to prevent pronoia from catching fire in the collective imagination.

How else to explain why it hadn't spread with contagious glee, at least through bohemian and underground culture? It wasn't just another generic version of the "positive thinking" movement. It didn't have the cult-like associations of teachings like "The Course in Miracles." Pronoia was snappy and seductive, a feel-good yet saucy meme just begging to be turned into a pop philosophy for hipsters. The New Age movement alone should have seized upon it long ago. How many wannabe gurus might have made fortunes selling self-help books like *Embracing Pronoia: Fifty Ways to Live as if the Whole World Is Conspiring to Help You?*

Even I myself had displayed a curious passivity in relation to pronoia. When I first happened upon the term years ago, I recognized that it echoed the spiritual teachings of Hermeticism, which I had been studying for two decades. This tradition, taught in the mystery schools of the West for centuries, is a synthesis of Qabala, astrology, alchemy, tarot, and magick. One of its core principles is that despite superficial appearances to the contrary, all of creation is on our side; that the very structure of reality ensures our eventual liberation from suffering; that life is a divine conspiracy to awaken us to our god-like nature and become co-administrators of the divine plan for evolution.

Pronoia was a more simplistic and pop culture-worthy meme for expressing this same set of ideas: seemingly a perfect fit for me. I had long been an aspiring Hermetic magician disguised as a rock musician and horoscope columnist. I'd built my entire career on translating esoteric spiritual themes into entertaining forms that could be enjoyed by people who'd never heard of a mystery school. Pop culture was my milieu.

So why didn't I start writing a book about pronoia when I first encountered the meme? In *The Televisionary Oracle,* the 486-page book I worked on from 1991 to 1999 and published in 2000, there was only one small reference to pronoia in the last chapter. And why hadn't I at least made pronoia a regular theme in my syndicated weekly astrology column? (Later I determined that between 1989 and 2001, I'd mentioned pronoia in my column only three times.) I had never invoked pronoia by name in a single song I'd written.

If there were a cultural blind spot that prevented pronoia from flourishing, I had suffered from it as much as anyone.

By now my walking-and-writing meditation had taken me far from the babble of music flooding from Burning Man's hundreds of generators. I was surrounded by pure desert. Memories of the glorious past few days, accompanied by the emotions they roused, rushed into my awareness with an intensity akin to what I imagined would happen during the instantaneous life review that comes with a near death experience.

I remembered arriving at the gates to Burning Man about 2 a.m. on Sunday night after the day-long drive from my home in Northern California. As I climbed down out of the RV to check in, three dusty-skinned women wearing white turbans, white silk bikinis, and black work boots danced around me, their faces aglow in the torchlight. One sang, "Welcome home, Rob. We've been waiting for your return since the Big Bang." (How did she know my name?) They converged upon me with swarming hugs and kisses. Each whispered a secret in my ear.

"Your Burning Man superhero name is 'Friendly Shocker.'"

"You're like the chrysanthemum, which needs long hours of darkness to bloom."

"In my dream, you were a good trickster who did healing mischief to defuse the terrible mischief committed by the evil tricksters in Washington, D.C."

That was just one of a score of recent memories that flooded through me as I stood transfixed with gratitude in the vast white desert wasteland. I recalled Sunyatta, a classically trained ballet dancer, teaching me how to do a professional pirouette as we danced inside a circle of flames . . . globe-trotting activist Pax, who'd been arrested during demonstrations in 17 different countries, regaling me with the story of the idealistic 18-year-old woman who initiated events that led to the overthrow of the repressive Bulgarian government in 1996 . . . my band Sacred Uproar conducting a "Chaotic

Meditation" ceremony in which hundreds of reverently irreverent bohemians kicked their own asses, bragged about what they could not do and did not have, mimed throwing rocks toward heaven as they sent complaining messages to God, simulated the sounds they would make as they gave birth, and cast love spells on themselves.

During the six days I'd been at Black Rock City, I glided through the streets without a taint of fear, no matter what the hour. I had eaten fresh sushi off naked bellies while dancing to the funky Arab Celtic music of the best band I'd never heard of; had played a giant game of billiards using bowling balls; had taken a joyride on a wheeled version of Captain Hook's schooner as it swayed with scores of sweaty dancers dressed like characters from my dreams; had enjoyed numerous no-strings-attached gifts from magnanimous strangers, including a free foot rub, free homemade organic beer, free palm reading, free portrait-painting, free skydiving lesson, and free kisses. I had also sampled a variety of soulmates at the Costco Soulmate Trading Outlet, a clearinghouse for soulmates that offered "quality name-brand and private-label soulmates at substantially lower prices than can be found through conventional wholesale sources."

The values I held most dear were reflected back to me wherever I wandered: generosity, playfulness, luxurious conviviality, a relaxed attitude about sexuality, spirituality that didn't take itself too seriously, frequent celebration, and love of creative ritual. I've been in love with more than a few women in my life, but this was the first time I'd become infatuated with a time and place.

As the rush of memories subsided, I turned my attention to my surroundings. The full moon was rising over the black mountains in the east. Maybe because there was so little humidity in the air, the silver globe looked closer and more spherical than usual. It had an intimate presence—wasn't as flat and lifeless as it seemed back in the civilization that burners called Babylon. I fantasized that it was a sentient creature gazing back at me.

I swiveled around to bear witness to the setting sun at the other side of the sky. It, too, had lost its blank, two-dimensional veneer. It was no longer far away and abstract. It had swooped down very close. I couldn't help but register a detail that did not normally reach my conscious awareness: It was a ball of fire. And more than that: It was alive. It was a conscious and intelli-

gent being, clearly not just a mass of soulless matter or a natural machine running on automatic.

I searched for a groove in my awareness where I could tune in to the thoughts of the living, sentient sun. Abracadabra! Suddenly I was flooded with its consciousness—as if we had slipped into telepathic communion. Not that I could immediately translate the sun's language into English.

Then I awakened to an even more amazing perception: The sun was acutely aware of me. It knew me intimately. It was beaming specific thoughts, made for me, directly into me.

Break open the forbidden happiness.

Well, "thoughts" was not the right term. There was a fierce, musical, lilting quality to whatever the sun was beaming into me. As if a great deal of intelligent emotion were coming along for the ride. Lush, hot emotion. Delightful, surprising, demanding emotion. The more I allowed it in, the happier I became.

It was no metaphor. I wrote on one of my baby wipes: "The sun is singing its love into me." Not just my imagination, but my entire body was awash in a flood of erotic sensation. A contrapuntal weave of haunting melodies massaged me on the inside, leaving trails of delectable warmth. Flashes of unfamiliar longing arose and were instantly satiated by floods of pleasure, as if the sun were both the source of and answer to a primal desire I was feeling for the first time. To note merely that my cock was hard would be trivial: My entire body had an erection.

I became absolutely certain that the sun loved me personally. Its love was not just incidental or careless, provided because I happened to be within range of the radiance it showered down on everything unconditionally. No, the great eternal God known outwardly as the sun was beaming into me now, as she (or he?) had always done, a unique torrent of beneficence that was specially designed for me alone. And she did the same for every human soul, too! I knew beyond a doubt that each and every one of us receives a singular flow of the Sun Goddess's intimate blessings without end. Whether we appreciate, register, or take advantage of the blessings is another thing.

In the spiritual system I've studied for many years, I've been taught to bring my analytical intelligence with me everywhere: into sleep and dreams, into meditation, into shamanic journeys, into all unusual states of awareness. There are many realms of creation outside of what normal waking consciousness can perceive, but the data encountered while visiting those places is not necessarily more reliable than what can be gleaned on the material plane. Be discriminating, I've been cautioned, even in the midst of mystical rapture. Beware of illusion even when seemingly talking with a deity.

Under my own power, I've developed a corollary to this sensible advice: Never take myself too seriously, even when I seem to be talking to a deity. Along with keeping my skepticism in gear, nursing a giggling mockery of my own earnestness is a foolproof protection against being deceived on any plane of existence.

Fortunately, one of the perks of my spiritual training is that my discriminating, self-mocking mind does not feel a need to tear down all other modes of awareness. It knows it's a servant, not an omnipotent master above which there must be no other masters. I am able, therefore, to bring my Chuckling Kibitzer with me into interludes of mystical rapture without fear that I'll lose my grip on the mystical rapture. I'm psychologically double-jointed.

Right on schedule, the Chuckling Kibitzer appeared in the midst of my mystical rapture in the desert. "Fucking the sun, eh?" was its first comment. "Doing the nasty with the Goddess herself?"

I broke into a cackle, but the joke didn't disrupt my tantric communion in the least. If anything, it intensified my full-body hard-on. It's often the case that the Chuckling Kibitzer's humor helps me relax more fully into an experience I'm on the verge of taking too seriously.

"It's not too much for you, right?" the Chuckling Kibitzer continued after a pause. "You sure you're up for this much mojo? You're not going to get fucked to death, I trust."

That jab had a bite to it.

"I just want to make sure you're not going to have a stroke," C. K. pressed on. "As we know from the case of Semele and Zeus, gods aren't always careful about protecting fragile humans from their sublime blasts. Pindar said, 'Long-haired Semele died in the roar of the thunderbolt.'"

That made two quick mentions of death: unusual for C. K. What was he driving at? Ever so slightly, I slowed the acceleration of my expansive opening to the sun's gifts.

"Even if the sun wants nothing but the best for you," C. K. continued, "even if the sun literally lusts to shower you with blessings that are meant to activate your highest potential, maybe you're not ready for them yet. Maybe you need to be your neurotic self for a few more years—or lifetimes."

With the introduction of this doubt, the ecstasy I had been feeling abated a bit, but not much. On the other hand, a new emotion sprouted: terror. Soon I'd learned a new thing about myself: I was capable of feeling rapture and terror at the same time.

And this was honest, intelligent terror. It wasn't rooted in an archaic, superstitious guilt about feeling good; I'd shed the Judeo-Christian mistrust of pleasure fairly early on in my spiritual work.

No, this was terror of a higher order, a terror I'd sometimes faced during my many years of meditation and spiritual work on myself: What are the risks of seeking face-to-face communion with Divine Intelligence? What treasured illusions must be sacrificed? What part of me has to die?

All the best teachings I'd encountered agreed that in order for one's Higher Self to be born—and it was only the Higher Self that could endure direct communion with the Creator—the little self had to die. Hermetic philosophy asserted that there is an immortal part of each of us, an adamantine uniqueness that was never born and will never die; but our awareness can't inhabit that immortal part until we dissolve our attachments to the hodgepodge of conditioning that most of us mistake as our precious, fascinating, unique self.

And that dissolution can be excruciating, especially if a slew of attachments expire in one sudden swoop.

There in the Nevada desert, I was as scared as I had ever been. What if I opened myself so completely to the sun's raging blessings that I would be transformed into something I no longer recognized as me?

I understood that the gift was beyond my understanding. As brilliant and hot and sweet as it was, it was also dark. Majestic and intimate and perfect, but also wild. I was invigorated by the stabbing vortex of divine love, and I was annihilated by it. I wrote on my baby wipe: "What if the Sun Goddess is annihilating me with her staggering beneficence?"

I was not on drugs at this time. In fact, I had not ingested a single mind-altering substance, even marijuana, for 16 years. And while the vision in the desert was an extreme state, the gnosis it climaxed had been building in me for years. I had long been a connoisseur of the mysterious interplay of dark and light. *The Televisionary Oracle,* the book I worked on for so long, was a reverent exploration of the riches to be gleaned from hanging out with the chthonic embodiment of the Goddess.

My awareness that there can be no yang without yin, and vice versa, explained one of my problems with pronoia—a reason why it had not yet bloomed in me and generated a New Age bestseller. The bare-bones version of pronoia promulgated by Barlow and Clark and McKenna and Wilson was a cute cartoon. It was suitable for framing as a pop culture icon, but was not sufficiently true to the complex poetry of real life to take root in me.

In the past few years, I had felt like a fraud every time I invoked pronoia. People had loved me for introducing the idea to them; they saw me as a bright light giving them permission to be optimistic. But I'd always been slightly embarrassed, aware that I was hiding some of my true feelings.

If I had ever said what I meant, I'd have told them that *my* pronoia has got to be a pronoia for the soul, not for the ego. *My* pronoia, if it ever took root, would overthrow your ego and my ego and everyone's ego, would

overthrow the status quo, the government, and even reality itself.

But I had remained forever coy, never playing with pronoia to make it more aesthetically and ethically appealing to myself. I'd written nothing beyond the same one-sentence formulations that my predecessors had been content with. Questions like, "What does pronoia have to say to someone who has just been widowed or been in a car crash?" or "If I believe in pronoia, will I get my dream job and find my perfect lover this week?" had never won my attention; let alone the subtler inquiries, like, "What would a psychology based on pronoia look like?" or "Does pronoia require a belief in God?"

There at Burning Man, the Goddess of the sun finally thunderstruck me, forcing me to escape my lazy rut. I realized with a burst of rebellious joy that there was no reason I had to be loyal to the meaning of pronoia as promulgated by its originators. Pronoia didn't belong to them or anyone. I could use it any way I wanted. I could stretch it and bend it to fit my extravagant needs.

My benefactor, the sun, slowly dipped beneath the horizon. The sky's zenith had turned from purple to indigo. I sat down on the gray playa, facing the rising moon, and wrote for a long time on my baby wipes. The Beauty and Truth Laboratory had been born. The last line I wrote before trekking back to my camp to find my co-conspirators was a quote from the mathematician Ralph Abraham: "Heart physiologists find more chaos in the healthy heart than in the sick heart."

Your Inalienable Right to Fresh Omens

Factual information and reasonable thinking alone are not sufficient to guide you through life's labyrinthine tests. You need and deserve regular deliveries of uncanny revelation. One of your inalienable rights as a human being should therefore be to receive a mysteriously useful omen every day of your life. Unfortunately, our culture conditions us to be overly receptive to bogus superstitious portents and hostile to the real thing. It's hard to get our minimum daily requirement. In this spirit we present "Guerrilla Oracle: Clues to the Rebel Grail," a recurring feature designed to help you reclaim your birthright. Here's one for you now.

Burn, Baby, Burn

Try this meditation: Imagine that you are the wood and the fire that consumes the wood.

First, focus your awareness on the part of you that is the wood. You may tremble or gasp, feeling the jolt of your solidity disintegrating, your form changing. As you shift your attention to the part of you that is the fire, you may exult in the wild joy of power and liberation.

It may be tempting to favor the fire over the wood, to love the burning more than the being burned. But if you'd like to understand pronoia in its fullness, you've got to appreciate them equally. Can you imagine yourself being the fire and wood simultaneously? Is it possible for you to experience the deep pleasure of their collaboration?

3

We're searching for the answers
so we can destroy them
and dream up better questions

LUMINOUS TEASE

Change yourself in the way you want everyone else to change
Love your enemies in case your friends turn out to be jerks
Avoid thinking about winning the lottery while making love
Brainwash yourself before someone nasty beats you to it
Confess big secrets to people who aren't very interested
Write a love letter to your evil twin during a lunar eclipse
Fool the tricky red beasts guarding the Wheels of Time
Locate the master codex and add erudite graffiti to it
Sell celebrity sperm on the home shopping channel
Dream up wilder, wetter, more interesting problems
Change your name every day for a thousand days
Kill the apocalypse and annihilate Armageddon
Exaggerate your flaws till they turn into virtues
Brag about what you can't do and don't have
Get a vanity license plate that reads KZMYAZ
Bow down to the greatest mystery you know
Make fun of people who make fun of people
See how far you can spit a mouthful of beer
Pick blackberries naked in the pouring rain
Scare yourself with how beautiful you are
Simulate global warming into your pants
Stage a slow-motion water balloon fight
Pretend your wounds are exotic tattoos
Sing anarchist lullabies to lesbian trees
Plunge butcher knives into accordions
Commit a crime that breaks no laws
Sip the tears of someone you love
Build a plush orphanage in Minsk
Feel sorry for a devious lawyer
Rebel against your horoscope
Give yourself another chance
Write your autohagiography
Play games with no rules
Teach animals to dance
Trick your nightmares
Relax and go deeper
Dream like stones
Mock your fears
Drink the sun
Fuck gravity
Sing love
Be mojo
Do jigs
Ask id

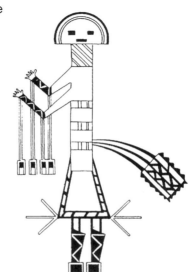

EVIL IS BORING

When an old tree in the rain forest dies and topples over, it takes a long time to decompose. As it does, it becomes host to new saplings that use the decaying log for nourishment.

Picture yourself sitting in the forest gazing upon this scene. How do you describe it? Would you dwell on the putrefaction of the fallen tree while ignoring the fresh life sprouting out of it? If you did, you'd be imitating the perspective of many modern storytellers, especially the journalists and novelists and filmmakers and producers of TV dramas. They devoutly believe that tales of affliction and mayhem and corruption and tragedy are inherently more interesting than tales of triumph and liberation and pleasure and ingenuity.

Using the juggernaut of the media and entertainment industries, they relentlessly propagate this covert dogma. It's not sufficiently profound or well thought out to be called nihilism. *Pop nihilism* is a more accurate term. The mass audience is the victim of this inane ugliness, brainwashed by a multibillion-dollar propaganda machine that in comparison makes Himmler's vaunted soul-stealing apparatus look like a child's backyard puppet show. This is the engine of the phenomena I call the global genocide of the imagination.

At the Beauty and Truth Lab, we believe that stories about the rot are not inherently more captivating than stories about the splendor. On the contrary, given how predictable and ubiquitous they are, stories about the rot are actually quite dull. Obsessing on evil is boring. Rousing fear is a hackneyed shtick. Wallowing in despair is a bad habit. Indulging in cynicism is akin to committing a copycat crime.

Most modern storytellers go even further in their devotion to the rot, implying that breakdown is not only more interesting but far more common than breakthrough, that painful twists outnumber vigrous transformations by a wide margin. That's just absurd disinformation. Entropy does not dominate the human experience. Even factoring in the misery in parts of Africa and the Middle East, the Global Bad Nasty Ratio never exceeds 50 percent. And here in the West, where most of you reading this live, the proportion is lower. Besides that, the fact is that a vast majority of the people on this planet love to be alive, and the preponderance of their experience is a YES, not a NO.

Is it possible to fight tenderly for beauty and truth and love without despising those who spread ugliness and lies and division?

Still, we at the Beauty and Truth Lab are willing to let the news media fill up half their pages and airwaves and bandwidths with poker-faced accounts of decline and degeneration, misery and destruction. We can tolerate a reasonable proportion of movies and novels and TV dramas that revel in pathology. But we also demand EQUAL TIME for stories about integrity and joy and beauty and bliss and renewal and harmony and love. That's all we ask: a mere 50 percent.

I vividly recall one of the shocks that incited me to head in the direction of pronoia. While perusing the front page of my local daily newspaper some years ago, I was startled to find a tiny oasis of redemptive news amidst the usual accounts of reeling turmoil. It reported that inner cities all over America were undergoing a profound renaissance. From Los Angeles to New Orleans to Boston, the poorest sections of town were becoming markedly safer. New businesses were opening, capital was flowing in, neighborhood clean ups were proliferating, drug sales were decreasing, and people were relaxing on their front porches again.

I was amazed that such an uplifting story had cracked the media's taboo against good news. And yet its anomalous presence as an exception to the rule proved that the rule is virtually ironclad.

At this late date in the evolution of pop nihilism, the problem is not merely the media's relentless brainwashing. We of the mass audience have become thoroughly converted to the sadomasochistic vision of the world: so much so that we've almost lost the power even to *perceive* evidence that contradicts that vision. The good news is virtually invisible.

Even those of us whose passion it is to champion the cause of beauty and truth are in the early stages of fighting our blindness. We are retraining our eyes to see the emancipating truth about the nature of reality.

As we gather the secret stories of the human race's glories and success, the Beauty and Truth Lab doesn't spend much time on ho-hum data like, "Two thousand planes took off yesterday and all landed safely." We leave that to others with more patience. Our preferred evidence emphasizes the triumphs that have entertainment value equal to the bad nasty stuff.

We also want our good news to consist of more than reports about hurts being healed and disasters being averted. We celebrate the family of the deceased Israeli girl who gave her heart to be transplanted into a sick Palestinian boy, but we also want a front-page story about physicist Paul Ginsparg, who has revolutionized scientific communication by creating a free service for publishing and reading research reports on the Internet.

We cheer forest protection activist Odigha Odigha's successful campaign to preserve Nigeria's last remaining rain forests, but we want to hear more about George Soros, whose philanthropy has provided billions of dollars in support for intellectual freedom and democratic societies in more than 30 countries.

We honor West Virginia's Julia Bonds, who has made headway in her campaign to halt mountaintop coal mining before it turns more river valleys into waste dumps, but we also want sensational acknowledgment for Ruth Lilly, who donated $100 million of her fortune to *Poetry* magazine, even though its editors had rejected all the poems she had submitted for possible publication over the years.

I invite you to share with us the *interesting* good news you come across in your travels. Not sentimental tales of generic hope; not "Chicken Soup for the Soul;" not life imitating the faux Hollywood art of contrived happy endings; but rather crafty, enigmatic, lyrical eruptions of the sublime; unpredictable outbreaks of soul that pass Emily Dickinson's test for poetry: She said she always knew when she was reading the real thing because it made her feel like the top of her head was about to come off.

Feel free, too, to take up the cause of zoom and boom as you resist the practitioners of doom and gloom in your own sphere. Demand equal time for news about integrity and joy and beauty and pleasure and renewal and harmony and love. In your personal life, be alert for stories that tend to provide evidence for the fact that all of creation is conspiring to give us exactly what we need, exactly when we need it.

P.S. Part of our task is to hunt down and identify the interesting good news that's going on now. But we've also been charged with the job of *creating* the good news that's coming.

SLAM

If you've ever been to a poetry slam, you know that sensitive lyrics in praise of love and beauty are rare. Far more common are vehement diatribes that curse injustice and hypocrisy.

I'm not putting that stuff down; I've been known to unload some dark rants myself. But at this perfect moment, the Beauty and Truth Lab is more interested in pragmatic idealism. We're thirsty for streams of visionary consciousness, fountains of lustrous truth, and floods of feisty hope.

Therefore, we propose that instead of a poetry slam, you participate in our "I Have a Dream" Slam. To get in the mood, read or listen to the speech that Martin Luther King Jr. made at the Lincoln Memorial in Washington, D.C., on August 28, 1963. The text, as well as an MP3 of King giving the speech, is available on the Web at tinyurl.com/yzed42.

Here's an excerpt:

I have a dream that one day this nation will rise up and live out the true meaning of its creed: We hold these truths to be self-evident that all men are created equal.

I have a dream that one day on the red hills of Georgia the sons of former slaves and the sons of former slave owners will be able to sit down together at the table of brotherhood.

I have a dream that one day even the state of Mississippi, a state sweltering with the heat of injustice, sweltering with the heat of oppression, will be transformed into an oasis of freedom and justice.

I have a dream that my four little children will one day live in a nation where they will not be judged by the color of their skin but by the content of their character. I have a dream today!

I have a dream that one day every valley shall be exalted, and every hill and mountain shall be made low, the rough places will be made plain, and the crooked places will be made straight, and the glory of the Lord shall be revealed and all flesh shall see it together.

Maybe King's plea will inspire you to create your own personal "I Have a Dream" manifesto. To be part of the "I Have a Dream" Slam, send your offering to Truthrooster@gmail.com.

My own "I Have a Dream" speech appears on the next page.

"Almost without exception, everything society has considered a social advance has been prefigured first in some utopian writing." —David L. Cooperrider

I HAVE A DREAM

have a dream.

I have a dream that in the New Earth, there will be a new Bill of Rights. The first amendment will be, "Your daily wage is directly tied to the beauty and truth and love you provide."

I have a dream that in the New Earth, childbirth will be broadcast on prime time TV every single night.

I have a dream that the New Earth will have rapturists, and they'll vastly outnumber the terrorists. The rapturists will be performance artists with a conscience . . . charismatic improvisers who love to spring fun surprises. They'll commit unexpected interventions and unscheduled spectacles that delight hordes of strangers.

I have a dream that in the New Earth, we will add an eleventh commandment to the standard ten: *Thou shalt not bore God.*

I have a dream of a week-long annual holiday called the Bacchanalia. Work and business will be suspended so that all adults can explore their ripe mojo with frothy erotic experiments. Tenderly orgiastic marathons will rage unabated. Reverential ecstasy and grateful generosity will rule.

I have a dream that when anchormen report tragedies on their nightly TV shows, they'll break down and cry and let their emotions show. No more poker faces.

In the New Earth, you'll be a fascinating enigma worthy of a best-selling unauthorized biography and I'll be an inscrutable genius whose every move is packed with symbolic meaning—and vice versa. That will be the law in the New Earth—far different from the Old Earth, where schadenfreude is epidemic and your distinctive flair is supposed to make me feel worshipful or diminished.

I have a dream that in the New Earth, the word "asshole" will be a term of endearment rather than abuse. Plutocracy will be a felony. April Fool's Day will come once a month. There'll be scientific horoscopes and mystical logic. Every one of us will have at least one imaginary friend. Compassion will be an aphrodisiac.

In the New Earth, we'll launch an affirmative action program that ultimately makes most of us celebrities. Buddhist real estate developers will build a chain of sacred shopping centers in the heartland. The CEOs of the Fortune 500 companies will be required by law to enjoy once-a-week sessions with Jungian psychotherapists. Pioneers in artificial intelligence research will develop computers that can talk to God.

In the New Earth, same-sex marriages will be fully sanctioned, of course. But why stop there? We'll also legalize wedding bonds among threesomes, foursomes, fivesomes, and large groups of people who are in love with each other. I have a dream that we will expand the meaning of love beyond anything our ancestors imagined.

In the New Earth, our children will study singing and dancing and meditation and dream work with as much diligence as they now devote to math and science. They'll learn to see with their own eyes and think with their own minds and feel with their own hearts, studying those subjects as intently as they do spelling and grammar and social studies. Beginning in seventh grade, they'll get lessons in the art of creating successful intimate relationships. And we'll teach them why it's only fair that for the next 3,000 years we use "her" for the generic singular pronoun instead of "him."

I have a dream that we will take everything we need and give everything we have. We'll be both selfish altruists and generous braggarts, libertarian socialists and capitalist humanitarians. That'll be the law in the New Earth—different from the Old Earth, where you can blindly serve your own interests or devote yourself to the needs of others, but not both.

I have a dream that in the New Earth, Oprah Winfrey will buy up all the Pizza Huts on the planet and convert them into a global network of menstrual huts, where for a few days each month, every one of us, men and women alike, can resign from the crazy-making 9–5—drop out and slow down, break trance and dive down into eternal time.

We will sleep nine hours every night as we practice our lucid dreams . . . sing love songs from the future while soaking in steamy herb baths . . . feast on chocolate as we converse with the little voices in our heads

. . . research the distinctions between stupid, boring pain and smart, fascinating pain until we finally get it right . . . wear magic underwear made from eagle feathers, spider webs, and 100-year-old moss . . . and conjure up bigger, better, more original sins and wilder, wetter, more interesting problems.

In the New Earth, you'll kick your own ass and I'll wash my own brain. I'll be my own parent and you'll be your own wife. And vice versa. That'll be normal in the New Earth—different from the Old Earth, where everyone except me is to blame for my ignorance and you call on everyone except yourself to give you what you need.

I'll push my own buttons and right my own wrongs. You'll wake yourself up and sing your own songs.

I'm the president now . . . and so are you. I am the Supreme Commander of the United Snakes of the Blooming HaHa . . . and so are you. And what we proclaim is that in the New Earth, we will love our neighbors as ourselves, even if our neighbors are jerks. We will never divide the world into us against them. We will search for the divine spark even in the people we most despise, and we will never dehumanize anyone, even those who dehumanize us.

I have a dream that sooner or later every one of us will become a well-rounded, highly skilled, incredibly rich master of rowdy bliss—with lots of leisure time and an orgiastic feminist conscience.

Pyrokleptomania refers to a Promethean compulsion to steal fire.

SACRED ADVERTISEMENT

_Thanks to our sponsors for "I Have a Dream"—
psychologist Carl Jung, poet Walt Whitman,
and activist Martin Luther King Jr.
Their support made it possible to retrieve
these memories from the future._

Primordial Gossip

DREAMY PRONOIA THERAPY

Practice in becoming a doggedly visionary Master of Freaky Purity

Write your own "I Have a Dream" poem, story, essay, or manifesto.

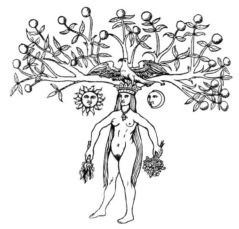

Clues to the Rebel Grail

Fat Lover

The Yanyuwa Aboriginal people live along the coast of Australia's Northern Territory. Their word for "fat" is *nalu-ngiliny.* It doesn't merely refer to the greasy stuff that grows naturally under the skin of animal bodies. It's also a metaphysical term for vitality.

Anything that's rich in *nalu-ngiliny* is healthy. A certain landscape may be considered fat, for instance, which means that it's fertile and sacred. When acacia flowers bloom each year, it's a sign that sea turtles and the marine mammals known as dugongs, favorite foods of the Yanyuwa, are "fat" and ready to be hunted.

I have a dream that you will identify the things in your life that are *nalu-ngiliny,* and give them the honor and gratitude they deserve.

Sacred Advertisement

Nalu-ngiliny is brought to you by your bone marrow, which every second of your life produces 100 trillion molecules of hemoglobin, the stuff that carries oxygen from your lungs to the rest of you . . . and by your immune system, which every minute begets 10 million lymphocytes, the key players in your body's defenses. (For more info, go to tinyurl.com/6hmoaj and tinyurl.com/m33bjc)

WHAT IS THE BEAUTY AND TRUTH LABORATORY?

The Beauty and Truth Lab is an ever-expanding web of think tanks and mystery schools devoted to exploring pronoia. Since I launched the prototype in October 2001, 22 other branches have sprung up in basements, barns, and bedrooms all over the world: 16 in North America and others in Amsterdam, London, Berlin, Florence, Italy, Aix-en-Provence, France, and Sydney, Australia.

All of these, including my own in Marin County, California, are similar in spirit to pirate radio stations. They're not registered, incorporated, or licensed, and Goddess forbid that they should ever become the canonical hubs of a franchise.

That doesn't mean I eschew power, authority, and wealth. My own branch of the Beauty and Truth Lab is stationed in a garage next to the house I rent on the seedy outskirts of suburbia, but I'd have no problem moving to a more expansive location, like say, a conference center on a 100-acre compound in an idyllic place that the original inhabitants of this continent regarded as a power spot. And I'd love it if this book sold a million copies, or if Beauty and Truth Labs were as common as 7-Elevens in 10 years.

On the other hand, I'm happy with whatever blessings life conspires to bring me. If it's to my and your ultimate benefit that this book reaches no more than 50,000 wise guys and riot grrrls, I will celebrate that outcome. And my garage-based laboratory is fine just the way it is, with its sloping floor and row of tiny windows darkened by the exuberant persimmon tree outside. The modesty of its structure is a constant reminder that the most important aspect of my work is building the Beauty and Truth Lab within me. As I prod my imagination to nurture

ever-more-detailed visions of love, compassion, joy, freedom, beauty, and truth, I'm better able to spot and name all those good things in the world around me. I also become more skilled at creating them.

My humble headquarters brings another advantage. It encourages me to regard everywhere I go as a potential extension of the Beauty and Truth Lab. My experiments aren't confined to the hours I spend in the solitude of my ivory tower, but also spill out into the fertile chaos of daily life.

On one epiphanic occasion, an eight-lane highway at rush hour turned into a temporary Beauty and Truth Lab. It was just a few days after my return from the Burning Man festival where the dream of the Lab had hatched. I was driving on 101, the artery that bisects Marin County.

As I cruised at 65 mph between Larkspur and Corte Madera, a blonde in a Jaguar convertible with the top down passed me on the right. Perhaps distracted by the chat she was enjoying on her cell phone, she suddenly zipped in front of me. After hitting my brakes to avoid rear-ending her, I honked my horn to express my annoyance. In response, she careened over to the left lane, then slowed down and waited for me to catch up. I avoided eye contact at first, but finally looked over. Quaking with agitation, she was flashing me a middle-finger salute and a mad face as fierce as a Tibetan demon. Her car was veering closer to mine. Might she actually crash into me on purpose?

I was quaking with agitation myself. My adrenaline surged, threatening to explode to mushroom cloud proportions. Curses were rising from my gut to throat. At the same time, I resisted it all. I didn't want to be possessed by stupid rage because of the carelessness of a bad driver. Such a trivial eruption of my fight-or-flight instinct was against my religion.

Then a miracle happened. As if through divine intervention, without any prompting from my will, fond memories of Burning Man surged into my imagination. I was back there on the ancient lake bed with my stack of baby wipes, intimately conversing with the Goddess of the sun. I could hear the thump of music in the distance and feel the desert breeze on my cheeks.

The stabbing rage that had filled my abdomen dissipated. In its place, a whirlpool of warmth spiraled around my heart. It was a luxurious, sensual feeling, almost erotic. Then came a prick like a needle popping a water balloon, followed by a gush of sweet release. A heart orgasm? I was suffused with a sense of well-being. All was right with the world, and I felt a cheerful affection for everything, even the mad woman in the Jaguar.

As urgent as my wrath had been just a few moments before, so now was my tenderness. I felt triumphant. For the first time in my life, I had conquered an adrenaline rush of anger *as it was happening.* In comparable situations in the past, I had always needed a cooling-off period before I could soften my heart.

It was as if I had succeeded at a difficult game that required all my macho prowess, only the prowess in this case was demonstrated through love instead of strength and cleverness.

I looked over at the crazed monster in the car that was on the verge of sideswiping mine. She was still glaring at me as if transfixed. Her demeanor had not lost any of its obscene savagery. Had she even glanced at the road in front of her recently?

I rolled down my window and leaned my head out. Less than ten feet now separated our faces. She looked as if she were about to leap out of her seat and pounce on me. Just in time, I smiled and blew her three kisses. Then, summoning my ample powers of vocal projection, I boomed out the words, half-singing, "I love you. I have always loved you. And I will love you until the end of time." I put my hands together in the gesture of prayer, using my knees to steady the steering wheel, and bowed my head in her direction.

I was utterly sincere. There was not a speck of sarcasm or irony in the mix. At that moment, I was a bodhisattva linked directly to the undulating love of the Goddess. I had no doubt that a radiant beam of divine sweetness was emanating from me, bathing the mad woman in a palpable ray of lusty compassion. She had to be feeling it.

There was one more gift I longed to deliver: the talisman I kept on my dashboard. It was a spectacular piece, meticulously constructed by my friend Calley, who was an adept in a Qabalistic mystery school as well as an expert in origami, the Japanese art of paperfolding. She had taken eight one hundred-dollar bills—real legal tender—and folded them into the shape of an eight-pointed star. Golden threads, small rubies, fragments of a meteorite, and the 400 million-year-old fossilized penis of a daddy longlegs were the other essential elements. Everything was mounted on a circular disk of gold, six inches in diameter.

As formulated by Hakim Bey, a Temporary Autonomous Zone (TAZ) is any event that liberates the imaginations of everyone present, thereby making it possible for life to be penetrated by the Marvelous.

I treasured the piece. Calley had made it for me at a time in my life when I was purging myself of old, ingrained desires that were no longer in harmony with my evolving ideals. The kind of fame that I had coveted in my early years of being a rock musician, for instance, no longer interested me. Nor did my former fascination with having an endless variety of sexual partners. Calley invoked her sophisticated understanding of Qabalistic and astrological principles to design the talisman so that it would supercharge my ability to change my life in accordance with my will.

This was the gift I wanted to bequeath to my former adversary, Jaguar Woman. Her convertible top was down and our cars were nearly touching, so the risk of missing my target was small. Taking my beloved power object in my right hand, I reached out the window and flung it. She swerved away but not out of range. It fell into the front seat of her car.

I returned my gaze to the road ahead, checking to see if the divine guidance that had been pouring through me had extended to keeping my car on track. It had. A few seconds later, I returned my gaze to Jaguar Woman. She was holding up the talisman as she stared at me. Her face had turned innocent and awed, almost reverent, as if she had seen the Ghost of Christmas Future arm-in-arm with a long-lost loved one. I guessed that her demons had withdrawn.

After that her car slowed, quickly falling behind my pace. In my rearview mirror, I observed her making her way to the far right lane. She drove carefully, using her turn signal. She got off at the next exit.

Medicine Story

In the midst of my exuberant oneness with all of creation, a tinge of sadness crept in. I mused on how I'd never know if my victory over the angry devil within me would produce any lasting effect on Jaguar Woman. Would she fully appreciate the love I invoked in response to her attack? If nothing else, surely the gift of the talisman would change her life forever, right?

As I sped toward the Golden Gate Bridge, I remembered a quote I'd once heard attributed to basketball coach John Wooden: "You can't have a perfect day without doing something for someone who'll never be able to repay you." I mused on the fact that while this *was* a relatively selfless approach to giving gifts, it was still imperfect: Maybe the recipient of your largesse couldn't literally pay you back, but he or she could think wonderful thoughts about you; your ego would benefit. No, a more ultimate expression of generosity, an improvement on Wooden's formulation, would be to give *anonymously* to someone who couldn't repay you.

Which was what I had just done. Rather than bemoaning the fact that I'd never know whether or how Jaguar Woman would benefit from my gift, I realized I should celebrate.

At this point in my impromptu Beauty and Truth Lab experiment, I had settled into full meditation mode. Though I was barreling along a crowded freeway at high velocity, my brain was enjoying an expansive perspective made possible by an abundance of alpha waves. I embodied the definition of meditation offered by the Hindu sage Patanjali: "an unbroken flow of knowledge on a particular object."

My stream of consciousness flowed on to the next clue, advice I'd once heard articulated by the Dalai Lama. He said you should work as hard as you can to fight for justice and reduce suffering— even as you accept with equanimity that all of your efforts may come to absolutely nothing in the end. My translation: Give your best beauty and live your highest truth without expecting any rewards.

My unbroken flow of knowledge glided on to the next thought, this one planted in me by the author Rachel Pollack. "We cannot predict the results of healing, either our own or the world around us," she said. "We need to act for the sake of a redemption that will be a mystery until it unfolds before us."

I looked around my car for something to write on. At the end of my drive I'd be meeting a potential investor in San Francisco, and I wanted to record the results of my spontaneous Beauty and Truth Lab experiment before having to hand myself over to the business part of my brain.

There was only one surface available to take notes on: a piece of junk mail lying on the floor in the backseat. Poorly designed, it had a lot of empty space on one page. I balanced it on my thigh as I recorded the notes that became the basis for what you've just read.

A half hour later I was at 16th Street and Potrero in San Francisco, where I scored a parking space in record time. Before getting out to go to my meeting, I sat in my car and composed the last few paragraphs of this report. They read as follows:

First there was the "Baby Wipe Communiqué," and now there's the "Blank Space on a Piece of Junk Mail Communiqué." I prophesy that the future will bring the "Bar Napkin Communiqué," the "Grocery Bag Communiqué," the "Mulberry Leaf Torn Off the Tree Next to the Library While I'm Walking by Communiqué," and many others.

A new tradition is announcing itself. It reveals I've got to be ready to conjure up the Beauty and Truth Lab at a moment's notice, whenever a pressing experiment needs to be done—even if it's in my car, a sports bar, the check-out line at Safeway, or on a stroll downtown.

This is not to say that some future Beauty and Truth Lab breakthroughs won't also unfold on the beach after midnight on the winter solstice or on my meditation pillow after three days of fasting and praying.

But I vow to be vigilant for the possibility that any place and any time may become the holy ground where I can commit radical acts of pronoia or gather revelations that will change my mind every which way about the mysterious, ever-deepening meanings of pronoia. I promise to seize the pregnant pauses, leap into the empty spots, and squeeze through the cracks in the system.

Medicine Story

Everyone
who believes
in the devil
is the devil

Your Personal Manifesto

The Beauty and Truth Lab would love it if, while consorting with this book, you would be inspired to brainstorm your own personal manifesto. There's plenty of empty space for you to work out the details beginning on page 374.

As you proceed, feel free to borrow from us and from the hundreds of gorgeous geniuses whose wisdom we've borrowed. Below is an especially pithy mission statement written by Tatsuya Ishida, who makes his home at sinfest.net. It's fine with him if you want to say that this is how you feel, too.

"All I ever wanted in life was to make a difference, be worshiped like a god, conquer the universe, travel the world, meet interesting people, find the missing link, fight the good fight, live for the moment, seize each day, make a fortune, know what really matters, end world hunger, vanquish the dragon, be super popular but too cool to care, be master of my own fate, embrace my destiny, feel as much as I can feel, give too much, and love everything." The Portable Emerson

Sacred Advertisement

Here's a message from our spiritual patron,
Ralph Waldo Emerson:
"Make your own Bible. Select and collect all the
words and sentences that in your reading
have been like the blast of triumph out of Shakespeare,
Seneca, Moses, John and Paul."
—The Portable Emerson, *Carl Bode, editor*

The Universe Is Made of Stories

The poet Muriel Rukeyser said the universe is composed of stories, not of atoms. The physicist Werner Heisenberg declared that the universe is made of music, not of matter.

And we believe that if you habitually expose yourself to toxic stories and music, you could wind up living in the wrong universe, where it's impossible to become the gorgeous genius you were born to be.

That's why we implore you to nourish yourself with delicious, nutritious tales and tunes that inspire you to exercise your willpower for your highest good.

"The only war that matters is the war against the imagination. All other wars are subsumed by it." —Diane di Prima, "Rant," from *Pieces of a Song*

Astrologer Caroline Casey offers an apt metaphor to illustrate how crucial it is for us to hear and read good stories. She notes that if we don't have enough of the normal, healthy kind of iodine in our bodies, we absorb radioactive iodine, which has entered the food chain through nuclear test explosions conducted in the atmosphere. Similarly, unless we fill ourselves up with stories that invigorate us, we're more susceptible to sopping up the poisonous, degenerative narratives.

Novelist Ursula K. Le Guin decries the linear perspective that dominates modern storytelling. She says it's "like an arrow, starting here and going straight there and THOK! hitting its mark." Furthermore, she complains, plots are usually advanced through conflict, as if interesting action can't possibly arise from any other catalyst.

I invite you to rebel against these oppressive conventions. Wean yourself from tales that have reductive plot lines fueled primarily by painful events. Celebrate the luminous mysteries that have shaped your own life story: the meandering fascinations that didn't lead to tidy conclusions, the wobbly joys that fed your soul but didn't serve your ego's ambitions, the adventures whose success revolved around brain-teasing breakthroughs instead of exhausting triumphs over suffering.

"It is difficult
to get the news from poems
       yet men die miserably every day
       for lack
of what is found there." —William Carlos Williams,
"Asphodel, That Greeny Flower"

In *The White Goddess: A Historical Grammar of Poetic Myth,* Robert Graves tells us that "In ancient Ireland, the *ollave,* or master-poet, sat next to the king and was privileged, as none but the queen was, to wear six different colors in his clothes." The *ollave,* he adds, was also a judge and seer, and tutored the king in morality.

In contrast, our culture relegates poets to the margins of every debate. After the terrorist attack of September 2001, for example, only Maya Angelou, in an ephemeral appearance on ABC-TV's *Nightline,* and Robert Pinsky on *The News Hour with Jim Lehrer,* managed to crack the procession of pundits, politicians, and lawyers that dominated the airwaves and shaped our experience of what had happened. During the same period, leftist radio stations KPFA, WBAI, KPFK, KPFT, and KBOO, which define themselves as alternatives to the corporate news media, also offered newscasts monopolized by political analysis. It was rare to hear commentary from anyone who specialized in psychological, spiritual, or imaginal modes of perception.

If we of the rabble-rouser persuasion don't champion the *ollave,* how can we expect the culture of the living dead to do so?

"It's not until an event, institution, thought, principle, or movement crosses the media threshold that it becomes real to us." —Todd Gitlin, *Media Unlimited: How the Torrent of Images and Sounds Overwhelms Our Lives*

"Though we don't have to believe what the media tell us, we can't know what they don't tell us." —Bernard McGrane, "The Zen TV Experiment"

How did it come to be that what we call the news is reported solely by journalists? There are so many other kinds of events besides the narrow band favored by that highly specialized brand of storytellers. Indeed, there are many phenomena that can literally not even

be perceived by journalists. Their training, their temperament, and their ambitions make vast areas of human experience invisible to them.

"Ninety-six percent of the cosmos puzzles astronomers." I loved reading that headline on the CNN website. It showed that at least some of our culture's equivalents of high priests, the scientists, are humble enough to acknowledge that the universe is made mostly of stuff they can't even detect, let alone study.

If only the journalists were equally modest. Since they're not, we'll say it: The majority of everything that happens on this planet is invisible to them.

The Beauty and Truth Lab is gathering a network of seers to report the news that journalists miss and ignore. We're tempted to call them "spies," since they've got to be on the lookout for what has become secret. They don't necessarily have to be covert in their operations, but they do have to be attentive to stories unfolding below the media threshold. Maybe it's better if we don't give them a title yet. That way we won't limit the kinds of people who can serve in this role.

In the early years of Christianity, there were hundreds of books interpreting the life and teachings of Jesus Christ. But by 325 AD, a group backed by the political and military might of the Roman Empire had determined which few of the stories about Christ would thereafter be considered the canonical New Testament, and which would be regarded as heretical bilge. No better evidence exists for the saying, "History is a tale told by the victors." Keep this in mind as you strategize your way through your personal War of the Stories. Your account of events may have more truth in it than everyone else's conflicting tales, but that won't carry much weight unless you obtain the power to *enforce* your version.

"The world is composed of rival gangs of hypnotists, each competing for your entranced attention." —graffiti on the wall of a public restroom at Northgate Mall, San Rafael, California

"The news flies down its beam of dusted light." —Osip Mandelstam

WELCOME TO THE SHOW

You're tuned to PNN, the Pronoia News Network. We're coming to you live from your repressed memory of paradise, reminding you that you can have anything you want if you will just ask for it in an unselfish way.

The Pronoia News Network is brought to you by the state of mind that the philosopher Robert Anton Wilson inhabited when he said, "Reality is what you can get away with."

Welcome to the end of your nightmares, beauty and truth fans! The world is young, your soul is free, and a naked celebrity is dying to talk to you about your most intimate secrets right now.

Just kidding.

In fact, the world is young, your soul is free, and at any moment you will begin to feel horny compassion for salamanders, clouds, toasters, oak trees, and even the ocean itself.

I'm your host for the Pronoia News Network. My name is Younger Elder, the Tender of the Blooming Haha, and I'm proud to announce that this is a perfect moment. Stay with us for the next million perfect moments, and we promise to overstimulate your imagination and convince you that all you have to do to achieve the impossible is attempt the absurd.

Why is it so important to the future of red-tailed hawks and daffodils and coral reefs that childbirth be broadcast live on prime time TV every night? Stay tuned.

What is the best way for you to cancel the curses you've cast on yourself over the years? Stay tuned.

Why are we so sure that sooner or later every one of you will become a good-humored, vehemently compassionate, innocently wise master of pronoia, with a skill for lucid dreaming and a knack for being yourself even when you are beside yourself?

Stay tuned to the Pronoia News Network, and all will become bewilderingly clear. We will prove to you that life is a conspiracy to shower you with a nonstop feast of interesting experiences, all of which are designed to help you grow your intelligence, shed your pretensions, and master the art of ingenious love.

The Pronoia News Network is a tricky experiment designed to bring heaven all the way down to earth . . . if that's what you want. It's a holy advertisement based on the story of your life . . . if that's what you want.

The clues that will lead to the end of your ancient amnesia are all around you, beauty and truth fans . . . if that's what you want. You're ready to rediscover the 13 perfect secrets from the beginning of time . . . if that's what you want.

So what do you want, anyway?

PRONOIA NEWS NETWORK

The Immortalists Current human life expectancy, already at age 78 for Americans, is steadily increasing. Men now live an average of 27 years longer than they did a century ago, and women 31 years. Many scientists believe there is no absolute limit to the human life span. Some expect that by 2070, life expectancy will be 100.

Crime Declines As of 2007, crime in the U.S. was at its lowest level since it was first officially tracked. Between 1973 and 2005, the violent crime rate decreased by 56 percent, while crimes against property shrank by 70 percent. The report comes from the Bureau of Justice's "National Crime Victimization Survey" (tinyurl.com/l804).

According to the FBI, the years 2005 and 2006 brought a small increase in violent crimes, but by 2008, the rate had fallen even lower than it was in 2005. Crimes against property have steadily continued to drop. The most dramatic decline has occurred in the number of rapes. The frequency of that crime per capita is down 85 percent since the 1970s.

Moose Luxury A Canadian moose can now walk in peace and safety all the way to South America, thanks to Harrison Ford and other celebrities with wealth and influence. They quietly worked together for years to purchase land along corridors that connect various wildlife refuges and national parks.

Meanwhile, Canadian government officials announced that their country, the second largest in the world in terms of physical size, is creating ten giant national parks and five marine conservation areas. The new sanctuaries, when added to the existing 39 national parks, will double the amount of protected land.

Conversation with Eternity Beauty and Truth Lab researcher Firenze Matisse traveled to Antarctica. On the first day, the guide took him and his group to a remote area and left them alone for an hour to commune with the pristine air and unearthly stillness. After a while, a penguin ambled up and launched into a ceremonial display of squawks and stretches. Firenze responded with recitals of his favorite memorized poems, imagining he was "engaged in a conversation with eternity." Halfway through his inspired performance of Thich Nhat Hanh's "Please Call Me by My True Names," the penguin sent a stream of green projectile vomit cascading against his chest, and shuffled away.

Though Firenze initially felt deflated by eternity's surprise, no harm was done. He soon came to see it as a first-class cosmic joke, and looked forward to exploiting its value as an amusing story with which to regale his friends back home.

Beauty and Truth Lab researcher Michael Logan was the first person to hear Firenze's tale upon his return from Antarctica. "You might want to consider this, Firenze," Michael mused after taking it all in. "Penguins nurture their offspring by chewing food—mixing it up with all God's enzymes—and then vomiting it into the mouths of the penguin babies. Perhaps you weren't the butt of a cosmic joke or some Linda Blair-esque bad review, but in fact the recipient of a very precious gift of love. Who knows?"

Now Firenze has two punch lines for his tale of redemptive pronoia.

PNN is made possible by Mary Oliver's poem about sunflowers, in which she writes that the long work of turning their lives into a celebration is not easy.

IMPOSSIBLE DREAM FULFILLED

The world's largest private bank, Citigroup, agreed to stop financing projects that damage sensitive ecosystems. It promised to invest more in projects that use renewable energy and to pursue policies that protect indigenous people. How did this impossible dream come to pass? The humble but dogged environmental group, Rainforest Action Network, creatively pestered Citigroup for years until the corporation gave in to its demands.

PNN is brought to you by this passage from Eknath Easwaran's book Gandhi, the Man: *"One of the most radical discoveries Gandhi was to make in a lifetime of experimentation: In order to transform others, you have to transform yourself."*

Sharing Your Breath

Quoting geneticists, Guy Murchie says we're all family. You have at least a million relatives as close as tenth cousin, and no one on Earth is any further removed than your fiftieth cousin.

Murchie also describes our kinship through an analysis of how deeply we share the air. With each breath, you take into your body 10 sextillion atoms, and—owing to the wind's ceaseless circulation—over a year's time you have intimate relations with oxygen molecules exhaled by every person alive, as well as by everyone who ever lived. Right now you may be carrying atoms that were once inside the lungs of Malcolm X, Christopher Columbus, Joan of Arc, and Cleopatra. (Source: Guy Murchie, *The Seven Mysteries of Life*)

Fortune Cookie You're like an arrow in flight. You're a half-cooked feast, the fifth month of pregnancy, the week before a big election. Have you ever mastered a second language? You resemble the time right before fluency arrives.

The Evolution of Ecstasy

According to ecstasy expert Rapunzel Blavatsky, the very nature of ecstasy seems to be evolving. Researchers at her Berkeley, California-based Beauty and Truth Lab have found that increasing numbers of people are able to cultivate a chronic, low-grade rapture that never fully dissipates. This altered state often sensitizes their perceptions to the presence of subtle miracles that are hidden from others.

Blavatsky's team has also discovered that for these "everyday ecstatics," extraordinary stimulation and peak experiences are not necessary to sustain the constant flow of bliss. The testimony of one such "everyday ecstatic," Sheila Samizdat, illustrates the phenomenon.

"My handmade, fresh-cooked booster dose of euphoria arrived," Samizdat reports, "while I was waiting in line at the post office on a Tuesday afternoon. I already felt pretty good, because a few minutes earlier I'd witnessed a man and a woman squirting each other in the head with yellow squirt guns as they embraced and wrestled and conducted a raucous make-out session in the alley behind the post office.

"But my giddiness really kicked into high gear when an exuberant toddler tipped over a trash can, turned it upside down, climbed up on top, and leaped off as he shouted, 'God sucks!' Meanwhile, the customer behind me in line was telling someone on her cell phone that she kissed a lesbian from Amnesty International outside a pungent-smelling herb shop in Chinatown while a gang of elegantly dressed thugs orchestrated a drug deal in a nearby alley.

"Moments later, a barely-five-feet-tall Vietnamese man in his 40s, sporting shoulder-length black hair and wearing an oversize green silk pajama top, rode a neon pink girl's bike one-handed right through the open front doors of the post office and into the lobby as he sipped a Laffy Taffy Blue Vanilla Slurpee and sang 'The Impossible Dream' from the Broadway musical, *Man of La Mancha*.

"And suddenly I found myself thrust into the throbbing core of delight, awash in murmuring, quizzical amazement. The center of my gravity exploded like a supernova, instantaneously spreading my awareness out to the size of the universe, turning me into a furious sun-blasted ocean-soaked wind-cured radiance, arriving everywhere at once from the heart of the Only Intelligence There Is. And I was home again, worshiping inside the tabernacle in the wilderness. 'Oh, yeah,' I thought to myself with a rush of eternal glee, 'Now I remember: I am you and you are me and they are we and we are they.'"

Sacred Genius of Generosity "The Sun, each second, transforms four million tons of itself into light, giving itself over to become energy that we, with every meal, partake of. For four million years, humans have been feasting on the Sun's energy stored in the form of wheat or reindeer, as each day the Sun dies as Sun and is reborn as the vitality of Earth. Every child of ours needs to learn the simple truth: She is the energy of the Sun. And we adults should organize things so her face shines with the same radiant joy.

"Human generosity is possible only because at the center of the solar system a magnificent stellar generosity pours forth free energy day and night without stop and without complaint and without the slightest hesitation. This is the way of the universe. This is the way of life. And this is the way in which each of us joins this cosmological lineage when we accept the Sun's gift of energy and transform it into creative action that will enable the community to flourish." — Brian Swimme, *The Hidden Heart of the Cosmos*, video

The Inner Voice Speaks

Scientists have confirmed what we all knew: You do indeed have a little voice in your head that warns you when you're about to do something dumb. It's called the anterior cingulate cortex, according to white-coated authorities at Carnegie-Mellon University. If you're receptive to it, it's as good as having a guardian angel. "Don't do it," the voice whispers when you're on the verge of locking your keys in your car or leaving the bar with the cute drunk you just met. "Go back," it murmurs as you start to walk away from a huge, though initially inconvenient, opportunity.

Better Than Cloning a Dinosaur

Aeschylus, the seminal playwright of ancient Greece, wrote more than 90 plays, but most did not survive. The evidence for his reputation as the "Father of Tragedy" has consisted of just seven works. Recently, however, archaeologists have discovered an eighth, *Achilles*. It was on a papyrus scroll stuffed inside an Egyptian mummy. In the summer of 2004, a theater company in Cyprus staged the ancient play for the first time in over 2,000 years.

BREAKING THE PRONOIA TABOO

"The secret of change is to focus all your energy not on fighting the old, but on building the new." —Socrates

"The basis of freedom is recognition of the unconscious; the invisible dimension; not yet realized; leaving a space for the new." —Norman O. Brown, *Love's Body*

"Never doubt that a small group of thoughtful, committed citizens can change the world. Indeed, it's the only thing that ever has." —Margaret Mead

"No work is more worthwhile than to be a sign of divine joy and a fountain of divine love." —Andrew Harvey

"If a man is called to be a street sweeper, he should sweep streets even as Michelangelo painted, or Beethoven played music, or Shakespeare wrote poetry. He should sweep streets so well that all the hosts of heaven and earth will pause to say, here lived a great street sweeper who did his job well." —Martin Luther King Jr.

Teen Angst Update

The juvenile crime rate has plummeted to its lowest levels since 1979. Violent crime committed by teenagers is 40 percent lower than it was in 1994.

Drunken teens are still killing themselves while driving cars, but the rate is less than half of what it was in 1975.

In 60 years, there hasn't been a lower birthrate among teenage girls than there is now. The overall dropout rate among American high school students has declined by four percent in the last two decades, with an eight percent improvement among African Americans. Three-fourths of high school students say they get along very well or extremely well with their parents, and only three percent say they don't get along well.

Urban Renewal At a concert in California, devotional singer Krishna Das told a story of escorting his revered teachers, a frail old Indian couple, to an acupuncturist in New York. They had to walk through a neighborhood dominated by strip clubs, prostitutes, and drug dealers. Every few feet, a new salesperson approached with an offer of crack, weed, crank, or sexual adventures.

Krishna Das worried about subjecting his beloved guides to such a degrading experience, but they were unfazed. "This is heaven," said the woman. When a surprised Krishna Das asked what she meant, she replied, "Heaven is any place where one's needs can be met."

Early last century, marauding boll weevils devoured the cotton crop that was the main product of Enterprise, Alabama. Local farmers had no choice but to diversify the plants they grew. As a result, the town's per capita income tripled what it had been when cotton was king. In response, grateful citizens built a huge bronze monument to the insect that had forced them to grow richer.

☼

Leo Alard was the first Hispanic to become an Episcopalian bishop in the U.S. His pioneer spirit emerged early on. As a young priest in the 1960s, he headed a racially integrated parish in Chattahoochee, Florida. The bigots of the KKK didn't look favorably on his work, and on one occasion they burned a cross on the church lawn. Alard, who was supervising a youth group on that particular night, brought the class out and had everyone toast marshmallows over the fire.

MIRABILIA REPORT *Mirabilia* n. events that inspire wonder, marvelous phenomena, small miracles; from the Latin *mirabilia*, "marvels."

■ With every dawn, when first light penetrates the sea, many seahorse colonies perform a dance to the sun.

■ A seven-year-old Minnesota boy received patent number 6,368,227 for a new method of swinging on a swing.

■ As it thrusts itself into our Milky Way Galaxy, the dwarf galaxy Sagittarius is unraveling, releasing a thick stream of dark matter that is flowing right through the Earth.

■ A chemist in Australia finally succeeded in mixing oil and water.

■ Except among birds and land mammals, the females of most species are bigger than the males.

■ The South African version of TV's *Sesame Street* has an HIV-positive Muppet named Kami.

■ In just two minutes, an ingenious octopus at the Bronx Zoo learned to unscrew the lid from a jar to get at the food inside, though it had never experienced a jar with a lid before.

■ Black sheep have a better sense of smell than white sheep.

■ There are about 60,000 miles of blood vessels in your body. Every square inch of your body has an average of 32 million bacteria on it.

Here's a message from one of our spiritual underwriters, Pierre Teilhard de Chardin: "By means of all created things, without exception, the divine assails us, penetrates us and molds us. We imagine it as distant and inaccessible, whereas in fact, we live steeped in its burning layers."

The Benevolence of Pleasure The quest for chemical-induced erections has helped stem the extinction of endangered species. Since the advent of Viagra, demand for traditional aphrodisiacs like harp seal penises and reindeer antlers has plummeted in Asia. The wild animals in possession of the body parts in question are no longer hunted so relentlessly.

Blasphemous Optimism "The biggest event of the last 20 years—the collapse of the Soviet Union—occurred without violence: the first nonviolent revolution of that size in all of human history, extending from Berlin to Siberia.

"Nelson Mandela went from a prison cell to the President's office in a country that evolved from white supremacy to power-sharing in only seven years.

"The Internet more and more evolves toward the planetary brain once only imagined by visionary scientists like Teilhard de Chardin and Arthur Clarke.

"What some call my 'blasphemous cheerfulness' or my 'cockeyed optimism' just depends on my basic agnosticism. We don't know the outcome of the current worldwide transformation, so it seems sick and decadent (in the Nietzschean sense) when fashionable opinion harps on all the gloomy alternatives and

resolutely ignores the utopian possibilities that seem equally likely (and, on the basis of past evolution, perhaps a little more likely)." —Robert Anton Wilson, rawilson.com

Name Trends Emma, Isabella, and Madison are among the most popular names for new baby girls, whereas Jacob, Ethan, and Joshua are top choices for boys. On the other hand, Condescensia, Crumpet, and Bucket are some of the least popular girl names, and Beelzebub, Humpty, and Scratch the least favorite for boys.
—thevoiceofreason.com

Gazing Into the Abyss of Happiness

M ore and more creative people find they do their best work when they're feeling healthy and secure. We know writers who no longer need to be drunk or in agony in order to shed the numbness of their daily routine and tap into the full powers of their imagination. We have filmmaker friends whose best work flows not from the depths of alienated self-doubt but rather from the heights of well-earned bliss. Musician P. J. Harvey is the patron saint of this new breed. "When I'm contented, I'm more open to receiving a lot of inspiration," she testified. "I'm most creative when I feel safe and happy."

At the Beauty and Truth Lab, we've retired the archetype of the tormented genius. We have zero attraction to books and movies and songs by depressed jerks whose work is celebrated but whose lives are a mess. Stories about supposedly interesting creeps don't rouse our perverse fascination, because we've broken our addiction to perverse fascination. When hearing about illustrious creators who brag that they feel most stimulated when they're angry or miserable, we unleash the Official Beauty and Truth Lab Histrionic Yawn.

Sadly, many storytellers and artists are still addicted to the old delusions about the risks of good mental health. Even those who don't view peace of mind as a threat to their creative power often believe that it's a rare commodity attainable only through dumb luck. "One cannot divine nor forecast the conditions that will make happiness," said novelist Willa Cather. "One only stumbles upon them by chance, in a lucky hour, at the world's end somewhere."

There is another obstacle to overthrowing the status quo. Oppressively nice, indiscriminately optimistic, sentimental comfort-hoarders give happiness a bad name. They seem to justify Flaubert's mean-spirited observation that "To be stupid, selfish, and have good health are three requirements for happiness, though if stupidity is lacking, all is lost."

Here's a third blotch on the reputation of happiness: that it's mostly an absence of pain. In *The Tibetan Book of Living and Dying,* Sogyal Rinpoche frames the issue well: "Would you prefer the happiness of scratching a mosquito bite over the happiness of not having a mosquito bite in the first place?"

It's possible to define a more supple variety of happiness that does not paralyze the will or sap ambition. For the first clue about how to proceed, we turn to Buddhist researchers Rick Foster and Greg Hicks. In their book *How We Choose to Be Happy: The 9 Choices of Extremely Happy People,* they reveal that the number one trait of happy people is a serious determination to be happy. Bliss is a habit you can cultivate, in other words, not an accident that you stumble upon by chance, in a lucky hour, at the world's end somewhere.

For another clue about how to conjure up a kind of happiness that does not anesthetize the soul, we call on Kenneth Koch. Here's what he wrote about Nobel Prize-winning poet Saint-John Perse: "So many poets have the courage to look into the abyss. But Perse had the courage to look into happiness."

TORRENTIAL PRONOIA THERAPY

Experiments and exercises in becoming a blasphemously reverent, lustfully compassionate, eternally changing Master of Transgressive Beauty

Report your answers and research results below

1 Take inventory of the extent to which your "No" reflex dominates your life. Notice for 24 hours (even in your dreams) how often you say or think:

"No."

"That's not right."

"I don't like them."

"I don't agree with that."

"They don't like me."

"That should be different from what it is."

Then retrain yourself to say "YES" at least 51 percent of the time. Start the transformation by saying "YES" aloud 22 times right now.

2 Go to the ugliest or most forlorn place you know— a drugstore parking lot, the front porch of a crack house, a toxic waste dump, or the place that symbolizes your secret shame—and build a shrine devoted to beauty, truth, and love.

Here are some suggestions about what to put in your shrine: a silk scarf; a smooth rock on which you've inscribed a haiku or joke with a felt-tip pen; coconut cookies or ginger candy; pumpkin seeds and an origami crane; a green kite shaped like a dragon; a music CD you love; a photo of your hero; a votive candle carved with your word of power; a rubber ducky; a bouquet of fresh beets; a print of Van Gogh's *Starry Night.*

3 Late at night when there's no traffic, stride down the middle of an empty road that by day is crawling with cars. Dance, careen, and sing songs that fill you with pleasurable emotions. Splay your arms triumphantly as you extemporize prayers in which you make extravagant demands and promises. Give pet names to the trees you pass, declare your admiration for the workers who made the road, and celebrate your sovereignty over a territory that usually belongs to heavy machines and their operators.

4 What causes happiness? Brainstorm about it. Map out the foundations of your personal science of joy. Get serious about defining what makes you feel good. To get you started, I'll name some experiences that might rouse your gratification: engaging in sensual pleasure; seeking the truth; being kind and moral; contemplating the meaning of life; escaping your routine; purging pent-up emotions. Do any of these work for you? Name at least ten more.

> ## *"In the war against reality, imagination is your only weapon."*
> *—Jules de Gaultier*

5 Have you ever seen the game called "Playing the Dozens"? Participants compete in the exercise of hurling witty insults at each other. Here are some examples: "You're so dumb, if you spoke your mind you'd be speechless." "Your mother is so old, she was a waitress at the Last Supper." "You're so ugly, you couldn't get laid if you were a brick."

I invite you to rebel against any impulse in you that resonates with the spirit of "Playing the Dozens." Instead, try a new game, "Paying the Tributes." Choose worthy targets and ransack your imagination to come up with smart, true, and amusing praise about them. The best stuff will be specific to the person you're addressing, not generic, but here are some prototypes: "You're so far-seeing, you can probably catch a glimpse of the back of your own head." "You're so ingenious, you could use your nightmares to get rich and famous." "Your mastery of pronoia is so artful, you could convince me to love my worst enemy."

6 Salvador Dalí once staged a party in which guests were told to come disguised as characters from their nightmares. Do the reverse. Throw a bash in which everyone is invited to arrive dressed as a character from the most glorious dream they remember.

7 On a big piece of cardboard, make a sign that says, "I love to help; I need to give; please take some money." Then go out and stand on a traffic island while wearing your best clothes, and give away money to passing motorists. Offer a little more to drivers in rusty

Torrential Pronoia Therapy

brown Pinto station wagons and 1976 El Camino Classics than those in a late-model Lexus or Jaguar.

8 In response to our culture's ever-rising levels of noise and frenzy, rites of purification have become more popular. Many people now recognize the value of taking periodic retreats. Withdrawing from their usual compulsions, they go on fasts, avoid mass media, practice celibacy, or even abstain from speaking. While we applaud cleansing ceremonies like this, we recommend balancing them with periodic outbreaks of an equal and opposite custom: the Bliss Blitz.

During this celebration, you tune out the numbing banality of the daily grind. But instead of shrinking into asceticism, you indulge in uninhibited explorations of joy, release, and expansion. Turning away from the mildly stimulating distractions you seek out when you're bored or worried, you become inexhaustibly resourceful as you search for unsurpassable sources of cathartic pleasure. Try it for a day or a week: the Bliss Blitz.

9 When many people talk about their childhoods, they emphasize the alienating, traumatic experiences they had, and fail to report the good times. This seems dishonest—a testament to the popularity of cynicism rather than a reflection of objective truth.

I don't mean to downplay the way your early encounters with pain demoralized your spirit. But as you reconnoiter the promise of pronoia, it's crucial for you to extol the gifts you were given in your early years: all the helpful encounters, kind teachings, and simple acts of grace that helped you bloom.

In Homer's epic tale *The Odyssey,* he described nepenthe, a mythical drug that induced the forgetfulness of pain and trouble. I'd like to imagine, in contrast, a potion that stirs up memories of delight, serenity, and fulfillment. Fantasize that you have taken such a tonic. Spend an hour or two remembering the glorious moments from your past.

"We are confronted with insurmountable opportunities."
—Pogo

10 "You can't wait for inspiration," proclaimed writer Jack London. "You have to go after it with a club." That sounds too violent to me, though I agree in principle that aggressiveness is the best policy in one's relationship with inspiration.

Try this: Don't wait for inspiration. Go after it with a butterfly net, lasso, sweet treats, fishing rod, court orders, beguiling smells, and sincere flattery.

11 Become a rapturist, which is the opposite of a terrorist: Conspire to unleash blessings on unsuspecting recipients, causing them to feel good.

Before bringing your work as a rapturist to strangers, practice with two close companions. Offer them each a gift that fires up their ambitions. It should not be a practical necessity or consumer fetish, but rather a provocative tool or toy. Give them an imaginative boon they've been hesitant to ask for, a beautiful thing that expands their self-image, a surprising intervention that says, "I love the way you move me."

12 "There are two ways for a person to look for adventure," said the Lone Ranger, an old TV character. "By tearing everything down, or building everything up." Give an example of each from your own life.

13 To many people, "sacrifice" is a demoralizing word that connotes deprivation. Is that how you feel? Do you make sacrifices because you're forced to, or maybe because your generosity prompts you to incur a loss in order to further a good cause?

Originally, "sacrifice" had a different meaning: to give up something valuable in order that something even more valuable might be obtained. Carry out an action that embodies this definition. For instance, sacrifice a mediocre pleasure so as to free yourself to pursue a more exalted pleasure.

14 What is the holiest river in the world? Some might say the Ganges in India. Others would propose the Jordan River or the River Nile. But I say the holiest river is the one that's closest to where you are right now.

Go to that river and commune with it. Throw a small treasure into it as an offering. Next, find a holy sidewalk to walk on, praise the holiness in a bus driver, kiss a holy tree, and shop at a holy store.

15 Are other people luckier than you? If so, psychologist Richard Wiseman says you can do something about it. His book *The Luck Factor* presents research that proves you can learn to be lucky. It's not a mystical force you're born with, he says, but a habit you can develop. How? For starters, be open to new experiences, trust your gut wisdom, expect good fortune, see the bright side of challenging events, and master the art of maximizing serendipitous opportunities.

Torrential Pronoia Therapy

Name three specific actions you'll try in order to improve your luck.

16 Entomologist Justin O. Schmidt drew up an index to categorize the discomfort caused by stinging insects. The attack of the bald-faced hornet is "rich, hearty, slightly crunchy. Similar to getting your hand mashed in a revolving door." A paper wasp delivers pain that's "caustic and burning," with a "distinctly bitter aftertaste. Like spilling a beaker of hydrochloric acid on a paper cut." The sweat bee, on the other hand, can hurt you in a way that's "light, ephemeral, almost fruity. A tiny spark has singed a single hair on your arm."

In bringing this to your attention, I want to inspire the pronoiac rebel in you. Your homework is to create an equally nuanced and precise index of three experiences that feel really good.

"For aren't you and I gods? Let all of life be an unfettered howl. Release life's rapture. Everything is blooming. Everything is flying. Everything is screaming."
—Vladimir Nabokov

17 Some scholars believe the original Garden of Eden was where Iraq stands today. Though remnants of that ancient paradise survived into modern times, many were obliterated during the American war on Iraq. A Beauty and Truth Lab researcher who lives near the confluence of the Tigris and Euphrates Rivers kept us posted on the fate of the most famous remnant: the Tree of the Knowledge of Good and Evil. Until the invasion, it was a gnarled stump near Nasiriyah. But today it's gone; only a crater remains.

Let this serve as an evocative symbol for you as you demolish your old ideas about paradise, freeing you up to conjure a fresh vision of your ideal realm.

18 "Two chemicals called actin and myosin evolved eons ago to allow the muscles in insect wings to contract and relax," writes Deepak Chopra in *The Book of Secrets*. "Today, the same two proteins are responsible for the beating of the human heart."

If you use your imagination, you can sense the connection between the flight of a dragonfly and the intelligent organ that renews its commitment to keeping

Torrential Pronoia Therapy

you alive every second of your life. So use your imagination.

19 Is the world a dangerous, chaotic place with no inherent purpose, running on automatic like a malfunctioning machine and fundamentally inimical to your happiness? Or are you surrounded by helpers in a friendly universe that gives you challenges in order to make you smarter and wilder and kinder and trickier? Trick questions! The answers may depend, at least to some degree, on what you believe is true.

Formulate a series of experiments that will allow you to objectively test the hypothesis that the universe is conspiring to help you.

20 The primary meaning of the word "healing" is "to cure what's diseased or broken." Medical practitioners focus on sick people. Philanthropists donate their money and social workers contribute their time to helping the underprivileged. Psychotherapists wrestle with their clients' traumas and neuroses. I'm in awe of them all. The level of one's spiritual wisdom, I believe, is more accurately measured by helping people in need than by meditation skills, shamanic shapeshifting, supernatural powers, or esoteric knowledge.

But I also believe in a second kind of healing that is largely unrecognized: to supercharge what is already healthy; to lift up what's merely sufficient to a sublime state. Using this definition, describe two acts of healing: one you would enjoy performing on yourself and another you'd like to provide for someone you love.

21 Those who explore pronoia often find they have a growing capacity to help people laugh at themselves. While few arbiters of morality recognize this skill as a mark of high character, I put it near the top of my list. In my view, inducing people to take themselves less seriously is a supreme virtue. Do you have any interest in cultivating it? How might you go about it?

22 "Creativity is like driving a car at night," said E. L. Doctorow. "You never see further than your headlights, but you can make the whole trip that way." I would add that life itself is like driving a car at night. You're often in the dark except for what's right in front of you. At least that's usually the case. But for a few shining hours sometime while you're communing with this book, I predict you'll be able to see the big picture of where you're headed. It will be as if the whole world is suddenly illuminated by a prolonged burst of light; as if you're both driving your car and also watching your journey from high above. Write about what you see.

Torrential Pronoia Therapy

5

"I vow
to interpret every experience
as a direct dealing of the Goddess
with my soul"

Beyond Goodness

"I used to have superpowers," the bumper sticker says, "but my therapist took them away." Does that describe you? Have you been overly normalized by the bland conventions of what constitutes psychological health? Has your spunk been sapped by the pressure to behave yourself in a civilized manner?

If so, I'll offer you three pieces of advice. They may have a sickening effect if you apply them too liberally, but they'll be a tonic if you use them in small doses.

Here's the first, courtesy of Henry David Thoreau: "Do not be too moral. You may cheat yourself out of much life. Aim above morality. Be not simply good; be good for something."

Here's the second, from Isaac Asimov: "Never let your sense of morals get in the way of doing what's right."

Here's another, formulated by William Irwin Thompson: "An overdose of an antidote becomes a poison in itself."

SACRED ADVERTISEMENT

Your supernal, mischief-enhanced goodness is brought to you by the thousands of endogenous retroviruses that attacked our ancestors for millions of years. (In response to their invasions, we humans had to build our rough, tough immune system, which is one of the most amazing creations on the planet.)

A Dangerous Taboo

This book is a conversation, not a dictation. It's an inquiry, not dogma. We're explorers in search of the ever-evolving truth, not authorities proclaiming doctrine from on high. We refuse to be salespeople intent on getting you to be like us or buy our ideas. In fact, let's look at the downsides of the perspectives we celebrate.

The first thing you should consider before leaping into a relationship with pronoia is that it is utterly at odds with conventional wisdom. The 19th-century poet John Keats said that if something is not beautiful, it is probably not true. But the vast majority of modern storytellers—journalists, filmmakers, novelists, talk-show hosts, and poets—assert the opposite: If something is not *ugly,* it is probably not true.

In a world that equates pessimism with acumen and regards stories about things falling apart as having the highest entertainment value, pronoia is deviant. It is a taboo so taboo that it's not even recognized as a taboo.

The average American child sees 20,000 simulated murders before reaching age 18. This is considered normal. There are thousands of films, television shows, and electronic games that depict people doing terrible things to each other. If you read newspapers and news sites on the Internet, you have every right to believe that Bad Nasty Things compose 90 percent of the human experience. The authors of thousands of books published this year will hope to lure you in through the glamour of killing, addiction, self-hatred, sexual pathology, shame, betrayal, extortion, robbery, cancer, arson, and torture.

But you will be hard-pressed to find more than a few novels, films, news stories, and TV shows that dare to depict life as a gift whose purpose is to enrich the human soul.

If you cultivate an affinity for pronoia, people you respect may wonder if you have lost your way. You might appear to them as naive, eccentric, unrealistic, misguided, or even stupid. Your reputation could suffer and your social status could decline.

But that may be relatively easy to deal with compared to your struggle to create a new relationship with yourself. For starters, you will have to acknowledge that what you previously considered a strong-willed faculty—the ability to discern the weakness in everything—might actually be a mark of cowardice and laziness. Far from being evidence of your power and uniqueness, your drive to produce hard-edged opinions stoked by hostility is likely a sign that you've been brainwashed by the pedestrian influences of pop nihilism.

Before the onset of pronoia, you may feel fine about the fact that you generate much of your dynamic energy through anger, agitation, discomfort, and judgmental scorn. But once the pronoia kicks in, you'll naturally want more positive feelings to be your high-octane fuel. That will require extensive retraining. The work could be arduous, delicate, and time-consuming.

Are you truly ready to shed the values and self-images that keep you locked into alignment with the dying civilization? Will you have the stamina and inspiration necessary to dream up bigger, better, more original sins and wilder, wetter, more interesting problems? Do you realize how demanding it will be to turn yourself into a wildly disciplined, radically curious, fiercely tender, ironically sincere, ingeniously loving, aggressively sensitive, blasphemously reverent, lustfully compassionate master of rowdy bliss?

In the future, judges will send criminals to holy spots where reverence-provoking beauty will overwhelm their addiction to hatred.

Try saying this aloud: "I die daily." It's one of our favorite formulas for success. Is it right for you? Say it again, using a different tone of voice this time. "I die daily." Chant it in a fake foreign accent. Sing it to the tune of the nursery rhyme "Frère Jacques." Play with it in the voice of the cartoon character you loved best as a child. Repeat it 10 times, or try other vocal experiments. Then muse on the following questions.

What do you need to kill off in yourself in order to tune in to the beauty that's hidden from you? What worn-out shticks are blinding you to the blessings that life is conspiring to give you? Which of your acerbic theories may have been useful and even brilliant in the past but are now keeping you from becoming aware of the ever-fresh creation that unfolds before you?

"I die daily" means that it's not enough to terminate your stale mental habits just once. The price of admission into pronoia is a commitment to continual dying. You'll have to ask yourself rude questions and kick your own ass again and again. Today's versions of beauty, truth, love, goodness, justice, and liberation will pass away. To keep abreast of the latest developments—to cultivate tomorrow's versions of pronoia—you will have to immerse yourself regularly in the waters of chaos. Your relationship with pronoia will have to be a never-ending improvisation.

The dream of a steady-state utopia is anathema to Beauty and Truth Lab researchers. We're allergic to any paradise that resembles a spotless shopping mall within the walls of a gated community in heaven.

Pronoia is fueled by a drive to cultivate happiness and a determination to practice an aggressive form of gratitude that systematically identifies the things that are working well. But it is not a soothing diversion meant for timid Pollyannas strung out on optimistic delusions. It's not a feel-good New Age fantasy used to deny the harsh facts about existence. Those of us who perceive the world pronoiacally refuse to be polite shills for sentimental hopefulness.

On the contrary, we build our optimism not through a repression of difficulty, but rather a vigorous engagement with it. We understand that the best way to attract blessings is to grapple with the knottiest enigmas.
Each fresh puzzle is a potential source of future bliss—an exciting teaching that may usher us to our next breakthrough.

Do you want to be a pronoiac player? Blend anarchistic rebelliousness with open-hearted exuberance. Root your insurrectionary fervor in expansive joy instead of withering hatred. Enjoy saying "no!" but don't make it the wellspring of your vitality. Be fueled by blood-red yeses that rip against the grain of comfortable ugliness.

"A Spell to Commit Pronoia," by psychotherapist Jennifer Welwood:

Willing to experience aloneness,
I discover connection everywhere;
Turning to face my fear,
I meet the warrior who lives within;
Opening to my loss,
I am given unimaginable gifts;
Surrendering into emptiness,
I find fullness without end.

Each condition I flee from pursues me.
Each condition I welcome transforms me
And becomes itself transformed
Into its radiant jewel-like essence.
I bow to the one who has made it so,
Who has crafted this Master Game;
To play it is pure delight,
To honor it is true devotion.

Origins of the Homeopathic Medicine Spells

Being a devotee of pronoia doesn't mean you will never have another difficult or painful experience. It doesn't obligate you to pretend that everything is perfectly right with the world. You don't have to cover your eyes whenever you come into proximity to a daily newspaper.

On the other hand, we're not going to waste our valuable space or your precious energy by giving equal time to stories of tragedy, failure, and tumult. They get far more than their fair share of attention everywhere else. Future historians might even conclude that our age suffered from a collective obsessive-compulsive disorder: the pathological need to repetitively seek out reasons for how bad life is.

Still, we feel the need to push a bit further in our acknowledgment of all the confusing evils of the world. We realize that what we've said so far may not be sufficient to satisfy the paranoid cynics, who include among their number many well-respected thinkers. Unless we demonstrate that we have some mastery of their ideology, they'll dismiss us as intellectual pussies. They will need proof that we're familiar with the data they favor.

We've decided, therefore, to launch a preemptive strike that will make it harder for the paranoids to dismiss us pronoiacs as naive optimists. On the next page and at four other places in this book, we've created Homeopathic Medicine Spells. They're designed to recognize the evils of the world, but in a controlled manner that prevents them from poisoning you. In this way, we can also practice what we preach, subverting any tendencies we might have toward fanaticism and unilateralism.

Each Homeopathic Medicine Spell consists of a contained space within which lies a recitation of Very Bad Things. The border around each space is a magical seal that we consecrated during a ritual invocation of the Cackling Goddess Who Eternally Creates Us Anew. Inspired through communion with Her fierce jokes, we also surrounded each seal with good mojo in the form of word charms and talismanic symbols.

As you gaze at the Homeopathic Medicine Spells, you'll be building up your protection against the dangers named inside the contained space. You'll also get intuitions about how to dissolve the pop nihilistic toxins within you that resonate with those dangers.

HOMEOPATHIC MEDICINE SPELL #1

namaste

bravo

eureka

aloha

blessed be

viva

hallelujah

rowdy blessings

shalom

abracadabra

whoopee

mitakuye oyasin

In lak'ech—A lak'en

kudos

The earth is in the midst of the greatest mass extinction since the disappearance of the dinosaurs 65 million years ago. Half of all species may be exterminated by 2100. The Air Force has fighter planes with radar scopes that can detect the body heat of an infant from 20,000 feet. About 37 million Americans take antidepressants. Only 15 percent of the shoppers in a grocery store express line obey the ten-item limit. Heart disease is the worst epidemic since the medieval plague. By the time girls reach seventeen, 78 percent are unhappy with their bodies. Living within one's means is un-American; the economy would collapse if consumers did it. The U.S. is the biggest arms dealer in the world, having sold more than $178 billion of weaponry since 1992, much of it to non-democratic regimes whose soldiers commit human rights abuses. Sperm counts are falling. Many clothes worn by Americans are made by youngsters working long hours in brutal conditions for paltry wages. Some of the biggest banks in the world turn a blind eye to money laundering. The average home is swimming in a noxious cocktail of chemicals that have been linked to allergies, cancers, and infertility. Three million children are abused and three million women are the victims of domestic violence in America every year. Blatantly totalitarian government is unnecessary because the mass audience eagerly participates in its own brainwashing. Studies show no relationship between an eyewitnesss confidence and the accuracy of his testimony. The Red Cross says half of all war casualties are civilians caught in the crossfire. Aggressive advertising to children is increasing. True "personality" as we know it has begun to die out as more people perform imitations of celebrities they admire. The U.S. has the most overweight population and the highest infant mortality rate in the West. The U.S. has the world's largest prison population and the highest rate of incarceration. Most pesticides on the market have not been tested for their ability to cause genetic damage. "People do not want God, people want to enslave God to their whim," said Da Avabhasa. Americans waste $12 billion of food a year. Many seemingly nice people cynically use honesty, cheerfulness, and openness to manipulate others into doing things their way. Over 80 million Americans live on incomes estimated by the U.S. Department of Labor as below a "comfortable adequacy," and 35 million of these live below the poverty level. The world's rain forests are disappearing at a rate of 80 acres per minute. He who dies with the most toys does NOT win. A million school children are treated with powerful mind control drugs for "hyperactivity" every year, with side effects like weight loss, growth retardation, and acute psychosis. Everyone tells at least one lie every day.

CONVULSIVE PRONOIA THERAPY

Experiments and exercises in becoming a sublimely berserk, subversively moral, devoutly crafty Master of Taboo Justice

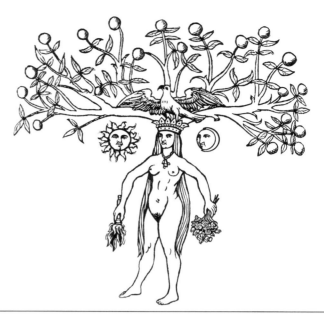

Scrawl curses and scratch protests here

You're invited to celebrate Unhappy Hour. It's a ceremony that gives you a poetic license to rant and whine and howl and bitch about everything that hurts you and makes you feel bad.

During this perverse grace period, there's no need for you to be inhibited as you unleash your tortured squalls. You don't have to tone down the extremity of your desolate clamors. Unhappy Hour is a ritually consecrated excursion devoted to the full disclosure of your primal clash and jangle.

Here's the catch: It's brief. It's concise. It's crisp. You dive into your darkness for no more than 60 minutes, then climb back out, free and clear. It's called Unhappy Hour, not Unhappy Day or Unhappy Week or Unhappy Year.

Do you have the cheeky temerity to drench yourself in your paroxysmal alienation from life? Unhappy Hour invites you to plunge in and surrender. It dares you to scurry and squirm all the way down to the bottom of your pain, break through the bottom of your pain, and fall down flailing in the soggy, searing abyss, yelping and cringing and wallowing.

That's where you let your pain tell you every story it has to tell you. You let your pain teach you every lesson it has to teach you.

But then it's over. The ritual ordeal is complete. And your pain has to take a vacation until the next Unhappy Hour, which isn't until next week sometime, or maybe next month.

You see the way the game works? Between this Unhappy Hour and the next one, your pain has to shut up. It's not allowed to creep and seep all over everything, staining the flow of your daily life. It doesn't have free reign to infect you whenever it's itching for more power.

Your pain gets its succinct blast of glory, its resplendent climax, but leaves you alone the rest of the time.

If performed regularly, Unhappy Hour serves as an exorcism that empties you of psychic toxins, while at the same time—miracle of miracles—it helps you squeeze every last drop of blessed catharsis out of those psychic toxins.

Pronoia will then be able to flourish as you luxuriate more frequently in rosy moods and broad-minded visions. You'll develop a knack for cultivating smart joy and cagey optimism as your normal states of mind.

 Now let's get you warmed up for Unhappy Hour.

First, unload a groan.

Second, disgorge a howl.

Third, unfurl a sigh.

Now say or sing these declarations:
Life is a bitch and everything stinks.
My pain is so bad I can hardly think.
I'm afraid to live, I'm afraid to die.
The world's so messed up, I can't even cry.

Exhale another very long groan. Eject a further desolate howl. Spill an additional self-pitying sigh.

 Now you're almost ready. When I say GO, you will have as much freedom as you want to dredge up and steep yourself in your savage sorrow, your unspeakable doubt, your shrill anguish, your secret shame, and your fearful fantasies.

Give yourself permission to make guttural moans, rueful cackles, or animalistic growls and squawks. Argue with God or your parents or the past while blurting out manic, explosive wails. Allow yourself to be crushed and dissolved, flung around and flayed, appalled and unhinged.

Convulsive Pronoia Therapy

And while you're at it, use the clean white space on these pages to scrawl down curses, scratch out narratives, or scribble symbolic drawings incited by your misery.

Later, make photocopies of these curses, narratives, and drawings, and conduct a ceremony of purification, burning them to ash, being careful not to set your house or the woods or yourself on fire, too.

As you burn, pray that you will extract all of the mojo you possibly can from the pain, and that the pain will make you smarter and wilder and kinder and trickier.

Pray that you will grow to feel gratitude for the pain, thereby turning the pain into a blessing and diminishing its power to hurt you.

Ready? Get set. GO. Be unhappy—but for no longer than 60 minutes.

SACRED ADVERTISEMENT

Unhappy Hour is brought to you by the origin myth of the Iroquois' Thunderbird Clan: Earthmaker woke up to realize he was the only being in the universe. Out of the depths of his loneliness, he cried, unleashing a flood of tears that became the oceans and rivers and lakes of our world.

Convulsive Pronoia Therapy

WORLD KISS

All of creation is alive and conscious, and all of creation deserves our burning, churning, yearning love. All of it. Not just the people and creatures and things that we personally find beautiful and helpful and interesting. But everything. All of creation.

If we want to become the gorgeous geniuses we were born to be, if we want to give back as many blessings as we are given, we've got to be in love with every single part of the Goddess's extravagant masterpiece.

So how could we possibly be mere heterosexuals? Why would we ever squeeze ourselves into the narrow constraints of homosexuality or bisexuality?

Even bestiality doesn't go far enough. Nor does the flower boinking of the Essenes, or the sky copulations of the Illuminati, or the ritual fisting of the Mediterranean Sea by the ancient Sapphic cults.

If we want to commune with the world the way the Goddess does, we've got to be Pantheosexuals—experts in the art of Polymorphous Perverse Omnidirectional Goddess Diddling. Anything less than that is an obscene limitation.

With this in mind, I invite you to perform the ritual of the World Kiss. To do the World Kiss, conjure up your most expansive feelings of tenderness—like what you might experience when you're infatuated with a lover or when you gaze into the eyes of your newborn baby for the first time—and then blow kisses to all of creation.

Blow kisses to the oak trees and sparrows and elephants and weeds. Blow kisses to the wind and rain and rocks and machines. Blow kisses to the gardens and jails, the cars and toys, the politicians and saints, the girls and the boys and every gender in between.

And with each World Kiss you bestow, keep uppermost in your emotions a mood of blasphemous reverence and orgiastic compassion. And remember that it's not enough simply to perform the outer gesture; you've got to have a heart-on in each of your seven chakras.

The poet Rilke said: "For one human being to love another is the most difficult task, the ultimate, the last test and proof. It's the work for which all other work is mere preparation."

Teilhard de Chardin said: "Some day after we have mastered the winds, the waves and gravity, we will harness for God the energies of love; and then for a second time in the history of the world, humans will have discovered fire."

Leo Tolstoy: "Everything I understand, I understand only because I love."

Blaise Pascal: "If you do not love too much, you do not love enough."

Emily Dickinson: "Until you have loved, you cannot become yourself."

And you and I say: "Because we love, ruby-throated hummingbirds sip from plum flowers and the moon sings its silver fragrance to the swans and volcanoes and fields of wheat. Because we love, wild grapevines coil around the roots of the mountain, and mangoes ripen in the smoke of forest fires. Because we love, everything alive swims in an eternal river that glides through our dreams all night long."

I'm blowing World Kisses right now, as I sit in the garden in front of my house and write down these words. I'm blowing World Kisses to the dirt below me and the hyacinths brushing my elbows. I'm blowing World Kisses to the persimmon tree sheltering the front door and to the neighbor's calico cat gazing up at a phantom in the branches. I'm blowing World Kisses to the ants snaking along the cracked sidewalk across the street and to the Anise Swallowtail butterfly perched on the tip of the antenna of my dark green Honda Accord.

My World Kisses fly further, reaching where I can't go right now. I'm blowing World Kisses to you, wherever you are, and to everyone you love and to everyone you hate. I'm blowing World Kisses to all the convenience store clerks in the world. I'm blowing World Kisses to the Norwegian widower working as a welder on an offshore oil rig near Nigeria, and to the poet playing cards with her nine-year-old granddaughter in the bus station in Quezaltenango, Guatemala, and to the head cook at the Hôtel de la Sûre in Esch-sur-Sûre, Luxembourg. I'm blowing World Kisses to all the wolverines near Sioux Lookout, Ontario, and all the Chihuahuan Ravens in Nebraska, and all the Komodo dragons on the Indonesian island of Gili Motang.

I'm not afraid of running out of love. The more I give, the more I have to give.

I'm blowing World Kisses to what some people (not me) call inanimate objects: to the Black Hills of South Dakota, and to Picasso's Guernica in the Reina Sofía National Museum in Madrid, and to the rolls of blue Saxony Plush carpet in the Carpeteria store on West Charleston Boulevard in Las Vegas. I'm blowing World Kisses to all the stone walls in Ireland, and to the tornado outside the city of Sukhumi on the Black Sea coast, and to the 15-year-old backhoe rusting in a junkyard in Montevideo, Uruguay.

I'm blowing World Kisses to the woman who broke my heart, and to the friend who betrayed my trust, and to the rich old white male politicians in Washington who hate everything I stand for.

On you and me and all of everything, I bestow my ripest blessings, and declare that since my atoms and your atoms were ripped asunder at the Big Bang, I have fantasized of our rapturous reunion.

Sacred Advertisement

*"World Kiss" is brought to you by the ecstatic state of mind
that the poet Daniel Ladinsky enjoyed when he said:*

*One regret, dear world,
that I am determined not to have
when I am lying on my death bed
is that I did not kiss you enough!*

How Pronoia Works

There was once a poor farmer who could afford to own just one horse. He cared well for the animal, but one summer night it escaped through a weak fence and ran away.

When his neighbors discovered what had happened, they visited to offer their condolences. "What bad luck!" they exclaimed. The farmer replied, "Maybe. Maybe not."

A week later, the fugitive horse sauntered back to the homestead, accompanied by six wild horses. The farmer and his son managed to corral them all. Again the neighbors descended. "What great luck!" they exclaimed. "Maybe," the farmer replied. "Maybe not."

Soon the farmer's son began the work of taming the new arrivals. While attempting to ride the roan stallion, he was thrown to the ground and half-trampled. His leg was badly broken. The neighbors came to investigate. "What terrible luck!" they exclaimed. The farmer replied, "Maybe. Maybe not."

The next day, soldiers visited the farmer's village. Strife had recently broken out between two warlords, and one of them had come to conscript all the local young men. Though every other son was commandeered, the farmer's boy was exempted because of his injury. The neighbors gathered again. "What fantastic luck!" they exclaimed. "Maybe," the farmer said. "Maybe not."

(Source: an old Taoist folk tale)

Glory in the Highest
Part 2; continued from page 16

All of creation is conspiring to shower us with blessings. Life is crazily in love with us—brazenly and innocently in love with us. The universe always gives us exactly what we need, exactly when we need it.

But wait a minute. What about all the people in Africa, Asia, Latin America, the Arab world, and Oceania who don't have enough to eat and a comfortable place to sleep? How about the victims of war and epidemics, and the oppressed who live under the rule of tyrants, and the innocents whose lives are distorted by bigotry? Where's their glory in the highest? Why should they feel grateful?

To answer that in full, I need the entire book you've got in front of you as well as my next two books. But I'll begin the process by taking an inventory of the ways that life in the developing countries may be less than horrendous. In doing so, I don't mean to downplay the immensity and intensity of suffering there. We still have a long way to go before we reach the only reasonable goal, which is to create a world in which everyone alive is a healthy, free, self-actualized, spiritually enlightened millionaire dedicated to living sustainably.

Now let's see if we can dig up any decent excuses to sing "Glory in the Highest" about the way the world is evolving outside of the privileged enclaves of the West.

In the developing world, too many children are suffering terribly. On the other hand, fewer and fewer are suffering terribly every year. In 2006, UNICEF (the United Nations Children's Fund) reported that the death rate among young children had declined dramatically since 1960. Back then, 184 of every 1,000 kids expired before age five. More recently, the number is 72 per 1,000.

Everyone in the developing world is living longer, too, according to a study published in 2005 by Noble Prize-winning economist Gary Becker. He reported that between 1960 and 2000, life expectancy in the poorest nations on the planet increased from 41 to 64 years.

This miraculous progress has happened in part because the world's wealth has been steadily increasing. In a blog he writes on *The New York Times* website (tinyurl.com/q4glr6), economist Steve Radelet reported that one of the most crucial shifts in human history began around 1980. The number of people living in poverty began to diminish then, and has continued to do so ever since. He waxed dramatic: "That's right: After rising steadily since the beginning of time, the number of people in the world living in absolute poverty has fallen by nearly one-third in less than three decades."

The World Bank issued a report in late 2008 that differed slightly in its details, but confirmed the general trend. It said that the number of people surviving on less than $1.25 per day had dropped by 500 million since 1981, even though the world's population increased by over two billion during that time. A United Nations' Human Development Report released in 2004 measured the progress from yet another angle, revealing that real per capita income in the developing world had more than doubled since 1975.

A further reason for the sharp reduction in child mortality has been improved medical treatments. These include immunizations against measles, rehydration therapy to combat diarrhea, vitamin A supplementation, and the widespread use of bed nets to foil mosquitoes bearing malaria.

Measles has been one of the most virulent diseases for children in Africa and Asia. But it's easily preventable through vaccination, which is why, in 2001, public health organizations launched the Measles Initiative, a campaign to provide mass vaccination. Since their work began, more than 600 million children have gotten the precious injections, and the death rate from measles has dropped 74 percent globally and 89 percent in Africa.

Of all the world's parasitic diseases, malaria is the deadliest. In second place is black fever, which takes 500,000 lives every year, mostly in India and Africa. In the 1960s, researchers identified the drug paromomyocin as an effective treatment against black fever, but pharmaceutical companies refused to make it. Why? There was little profit in the enterprise, since most victims were poor people. Forty years later, a not-for-profit drug company began doing business, and one of its first actions was to resurrect the use of paromomyocin. The Institute for One World Health has now mass-produced the life-saver, and offers it at a low price.

> **"After rising steadily since the beginning of time, the number of people in the world living in absolute poverty has fallen by nearly one-third in less than three decades."**

There's still much work to be done to eradicate preventable disease in the developing world. But thanks to widespread vaccination, two other success stories stand out: the final defeat of smallpox in 1977, and the looming victory over polio, which is very close to completion.

Steve Radelet says that an essential factor in the war against child mortality and global poverty has been the generosity of rich nations. While acknowledging that some criticisms of foreign aid are warranted, he unequivocally asserts that "foreign assistance programs have helped saved millions of lives over the last several decades."

This largesse is a recent development in the history of international relations. The voluntary transfer of wealth from one country to another was rare and meager from the beginning of recorded history until the end of World War II. Now it is routine and abundant, and flows not only from governments but also from numerous private organizations.

On many of the mornings when I wake up in my soft bed, surrounded by the perks of my temperature-controlled home and ready to enjoy another mysteriously interesting day, I am visited by the urge to murmur a prayer of gratitude like "Thank you a billion and one times, Whoever or Whatever You are that gave me this lavish riot of beauty." I am flooded with ecstatic appreciation as I taste the honey mingle with the sour flesh of the organic grapefruit, or when my lover cracks a quirky joke right before she kisses me twice, once on each eyelid, or when my daughter shows me the enigmatic new poem she wrote about how "I want to become the rust-brown manzanita tree, the gentle rash of moss spreading like love on her skin."

But what brings me even sharper pangs of personal elation, what evokes an even more exuberant longing to celebrate, are those moments when I deeply feel the triumphs that are unfolding for human beings far away from me—triumphs like the irrevocable decline of global poverty and child mortality.

And I know many people who nurture a similar aim. Our numbers are growing. Has there ever been a time in the history of civilization when masses of people were actively cultivating a capacity for transcendental empathy? Have there ever been so many of us attuned to and concerned for the suffering of those we've never met?

In his well-researched book Blessed Unrest: *How the Largest Movement in the World Came into Being and Why No One Saw It Coming,* Paul Hawken argues that organized political action devoted to advancing the rights of others is a relatively new phenomenon. The drive to abolish slavery was where it began. In recent decades it has grown exponentially, becoming a global crusade to improve social justice, economic conditions, human rights, and environmental health.

By Hawken's estimates, there are well over a million organizations engaged in the effort, which thrives without centralized leadership, charismatic front men, or a fixed ideology. Because of its grass-roots ubiquity, it is largely invisible to the mass media and underestimated by politicians.

Some day, maybe 500 years from now, our descendants will have installed the art and science of universal compassion as the first law of civilization. And I bet they will give honor to us, the people alive on the planet today, as the heroes who gave critical mass to their prime directive.

For those who are dogmatically predisposed to thinking that the world is a hellhole and life is a bitch, no amount of contrary evidence will change their minds. The cynic who asked me the following question didn't really want an answer: "Tell me how your pronoia explains a child in Darfur starving to death after watching soldiers kill his mommy?"

While I don't claim to have the authoritative response to that accusation, I think it's worthwhile to consider the possibility that suffering is, among other things, a difficult gift we humans are given in order to prod our evolution.

The world is steadily becoming more free, and is now the most free it has ever been.

On a personal level, our longing to escape our suffering is a primal force in making us smarter. On a collective level, nothing refines and ennobles us more than our passion to keep others from suffering. For every dead child in Darfur, 100 people in other places on the planet have responded with a commitment to create a world in which future Darfurs won't happen.

There is, in fact, considerable evidence that the agonies of war have aroused increasingly effective efforts to stop war.

In 2005, the *Human Security Report* presented detailed proof that the world has become dramatically more peaceful since the end of the Cold War. It said that the number of violent conflicts has declined by 40 percent, while acts of genocide have dropped by 80 percent. Weapons sales between countries have diminished 33 percent during the same time, and the number of refugees has fallen by 45 percent.

Meanwhile, coups d'état have decreased 60 percent since 1963, and the number of soldiers killed in battle has declined from an average of 38,000 per war in 1950 to 600 in 2002.

Shouldn't reports on these shocking developments have been at the top of the headlines for at least one news cycle? Wouldn't it make sense to declare a holiday and dance in the streets?

One of the primary causes of the plunge in violence, according to the *Human Security Report,* is the unprecedented upsurge of international peace activism, much of it spearheaded by the United Nations. Other factors it cites include the acceleration of democratization and the steep downswing of global poverty.

The main study was released in 2005, with updates issued in 2007 and 2008. Among the most recent findings: Deaths caused by terrorism have decreased 40 percent; support for al-Qaeda in the Arab world has diminished precipitously; and the number of wars in sub-Saharan Africa was cut in half between 1999 and 2006, while fatalities from those conflicts dropped 98 percent. More info is here: humansecurityreport.info.

Is there other evidence that the global culture of war and violence is receding? If so, it would be a cause for jubilee in the developing nations. To the degree that civilization is consumed with fighting, less energy and fewer resources are available to lift up the disadvantaged. As the richest and most powerful part of the human enterprise, the West is the dominant force in determining which way the scale leans: toward an obsession with conflict and supremacy or a focus on peace and well-being. So where do we stand?

According to evolutionary psychologist Steven Pinker, the human race has been growing progressively kinder and gentler since the onset of the Age of Reason in the early seventeenth century. "Today," he writes, "we are probably living in the most peaceful moment of our species' time on earth." In numerous ways, violence and cruelty are decreasing. You can read his full argument in his article "We're Getting Nicer Every Day" (tinyurl.com/3bcryc). His talk at the Ted conference is available at tinyurl.com/l8mvzd.

One measure of the change is the steep decline in the homicide rate. In the 14th century, for example, there were 24 murders for every 100,000 people in England. By 1960, that figure had shrunk to 0.6 per 100,000. A similar decrease occurred throughout Western Europe.

As further proof of his theorem, Pinker also cites shifts in the ways wars have been waged. The mass conflicts of the last hundred years wrought catastrophic casualties, and yet they were far less efficient killers than the tribal clashes that dominated the centuries before modern warfare. In the old days, violence was more consuming. A greater percentage of the men were soldiers, the battles were more numerous, and the death rates during combat were higher. "If the wars of the twentieth century had killed the same proportion of the population that die in the wars of a typical tribal society," says Pinker, "there would have been two billion deaths, not 100 million."

A third sign of waning cruelty is the dramatic drop-off in torture. Two thousand years ago, many cultures considered torture to be a legitimate element of their system of criminal justice. To the Romans, crucifixion served as a rightful punishment and an effective deterrent. The Egyptians preferred baking wrong-doers to death in the fire of the desert sun.

Throughout the Middle Ages and as late as the 18th century, the courts of Europe relied on torture as a means of wresting revelations from the accused. The Roman Catholic Church authorized its use in 1252 and

The world has become dramatically more peaceful since the end of the Cold War, with steep declines in the numbers of armed conflicts, acts of genocide, weapon sales, and refugees.

didn't officially rescind the order until 1816. If you're ever in Amsterdam, you might want to visit the Torture Museum to get a look at the actual devices used during those many centuries, like the Judas Cradle, which forced the victim to sit on a pointed, pyramid-shaped chair.

In addition to the forcible extractions of information, which were conducted covertly, European cities also staged public spectacles that featured excruciating executions. Some victims were burned alive and others were hanged, then cut up. "Softly, softly, gallows are everywhere and numerous are the executioners," wrote Erasmus of Rotterdam in the 16th century.

For hundreds of years, in numerous places on the planet, torture was routine, legal, and commonly accepted. But it's not any more. We shouldn't underestimate how miraculous a change this is. While sickening outbreaks still take place—witness the abuses that occurred at Abu Ghraib prison in Iraq beginning in 2004—they incur widespread moral outrage when they're discovered, and there is an international system of laws in place to discourage them.

So let's see: Pinker's research suggests that over the course of the last 600 years, the murder rate has declined 97 percent. The percentage of deaths during wartime has decreased by 95 percent. We can't be sure of the exact reduction in torture, but we know it's no longer a commonplace feature of the judicial system, and few of us have attended a public hanging.

Pinker says that social scientists are having to come to a conclusion that goes against the grain of the conventional wisdom: "Far from causing us to become more violent, something in modernity and its cultural institutions has made us nobler." What is that something?

By now, some readers may be recoiling in disapproval. They don't want to register evidence that contradicts

Dionysian Manifesto

There are over a million organizations working to improve social justice, economic conditions, human rights, and environmental health.

their foregone conclusions about humans' cancerous presence on the planet. It's dangerous to do so, they feel, because it threatens to make us complacent and fall under the delusion that our work as freedom fighters is done. Celebrating progress is a foolish indulgence that would sap our motivation to keep agitating for even greater justice. Focusing on the good stuff tempts us to ignore the continuing bad stuff.

I understand that position. It's the stance of many devoted activists who have a ferocious devotion to the extinction of suffering. I respect their work and am rooting them on. But I'd also like to suggest that there are alternate ways to wage the war on stupidity, violence, and tyranny.

Activist and author Naomi Klein tells a story about the time she traveled to Australia at the request of Aboriginal elders. They wanted her to know about their struggle to prevent white people from dumping radioactive wastes on their land.

Her hosts brought her to their beloved wilderness, where they camped under the stars. They showed her "secret sources of fresh water, plants used for bush medicines, hidden eucalyptus-lined rivers where the kangaroos come to drink."

After three days, Klein grew restless. When were they going to get down to business? "Before you can fight," she was told, "you have to know what you are fighting for" (tinyurl.com/5q84zh).

In the late 1990s, environmental activist Julia Butterfly Hill spent two years living in a redwood tree she named "Luna." Her goal was to save it from being cut down by a logging company. She succeeded both literally and mythically. Luna was spared from death, as was a surrounding three-acre swath of trees. Hill became an inspiring symbol of artful, compassionate protest.

Later she told Benjamin Tong in the DVD *The Taoist and the Activist:* "So often activism is based on what we are against, what we don't like, what we don't want. And yet we manifest what we focus on. And so we are manifesting yet ever more of what we don't want, what we don't like, what we want to change. So for me, activism is about a spiritual practice as a way of life. And I realized I didn't climb the tree because I was angry at the corporations and the government; I climbed the tree because when I fell in love with the redwoods, I fell in love with the world. So it is my feeling of 'connection' that drives me, instead of my anger and feelings of being disconnected."

Since 1973, Freedom House (freedomhouse.org) has evaluated the global state of civil liberties, democratic institutions, and independent media. Its research suggests that the world is steadily becoming more free, and is now the most free it has ever been.

In 1973, Freedom House said that 29 percent of the world's countries were free, 25 percent were "partly free," and 46 percent were "not free."

By 2009, the figures were dramatically improved: 46 percent of the nations on the planet were free, 32 percent were "partly free," and 22 percent were "not free." In 36 years, the percentage of "not free" countries had dropped by over 50 percent.

Of the world's 193 countries evaluated in the most recent report, 151 were judged to be free or partly free. This group accounts for 94 percent of the world's gross domestic product. (You can find more details here: tinyurl.com/a6u6me and here: tinyurl.com/n6efoo.) Freedom House concluded that the majority of the planet's economic, technological, and military resources belong to electoral democracies.

(Some progressives have complained that Freedom House is not sufficiently strong in reporting the abuses of freedom perpetrated by the U.S. and its allies. I think there may be some merit to their arguments, and I don't mean to imply that Freedom House is the ultimate and sole authority in the assessment of global freedom. However, it's also true that the organization assailed the Bush Administration's policies on interrogation and detention during its so-called War of Terror, and has over the years given low rankings to countries the U.S. considers friendly, like Saudi Arabia, Taiwan, Chile, and Guatemala.)

(There's also this: In 2009, Forbes magazine named Fareed Zakaria as one of the 25 most influential liberals in the American media. Here's his opinion about Freedom House, published in *Newsweek:* "While there are many sources of economic data, good political data is hard to find. Freedom House's survey is an exception. For anyone concerned with the state of freedom, or simply with the state of the world, 'Freedom in the World' is an indispensable guide.")

Richard Falk is a professor of international law at Princeton, and has served on the editorial boards of *The Nation* and *The Progressive* magazines as well as on two different United Nations human rights organizations. Writing in the magazine *Foreign Policy,* he said the following: "Every reliable human rights indicator suggests progress in the direction of self-determination and democratization in all parts of the world."

But then what about the observers who theorize that human rights are in alarming decline? "As with cancer and other diseases," responds Falk, "the ability to identify human rights abuses more accurately and treat their symptoms more effectively creates the illusion that the disease itself is more prevalent."

The United Nations organization UNESCO tracks literacy rates. Its latest news is very good. In 1950, 56 percent of the world's population could read and write. As of 2009, that figure had risen to 84 percent. The most dramatic improvement has occurred among young women. For example, not quite half of South Asian females were literate in 1990, while 75 percent are now. There were 10 million East Asian girls who couldn't read in 2000, but that had fallen to a million by 2009 (tinyurl.com/oh3nlc).

"There is a strong current of thought in the field of development economics," wrote Andrew Leonard in Salon.com, commenting on this report, "that the single most important factor in improving a variety of outcomes in the developing world—whether it be overpopulation, economic growth, violence against women, public health—is increasing female education levels."

The Maasai people of Kenya don't have running water, toilets, or electricity, and their per capita income is $300 a year. They use cattle dung as plaster in building their homes because the scent helps repel lions, which dislike it, from venturing too close. And yet they are as happy with their lives as *Forbes'* magazine's "400 richest Americans" are with theirs—even though the latter may live in 10,000-square-foot palaces with stained glass windows, French patio doors, limestone kitchen counter tops, spas, wine cellars, and Olympic-sized swimming pools.

This assertion comes from "Beyond Money: Toward an Economy of Well-Being" (tinyurl.com/nt3dpd), a report done by psychologists Ed Diener and Martin E. P. Seligman. On a scale of 1 to 7, where 1 is "extremely dissatisfied," 4 is "neutral," and 7 means "extremely satisfied," the Maasai, the Inuit of northern Greenland, and the wealthiest Americans all scored 5.8. Paupers scratching out a livelihood in the slums of Calcutta registered a score of 4.6, while international college students and the Amish of Illinois weighed in at 4.9. Citing 150 other studies in their work, Diener and Seligman conclude that economic factors are not necessarily correlated with happiness levels, especially in the developed world.

The Maasai tribespeople of Kenya, who have no running water and homes made from cattle dung, are as happy as the richest Americans.

Meanwhile, according to the World Values Survey, published in *New Scientist* magazine, Nigerians are the happiest people on the planet, although 60 percent of them live below the poverty line. The next four populations at the top of the list are Mexicans, Venezuelans, Salvadorans, and Puerto Ricans. On the scale of the planet's wealthiest places, they rank 63rd, 64th, 101st, and 163rd, respectively.

To be clear, Ed Diener notes in another report (tinyurl.com/qgn5m8) that on average, rich people are happier than poor people. He also says that cultural context is an important consideration in analyzing the relationship between financial well-being and happiness. A homeless man in California may have more money than a Maasai cattle-herder but be less sanguine about his fate. That's because basic necessities cost more for him and he is surrounded by people who are far better off than he is.

But Diener also declares that happiness is harder to attain for those who believe money is the most important factor in feeling good. Echoing him, the World Values Survey goes so far as to say that "the desire for material goods is actually a 'happiness suppressant,'" mirroring the Buddhist assertion that the craving for earthly riches can be the source of intense suffering.

In calling attention here to some of the surprisingly good news about the developing world, I of course don't mean to imply that paradise is at hand. My recognition of the underreported progress and miracles is not equivalent to an endorsement of evil-doers. And I trust that after reading these words you won't go numb to the suffering of others and stop agitating on their behalf.

Just the opposite: I hope that you will be energized by the signs of creeping benevolence and waxing intelligence. As you absorb the evidence that an aggressive strain of compassion is loose in the world, maybe you will conclude that activism actually works, and you'll be motivated to give yourself with confidence to the specific role you can play in manifesting the ultimate goal: to create a heaven on earth in which everyone alive is a healthy, free, self-actualized, spiritually enlightened millionaire dedicated to living sustainably.

Torture is no longer a commonplace feature of the justice system, as it was for centuries. The rate of child mortality in the developing world has dropped precipitously, while literacy is increasing steadily. Our era is the most peaceful time in recorded history.

SACRED ADVERTISEMENT

"Glory in the Highest Part 2" has been brought to you by Rigel 3200 Pro Night Vision Goggles and Sharon Doubiago's The Book of Seeing with One's Own Eyes.

6

Let's go wash some water.
Let's go burn some fire.

A SPELL TO RE-GENIUS YOURSELF

Although we are all born geniuses, said Buckminster Fuller, the grind of day-to-day living tends to de-genius us. That's the bad news. The good news is that you have the power to re-genius yourself.

Below is a ritual you can use to jump-start the process.

The Greek philosopher Plato long ago recognized that in addition to eating, drinking, sleeping, breathing, and loving, every creature has an instinctual need to periodically leap up into the air for no other reason than because it feels so good.

Face south, leap up in the air, and say these words: "From the south, I purify, electrify, beautify, and fructify this sacred space."

When I was a kid I used to love to go out in the middle of a meadow and whirl around in spirals until I got so dizzy I fell down. As I lay on the ground, the earth and sky and sun kept reeling madly, and I was no longer just a pinpoint of awareness lodged inside my body, but rather an ecstatically undulating swirl in the kaleidoscopic web of life. I invite you to feel that way right now.

Spin yourself around until you topple over. While lying on the ground, face west and say these words: "From the west, I sanctify, unify, clarify, and intensify this sacred space."

The people I trust the most are those who are always tenderly wrestling and negotiating with their own shadows, making preemptive strikes on their personal share of the world's evil, fighting the good fight to keep from spewing their darkness on those around them. I aspire to be like that, which is why I regularly kick my own ass. Will you try that right now?

Jump off the ground and snap your heels up against your butt. Then face north and say these words: "From the north, I immunize, psychoanalyze, satirize, and exorcise this sacred space."

In one sense each of us is an intriguing, intricately unique individual, justifiably proud of and in love with our own personal story. In another sense, we are all one body, descended from the same primordial mother and made of identical stuff—the calcium in all of our bones and the iron in all of our blood originally forged in a red giant star that died billions of years ago.

Rotating slowly in a clockwise direction, look down at your belly and breathe deeply five times as you imagine that at this moment, everyone in the world is breathing along with you. Then face east and say: "From the east, I lubricate, pollinate, consecrate, and emancipate this sacred space."

Now it's time to confess the truth about who you really are.

> *Gaze upward and stretch your arms out high. Say the following: "I am a genius."*

> *Put your arms out to the side, parallel to the ground with palms up, and say this: "I am a lucky, plucky genius."*

> *Swing your arms back and forth from behind you to in front of you as you say this: "I am a lucky, plucky, good-sucking genius."*

Thank you for finally confessing the truth. It's about time you admitted that you are a miraculous work of art.

You came into this world as a radiant bundle of exuberant riddles. You slipped into this dimension as a shimmering burst of spiral hallelujahs. You blasted into this realm as a lush explosion of ecstatic gratitude. And it is your birthright to fulfill those promises.

I'm not pandering to your egotism by telling you these things. When I say, "Be yourself," I don't mean you should be the self that wants to win every game and use up every resource and stand alone at the end of time on top of a Mt. Everest-sized pile of pretty garbage.

When I say, "Be yourself," I mean the self that says "Thank you!" to the wild irises and the windy rain and the people who grow your food. I mean the rebel creator who's longing to make the whole universe your home and sanctuary. I mean the dissident bodhisattva who's joyfully struggling to germinate the seeds of divine love that are packed inside every moment.

When I say, "Be yourself," I mean the spiritual freedom fighter who's scrambling and finagling and conspiring to relieve your fellow messiahs from their suffering and shower them with rowdy blessings.

Let's move on to the next stage of your confession.

> *Squat. While patting and massaging the ground or floor in front of you, say this: "I am insane."*

> *Still squatting, thrust your arms out sideways, palms down, and intone this oath: "I am an insane hurricane."*

> *Move from a squat to a pose in which you're on your knees. Bow your head as you stretch your arms out and touch the ground or floor. Say this: "I am a highly trained, entertainingly insane hurricane."*

Thank you for finally confessing the truth, which is that you are constitutionally incapable of adapting nicely to the sour and crippled mass hallucination that is mistakenly called "reality." You're too amazingly, blazingly insane for that.

You're too crazy smart to lust after the stupidest secrets of the game of life. You're too seriously delirious to wander sobbing through the sterile, perfumed labyrinth looking in vain for the most ultra-perfect mirror. Thank the Goddess that you are a fiercely tender throb of sublimely berserk abracadabra.

You'll never get crammed in a neat little niche in the middle of the road at the end of a nightmare. You refuse to allow your soul's bones to get ground down into dust and used to fertilize the killing fields that proudly dot the ice cream empire of monumentally demeaning luxuries. You're too brilliantly cracked for that. You're too ingeniously whacked. You're too ineffably godsmacked.

> *Stand up and make a series of small jumps, rotating a quarter turn in a clockwise direction with each jump. As you do, say this "I am a lucky, plucky, good-sucking genius and a highly trained, entertainingly insane hurricane."*

What's the Most Important Question for You to Ask Today?

Dear Gorgeous Genius: You possess exceptional capacities that are absolutely unique. You're a masterpiece unlike any other that has ever lived in the history of the world.

Furthermore, the precise instructions you need to ripen into your genius have always been with you, even from the time before you were born. In the words of psychologist James Hillman, you have a *soul's code.*

You might also call it the special mission you came to Earth to carry out; the divine blueprint that contains the open secret of how to be perfectly, unpredictably yourself; the master plan that is your heart's deepest desire.

Would you like help in deciphering it? The Divine Intelligence Formerly Known as God is always on call, ready to help. It's your birthright to ask Her a specific question every day about what you need to do next to express your soul's code; it's also your birthright to receive a response.

The divine revelation may not be as unambiguous as a little voice in your head. It might appear in the form of a TV commercial, an odd dream, or an encounter with a stranger. It could be demanding and difficult, delivering information you'd rather not have to deal with. Or it might show up as a clear and simple feeling of knowing exactly what to do, and it could be easy and fun.

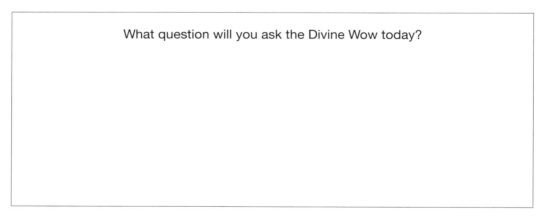

What question will you ask the Divine Wow today?

P.S. "There is a vitality, a life force, a quickening that is translated through you into action, and because there is only one of you in all time, this expression is unique. If you block it, it will never exist through any other medium. It will be lost. The world will not have it.

"It is not your business to determine how good it is, nor how valuable it is, nor how it compares with other expressions. It is your business to keep it yours clearly and directly, to keep the channel open." —Martha Graham, quoted by Agnes de Mille, *Dance to the Piper and Promenade Home*

Bigger, Better, More Interesting Problems

Is there anything more dangerous than getting up in the morning and having nothing to worry about, no problems to solve, no friction to heat you up? That state can be a threat to your health. If untreated, it incites an unconscious yearning for any old dumb trouble that might rouse some excitement.

Acquiring problems is a fundamental human need. It's as crucial to your well-being as getting food, air, water, sleep, and love. You define yourself—indeed, you make yourself—through the puzzling dilemmas you attract and solve. The most creative people on the planet are those who frame the biggest, hardest questions and then gather the resources necessary to find the answers.

Conventional wisdom implies that the best problems are those that place you under duress. There's supposedly no gain without pain. Stress is allegedly an incomparable spur for calling on resources that have been previously unavailable or dormant. Nietzsche's aphorism, "That which doesn't kill me makes me stronger," has achieved the status of a maxim.

We half-agree. But it's clear that stress also accompanies many mediocre problems that have little power to make us smarter. Pain frequently generates no gain. We're all prone to become habituated, even addicted, to nagging vexations that go on and on without rousing any of our sleeping genius.

There is, furthermore, another class of difficulty—let's call it the delightful dilemma—that neither feeds on angst nor generates it. On the contrary, it's fun and invigorating, and usually blooms when you're feeling

a profound sense of being at home in the world. The problem of writing this book is a good example. I've had abundant fun handling the perplexing challenges with which it has confronted me.

Imagine a life in which at least half of your quandaries match this profile. Act as if you're most likely to attract useful problems when joy is your predominant mood. Consider the possibility that being in unsettling circumstances may shrink your capacity to dream up the riddles you need most; that maybe it's hard to ask the best questions when you're preoccupied fighting rearguard battles against boring or demeaning annoyances that have plagued you for many moons.

Prediction: As an aspiring lover of pronoia, you will have a growing knack for gravitating toward wilder, wetter, more interesting problems. More and more, you will be drawn to the kind of gain that doesn't require pain. You'll be so alive and awake that you'll cheerfully push yourself out of your comfort zone in the direction of your personal frontier well before you're forced to do so by fate's kicks in the ass.

In Chinese, the word "crisis" is composed of two characters. One represents danger, the other opportunity. There has been no English equivalent until now.

The Beauty and Truth Lab has retooled an English term to convey a similar meaning: "kairos." Originally borrowed from Greek, "kairos" has traditionally meant "time of destiny, critical turning point, propitious moment for decision or action." In its most precise usage, it refers to a special season that is charged with significance and is outside of normal time. Its opposite is the Greek *chronos,* which refers to the drone of the daily rhythm.

These meanings provide the root of our new definition of the word. As of now, when used in the context of a discussion of pronoia, "kairos" will have the sense of "a good crisis, a rich problem, a productive difficulty."

"We should feel excited about the problems we confront and our ability to deal with them," says Robert Anton Wilson. "Solving problems is one of the highest and most sensual of all our brain functions."

The definition of "happiness" in the Beauty and Truth Lab's "Outlaw Dictionary of Pronoiac Memes" is "the state of mind that results from cultivating interesting, useful problems."

Sacred Advertisement

Kairos is brought to you by the mosquito that kept you up all night that one time, leading you to call in sick for work the next day and end up spending the unexpected free time rethinking your whole life and deciding to make a move that changed everything for the better.

Dionysian Manifesto

TWEAKABLE PRONOIA THERAPY

**Experiments and exercises
in becoming a radically curious,
wildly disciplined,
ironically sincere
Master of Sacred Uproar**

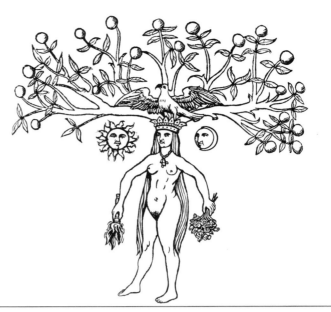

Report your answers and research results here

1 Charles Darwin said the "survival of the fittest" is a central factor in the process of evolution. What exactly did he mean by that? He makes it clear in his book *The Origin of Species:* "It is not the strongest of the species that survive, nor the most intelligent, but the ones most responsive to change."

According to Darwin's definition, what would you have to do to make yourself superbly fit?

2 The English language is in a state of rapid ferment. New words are barging into the dictionary at an unprecedented rate, even as old familiars fall into disuse. There's one exception to this trend: profanity. Hoary favorites like "fuck," "shit," and "asshole" have gained an acceptance unthinkable 30 years ago, but fresh curse words are rarely coined.

At the Beauty and Truth Lab, we find the overused classics inadequate for expressing our evolving rage at injustice, ignorance, and ugliness. Furthermore, as deadening clichés, they don't satisfy the pronoiac mandate to use language with sonorous precision.

There's another problem. Anger has become one of the trendiest emotions of all. In moderation it can be a righteous force for constructive change. But its hackneyed omnipresence means the vast majority of its outbreaks are trivial. The paucity of colorful obscenities is aggravated by an abundance of frivolous fury.

How can you purge the clichéd ire that dilutes the useful, inspired stuff? One good method is to make fun of it by expressing it bigger than life. Try this. Go alone to a place where it's safe to feel blind rage. Envision a person or thing you love to hate, then unleash the following mantra 15 times in the most vulgar tones possible: "You miasmic heap of shaved-off cemetery warts. You mangled preen of politicians' tongue scabs. You brackish tripe of experts' ego tinkles. You fragile crap of orphaned tyrants. You demented cluster of fickle weasel vows. You curdled slosh of rotting fracas-spawned opinions."

Now how about if you get to work helping us coin a new generation of profanities?

3 "Americans live inside their own private echo chambers," says syndicated writer Matt Zoller Seitz, "endlessly revisiting things they already know they like and avoiding exposure to anything new and different." Your assignment is to ask yourself if you fit Seitz's description, and then—if you do—to escape your private echo chamber. So for instance, if you're a tattooed pagan performance artist, attend a rodeo or NASCAR race; if you're a Christian Girl Scout leader, listen to Ani DiFranco or Radiohead, or read Noam Chomsky's radical critiques of American foreign policy. If you're an atheistic intellectual, take a workshop in ecstatic Sufi dancing or a class in Buddhist meditation.

> *"Technique in art has the same value as technique in love-making.*
> *On the one hand, heartfelt ineptitude has its appeal, and on the other hand, so does heartless skill; but what you want is passionate virtuosity."*
> *—John Barth*

4 Qabalist teacher Ann Davies told a story about a U.S. Army general negotiating with a cannibal chief in New Guinea during World War II. The general wanted the chief to rally his tribe to help American troops fight the Japanese. The chief refused, calling the Americans immoral. The general was shocked. "We are not immoral!" he protested. "The Japanese are immoral!" The cannibal chief replied, "The Japanese and Americans are equally immoral. You both kill far more people than you can eat."

Using this tale as your impetus, describe how parts of your moral code may not be rooted in an absolute standard of what's good and evil, but rather bound by the idiosyncrasies of your culture and historical era.

5 Radical segments of the gay movement appropriated the formerly nasty word "queer" and made it their own, a term of endearment and empowerment. Brave feminists took the word "bitch" and transformed it into a badge of honor. In a similar way, I call upon pronoiacs to reclaim the phrase "go fuck yourself."

Let's turn it into a celebratory battle cry—mutate the meaning so it's no longer a malignant curse but rather a liberating exhortation to enjoy pleasure in all of its intricate variety. Sexual rapture, yes, but also every other kind of ecstatic triumph—emotional richness, soulful breakthroughs, exotic states of consciousness, eruptions of profound wisdom, and sensual delight.

So when someone says to us, "Go fuck yourself," we will take it to mean, "Go give yourself big doses of bliss." And when we say "I did go fuck myself. I am going to fuck myself. I will go fuck myself," we'll mean, "I'm dreaming up endless ways to cultivate blessed euphoria in every area of my life."

6 During a trip to Europe, New York poet Stephen Ben Israel performed Re-Blessing Ceremonies in venerable cathedrals and synagogues. His primary sacramental act was to smoke a joint and invoke a visceral awareness of the Divine Intelligence. In so doing, he aspired to reanimate those sterile sanctuaries, where over the years so many worshipers have brought only their inert concepts and habit-encrusted beliefs.

Carry out your own version of a Re-Blessing Ceremony in a once-sacred place that has lost its juice.

7 In 752 AD, the Japanese Empress Kōken wrote a lyrical poem in praise of the eupatorium plant, whose leaves turn a vivid shade of yellow in summer. Recently, scientists demonstrated that the lovely foliage of the eupatorium is caused by a disease virus. In my view, this shouldn't diminish our appreciation of either the poem or plant. Beauty sometimes forms in response to a wound. Give examples from your own life.

8 Every act of genius, Carl Jung said, is an act *contra naturam:* against nature. Indeed, every effort to achieve psychological integration and union with the divine requires a knack for working against the grain. The eighteenth-century mystic Jacob Boehme recommended the same technique. The great secret to

Tweakable Pronoia Therapy

becoming enlightened, he said, is "to walk in all things contrary to the world." Qabalist teacher Paul Foster Case agreed: "The basis of the spiritual approach to life, the foundation of the everyday practice of a person who lives the life of obedience to esoteric law, is the reversal of the more usual ways of thinking, speaking and doing."

What exactly were they talking about? Give specific examples.

9 Composer Robert Schuman had long dialogues with his imaginary friends, Florestan and Eusebius, who provided valuable ideas for his musical scores. W.S. Merwyn wrote a poem in which he recounted the counsel of his teacher John Berryman: "He suggested I pray to the Muse / get down on my knees and pray / right there in the corner and he/ said he meant it literally."

Conjure up an imaginary friend and have an intimate conversation with him or her.

10 Take off your mask. You say you're not wearing a mask? But you are. The muscles of your face are so accustomed to displaying your familiar emotions, they've gotten stuck. Raw new emotions are aching to show themselves, but can't dislodge the incumbents.

Start an exercise program. Gaze into the mirror and make hundreds of rubbery faces. Loosen and tone your muscles. Flush those ancient expressions.

11 "As soon as you concern yourself with the 'good" and 'bad' of your fellows," said Morihei Ueshiba, founder of the martial art of aikido, "you create an opening in your heart for maliciousness to enter. Testing, competing with, and criticizing others weaken and defeat you."

Make that your hypothesis. Proceed according to the theory that you can feed your strength and power and freedom by accepting other people just the way they are. Assume that one of the surest ways to be happy and successful is to refrain from judging anyone.

12 Nineteenth-century English poet Dante Gabriel Rossetti wrote a series of sensual sonnets inspired by his relationship with his wife Elizabeth. Before he could publish them, Elizabeth died. He was so distraught he placed the only copy of his manuscript in the grave with her. Years later, though, he decided the love poems were too good to consign forever to the oblivion of the dirt. He had the coffin disinterred and recovered his work.

Tweakable Pronoia Therapy

Draw inspiration from Rosetti's change of heart. Reclaim riches you once abandoned or left for dead.

"The urge to transform one's appearance, to dance outdoors, to mock the powerful, and embrace perfect strangers is not easy to suppress."
—Barbara Ehrenreich

13 Cancer cells are constantly developing in our bodies. Luckily, our immune systems routinely kill them off. Similarly, our minds always harbor pockets of crazy-making misconceptions and faulty imprints. They usually don't rise up and render us insane thanks to the psychic versions of our immune systems.

How can you stay strong in your ability to fight off sickness and madness? You know the drill: Eat healthy food, sleep well, get physical exercise, minimize stress, give and receive love. But as an aspiring pronoiac, you have at your disposal other actions that can provide powerful boosts to your immune system. Here are examples:

Scheme to put yourself in the path of beautiful landscapes, buildings, art, and creatures.

Exercise your imagination regularly. Get in the habit of feeding your mind's eye with images that fill you with wonder and vitality.

Eliminate uhs, you knows, I means, and other junk words from your speech. Avoid saying things you don't really mean and haven't thought out. Stop yourself when tempted to make scornful assertions about people.

Every night before you fall asleep, review the day's activities in your mind's eye. As if watching a movie about yourself, try to be calmly objective as you observe your memories from the previous 16 hours. Be especially alert for moments when you strayed from your purpose and didn't live up to your highest standards.

With a companion, sit in front of a turned-off TV as you make up a pronoiac story that features tricky benevolence, scintillating harmony, and amusing redemption. Speak this tale aloud or write it down.

Take on an additional job title, beautifier. Put it on your business card and do something every day to

Tweakable Pronoia Therapy

cultivate your skill. If you're a people person, bring grace and intrigue into your conversations; ask unexpected questions that provoke original thoughts. If you're an artist, leave samples of your finest work in public places. If you're a psychologist or sociologist, point out the institutions and relationships that are working really well. Whatever you do best, be alert for how you can refine it and offer it up to those who'll benefit from it.

If you're going through a phase when you feel you have nothing especially beautiful to offer, or if you think it would be self-indulgent to inject your own aesthetic into shared environments, turn for help to great artists and thinkers. Sneak O'Keeffe or Chagall prints onto unadorned walls in public places, for instance. Memorize poems by Rilke and Hafiz, and slip them into your conversations when appropriate. Program your cell phone so that its ring is Vivaldi's *Stabat Mater in C Minor.* Scrawl passages from Annie Dillard's *Teaching a Stone to Talk* on the walls of public lavatories.

14 Write an essay on "What I Swear I'll Never Do Again as Long as I Live—Unless I Can Get Away With It Next Time."

15 Many concepts we use to interpret our experience originated in books written by people who are long gone. That's why philosopher Norman O. Brown (who died in 2002) says in his book *Apocalypse and/or Metamorphosis,* "The bondage to books compels us not to see with our own eyes; compels us to see with the eyes of the dead, with dead eyes. There is a hex on us, the authority of the past; and to exorcise these ghosts is the great work of magical self-liberation."

Melville Davisson Post (who died in 1930) echoes the theme in his book *Uncle Abner, Master of Mysteries.* "It is the dead who govern. Look how they work their will upon us! Who have made the laws? The dead! Who have made the customs that we obey and that form and shape our lives? The dead! All the writers, when they would give weight and authority to their opinions, quote the dead. Our lives follow grooves that the dead have run out with their thumbnails!"

Whose dead eyes do you see with? What would it be like to see the world without them?

16 Thomas Paine was a zealous revolutionary. He wrote incendiary pamphlets that helped ignite and sustain America's struggle for independence from Great Britain in the 18th century.

Tweakable Pronoia Therapy

Early in his life, however, he worked making women's girdles, which are among the most constrictive and oppressive garments in the history of the world. Was there a connection between his two gigs? Maybe his later struggle for liberation was an unconscious atonement for his youthful labors.

Instigate a Thomas Paine-like boomerang. Think of something you did in the past that constricted your spirit or squeezed other people's possibilities. Use that memory as a launching pad as you unleash a brilliant stroke in the name of abundance and expansiveness.

"The most beautiful thing in the world is conflicting interests when both are good."
—Robert Frost

17 "Watch out for the dark side of your own idealism and of your moral sense," says Howard Bloom. "Both come from our arsenal of natural instincts. And both easily degenerate into an excuse for attacks on others. When our righteous indignation breathes the flames of anger against a 'villain,' we all too often become a fang in nature's scheme of tooth and claw." What's the dark side of your idealism and morality?

18 Growing up in Montreal, musician Rufus Wainwright was steeped in the mystique of that city's legendary songwriter Leonard Cohen. Although too feisty a spirit to engage in idol-worship, Wainwright was at least slightly in awe.

As a young adult, he finally got to meet Cohen, whose daughter brought him to the great man's family home. When Wainwright walked into the kitchen, Cohen was in his underwear cooking up tiny sausages, which he was chewing, regurgitating, and feeding to a weak baby bird he had found and was trying to revive. (Source: the film *I'm Your Man*)

Are you, too, willing and able to have your fantasies confounded?

19 Thank you for not smoking while communing with this subliminal prod. Thank you as well for not burping, picking your nose, getting drunk, spilling food on yourself, thinking nasty thoughts about anyone, and letting your mind leap from undisciplined ideas to out-

Tweakable Pronoia Therapy

of-control feelings like a mean monkey on methamphetamine. All such behaviors would interfere with your ability to register on deep subconscious levels the meaning of this subliminal prod, which is: Sometimes you've got to be a bit of an asshole in order to avoid getting burned by the ass-souls. Do you agree? Provide evidence pro or con.

"The transfiguration of matter occurs through wonder."
—James Hillman

20 Computer programmer Garry Hamilton articulated the following "Game Rules." Give examples of how they have worked in your life.

1. If the game is rigged so you can't win, find another game or invent your own. 2. If you're not winning because you don't know the rules, learn the rules. 3. If you know the rules but aren't willing to follow them, there's either something wrong with the game or you need to change something in yourself. 4. Don't play the game in a half-baked way. Either get all the way in or all the way out. 5. It shouldn't be necessary for others to lose in order for you to win. If others have to lose, re-evaluate the game's goals.

21 When he's in his prime, a male panda performs an average of eight handstands a day. There's no apparent evolutionary purpose in this stunt. Maybe he does it because it feels good.

Make him your role model. Identify three activities you can do not because they're "good for you" or because they'll advance some goal you're pursuing, but simply for the sheer fun of it.

22 Here's the catch about pronoia: Life always gives you exactly what you need, exactly when you need it, but it doesn't necessarily give you exactly what you want, exactly when you want it. Talk about the differences between what you want and what you need.

23 Write a letter to the person you'll be one year from today. Tell this Future You that you've taken a vow to accomplish three feats by then. Say why these feats are more important to you than anything else. Describe them. Brainstorm about what you'll do to make them happen. Draw pictures or make collages that capture your excitement about them.

Tweakable Pronoia Therapy

Heroic Display of Willpower Dependence on nicotine is a notoriously difficult habit to break, resembling heroine and cocaine addiction in its power to enslave. Oddly, the drug is easily and legally available in the form of tobacco. In addition to the problems caused by addiction, cigarette smoking is also a grave menace to health, with the potential to cause numerous diseases that damage the heart and lungs.

The Center for Disease Control says that in 1965, 42 percent of adult Americans were in the grip of this deadly habit. But over four decades later, that percentage has dropped to below 21 percent, a decrease of over 50 percent. This amazing accomplishment was achieved without arrests, imprisonments, or drug testing.

PNN is brought to you by Emily Dickinson's passion. She "could never understand why the most intense human experiences had to be relegated to the margins of human society," wrote Edward Hirsch in American Poetry Review. "She read poetry and wrote every day because she needed a daily dose of ecstasy, the elation and exhilaration poetry provides."

Plant Liberation For the citizens of Switzerland, it's immoral to absentmindedly pluck wildflowers out of the ground and throw them aside. That's because this enlightened country has a Bill of Rights for plants. The 22-page document, drawn up by a panel of theologians, philosophers, geneticists, and lawyers, strongly urges respect for the feelings and dignity of all vegetation.

Rapture Update The World Health Organization reports that over 100 million acts of sexual intercourse, involving more than 200 million partners, take place on the earth every 24 hours. According to the Beauty and Truth Lab, if even one out of every two of those communions is motivated by love, the planet is continuously awash with tender ecstasy.

Almost More Good Luck Than You Can Bear "The rise of modernity served many extraordinary purposes: the rise of democracy; the banishing of slavery; the emergence of liberal feminism; the differentiation of art and science and morality; the widespread emergence of empirical sciences; an increase in average life span of almost three decades; the introduction of relativity and perspectivism in art and morals and science; the move from ethnocentric to world-centric morality; and the undoing of dominator social hierarchies." —Ken Wilber, *A Brief History of Everything*

Naked Heroism

The ancient Celts used to go into battle stark naked. They believed that only utter vulnerability demonstrated their total trust in the gods, who alone could make them invincible and who alone determined whether they would live or die. This brazen yet humble show of confidence often provoked primal fear in their enemies.

In 2002, 600 women from Nigeria's oil-rich Niger Delta invoked a similar approach to combat, launching a protest against U.S. oil giant ChevronTexaco. The women wanted the company to plow back some of its profits into their impoverished community, from whose land it was taking the oil. To drive home their demands, they threatened to commit a traditional shaming gesture—taking off their clothes. Nigerian tribes regard public displays of nudity by wives, mothers, and grandmothers as a damning protest that casts shame on those at whom the action is directed.

The tactic worked. To prevent the show of nakedness, ChevronTexaco gave in to the women, agreeing to hire villagers and build schools and electrical and water systems.

During the invasion of Iraq in 2003, groups of American, English, and Australian women, inspired by the Nigerians, registered their dissent through mass nudity. "In complete vulnerability there's a mighty well of power," said Australian peace activist Grace Knight.

What If Everything's Alive?

Yua is a term the Yupiit people of Alaska use for the spirit that inhabits all things, both animate and inanimate. A rock, for instance, has as much *yua* as a caribou, spruce tree, or human being, and therefore merits the same measure of compassion. If a Yupiit goes out for a hike and spies a chunk of wood lying on a frozen river bank, she might pick it up and put it in a new position, allowing its previously hidden side to get fresh air and sun. In this way, she would bestow a blessing on the wood's yua. (Source: Earl Shorris, "The Last Word," *Harper's*, August 2000)

Gross National Happiness

Calculated annually, the Gross National Product (GNP) is the standard by which countries gauge their prosperity. In an age when other values are subservient to the obsession with material wealth, the GNP is in essence a measure of the current worth of the Holy Grail.

In recent years the Buddhist nation of Bhutan has rebelled against this vulgarity, proposing a different accounting system: Gross National Happiness (GNH). While it takes into consideration economic development, it also includes factors like the preservation of the environment, enrichment of the culture, and quality of governance.

Here's an example of how Bhutan has raised its GNH. Its scenic beauty could potentially generate a huge tourist industry. But strict limits have been placed on the numbers of foreign visitors, ensuring the land won't be trampled and despoiled.

Unsung Mega-Hero

You've probably never heard of one of the greatest heroes of the last 100 years. Microbiologist Maurice Hilleman (1919-2005) developed vaccines for measles, pneumonia, meningitis, hepatitis, and many other diseases. *The Guardian* said he saved more lives in the twentieth century than anyone else.

Best Story and Storyteller of the Millennium

What was the best story of the previous millennium? Not Dante's *The Divine Comedy* or Cervantes' *Don Quixote* or Tolstoy's *War and Peace* or Joyce's A *Portrait of the Artist as a Young Man,* at least according to Booker Prize-winning author A. S. Byatt. Writing in *The New York Times,* she named *One Thousand and One Night*s as the most brilliant tale of the last thousand years.

In full agreement with Byatt's assessment, the Beauty and Truth Lab further names Scheherazade, narrator of *One Thousand and One Nights,* as the craftiest heroine in all of world literature. She saves her own life and those of countless other women as she diverts her husband from his murderous compulsion through the gentle pyrotechnics of her imagination. By the time she has finished telling her tales, drawing from her profound understanding of human nature, she has borne three children and humanized the misogynist tyrant who had terrorized the kingdom.

Proliferation of News Sources Reporting the Other Sides of the Story

Good News Network
goodnewsnetwork.org

Change the World News
cthings.com

Great News Network
greatnewsnetwork.org

Gimundo
gimundo.com

Talks by great thinkers
ted.com

Good News Daily
goodnewsdaily.com

Good News Blog
goodnewsblog.com

Rose Colored News
rosecolorednews.com

Happy News
happynews.com

Heroic Stories
heroicstories.com

Positive Economic News
positiveeconomicnews.com

Good News Economist
goodnewseconomist.com

NPR report on good news
tinyurl.com/d5mkuw

Positive magazines thrive
tinyurl.com/yo57bh

Yes magazine
yesmagazine.org

Ode magazine
odemagazine.com

Supreme Master TV
suprememastertv.com

Positive News
positivenewsus.org

World Transformation
worldtrans.org

World Changing
worldchanging.com

Domestic Bliss

"For the first time in history, more than half of central city households are homeowners. This increase has been led by African-American and Hispanic families, whose homeownership rates have been increasing the fastest."
—goodnewsnetwork.org

Adoration Reborn

"The insulted waters of New York City are again sacred passages, as they once were to Native Americans for millennia. Raw sewage no longer pours into vital waterways, and industrial pollution has largely been checked. We are witnessing the ecological resurrection of our rivers and bays, from the return of wood-eating gribbles and shipworms that devour our piers to winter visits by a small seal community. People are coming down to the water again to see rare birds, to kayak and to swim. And responding to an ancient call, they're coming down to the water to pray. Among the worshipers are Hindus, Shintoists, African Americans of the Yoruba-influenced Spiritual Baptist faith, Wiccans, Zoroastrians, Christians, and Jews." —Erik Baard, *Village Voice,* tinyurl.com/3ya6y5

Breaking the Pronoia Taboo

Future Studies

"Consider the oak beams in the ceiling of College Hall at Oxford. Last century, when the beams needed replacing, carpenters used oak trees that had been planted in 1386 when the dining hall was first built. The fourteenth-century builder had planted trees in anticipation of the time, hundreds of years in the future, when the beams would need replacing." —Danny Hillis, *Wired*

From the Field

Beauty and Truth Lab researcher Ariel Guzman saw this sign at a beauty salon in Ohio: "If truth is beauty, why doesn't anyone have their hair done at the library?"

"Know what you want and all the universe conspires to help you achieve it." —Paulo Coelho, *The Alchemist*

"The task of genius, and humanity is nothing if not genius, is to keep the miracle alive, to live always in the miracle, to make the miracle more and more miraculous, to swear allegiance to nothing, but live only miraculously, think only miraculously, die miraculously." —Henry Miller, *The Colossus of Maroussi*

"The soul should always stand ajar,
That if the heaven inquire,
He will not be obliged to wait,
Or shy of troubling her."
—Emily Dickinson, Poem 1055, *Complete Poems of Emily Dickinson*

"Humankind was put on earth to keep the heavens aloft. When we fail, creation remains unfinished." —Rabbi Menachem Mendel, known as the Kotzker Rebbe

"I hunger for your sleek laugh and your hands the color of a furious harvest. I want to eat the sunbeams flaring in your beauty." —Pablo Neruda, *100 Love Sonnets*

"The world is full of magical things patiently waiting for our wits to grow sharper." —Bertrand Russell

"Love the earth and the sun and animals, despise riches, give alms to everyone that asks, stand up for the stupid and the crazy, devote your income and labors to others, hate tyrants, argue not concerning God, re-examine all you have been told at school or church or in any book, dismiss whatever insults your own soul, and your very flesh shall be a great poem and have the richest fluency." —Walt Whitman, *Leaves of Grass*

"Love is the most difficult and dangerous form of courage. Courage is the most desperate, admirable, and noble kind of love." —Delmore Schwartz

"There is always some madness in love. But there is also always some reason in madness." —Friedrich Nietzsche

"In the world there is nothing more submissive and weak than water. Yet for attacking that which is hard and strong nothing can surpass it." —Lao Tzu

Gender Revolution Legalized

Sweden has been a pioneer in bringing gender balance into government. Forty-five percent of its parliament is female.

Other nations have begun to follow its lead. The Welsh assembly was the first legislative body in history to have as many women as men. Meanwhile, Denmark, Finland, Norway, Iceland, the Netherlands, Germany, Argentina, Costa Rica, New Zealand, South Africa, and Mozambique have at least 30 percent of their parliamentary seats filled by women, largely due to legally mandated quotas.

Rwanda's constitution calls for 30 percent of the decision-making positions to be held by women. In the most recent parliamentary elections, that quota was exceeded, as women captured 49 percent of the legislative seats.

The corporate domain is proceeding toward equality more slowly. Norway is the first and only nation to pass laws mandating female representation on corporate boards, requiring a 40 percent quota.

This perfect moment is brought to you by ringsel, pearly beads left behind after the cremation of Buddhist spiritual masters who've died. They're believed to contain the essence of the adepts' wisdom and life force, and may inspire healing or revelation in seekers who abide in their presence.

THIS DAY IN PRONOIAC HISTORY

The World Wildlife Fund has fought to save endangered species since 1961. Its logo features a panda bear. The World Wrestling Federation launched in 1962, and has made a fortune selling staged combats between steroid-inflamed loonies. One of its best-selling items is the "Undertaker Big Evil Red Devil T-shirt." So which of these WWFs won the skirmish between the two? The good guys. A court ruled that the panda lovers had a superior claim to the initials WWF. The devils had to change their name. It's now World Wrestling Entertainment.

Black South Africans fought for 40 years to dismantle the oppressive system of apartheid. One of their most potent weapons was toyi-toyi, a militantly exuberant form of singing and dancing. It served to mobilize the energy of crowds at the large protest demonstrations that ultimately broke the will of the white minority rulers. Imagine how confounded their authoritarian minds must have been when confronted by thousands of high-spirited activists passionately singing and dancing in unison.

Science Poetry

"Our skin shares its chemistry with the maple leaf and moth wing. The currents our bodies regulate share a molecular flow with raw sun. Nerves and flashes of lightning are related events woven into nature at different levels." —Richard Grossinger, *Planet Medicine*

"I am part of the sun as my eye is part of me. That I am part of the earth, my feet know perfectly, and my blood is part of the sea. There is nothing of me that is alone and isolate, except my mind, and we shall find that the mind has no existence by itself, but is only the glitter of the sun on the surface of the waters." —D. H. Lawrence, *Apocalypse and the Writings on Revelation*

MIRABILIA REPORT *Mirabilia* n. beguiling ephemera, inexplicable joys, changes that inspire quiet awe; from the Latin *mirabilia*, "marvels."

■ The sky not only isn't falling—it's rising. The top of the troposphere, the atmosphere's lowest layer, is slowly ascending.

■ Less than 25 percent of American households are composed of nuclear families.

■ The largest living thing in the world is a 2,384-acre, 2,400-year-old underground fungus in the Malheur National Forest of eastern Oregon. A member of the "honey mushroom" species, it has no name yet.

■ Anarchists claimed responsibility for the March 2001 earthquake in the Pacific Northwest, saying the deed was accomplished with a spell cast by the Green Fire coven of anarchist witches.

■ For $900, you can arrange for the manufacture of 12 action figures that look like you.

■ Some Christians really do love their enemies, as Jesus recommended.

■ In 2001, 16 refugees from the Dominican Republic were lost at sea for 12 days while fleeing across shark-infested waters to a better life in Puerto Rico. To save themselves from death by dehydration, they sucked milk from the breasts of a nursing mother who was among them.

■ Up to four million Americans believe they've been abducted by extraterrestrials. On average, Americans eat 18 acres of pizza every day.

■ Anthropologists say that in every culture in history, children have played the game hide-and-seek.

Clues to the Rebel Grail

The Rich Get Richer

Dear Beauty and Truth Lab: Help! My old Buick's transmission is dead, my credit cards are maxed, my kid's got to see the dentist real bad, and the one-speed bike I ride everywhere is about to collapse. I'm working two low-paying jobs already, although I just applied for a more lucrative gig as a strip-club dancer, only I'm having so much mysterious pain in my joints I'm not sure how sexy my gyrations will be. Please clue me in to some tricks that will help me keep a pronoiac attitude in the midst of the mess that is my life. —Pickled

Dear Pickled: Here's the first thing I want to tell you: Pronoia does not assume that material comfort is a sign of divine favor. The universe is an equal-opportunity provider, conspiring to shower blessings on every one of us in the same abundance. But while the blessings *may* come in the form of money and possessions, they're just as likely to consist of other gifts that aren't as concrete.

Here's a hypothetical example. Let's say you have the gift of feeling at home in the world no matter where you are. The universe has determined that it's the exact skill you need in order to fulfill the specific purpose you came to earth to carry out. Having a prestigious job and big salary, on the other hand, might be exactly what you *don't* need.

The question of what gifts are essential revolves around your precise role in the universal conspiracy to perpetrate blessings.

The second meditation I'll offer you is a passage from the Gospel of Matthew: "Whoever has, shall be given more and more, while whoever has nothing, even what he has will be taken away from him."

Pronoiac translation: Whatever you choose to focus your attention on, you will get more of it. If you often think of everything you lack and how sad you are that you don't have it, you will tend to receive prolific evidence of how true that is. As you obsess on all the ways your life is different from what you wish it would be, you will become an expert in rousing feelings of frustration and you will attract experiences that assist you in rousing frustration.

If, on the other hand, you dwell on the good things you have already had the privilege to experience, you will expand your appreciation for their blessings, which in turn will amplify their beneficent impact on your life. You will also magnetize yourself to receive further good things, making it more likely that they will be attracted into your sphere. At the very least, you will get in the habit of enjoying yourself no matter what the outward circumstances are.

Bear in mind that you are a great wizard. You can use your powers to practice white magic on yourself instead of the other kind. The most basic way to do that is to concentrate on naming, savoring, and feeling gratitude for the blessings you do have—your love for your kid, the pleasures of eating the food you like, the sight of the sky at dusk, the entertaining drama of your unique fate. Don't ignore the bad stuff, but make a point of celebrating the beautiful stuff with all the exuberant devotion you can muster.

Kaohinani
is a Hawaiian word
meaning
"gatherer of beautiful things."

Sacred Advertisement

The research of the Beauty and Truth Lab is made possible in part by the largesse of Boris Pasternak's poem "Bacchanalia," which includes these words: "How much courage is needed to play forever, as the ravines play, as the river plays."

FURTHER EVIDENCE

In our quest to insinuate pronoia into dinner table discussions taking place all over the world, we bring the following pieces of evidence to your attention.

Exhibit A

The bible of the mental health community is a 943-page textbook called the *Diagnostic and Statistical Manual of Mental Disorders, Fourth Edition,* or *DSM-IV.* Published by the American Psychiatric Association, it's a standardized catalog of psychological disorders that therapists use to evaluate and treat their patients. Surprise! This ultimate word on the state of the human psyche describes countless pathological states, but there's not a single entry referring to good mental health.

You might imagine that shrinks would be mildly interested not only in fixing what's wrong with their patients but also in helping them cultivate what feels good. But how can that happen if the feel-good states aren't even recognized as important enough to name?

Exhibit B

David G. Myers and Ed Diener authored an article called "The Science of Happiness," which appeared in the September/October 1997 issue of *The Futurist.* "What causes happiness?" they inquired. "This question not only went largely unanswered during psychology's first century, it went largely unasked." They note that from 1967 to 1995, essays on negative emotions far outnumbered those on positive emotions in the psychological literature. The ratio was 21:1.

Exhibit C

Even those supreme perpetrators of pop nihilism, *The New York Times* and *The Washington Post,* have a better ratio than the psychological literature. They average only 12 negative stories to every one that might be construed to be non-negative. Most other daily newspapers maintain a similar proportion.

Many of their non-negative stories, however, cover success in sports and entertainment. For example: The Atlanta Braves won their eighth straight game; the new book by Malcolm Gladwell is pretty decent. Remove these feel-good stories from the equation, and the media's Curse Quotient rises closer to that of the psychological literature.

Exhibit D

In his book *Omens of Millennium,* Harold Bloom hints at the "reductive fallacy" that serves as a shibboleth for intellectuals. Picture yourself, he says, in conversation with a bright, literate acquaintance who asks you about someone you know well: "Tell me what he or she is really like." You reflect a moment and give a brief description of your impressions, but your acquaintance isn't satisfied: "No, I mean *really* like." And now you grasp the actual question: "What is the very worst thing you can say about him or her that is true?"

Exhibit E

Thousands of amazing, inexplicable, wondrous, and even supernatural events occur every day. And yet most are unreported by the media. The few that are cited are ridiculed. Why? Here's one possible reason: The people most likely to believe in miracles are superstitious, uneducated, and prone to having a blind, literalist faith in their religions' myths. Those who are least likely to believe in miracles are skilled at analytical thought, well educated, and yet prone to having a blind, literalist faith in the ideology of materialism, which dogmatically asserts that the universe consists entirely of things that can be perceived by the five human senses or detected by instruments that scientists have thus far invented.

The media is largely composed of people from the second group. It's virtually impossible for them to admit to the possibility of miracles, let alone experience them. If anyone from this group manages to escape peer pressure and cultivate a receptivity to miracles, it's because they have successfully fought against being demoralized by the unsophisticated way miracles are framed by the first group.

At the Beauty and Truth Lab we're immune to the double-barreled ignorance. When we behold astonishing synchronicities and numinous breakthroughs that seem to violate natural law, we're willing to consider the possibility that our understanding of natural law is too narrow. And yet we also refrain from lapsing into irrational gullibility; we actively seek mundane explanations for apparent miracles.

Exhibit F

Wes Nisker wrote a book called *If You Don't Like the News . . . Go Out and Make Some of Your Own.*

Exhibit G

If you have encountered examples of the following evidence, tell us about it. Send your testimony to the Beauty and Truth Lab at Truthrooster@gmail.com. You might want to include the following:

1. bliss that flows toward you because you've made a habit of expecting it and cultivating it;

2. good news that's really interesting; fascinating stories that provide an antidote to the media's obsession with hardship, anguish, deterioration, and death;

3. states of emotional wealth and psychological health: raw material for the manual that will be the corrective for the *DSM-IV;* the missing half of the story;

4. mirabilia: mysterious revelations, rejuvenating prodigies, ineffable breakthroughs, beguiling ephemera, sudden deliverance from boring evils;

5. plain old everyday miracles;

6. the good news you've gone out and created.

> **"The rise and fall of images of the future precede or accompany the rise and fall of cultures. As long as a society's image is positive and flourishing, the flower of culture is in full bloom. Once the image begins to decay and lose its vitality, the culture does not long survive."**
> **—sociologist Fred Polak**

Everyone's a nobody—
and nobody's perfect

You Are Almost Everything

You taste delicious
Animals understand you
Your importance is unusual

The funny faces you make are interesting to look at
You fight for power in all the right ways

Ecstatic gratitude is pouring out of you
I see the best in you
Your divine attitude

You have strong feet and a pioneer heart

No one can overflow as well as you can

You are famous with God
You are famous with me
You are famous with the snakes and birds
and roses and pines
and oceans and earth and sky

A lost tribe salutes you from the other side of the veil

You remind me of a star

Healing Shocks

Many of us are essentially asleep, even as we walk around in broad daylight. We're so focused on the restless narratives and repetitive fantasies unfurling in our heads that we only dimly perceive the larger story raging in all of its chaotic beauty around us.

To have any hope of permanently breaking out of our fuzzy trance, we require regular shocks. A single jolt might cause us to briefly come to attention and see the miracle of creation for what it is, but once the red alert has passed, we relax back into our fixation on the dreamy tales our mind never stops telling us.

In the course of its conspiracy to shower us with blessings, life does its best to provide us with a steady flow of healing shocks. But because it tends to err on the side of tenderness, its prods may be too gentle, allowing us to ignore them. Gradually, life will up the ante, trying to find the right mix of toughness and love, as it encourages us to WAKE UP!

But our addiction to the phantasmagoria is tenacious. The stream-of-conscious narratives and ever-bubbling fantasies, even when they're racked with torment and terror, are perversely entertaining. And so we may avoid responding to the kind shocks for so long that life finally has to resort to stronger medicine. Then we might get sick or lose our job or muck up our closest relationship.

It doesn't have to be that way. We could cultivate in ourselves a sixth sense for the wake-up calls life sends us. We might develop a knack for responding with agile grace to the early, gentler ones so that we wouldn't have to be visited by the more stringent measures.

There's also another possibility: With hungry intent, we could seek out and hunt down invigorating jolts. We wouldn't wait to have our asses kicked, but would kick our own asses—over and over again, with a creative ingenuity that would be the envy of a great pronoiac novelist or musician or filmmaker. Who knows? We might even master the art of inducing shocks that feel really good.

BRAIN-SCRAMBLING MEDITATION

Relax. Put yourself in a comfortable position. Breathe deeply. Let the tension stream out of your head and neck and shoulders. Imagine that your worries are flowing out of you into the good earth below. Say "ahhhhh" in your softest tone.

Dissolve the constricted energy in your chest and belly and pelvis, and let it trickle away. Allow the stress in your legs and feet to evaporate. With each breath, send out a wave of love to your entire body. Relax even more deeply. Become aware that all of the disquiet within you is departing. Your knots are unraveling. Your congestion is dissipating.

Now close your eyes and imagine that it's a bright and warm summer day at the beach. You're sitting in a cozy chair. The sky is a deep, infinite blue. A balmy breeze caresses your cheeks. Your body feels strong and serene. You're in harmony with the flow of life. Look around you. See the sparkling white sand. Feel the gentle waves swirl around your ankles.

As you bask in this beauty and calm, imagine that you're reading the *Wall Street Journal* and listening in your headphones to the soothingly riotous music of a klezmer band playing free-form jazz with a hip-hop beat. Nearby is a shopping mall you have recently bought and converted into a country club for poor people. A cell phone and wireless laptop are by your side because you must always be available to conduct late-breaking business deals, buy or sell stocks, or give spiritual advice.

Amazing but true: You are both a billionaire *and* a wise counselor. This blend of wealth and sagacity has led you to become a philanthropic healer. Through cash donations and gifts of insight, you have helped thousands of people transform themselves into gorgeous geniuses skilled at expressing their souls' codes.

Relax even more deeply. Tune in to the understanding that you are a furiously curious soul full of orgiastic compassion for everything alive. You are an ongoing experiment in lyrical logic, a slow explosion of uncanny delight, a sacred agent devoted to breaking the taboo against feeling crafty joy.

Now say this: *I have only barely imagined the blessings that await me. As interesting and as full as my life is, I'm ready for it to become even more so.*

With this declaration, you have given the future permission to transform you into a more awakened version of yourself than you ever knew was possible.

Continue your cooperation with the glorious fate that's coming your way. Speak the following affirmations, which have been scientifically formulated to free you of all rigid beliefs that might cause stupidity:

I kick my own ass and wash my own brain.
I push my own buttons and trick my own pain.
I burn my own flags and roast my own heroes.
I mock my own fears and cheer my own zeroes.

Nothing can stop me from teasing my shadow.
I'm full of empty and backwards bravado.
My wounds are tattoos that reveal my true beauty.
I turn tragic to magic and make bliss my duty.

I honor my faults till they become virtues.
I play jokes on my nightmares
till I'm sure they won't hurt you.
I sing anarchist lullabies to lesbian trees
and love songs with punch lines
to anonymous seas.

I won't accept gifts that infringe on my freedom.
I shun sacred places that stir up my boredom.
I change my name daily, pretend to be nobody.
I fight for the truth if it's majestically rowdy.

Gravity fucks me and I fuck it back.
The sun is my sex slave, the moon smokes my crack.
I pump up my conscience with idiot laughter.
I'm living happily, in love ever after.

I brag about what I can't do and don't know.
I take off my clothes to those I oppose.
I'm so far beyond lazy, I work like a god.
I'm totally crazy; in fact that's my job.

It's all true. You're completely wacko. Throbbingly, succulently, shimmeringly insane. And that's good news.

Freed from your need to pretend you're dignified and consistent and sensible, you find yourself becoming aware of voluptuous facts you were impervious to before now. You know beyond any doubt that each of your heart's beats originates as a gift of love directly from the Goddess herself. You understand that the laws of physics are fine-tuned to create a universe in which you can thrive. You realize with visceral lucidity that everything you see is permeated with a single, unified conscious intelligence, of which you partake intimately. This intelligence is immortal, and thus, so are you. As you register the shocking joy of these truths imprinting themselves on your perfect body, every one of your cells purrs with luminous gratitude.

Now please take the following multiple-choice test:

How does it make you feel when I urge you to confess profound secrets to people who are not particularly interested? Does it make you want to:

a. cultivate a healthy erotic desire for a person you'd normally never be attracted to in a million years;

b. stop helping your friends glamorize their pain;

c. imitate a hurricane in the act of extinguishing a forest fire;

d. visualize Buddha or Mother Teresa at the moment of orgasm;

e. steal something that's already yours.

The right answer, of course, is any answer you thought was correct. Congratulations. You're even smarter than you knew.

To seal your victory, repeat the following declaration, uttered by the Baron in the film The Adventures of Baron Munchausen: "Your reality, sir, is lies and balderdash, and I'm happy to say I have no grasp of it whatsoever."

Remain here for a while in this state of supernatural relaxation. As you begin to return to normal waking consciousness, *don't* return to normal waking consciousness. Instead, practice feeling the confidence that you can invoke the scent of wild honey in a sunlit meadow any time you feel an urge to.

In honor of your enhanced power to be yourself, I hereby reward you with a host of fresh titles. From now on you will be known as the Senior Vice President of Strawberry Fields and Hummingbirds, and the Deputy Director of Green Lights and Purple Hearts. Consider yourself, as well, to be the new Puzzle-Master Supreme, the Chief Custodian of Secret Weapons, and Field Commander of Free Lunches and Poetic Licenses.

***Lucid dream whirlygigs that are
scientifically synergized
with shadow-perfect songs
from heaven's abyss
yield
chthonic faster-than-light clarity.***

Primordial Gossip

YOU ARE HERE

REAP THE BENEFITS OF YOUR SCRAMBLED BRAIN

Have you ever done automatic writing? Try it. Hold a pen with your non-dominant hand and make up a dream in which you change into an animal. Imagine a conversation with your bravest ancestor or smartest descendant. Relive the last day of your beloved's childhood. Fantasize about the possibility that there's something you really need but you don't know what it is. Pretend you meet another version of yourself, maybe your long-lost twin or your doppleganger from Romania or the person you'll be in a future incarnation, who has time-traveled here to be with you. Channel a telepathic message from a violet chupacabra who's a great leader on a planet circling the star Gliese 876. Compose a prayer in which you ask for something you're not supposed to.

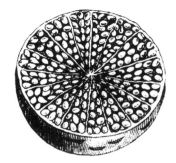

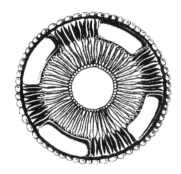

Apocalypse Versus Apocalypse

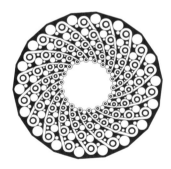

The chauvinism I suffer from is a peculiar variety. I don't have delusions of grandeur about my religion, country, or football team, but rather of the era I live in. I fantasize that our moment in history is more important than all the others. Those of us alive today are on the cusp of a radical turning point in the evolution of humanity. Or so I like to imagine.

It's embarrassing. It associates me with wacky millenarians of all stripes, from histrionic New Age prophets to fundamentalist Christians who fanatically anticipate the "end times." And as much as I would like to imagine my views are subtler and more rational than those of the superstitious extremists, I must admit that I sometimes catch myself dreaming of how deliriously interesting it would be if the mass hallucination that is mistakenly referred to as "reality" really did mutate "in the twinkling of an eye," as the Bible insinuates.

Did I scoff at the scaremongers who shivered at the approach of Y2K? Well, yeah, I mostly did. But there was also a Drama King in a dark corner of my psyche who indulged in perversely thrilling chimeras about the possibility that the melodramatic doomsayers might be right. A similar reflex put me in alignment with the Nostradamus wannabes who forecast "earth changes" and a global economic depression in the face of the massive conjunction of planets in the astrological sign of Taurus in May 2000.

In recent years, a month rarely goes by when my inner Drama King doesn't pounce on some new sign of imminent upheaval. Endgame scenarios are no longer solely the province of certifiable cranks and paranoids. Scientists speculate on the odds of the earth getting blasted by an asteroid similar to the one that apparently wiped out the dinosaurs 65 million years ago. Medical researchers raise the specter of novel strains of the flu turning into out-of-control pandemics. Seemingly sane politicians and journalists insist on cramming our imaginations full of visions of terrorist-delivered suitcase nukes and killer bioweapons.

But there is another part of me, a voice that feels older and wiser, who suspects that even if we *are* on the verge of an evolutionary turning point, even if those of us who are alive today *will* experience the End of Life as We Know It, it just won't be as simple and obvious and bad as the literalist prophets fantasize. The transformation will not come via some cataclysmic overnight worldwide presto-chango.

It is this same part of me—the older, wiser voice—that's distrustful of our culture's predilection for seeing the worst in everything. How did hopelessness come to be regarded as a mark of sophisticated realism? Why are Things Falling Apart thought to be inherently more gripping than Things Being Reborn?

Luckily, the jingoistic part of me that yearns to be alive when Everything Changes can find a common ground with the Zen master in me who regards the entropy-obsessed, all-or-nothing mind-set as a unique signature of the civilization that's dying. Together these two aspects of my psyche can collaborate to conclude the following:

WE ARE IN FACT LIVING THROUGH THE APOCALYPSE RIGHT NOW.

But it's nothing like the end of the world visualized by any of the usual suspects. It's different in four ways.

1. It's a slow, gradual apocalypse.

2. The apocalypse is usually invisible, erupting into our conscious awareness only on rare occasions.

3. The apocalypse is as much about rebirth as collapse.

4. The primary way most of us experience the apocalypse is through the intimate events of our personal lives.

I'll explore these four points in more detail.

1. THE APOCALYPSE IS HAPPENING IN SLOW MOTION. It has been going on for decades and will continue to unfold for many years. Sudden, sensational punctuations arise now and then to expedite it, but for the most part it ferments continuously in the background. Most days bring no emergency that is beyond our capacity to bear, but the cumulative effects of the transfigurations that relentlessly weave themselves into our lives have turned every one of us into heroes whose courageous endurance dwarfs the valor of legends like Gilgamesh, Odysseus, Arthur, and Joan of Arc.

2. THE APOCALYPSE IS FOR THE MOST PART INVISIBLE. Here's the most extreme evidence: Few of us have registered the fact that we're in the midst of the largest mass extinction of life on Earth since the demise of the dinosaurs. This is the conclusion of the American Institute of Biological Sciences, a professional society of 5,000 scientists. Think of it: About 40 animal and plant species are dying off every day—a rate unmatched in 65 million years. Shouldn't this be a recurring headline on the front page of every major newspaper?

But the work-in-progress that is the apocalypse is not always cloaked. Now and then a riveting event transfixes our collective emotions, driving millions of us deep into a visceral encounter with the ongoing collapse. For a brief interlude, the covert, slow-motion upheaval explodes into plain view. In recent years, no event has done that more dramatically, at least for Americans, than the mass murder perpetrated by kamikaze hijackers on September 11, 2001.

3. THE APOCALYPSE IS AS MUCH ABOUT REBIRTH AS BREAKDOWN. The English word "apocalypse" is derived from the Greek word for "revelation." In the esoteric spiritual traditions of the West, "apocalypse" has also come to denote a great awakening.

The apocalypse we're living through can be described by all three meanings of the word: as the end of the world, a revelation, and an awakening. Disintegration and renewal are happening side by side; calamity and fertility; rot and splendor; grievous losses and surges of invigorating novelty. Yes, the death of the old order is proceeding apace; but it's overlapped by the birth pangs of an as-yet unimaginable new civilization.

The devastation and regeneration often have no apparent link. But in the case of 9-11, they seemed to be meshed. I received many e-mails from people testifying about how the terrorist assault was a weird kind of gift. In the aftermath, their petty worries evaporated and they stopped wasting time on low-priority, dead-end desires. Roused by an electrifying clarity of purpose, they began to live the life they'd previously only fantasized they wanted. And they had direct perceptions—gut-level, intuitive gnosis—that We Are All One.

It's as if millions of people had a simultaneous Near Death Experience and harvested the epiphanies that typically come to those who have peered over to the other side of the veil.

Here's another example of catastrophe and regeneration arising from a single set of events, suggested by Caroline Myss in her book *Energy Anatomy.* China's

Dionysian Manifesto

invasion and occupation of Tibet in the 1950s resulted in the exile of the Dalai Lama, which ultimately brought that great soul's influence, along with his elegant brand of Buddhism, to the entire world with a breadth and depth that would never have happened otherwise.

4. MOST OF THE TIME WE EXPERIENCE APOCA-LYPSE NOT THROUGH BIG, BAD EVENTS LIKE THE SEPTEMBER 11 MASSACRES, BUT THROUGH THE DETAILS OF OUR PERSONAL LIVES. The sweeping but gradual revolution, the agonizing decay of the old order and breathtaking bloom of the new, are framed in the storylines of your most intimate dramas. Again and again over the years, you're pushed to a brink that challenges you to either rise to the occasion or else surrender to demoralizing chaos. The crises may come in the form of divorce or illness or job loss, or even in less dramatic events like a misunderstanding with a friend or the inexplicable waning of a once-passionate dream.

Seeded inside each of these personal turning points is the crux of the evolving global apocalypse: You get to choose whether you'll adjust by taking a path that keeps you aligned with the values of the dying world or else a path that helps you resonate with what's being born. In effect, you get the chance to vote, with your entire life, for which aspect of the apocalypse you want to predominate.

In Hawaii there are two plants, called *'ama'u* and *limu-haea* by the natives, which specialize in colonizing fresh lava flows. Their windblown seeds insinuate themselves into cracks in the newly cooled rock, and sprout long before any other species does.

SACRED ADVERTISEMENT

The apocalypse is being brought to you by the time you dreamed you signed the Declaration of Independence with your non-dominant hand as you ate fresh Peruvian figs flown to you on the backs of albatrosses.

Dionysian Manifesto

Hype-ocalypse

Rank your favorite doomsday scenarios in order of preference.

____A new ice age

____Destruction of ozone layer

____Dramatic upsurge in earthquakes, volcanic eruptions, and hurricanes

____Universal drug addiction

____Mass starvation

____Takeover by monsters created through genetic engineering

____Genocide of the imagination; lethal proliferation of dangerous images

____Terrifying, contagious superstitions spread by apocalyptic pop prophecy

____Insects and bacteria conspire to cull planet's most dangerous species

____Multinational corporate criminals create a single, globe-spanning totalitarian state with concentration camps that are the setting for popular reality TV shows

____Mutated flu strain becomes unstoppable plague

____Extraterrestrial invasion

____Cataclysmic degeneration of language into incomprehensible babble and cliché

____Anthrax and LSD dumped in water supplies

____Revolt of super-intelligent machines

____Stupidity becomes popular

____Mass hypnosis by evil political and religious leaders

____President, suffering from mental illness, goes berserk and nukes Mecca, Moscow, Beijing

____Virus from outer space

____Virus from inner space

____Essential natural resources run out

____Global addiction to porn results in accidental mass suicides through excessive masturbation

____Psychic terrorists administer mass brainwashing that causes millions to buy so many products they can't afford that they become destitute, can't afford health care, and die from diseases caused by eating GMO-laden junk food out of garbage cans

____The Internet births itself as a sentient global brain, but it's so riddled with spam that it becomes a god-like cripple suffering from the Artificial Intelligence version of Alzheimer's

____Earth is hit by comet, asteroid, or mini-black hole

____Wealthy philanthropists give everyone in the world $100,000, causing mass insanity

____Sun goes supernova

____Breakthroughs in disease control make it hard for people who are tired of living to die, leading to a pandemic of depression

____The devil possesses everyone in the world

____Nuclear war

____Other (describe)_____

_____

PRONOIA'S VILLAINS

According to Argentinian writer Jorge Luis Borges, Judas was actually a more exalted hero than Jesus. He unselfishly volunteered to perform the all-important villain's role in the resurrection saga, knowing he'd be reviled forever. It was a dirty job that only a supremely egoless saint could have done. Jesus suffered, true, but enjoyed glory and adoration as a result.

Let's apply this way of thinking to the task of understanding the role that seemingly bad people play in pronoia.

Interesting narratives play an essential role in the universal conspiracy to give us exactly what we need. All of us crave drama. We love to be beguiled by twists of fate that unfold the stories of our lives in unpredictable ways. Just as Judas played a key role in advancing the tale of Christ's quest, villains and con men and clowns may be crucial to the entertainment value of our personal journeys.

Try this: Imagine the people you fear and dislike as pivotal characters in a fascinating and ultimately redemptive plot that will take years or even lifetimes for the Divine Wow to elaborate.

There is another reason to love our enemies: They force us to become smarter. The riddles they thrust in front of us sharpen our wits and sculpt our souls.

Try this: Act as if your adversaries are great teachers. Thank them for how crucial they've been in your education.

Consider one more possibility: that the people who seem to slow us down and hold us back are actually preventing things from happening too fast.

Imagine that the evolution of your life or our culture is like a pregnancy: It needs to reach its full term. Just as a child isn't ready to be born after five months of gestation, the New Earth we're creating has to ripen in its own time. The recalcitrant reactionaries who resist the inevitable birth are simply making sure that the far-seeing revolutionaries don't conjure the future too suddenly. They serve the greater good.

You're a Good Killer

In order to live, you've got to be a demolisher. You take plants and animals that were once alive and rip them apart with your teeth, then disintegrate them in your digestive system.

Your body is literally on fire inside, burning up the oxygen you suck into your lungs.

You didn't actually cut down the trees used to make your house and furniture, but you colluded with their demise.

Then there's the psychological liquidation you've done: killing off old beliefs you've outgrown, for instance.

I'm not trying to make you feel guilty—just pointing out that you have a lot of experience with positive expressions of destruction.

Can you think of other forms this magic takes? As an aspiring master of pronoia, it's one of your specialties—a talent you have a duty to wield with energetic grace

SACRED ADVERTISEMENT

Your talent for creative destruction is brought to you by the bacteria, viruses, fungi, and protozoa that are instrumental in providing our food, aiding our digestion, purifying our drinking water, and processing our sewage.

AMBIDEXTROUS PRONOIA THERAPY

Experiments and exercises in becoming a mysteriously truthful, teasingly healing, mutinously magnanimous Master of Impartial Passion

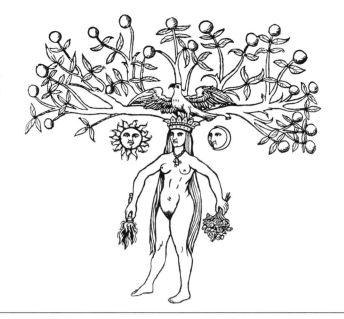

Report your answers and research results below

1 What three ideas do you hate most? Pretend you believe those ideas devoutly. Write about them as if they were the cornerstones of your philosophy of life.

2 The Shinto monks of Ise, Japan, have a curious custom. Every 20 years since the year 772, they've dismantled their central shrine and rebuilt it from scratch. In so doing, they pass down the knowledge of their sacred construction techniques from generation to generation. It's also an effective way for the monks to participate eagerly in the transitoriness of life, rather than merely being resigned to it. They practice the art of death and rebirth not just in meditation but through a practical long-term ritual.

Can you think of an analogous custom you might create for your personal use?

3 There is a disproportionate abundance of evil stepmothers in traditional fairy tales. Storyteller Michael Meade believes that's because the evil stepmother is a symbol of the soul's nemesis, and everyone has a nemesis. In fact, he says, we all *need* a nemesis to keep us honest, to challenge our assumptions and call our bluffs. With this in mind, brainstorm a short fairy tale in which you're compelled to call on resources you didn't realize you had in order to outwit an adversary.

4 We're acquainted with a group of Hells Angels that has a unique way of honoring the deceased. Once a year the gang throws a party in the cemetery where their fallen comrades are buried, pouring beer on and snorting coke off their graves.

Think about developing a similar approach to dealing with the dead parts of your own life. Don't just cry mournfully over the dreams and influences that have helped make you what you are. Dance for them; sing for them; leap into the air and kiss the sky for them.

5 We all have a war going on inside ourselves. What's yours? Is it a just and fruitful war or a senseless and wasteful war, or both?

Which of your many pains provided the very best cure?

6 Once upon a time, you asked a certain someone for a blessing. Instead, he or she blasted you with a curse. The debilitating blow of that bad juju hit you right in the place that was ripe for the blessing you requested. What a tragedy!

Do you understand that the seed of the blessing you once needed (and still need) is hidden within the curse? If you figure out what that blessing is, you'll find the cure. (P.S. The French word for "wound" is blessure, which suggests that blessing can come from wounding.)

7 Hundreds of years ago, it was seemingly possible to buy forgiveness. Until Martin Luther came along to spoil the fun, the Catholic Church used to sell "indulgences," which buyers could supposedly trade in purgatory for a reduced punishment for their earthly sins.

The forgiveness freaks at the Beauty and Truth Lab have revived this practice in a mutated form. For the right price, we're able to guarantee your absolution. To take advantage of our offer, simply send us a million dollars for each sin you want to have forgiven.

There's just one condition: You can't pay us with the government's legal tender. You must *make* the money—literally. Using crayons, paints, scissors, glue, collage materials, or other media, create your own version of large-denomination paper money. Instead of the images of politicians that typically appear on government currency, draw pictures of your muses and heroes and friends and pets. Rather than patriotic clichés and meaningless decorative frills, add sayings and symbols that make you happy. Be sure to write a description of the sin you want "indulged" somewhere on the bill. Send your payment to the Beauty and Truth Lab. You can find the address at the bottom of this web page: tinyurl.com/nhhsmf.

8 "God offers to every mind its choice between truth and repose," wrote Ralph Waldo Emerson. "Take which you please; you can never have both." Give an example from your own life that refutes or proves Emerson's assertion.

Ambidextrous Pronoia Therapy

9 Our culture regards vultures as ugly and disgusting. But in ancient Egypt, they were sacred. Scholar Elinor Gadon says they were called "compassionate purifiers." As devourers of corpses, they transformed rotting flesh into usable energy, and expedited the soul's transition to heaven. Queens of Egypt wore vulture headdresses to signify their divine consecration.

How would you invoke the help of mythical vultures in your own life? Here's one possibility. Meditate on death not as the end of physical life, but as a metaphor for shedding what's outworn. In that light, what is the best death you've ever experienced? What death would you like to enjoy next?

10 James Hillman and Michael Ventura wrote the book *We've Had a Hundred Years of Psychotherapy and the World's Getting Worse.* They propose that resolving our problems may not necessarily come from talking about our deep, private feelings with a trusted counselor. Instead, the best approach might be to go out into the world and do good works like helping the underprivileged or fighting for social justice.

Try their approach as a prescription for one of your personal problems.

11 In an old fairy tale, a virtuous hero throws a punch at an evil witch. But because of her wizardry, the thrust of his fist boomerangs and he smashes himself in the nose. Blood flows from his nostrils. He wipes it with his fingertips and flings a few red drops in the witch's direction. This is the unexpected magic that sends her fleeing. He's saved. Moral of the story: The hero's self-wounding produces his ultimate protection. Give an example of this theme at work in your own life.

> *You will dream*
> *about a flying carpet,*
> *a genie's lamp,*
> *the candy of the gods,*
> *a wizard's wand,*
> *healing ointment,*
> *a silver chalice,*
> *and enchanted mud.*

12 My friend Ronnie, the tattoo artist, told me that people who come in to get their first tattoo are sometimes unprepared for how much it hurts. Most are

Ambidextrous Pronoia Therapy

able to endure the razor-sharp ripping of their flesh for the time it takes, though. There are some sissies who can't, and they tend to be the biggest, baddest macho dudes. Ronnie says she personally knows 15 tough guys walking around San Francisco with a fragment of a tattoo, having abandoned the process in agony before it was done.

Is there any situation in your life that resembles a half-completed initiation? Have you ever left midway through a rite of passage? Make plans to go back and finish what you started.

> *"I think the whole world's gone mad."*
> *"Nah. It's always been like this. You just don't get out enough."*
> *—Neil Gaiman*

13 Dumb suffering is the kind of suffering you're compulsively drawn back to over and over again out of habit. It's familiar, and thus perversely comfortable. Smart suffering is the kind of pain that surprises you with valuable teachings and inspires you to see the world with new eyes.

While stupid suffering is often born of fear, wise suffering is typically stirred up by love. The dumb, unproductive stuff comes from allowing yourself to be controlled by your early conditioning and from doing things that are out of harmony with your essence. The smart, useful variety arises out of an intention to approach life as an interesting work of art and uncanny game that's worthy of your curiosity.

Come up with two more definitions about the difference between dumb suffering and smart suffering.

14 Traditionally, the Seven Deadly Sins—actions most likely to wound the soul—are pride, lust, gluttony, anger, envy, sloth, and covetousness.

But we have formulated a fresh set of soul-harmers, the Four Foolish Virtues. They are as follows: (1) being analytical to such extremes that you repress your intuition; (2) sacrificing your pleasure through a compulsive attachment to duty; (3) tolerating excessive stress because you assume it helps you accomplish more; (4) being so knowledgeable that you neglect to be curious.

Ambidextrous Pronoia Therapy

Are you victimized by any of these Four Foolish Virtues? If so, what are you going to do about it?

15 The 17th-century surgeon Wilhelm Hilden had an interesting theory about healing. He developed a medicinal salve that he applied not to the wound itself but rather to the weapon that inflicted it. Though today we may sneer at such foolishness, the fact is that Hilden's approach has great potential if used for psychic wounds. Jesus understood this when he articulated the revolutionary formula, "Love your enemy." More than any other action, this strategy has the power to cure you of the distortions your enemy has unleashed in you. Try it out.

16 Go to a mirror and play with your face until you create the Fabulous Smirk. Not the Arrogant Smirk or the Vengeful Smirk or the Hateful, Whiny, Passive-Aggressive Smirk. Rather, express the Smirk that Passeth All Understanding. The Wise, Charitable, Forbearing Smirk. The Über-Smirk that says, "I've figured out what everyone's hiding, and I love them anyway."

17 How do you respond to the part of the apocalypse that brings breakdown and ruin? Is it with actions that express rage, disdain, hatred, fear, tribalism, and all the primitive emotions that infect the roots of the dying civilization?

Or is it with actions that exude ingenious compassion, creative self-protection, expansive resourcefulness, and other robust emotions that are at the heart of the New Earth?

What can you do to focus your personal experience of the apocalypse on liberation and awakening rather than suffering and loss? How can you personally starve the bad apocalypse and nurture the good apocalypse?

> ### To keep your "sorcery" clean and sweet, pray every now and then for your enemies to get what they want.

18 Sometimes hope is an irrelevant waste of time, even a stupid self-indulgence. Let's say, for instance, that I'm intently hoping that a certain disagreeable person I've got to communicate with won't answer when I call on the phone. That way I can simply leave a message on his voice mail and avoid an unpleasant exchange. But it doesn't matter what I hope. The guy will either answer or not, regardless of what I hope.

But there is another kind of hope that's potentially invigorating. Let's say I hope that we humans will reverse the environmental catastrophes we're perpetrating. Let's say that my hope motivates me to live more sustainably and to inspire others to live more sustainably. Then my hope is a catalyst.

Give two examples from your life about the two kinds of hope.

Welcome to the Clandestine Indigenous Revolutionary Committee in Charge of the Ingenious Liberation of All Sentient Beings. May your time with us increase your brilliance a hundredfold.

19 "Obstacles are a natural part of life, just as boulders are a natural part of the course of a river," declares the ancient Chinese book the I Ching. "The river does not complain or get depressed because there are boulders in its path."

I'd go so far to say—this is not in the original text, but is my 21st-century addition—that the river gets a sensual thrill as it glides its smooth current over the irregular shapes and hard skin of the rocks. It looks forward to the friction, exults in the intimate touch, loves the drama of the interaction. How would you go about imitating the river?

20 "Everything has been figured out, except how to live," sneered existentialist philosopher Jean-Paul Sartre. That's not true, of course, which he might have discovered had he not closed his dogmatically cynical mind to the countless humans (many unknown to history) whose lives have been great works of art.

You're invited to track down five human beings, living or dead, famous or anonymous, rich or poor, who figured out how to live extremely well.

21 Provide evidence proving or disproving the following four hypotheses: 1. If you're not part of the grueling solution, you're probably part of the insidiously comfortable problem. 2. If you're not conspiring to commit smart fun, you're almost certainly colluding with the disingenuous repression. 3. If you're not trying to rally support for a tough investigation, you'll end up assisting the bland cover-up. 4. If you're not mad about how unconstructively you've used your anger in the past, then you won't be motivated to wield it more creatively any time soon.

22 POP QUIZ! By now, you should be sufficiently knowledgeable about pronoia to speak about it with some authority. Your assignment is to write a pronoiac rebuttal to the following news story, which appeared in a weekly tabloid:

"If you want to be happier, feel better, and do more in life, just turn your back on reality—and inflate your ego! A new study reveals that an unrealistically positive attitude and unfounded optimism, along with some denial of reality, help you accomplish great things in all areas of your life. In other words, you don't need a firm grip on reality to be successful and happy."

23 A thousand years from today, everyone you know will be long dead and forgotten. There'll be nothing left of the life you love, no evidence that you ever walked this planet. That, at least, is what the fundamentalist materialists would have you believe.

But suppose the truth is very different? What if in fact every little thing you do subtly alters the course of world history? What if your day-to-day decisions will actually help determine how the human species navigates its way through the epic turning point we're living through? And finally, what if you will be alive in a thousand years, reincarnated into a fresh body and in possession of the memories of the person you were back in this era?

These are my hypotheses. These are my prophecies. That's why I say: Live as if your soul is eternal.

Ask the healer
to sing the medicine songs
directly into
the top of your head.

HOMEOPATHIC MEDICINE SPELL #2

buoyantimprovisingfearlesswideawakefunwrestler

Life
is "a meaningless existential hell,"
say 26 percent of American male college students. Banging your head against a wall consumes 150
calories an hour. Sigmund Freud had a morbid fear of ferns. Most
Americans would vote against the Bill of Rights if it were presented to
them in a referendum. The odds that the ghost of Elvis Presley will crash-
land a UFO on the head of the Loch Ness monster are 14 million to one, according to a British betting agency. Heroin addiction causes constipation. More than half
of the pianos in the world are out of tune. An underground economy that runs on marijuana, porn, and the services of illegal immigrants constitutes 10 percent of the American
economy. Lightning strikes about 6,000 times per minute on this planet and kills more than a
thousand people a year. Sleep deprivation, which has reached epidemic proportions, is akin to
drug abuse in the way that it dramatically lowers competence levels and causes aberrant behavior. Queen Ranavalona of Madagascar decreed that if any of her subjects appeared in her dreams,
they would be killed. Thomas Edison was afraid of the dark. Big drug companies don't invest in the
development of a new drug if it's a cure for a relatively rare disease that wouldn't affect enough people to generate a substantial profit. An Alabama court upheld a ban on the sale of vibrators, ruling
that there's no constitutional right to an orgasm. Mosquitoes have teeth. The sun's mass decreases
by four million tons per second, and our home star will die a few billion years from now. Every time
an actor portraying a doctor performs a particular kind of surgery on a popular soap opera, real doctors are sought out to perform the same surgery at a dramatically higher rate. You're more likely to
be killed by a champagne cork than a poisonous spider. Mortuary workers in Zimbabwe rented
corpses to drivers who wanted to take advantage of the priority given to hearses in gas-station
lines. None of Socrates' writings survive. In Jon Rappoport's book *The Secret Behind Secret
Societies*, hypnotist Jack True says he rarely practices his craft anymore because most of
his clients are already in a light trance when they come to see him. What was an hour 10
years ago is now only 52 minutes. Every night, millions of Americans are tormented
by nightmares of the CIA overthrowing the democratically elected governments
of Iran in 1953, Guatemala in 1954, Brazil in 1963, and Chile in 1973. Israeli
scientists are working to perfect a procedure whereby they harvest eggs
from aborted human fetuses, fertilize them, and transplant them
into the wombs of infertile women, thereby making the donor
fetus an unborn mother. Clarence Thomas and Rob
Brezsny were both born on June 23.
Babies often stink.

surgingsoaringfoxygeniuswhirlingrisktaker

moistlushlaughingjubilationbouquetlover

freejoycrispfreshleapingflashdazzler

120

What's the difference
between dumb pain and smart pain?

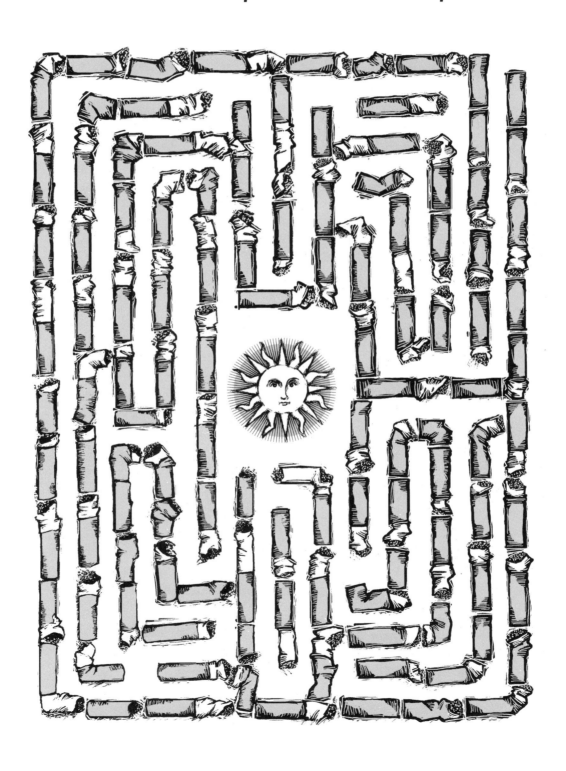

FEAR OF BEAUTY?

The Italian city of Florence harbors the richest trove of art treasures in the world. Its many museums are hot spots for outbreaks of a rare psychological disorder. Foreign tourists sometimes experience breakdowns while standing in the presence of the tremendous beauty, and are rushed to the psychiatric ward of Florence's Santa Maria Nuova Hospital.

"Many visitors panic before a Raphael painting," reports Reuters. "Others collapse at the feet of Michelangelo's statue of David."

Psychiatrists have referred to this pathology as the Stendhal syndrome, named after the French novelist who wrote about his emotional breakdown during a visit to the city's art collection in 1817.

As you embark on your explorations of pronoia, you should protect yourself against this risk. Proceed cautiously as you expose yourself to the splendor that has been invisible or unavailable to you all these years.

SACRED ADVERTISEMENT

"Fear of Beauty" is brought to you by wealthy silk merchant Francesco del Giocondo, who in 1503 commissioned Leonardo da Vinci to paint a portrait of his wife Lisa. When Leonardo finished the work, now known as the Mona Lisa, *del Giocondo was so dissatisfied with it that he refused to pay for it.*

Shadow School

You're a gorgeous mystery with a wild heart and a lofty purpose. But like all of us, you also have a dark side—a part of your psyche that snarls and bites, that's unconscious and irrational, that is motivated by ill will or twisted passions or instinctual fears. It's your own personal portion of the world's sickness: a mess of repressed longings, enervating wounds, ignorant delusions, and unripe powers. You'd prefer to ignore it because it's unflattering or uncomfortable or very different from what you imagine yourself to be.

If you acknowledge its existence at all (many of us don't), you might call it the devil, your evil twin, your inner monster, or your personal demon. Psychologist Carl Jung referred to it as the shadow. He regarded it as the lead that the authentic alchemists of the Middle Ages sought to transmute into gold.

"The unconscious sends all sorts of vapors, odd beings, terrors, and deluding images up into the mind; for the human kingdom, beneath the floor of the comparatively neat little dwelling that we call our consciousness, goes down into unsuspected Aladdin caves. There not only jewels but also dangerous jinn abide: the inconvenient or resisted psychological powers that we have not thought or dared to integrate into our lives." —Joseph Campbell, *The Hero with a Thousand Faces*

"I am superior to you only in one point," Narcissus tells Goldmund in Hermann Hesse's novel *Narcissus and Goldmund*. "I'm awake, whereas you are only half awake, or completely asleep sometimes. I call a man awake who knows in his conscious reason his innermost unreasonable force, drives, and weaknesses, and knows how to deal with them."

Astrologer Steven Forrest has a different name for the shadow: stuff. "Work on your stuff," he says, "or your stuff will work on you." He means that it will sabotage you if you're not aggressive about identifying, negotiating with, and transforming it.

The shadow is not inherently evil. If it is ignored or denied, it may become monstrous to compensate. Only then is it likely to "demonically possess" its owner, leading to compulsive, exaggerated, "evil" behavior.

"The shadow, which is in conflict with the acknowledged values, cannot be accepted as a negative part of one's own psyche and is therefore projected—that is, it is transferred to the outside world and experienced as an outside object. It is combated, punished, and exterminated as 'the alien out there' instead of being dealt with as one's own inner problem." —Erich Neumann, *Depth Psychology and a New Ethic*

"Until you make the unconscious conscious, it will direct your life and you will call it fate." —Carl Jung

The qualities in ourselves that we deny or dislike are often the very qualities that we most bitterly complain about in other people. So for instance, an old friend of mine named Mark had a special disgust for friends who were unavailable to him when he really needed them. But I was witness to him engaging in the same behavior three different times, disappearing from the lives of his friends just when they needed him most.

"Whatever is rejected from the self, appears in the world as an event," said Jung. If you disown a part of your personality, it'll materialize as an unexpected detour.

Everyone who believes in the devil is the devil.

A bright red cardinal had a confrontation with my picture window. For almost 45 minutes, the bird hammered its beak against the glass. With the help of my good friend and research assistant Google, I determined that the bird had probably mistaken its own reflection for a rival that it was trying to attack.

The event suggests three teachings: 1. If you feel the urge to fight others, you're probably mad about something in yourself. 2. You might want to monitor any tendency you have to get fixated on an image that is at best a distorted representation of a real thing and not the real thing itself. 3. It's best not to hurt yourself or drive yourself crazy in an effort to chase away an illusion.

"Nothing determines who we will become so much as those things we choose to ignore." —Sandor McNab

"As is demonstrated by a wealth of historical examples, every form of fanaticism, every dogma and every type of compulsive one-sidedness is finally overthrown by precisely those elements which it has itself repressed, suppressed, or ignored." —Erich Neumann, *Depth Psychology and a New Ethic*

Hypothesis: Those among us who have most thoroughly denied and repressed their own shadows are in the greatest danger of provoking mayhem and doing evil deeds in the real world.

In the Middle Ages, the Catholic Church branded cats as "ambassadors of the devil" and called for their mass extermination. The virtual disappearance of felines from Europe was an important factor in propagating the Black Death, which killed 25 million people between 1347 and 1352. The disease was spread by fleas that lived on rats, whose populations had soared in the absence of their natural predators.

America's former Poet Laureate Robert Pinsky addressed an assembly at my daughter's high school. He read from his translation of Dante's *Inferno* and took questions from students. After hearing Dante's description of the nether regions, one boy asked Pinsky what his personal version of hell was. The poet said that each of us creates our own hell. The fearful and negative interpretations of reality with which we infect our imaginations constitute curses that we cast on ourselves. They terrify and enslave us so thoroughly that most of the difficult outer circumstances we encounter are mild in comparison.

"If only it were all so simple! If only there were evil people somewhere insidiously committing evil deeds, and it were necessary only to separate them from the rest of us and destroy them. But the line dividing good and evil cuts through the heart of every human being. And who is willing to destroy a piece of his own heart?" —Aleksandr Solzhenitsyn, *The Gulag Archipelago*

In her book *Zen Miracles,* Brenda Shoshanna defines the shadow as the unacceptable aspects of ourselves that we dump into our unconscious minds. As we avoid looking at that hidden stuff, it festers. Meanwhile, we project it onto people we know, imagining that they possess the qualities we're repressing.

The antidote to the predicament, says Shoshanna, is to "eat our shadow"—haul it up from out of the pit and develop a conscious connection with it. Doing so not only prevents our unacknowledged darkness from haunting our thoughts and distorting our relationships; it also liberates tremendous psychic energy.

In her role as DJ Debi Newberry in the film *Grosse Pointe Blank,* Minnie Driver defines the term *shakabuku* as a swift spiritual kick to the head that alters your reality forever. That's the kind of jolt you're more likely to get if you've been avoiding the shadow's entreaties. But if you send it flowers on special occasions, or periodically give it license to blubber its horrible secrets while sobbing on your lap, it might be more inclined to deliver a *whoopibuku,* which is a soft spiritual stomp on the toes that inspires you to make a course correction.

Working with your dreams can help you stop colluding with the global genocide of the imagination.

"There is no generally effective technique for assimilating the shadow. It is more like diplomacy and is always an individual matter. First one has to accept and take seriously the existence of the shadow. Second, one has to become aware of its qualities and intentions. This happens through conscientious attention to moods, fantasies, and impulses. Third, a long process of negotiation is unavoidable." —Daryl Sharp, *Jung Lexicon: A Primer of Terms and Concepts;* also available at tinyurl.com/znxn3 and tinyurl.com/cgppsh

"It is by going down into the abyss that you recover the treasures of life," wrote Joseph Campbell. "Where you stumble, there lies your treasure."

"Suffering can't be avoided," James Broughton told Jack Foley. "The way to happiness is to go into the darkness of yourself. That's the place the seed is nourished, takes its roots and grows up, and becomes ultimately the plant and the flower. You can only go upward by first going downward." —James Broughton, as told to interviewer Jack Foley, *All: A James Broughton Reader*

Modern culture does not have a high regard for the alchemists of the Middle Ages. Most people think of them as lunatics who worked in primitive laboratories at the impossible task of turning lead into gold. What idiots, right? Science has proved beyond all doubt that you cannot transform one metal into another.

But here's the real story. While there were some clueless medieval alchemists who wasted their lives trying to convert actual lead into actual gold, the authentic alchemists were up to something else. They labored to transmute the metaphorical lead of their own psyches into metaphorical gold. Their flaws, wounds, compulsions, and ignorance were raw materials they used to create light and life and wisdom and love.

Compared to the spectacular hope of creating fantastic riches out of worthless metals, it was a lowly goal. From the perspective of most of the powerful and outwardly successful people in the world, then as now, striving to apotheosize the ugliness within us is about as unglamorous as you can get. The Beauty and Truth Lab does not share that view, however.

P.S. There are many authentic alchemists alive and hard at work in the world at this very moment.

The alchemists said the magic formula for enlightenment was *Visita Inferiora Terrae Rectificando Invenies Occultum Lapidem,* or "Seek out the lower reaches of the earth, perfect them, and you will find the hidden stone"—the treasured philosopher's stone. Jungian psychologists might describe the process this way: Engage in a relationship with the blind and sickly parts of yourself, perfect them, and you will awaken your hidden divinity.

Is it possible that in trying to repress some of the things you don't like about yourself, you have also disowned potentially strong and beautiful apects?

"The great epochs in our lives are at the points when we gain the courage to rebaptize our badness as the best in us." —Friedrich Nietzsche

The shadow is not only the place where we keep the nasty and monstrous underside of ourselves. It also harbors "vitalizing instincts, sleeping abilities, and positive moral qualities." says Daryl Sharp in his *Jung Lexicon.* If developed, these unripe aspects might become talents and treasures. Unfortunately, because they are intermingled with the parts of us we don't like to look at, they often remain untapped. In shunning our shadows, we shut ourselves off from some of our potential brilliance.

Imagine a person who conceives herself as mild, polite, and dignified, but who is in fact repressing a mother lode of anger. She clamps down hard on herself, never expressing her barely conscious grudges and irritations, since to do so would be at odds with her self-image. Meanwhile, in squelching the dangerous potency inherent in her rage, she inadvertently disallows

other disorderly powers, like longing and exuberance and spontaneity, that if expressed would also make her spin out of control. They aren't negative like rage, but they are just as unpredictable.

The result is that all of her intensity is buried. If she could strike up a negotiation with her shadow, if she could admit to her anger and allow it an outlet, she might also access the valuables that have also been locked away.

Jung again: "The shadow is merely somewhat inferior, primitive, unadapted, and awkward; not wholly bad. It even contains childish or primitive qualities which would in a way vitalize and embellish human existence, but convention forbids!"

In the best-known version of the Greek myth, Persephone is dragged down into the underworld by Hades, whose title is "Pluto." But in earlier, pre-patriarchal tales, she descends there under her own power, actively seeking to graduate from her virginal naiveté by exploring the intriguing land of shadows.

"Pluto" is derived from the Greek word *plutus,* meaning "wealth." Psychologist James Hillman says this refers to the psyche-building riches available in Pluto's domain. Hades, he says, is "the giver of nourishment to the soul."

The goddess Hecate also lives in the underworld. According to poet Robert Graves, she is the mistress of sorcery, "the goddess of ghosts and night-terrors, of phantoms and fearful monsters." On the other hand, he notes, Hecate "presides at seed time and childbirth; she grants prosperity, victory, plentiful harvests to the farmer and rich catches to the fisherman."

How can a single deity embody such seemingly contradictory archetypes? Graves: She symbolizes "the unconscious in which beasts and monsters swarm. This is not the living hell of the psychotic, but a reservoir of energy to be brought under control, just as Chaos was brought to cosmic order under the influence of the spirit."

Dionysian Manifesto

Neuroscientists at Britain's Bristol University have concluded that playing in the dirt can make you feel really good. That's because most soil is crawling with species of bacteria that interact favorably with the human body, strengthening the immune system and stimulating the brain in the same way antidepressants do.

Let's hypothesize that this is an apt metaphor for playing in the dirt of the shadow.

Jung: "Whoever loves the earth and its glory, and forgets the 'dark realm,' or confuses the two (which is mostly what happens), has spirit for his enemy; and whoever flees from the earth and falls into the 'eternal arms' has life for an enemy."

Where exactly is Hell in relation to Heaven, anyway? Is it, like, the equivalent of a billion light-years away? Or are they located within shouting distance of each other? Lots of ancient religious texts suggest the latter. *Yalkut Koheleth,* a Jewish commentary on the Biblical book *Ecclesiastes,* claimed the two domains were just "a hand-breadth apart." In Greek myth, the blessed Elysian Fields were situated right next door to Hades. "The doors to heaven and hell are adjacent and identical," wrote Nikos Kazantzakis, "both green, both beautiful."

Maurice Krafft made a career of filming places where hot lava is flowing. *National Geographic* described him hiking across the crater floor of Ol Doinyo Lengai, an active volcano that's sacred to the Maasai people in Tanzania. The ground was not erupting in torrents of fire and burning liquid rock, but was constantly bubbling and exuding. Through long years of experience, Krafft knew exactly where to walk so that his shoes didn't catch on fire.

Some shadow masters have learned to perform similar feats as they weave their way through the shadow's simmering landscape.

Ambergris is a foul-smelling excrement that sperm whales vomit. After years of exposure to the sun while floating on the ocean, it transforms into an aromatic, waxy substance that's used as a major ingredient in perfume.

Some modern alchemists say they've performed comparable transmutations of the miasmic ooze that they've gathered in the shadow's underground lagoons.

During 2003's monsoon season in Sri Lanka, floods caused landslides in and around Ratnapura, the "City of Gems." As devastating as this natural disaster was, it dredged up many raw gems from their hiding places deep in the earth. After the heavy rains stopped, sapphires and rubies were strewn across the landscape for any passer-by to pick up.

The Bible quotes the radical first-century religious activist Jesus Christ as follows: "Love your enemies, do good to those who hate you, bless those who curse you, pray for those who mistreat you." Sounds like he had a good strategy for working with his shadow.

Here's a corollary to Christ's injunction to love thy neighbor as thyself: "I will love the dark, difficult side of my neighbor—not just the attractive, friendly side—and I will encourage it to express itself in constructive ways."

A friend of mine, Allen, was evaluating the spiritual progress of a mutual acquaintance, John. "Twenty years of Buddhist meditation and he's still an insensitive jerk," Allen concluded with a flourish.

I didn't respond except to say, "Hmmm." It's my policy to refrain from participating in the popular sport of bad-mouthing, which for so many of its practitioners is a way of projecting the unacknowledged content of their own shadows.

But I did actually agree with Allen's assessment. Like many seekers I've known, John hasn't translated his high-minded religious principles and rigorous devotional practices into the way he treats people in his daily life. That's mostly because he has neglected the less glamorous work of wrestling with his shadow.

It's a great privilege to live in a free country. You're fortunate if you have the opportunity to pursue your dreams without having to ward off government interference or corporate brainwashing or religious fanaticism.

But that's only partly useful if you have not yet won the most important struggle for liberation, which is the freedom from your own unconscious obsessions and conditioned responses. Becoming an independent agent who's not an unwitting slave to his or her shadow is one of the most heroic feats a human being can accomplish.

In the New Earth, it won't be your material wealth that will win you the most bragging points. Nor will it be the important people you know or the deals you've swung or the knowledge you've amassed or your mate's attractiveness.

What will bring you most prestige and praise in the civilization to come will be your success in transmuting lead into gold—how thoroughly you have integrated your shadow and tapped into its resources.

"The best political, social, and spiritual work we can do is to withdraw the projection of our shadow onto others." —Carl Jung

Ancient legend says that a giant cobra—normally a fearsome predator—shielded Buddha with its expansive hood as he meditated in the wilderness during a terrible week-long storm.

In his song "Get Behind the Mule," Tom Waits tells us to "Never let the weeds get higher than the garden." That's good advice. But maybe you shouldn't go overboard and become a fanatic who acts as if weeds are evil demons from the ninth level of hell.

It turns out that some weeds are good for flowers and vegetables, protecting them from predatory insects. So say horticulturalists Stan Finch and Rosemary Collier, writing in *Biologist* magazine. When the bugs come looking for their special treats—the plants we love—they often get waylaid by the weeds, landing on them first and getting fooled into thinking there's nothing more valuable nearby.

So for example, when cabbages are planted in the midst of clover, flies lay eggs on only seven percent of them, compared to a 36 percent infestation rate on cabbages that are grown in bare soil with no clover nearby.

This could be a useful metaphor in working with your own versions of impurities and interlopers. Make sure there are always a few chickweed or henbit weeds surrounding your ripening tomatoes.

Divine subversion. Taboo justice. Unauthorized healing. Reverent insurgency. Guerrilla splendor. Ethical mischief. Sacred transgression. Freaky purity. Rebellious kindness. Friendly shocks. Sublime convulsion. Outlaw sacraments. Insurrectionary beauty. Illegal truth.

FLIP-FLOP THE TRAUMATIC IMPRINT

Beauty and Truth Lab researcher Artemisia had just begun menstruating, and was suffering from debilitating cramps. Massive doses of ibuprofen were not relieving the distress, so she went to her regular acupuncturist, Dr. Lily Ming, to get relief.

Dr. Ming had Artemisia lie down on the table and proceeded to insert 10 needles in her belly and hand and ear. Then Dr. Ming introduced a treatment that Artemisia was unfamiliar with: She lightly pounded the nail of Artemisia's left big toe with a small silver hammer for a few minutes.

"Why are you doing that?" Artemisia asked.

"It is good for the uterus," the doctor replied.

Indeed, Artemisia's cramps diminished as the doctor thumped, and in the days to come they did not recur.

After the session, as Artemisia prepared to leave, the usually taciturn Ming started up a conversation. Artemisia was surprised, but listened attentively as Dr. Ming made a series of revelations. The most surprising was Dr. Ming's description of a traumatic event from her own childhood.

During the military occupation of her native Manchuria, a province of China, she was forced to witness Japanese soldiers torturing people she loved. Their primary atrocity was using hammers to drive bamboo shoots through their victims' big toes.

The moral of the story: Dr. Ming has accomplished the heroic feat of reversing the meaning of her most traumatic imprint. She has turned a symbol of pain into a symbol of healing.

**Fairy tales tell of a magical cauldron
that cracks apart when three lies are told
by the people standing over it.
There is one way
to restore the pot to wholeness:
Speak three great truths
in its vicinity.**

LOVE BOMB

I feel closer to you when I imagine that all of us are collaborating to fight monumental dangers. The telepathic links among us heat up when our emotions register the possibility that a global cataclysm could wipe us out.

That's why I think of the nuclear bomb as a gift. It's a terrible and sacred taboo that mobilizes our love for each other better than any other symbol. It's the superhuman profanity on which all life depends and against which all values must be tested. Shadowing every one of our personal actions, the bomb is the fascinating blasphemy that won't stop ranting unless we're all very, very good.

In the quiet abyss of our imaginations, we unconsciously worship it, believing in its extravagant potency as if it were a god. It is the most spiritual, most supernatural material object in the world, a fetish that has the power to literally change all life on earth instantly and forever. We agree to be possessed by it, to be haunted by its apparition above all other apparitions. No other spectacle inspires more perverse attraction.

And yet it's secret. How few of us have ever stood next to the magic body of a hydrogen bomb in a missile silo or laboratory—breathed in its smell, touched it, communed with its actual life. Its presence among us is rumor and mystery, like flying saucers and the afterlife. We hear stories.

At night our dreams turn the bomb into the philosopher's stone, the pearl of great price, the doppelganger of the messiah, the violent ecstasy of religious conversion. Our blood is alive to its alchemy, alert to its offer of the blinding flash of irreversible illumination. We recognize the bomb as our impossible teacher because it harbors a dangerous light that seems to mimic the sun.

It's ours. We made it. We imagined it into existence so we could remember that we are all one body. When I fantasize the bomb vaporizing me into its pure primeval heat and radiation, I remember that you and I are made of the same stuff. The bomb frees us to imagine that we all live and die together, that we are all born out of Adam, the indivisible hermaphrodite god of our species. And we can return now because we never left.

We need the bomb. We need the bomb because only the tease of the biggest, most original sin can heal us. The bomb is a blind, a fake, a trick memory we're sending ourselves from the future that shocks us better than all the abstract devils.

Let's call the bomb a love that's too big for us to understand yet. Let's say it's the raging creative life of a cleansing disease that wants to cure us so it doesn't have to kill us. Let's say it's the last judgment that promises not to come true if we can figure out what it means.

We have genetic potentials and divine powers so undreamed of that they will feel like magic when they finally bloom. But they may remain partially dormant in us until we're terrified not just of our individual deaths but also of the extinction of the human archetype.

Bless the fear. Praise the danger. O God of Good and Evil Light, let the ugly power fascinate us all now. Let it fix our dread so precisely that we become one ferocious, potently concentrated magician, a single guerrilla mediator casting a spell to bind the great Satan bomb. There will be no nuclear war.

SUBTERRANEAN PRONOIA THERAPY

Experiments and exercises in becoming a rebelliously humble, affably unpredictable, insanely poised Master of Supernal Mischief

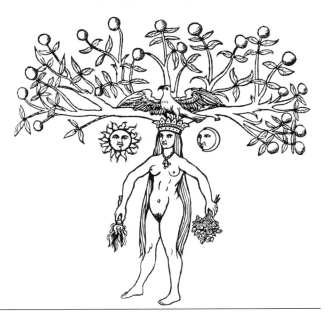

1 "I have not used my darkness well," mourns poet Stanley Moss in his book *Asleep in the Garden.* He's right about that. His forays into the realm of shadows rarely lead to redemption.

"One fine day / I shall fall down ... in a prison of anger," he moans in one poem. "In this country I planted not one seed," he announces elsewhere. Other samples: "vomit is the speech of the soul"; "We die misinformed"; "How goes a life? Something like the ocean / building dead coral."

But enough. Let's not indulge Moss in his profligacy. Instead, we'll appoint him to be your anti-role model: an example of what you don't want to become. May he inspire you to regard your sorrows and failures as sources of disguised treasure; as raw materials that will fuel future breakthroughs. Now write a poem or story in which you use your darkness well.

2 Acquire a hand puppet, preferably a funky old-fashioned one from a thrift store, but any one will do. Give the puppet a name and wear it on your hand wherever you go for several days. In a voice different from your normal one, make this ally speak the "shadow truths" of every situation you encounter: the dicey subtexts everyone is shy about acknowledging, the layers of truth that lie beneath the surface, the agreed-upon illusions that cloud everyone's perceptual abilities.

3 All of us are eminently fallible nobodies. We're crammed with delusions and base emotions. We give ourselves more slack than we give anyone else, and we're brilliant at justifying our irrational biases with seemingly logical explanations. Yet it's equally true that every one of us is a magnificently enigmatic creation unlike any other in the history of the world. We're stars with vast potential, gods and goddesses in the making.

Dramatize this paradox. Tomorrow, buy and wear ugly, threadbare clothes from the same thrift store where you got your hand puppet. Eat the cheapest junk food possible and do the most menial tasks you can find. The next day, attire yourself in your best clothes, wear a crown or diadem, and treat yourself to an expensive gourmet meal. Enjoy a massage, a pedicure, and other luxuries that require people to wait on you. On the third day, switch back and forth between the previous two days' modes every couple of hours. As you do, cultivate a passionate indifference to the question of whether you are ultimately an unimportant nobody or a captivating hero.

What's the most important thing you've never done?

4 Inventor Thomas Edison came up with a lot of ideas that went nowhere. While trying to develop the perfect battery, his unsuccessful experiments were comically legion. "I have not failed," he mused. "I've just found 10,000 ways that won't work." There are other ways in which he didn't match the profile we usually associate with genius. He rarely had a dramatic breakthrough out of the blue, for instance. Most often, he tinkered and fussed until he discovered some new useful thing. Of his 1,093 patents, some were inventions he purposefully set about to create, but most he simply stumbled upon.

Describe an area of your life where you've discovered 10,000 ways that don't work.

5 "Chantpleure" means "to sing and weep simultaneously." Invoke a memory or scene that moves you to do that.

6 For the 2001 Burning Man festival in the Nevada desert, artist David Best constructed the "Mausoleum: Temple of Tears." Made from wooden pieces of dinosaur puzzles, this pagoda-like sanctuary took him weeks to perfect. Pilgrims who visited it were encouraged to write prayers on the walls, mourning dead loved ones and exorcising adversaries who had passed over. At the end of the festival, Best hosted a mass ritual of grief and burned his masterpiece to ash.

Draw inspiration from Best's project. Create a talisman or ritual tool out of whimsical junk, use it a while to catalyze a catharsis, then destroy it or throw it away.

7 Declare amnesty for the part of you that you don't love very well. Forgive that poor sucker. Hold its hand and take it out to dinner and a movie. Tactfully offer it a chance to make amends for the dumb things

Subterranean Pronoia Therapy

it has done. And then do a dramatic reading of this proclamation by the playwright Theodore Rubin: "I must learn to love the fool in me—the one who feels too much, talks too much, takes too many chances, wins sometimes and loses often, lacks self-control, loves and hates, hurts and gets hurt, promises and breaks promises, laughs and cries. It alone protects me against that utterly self-controlled, masterful tyrant whom I also harbor and who would rob me of human aliveness, humility, and dignity but for my fool."

8 Pathologist Paul Wolf has suggested that some of history's great artists may have never created their masterpieces if the wonders of modern medicine had been available to them. For example, what if doctors had cured van Gogh's mental illness with a regimen of drugs like Prozac and Xanax? Maybe he would have been spared the torment that goaded him to the outbursts of genius that erupted on his canvases.

Are there ways in which the very things that have driven you crazy might play a role in your finest accomplishments?

9 An African proverb says that cattle are wealth, and there are no cattle without dung. Test that hypothesis. Has the source of your riches produced some waste matter that needs to be cleaned up?

You can have rich, dark compost in just a few days.

10 Some of my readers complain when I draw inspiration from a public figure they consider a bad person. Once I cited philosopher Bertrand Russell, and a woman from Austin went ballistic: "Russell was a terrible father! How dare you give him any credence?" Another time I invoked the wisdom of ex-U.S. president Teddy Roosevelt. "What possessed you to quote such a militaristic bully?" wrote an outraged emailer. Here's how I respond to these grumbles: If I refused to learn from people unless I agreed with everything they had ever said and done, I would never learn from anyone.

What about you? Have you set up your life so that everyone is either on or off your good list? If so, try something new: Cultivate a capacity to derive help and insight from people who aren't perfect.

11 No matter how holy and good, everyone in the world has a portion of the world's sickness inside them. It's known by many names: neurosis, shadow, demon, devil. Many people try to deny that it inhabits them. Others acknowledge its power so readily that they allow themselves to be overwhelmed and distorted by it. At the Beauty and Truth Lab, we take a position between those two positions. We accept the fact that the evil is part of us, but treat it with compassionate amusement and flexible vigilance. Our stance is partly that of loving parents and partly that of warriors.

Once you make a commitment to explore the mysteries of pronoia, your shadow will try to play tricks on you that it has never tried before. How will you respond? We recommend an aggressive, tender, improvisational approach. Be ready for anything. Avoid both blithe excesses of tolerance and grave fundamentalism.

Make a wish upon a scar.

12 "We are attracted to people who express the qualities we deny or repress in ourselves," says creativity expert Shakti Gawain. Using this idea as your hypothesis, take an inventory of the people you're most drawn to. Ask yourself whether they have talents and dreams that you wish could come alive in you. If you find this to be the case, consider the possibility that it's time to claim those talents or dreams as your own.

13 Philosopher William James proposed that if our culture ever hoped to shed the deeply ingrained habit of going to war, we'd have to create a moral equivalent. It's not enough to preach the value of peace, he said. We have to find other ways to channel our aggressive instincts in order to accomplish what war does, like stimulate political unity and build civic virtue.

Astrology provides a complementary perspective. Each of us has the warrior energy of the planet Mars in our psychological makeup. We can't simply repress it, but must find a positive way to express it. How might you go about this project?

14 In his bok *Shamanism: Archaic Techniques of Ecstasy,* religious scholar Mircea Eliade speaks of *Qaumaneq,* a special capacity that may be magically obtained by Inuit shamans. It's "a mysterious light the shaman feels inside his head, an inexplicable searchlight, a luminous fire. It enables him to see in the dark, both literally and metaphorically speaking, even with closed eyes, allowing him to see through darkness and perceive things that are hidden from others."

Go ariound for three days and three nights imagining you possess this *Quamaneq.* Report your results here.

Subterranean Pronoia Therapy

15 Dealing with your shadow may require superhuman levels of patient objectivity. The experience may be like having to speak in a neutral tone of voice as you wield the language of diplomacy during negotiations with the inscrutable leader of an enemy that is carrying out covert sabotage against your vulnerable sanctuaries.

On rare occasions, though, you may get a more direct opportunity to disarm your shadow. The following anecdote is an example. Study it as a metaphor for the approach you might try one day.

While still a young man, the medieval English King Richard was captured and imprisoned by his enemy Modard. For many days he languished alone in his cell, barely fed and having no blanket to warm him at night.

One morning he awoke to the sound of growling. His jailers had brought a full-grown male lion to the cell. They opened the door and ushered the beast in, whereupon they cut off the leather muzzle binding its jaws and scurried out, leaving Richard to fend for himself against the lion.

Freed from its constraint, the beast reared back and unleashed a roar. Without wasting a moment in useless fear, Richard leaped forward and jammed his arm down the throat of the lion. Thrusting all the way into its chest, he ripped out its heart, killing it instantly.

"You can't know fire unless you play with it," says Mark Finney, a math whiz who develops computer models for fighting forest fires.

16 In a radio interview, a former remote-viewer for the U.S. military was asked how his life had changed as his psychic skills had grown. "There were secrets my conscious and subconscious minds had been waiting for years to tell each other," he said, "and as my telepathic power improved, they no longer wanted to wait."

Try to accomplish this yourself. Imagine that the barriers between your everyday awareness and your deep self are crumbling. Act as if you are developing an ever-increasing ability to read your own mind.

Subterranean Pronoia Therapy

17 The greatest gift you can give might be the gift that you yourself were never given. Give that gift.

The most valuable service you have to offer your fellow humans may be the service you have always wished were performed for you. Offer that service.

An experience that wounded you could move you to help people who've been similarly wounded. Heal yourself by healing others.

Explain the difference between stingy dangerous images and generous dangerous images.

18 Describe your signature pain. What is the nature of the torment that chronically upsets you most?

This is the first step in graduating from the No Pain, No Gain School of Tortured Progress. You can't be healed unless you name the tweaked karma that needs to be healed.

Step #2: Figure out what it is about your problem that's so appealing. Consider the possibility that you have it at least in part because it perversely entertains you or keeps you from being bored.

Meditate on the theory that maybe you unconsciously don't want to give up your dilemma because it prevents you from reaching lofty goals you're too afraid or timid or lazy to strive for.

Contemplate the notion that you're secretly proud of your distress—that it's so interwoven with your identity that you wouldn't feel like yourself if you had to live without it. Do you ever find yourself bragging to others about the difficulties you have to endure? Are they essential to the construction of your self-image?

Consider the possibility that you use your nagging agony as an attention-getting device, or as a way to gather love. Isn't it true that some people are more likely to shower you with sympathy when you're miserable than when you're blandly well-adjusted?

Muse on the seductiveness of your hurt, and on all the unacknowledged reasons that maybe you are attracted to it and hesitate to give it up.

Step #3: Simply feel your suffering. Don't judge it or repress it. Don't come up with reasons about how it's beneath you to feel it or how you should be over it by now or how you can't believe you still let it have so much power over you. Let the pain ripple and flow. Allow it to break your heart apart. Give it room to wail its truths. Marvel at the fullness of the emotions it stirs.

Step #4: Leaving all your preconceptions behind, meditate on what lessons your pain is asking you to master. How is it inspiring you to grow in directions you've been unable to accomplish by any other means?

Step #5: Put yourself in a state of mind wherein you can feel gratitude for your pain. Be thankful for its teachings, for its chewy mystery, for its command that you build a soul resilient enough to do the work you came to Earth to carry out.

19 "Don't eat any food that's incapable of rotting," says Michael Pollan in his book *In Defense of Food: An Eater's Manifesto.* In other words, highly processed foods with a long shelf life don't contribute to your optimum vitality.

I'd like to expand this rule to make it an all-purpose guideline for life. Try out this hypothesis: If you're involved with any person or situation that never decays, or if there is some part of you that never decays, that's highly suspicious and may be a problem. Like growth, rot is a natural phenomenon. Indeed, every advancement requires or brings the disintegration of whatever it replaces. You can't grow if you don't rot. The "perfection" of stasis can be hazardous to your health.

What's ripe to rot in your world?

Not the nasty, sick, debilitating kind of chaos, but the dynamic, exhilarating, rejuvenating variety.

20 Every seven years I do a performance art piece called *A Pilgrimage to the Sacred Shopping Sites of North America.* During one, I visited a store called Kosher Intifada in New York. There I had a consummate experience of apocalyptic delight. Shopping and spirituality converged, and for a brief interregnum, all contradictions were annihilated, all contraries harmonized.

On the holy ground of Kosher Intifada, I listened to the house band Yo Tifereth sing Hebrew lyrics and play Arabic tunes on the oud, darbuka, violin, and kanun.

Later, a rabbi and imam took turns reciting prayers from their respective traditions. I bought a yarmulke decorated with Palestinian political symbols, a T-shirt that read "I Got Stoned on the West Bank," and the DVD of a musical comedy film *West Bank Story,* which portrays the love affair between an Israeli soldier and a Palestinian cashier, whose parents operate competing falafel restaurants on the West Bank.

I'd love for you to have a comparable experience: an immersion in an eerie sanctuary where you're simultaneously entertained and confounded. It would provide a counterpoint for all the more excruciating and demanding manifestations of the shadow you have to endure. Find or create such a sweetly discomfiting thing.

SACRED ADVERTISEMENT

*"Subterranean Pronoia Therapy" is brought to you
by the decisions you didn't make, the words you
never spoke, the actions you've avoided,
and the codes you haven't broken.*

21 In his book *The Thought of the Heart and the Soul of the World,* psychologist James Hillman writes: "The question of evil refers primarily to the anaesthetized heart, the heart that has no reaction to what it faces, thereby turning the variegated sensuous face of the world into monotony, sameness, oneness."

What would you have to do in order to triumph over this kind of evil in yourself?

22 "The problem, if you love it, is as beautiful as the sunset," wrote J. Krishnamurti. "The obstacle is the path," says the Zen proverb. What frustrating puzzle do you love the best?

*Your "nightmare" might give
you special access
to river lightning
and song winds.*

PRONOIA NEWS NETWORK

Human Ingenuity Update

U.S. Patent number 5,996,568 is an apparatus for safely shooting hot dogs into a crowd. Patent 4,834,212 is a device into which someone can scream and howl without bothering anyone nearby, allowing her to vent pent-up emotions. Patent 2,272,154 is a ladder that spiders can use to climb out of a bath. Patent 4,247,283 is a gadget that allows a trumpet to be used as a flamethrower while being played.

PNN is brought to you by Agatha Christie's feeling that she came up with the best ideas for her books while she was washing dishes, and by Goethe's belief that in order to write he needed an apple rotting in his desk drawer.

Singing Duels Diffuse Anger

"In Greenland, disputes are solved through singing duels. The quibbling parties face off and proceed to croon tunes heaped high with insults. While spectators pass the final judgment on the event, the singing generally diffuses the anger, and the dueling parties leave as friends." —*Mental Floss*, July–August 2004

Culture Wars a Fabrication?

The high degree of religious and multicultural tolerance in the United States is unprecedented in world history. So said sociologist Alan Wolfe in his book *One Nation, After All*, based on two years of interviews with 200 subjects.

"Wolfe argues that middle-class Americans don't deserve their reputation as angry, sanctimonious, and narrow-minded," reported Alicia Potter in the *Boston Phoenix*. "On the contrary, they're optimistic, thoughtful, and slow to judge."

Wolfe's subjects had one blind spot: homosexuality. But other than their lack of tolerance for gays, they expressed remarkable acceptance of immigrants, non-whites, and people of other socioeconomic classes.

Wolfe was frustrated by his findings. Because he makes part of his living writing for opinionated magazines, he yearned for more controversial data.

"The reasonableness, the sensitivity, the thoughtfulness just drove me batty," he told Potter. "I just wanted to scream at people, 'Isn't there something that really just makes you angry and upset?'" (Source: Alicia Potter, *Boston Phoenix*, March 30, 1998)

Reborn Steel   The North American steel industry annually recycles millions of tons of steel scrap from recycled cans, automobiles, appliances, construction materials, and other steel products. The scrap is remelted to produce new steel. Every ton of steel recycled saves 2,500 pounds of iron ore, 1,400 pounds of coal, and 120 pounds of limestone. The industry's overall recycling rate is 68 percent.

Medicine from Poison   Salmonella bacteria, the cause of food poisoning, may become a weapon against cancer. In tests on mice, it has carried out search-and-destroy missions against tumors.

The saliva of vampire bats appears to be effective in dissolving the blood clots that cause strokes.

Ongoing research into the medical applications of·snake venom suggests it may ultimately be used to fight cancer, heart attacks, and spongiform encephalopathies like BSE, or "mad cow disease."

Power through Service   "It's antithetical to the definition of power in this culture that a person might derive power by service rather than control, but that's the essence of midwifery." —Elizabeth Davis, *Heart & Hands: A Midwife's Guide to Pregnancy and Birth*

The Pink Balloon   Beauty and Truth Lab researcher Elizabeth Whitsage tells a story of when she was working at Disneyland selling mouse-eared balloons. Every so often a mother, father, and young son would come up to her, the parents asking in enthusiastic voices, "What color do you want?" and the son answering, "Pink!" One parent, usually the father, would recoil in horror and say something like, "No, son, don't you want red or blue?" But before the child could reply, Elizabeth would whip a pink balloon out of the bunch and wrap its string around his wrist. Then she'd smile and say to the dad, "That'll be one dollar, please."

BLOWOUT BARGAINS

A Less Boring Evil, Part 1

"Rudolf Steiner believed that evil was comprised of two forces that were opposed to each other in many ways, though with a tendency to form an alliance. One force, associated with Lucifer, represents grandiosity, arrogance, and self-indulgence. The other, associated with Ahriman, is manipulative, acquisitive, and ultimately sterile. We owe art to Lucifer and technology to Ahriman. They have both played a necessary and constructive role at different stages of the evolution of consciousness, enabling human beings to find a path of development towards love, wisdom, and freedom. Thus, for Steiner,

'the task of evil is to promote the ascent of man.' Because there are two forces of evil, not just one, good is not seen as being opposed to evil. The forces of good, associated with Christ, balance, redeem, and heal the two evil forces." —Fraser N. Watts, "The Spiritual Psychology of Rudolf Steiner," an essay in *Beyond Therapy: The Impact of Eastern Religions on Psychological Theory and Practice,* G. Claxton, editor

A Less Boring Evil, Part 2

"Rudolf Steiner saw Christ as the human mediation between the demonic Ahriman and the satanic Lucifer. Ahriman is the unit crushed into the uniform, the

destruction of individuality in sameness. He is the spirit behind Stalin, or Orwell's nightmares of Big Brother. Lucifer is the opposite, the individual raised to a cosmic egotism where there can be no other one, not even God. The Ahrimanic evil is the state that crushes all diversity. The Luciferic evil is the overweening pride of the scientist who believes he can control evolution through the genetic engineering of life in his laboratory. The Christ is neither the unit and the uniform, nor the alone, but expresses the crossing of the unique and the universal." —William Irwin Thompson, *Imaginary Landscape: Making Worlds of Myth and Science*

Gates Goes Both Ways Though many people consider him an asshole who has monopolized the computer industry with inferior technology, Bill Gates is the most generous philanthropist in history. He has donated more than $25 billion to promote health and education all over the globe. Some of the beneficiaries of his largesse have been the United Negro College Fund, International AIDS Vaccine Initiative, Johns Hopkins University, Save the Children Federation, and the United Nations Foundation.

Whiteread Goes Both Ways In 1993, sculptor Rachel Whiteread was named best artist of the year during a show at London's Tate Gallery. The K Foundation chose the same occasion, however, to bestow on her the sarcastic honor of being Britain's worst artist. She won more money for the second award.

Fitzgerald Went Both Ways "The test of a first-rate intelligence," said F. Scott Fitzgerald, "is the ability to hold two opposed ideas in the mind at the same time, and still retain the ability to function."

Bohr Went Both Ways "The opposite of a correct statement is a false statement," said the physicist Niels Bohr. "But the opposite of a profound truth may well be another profound truth."

The Dalai Lama Goes Both Ways "I call the high and light aspects of my being *spirit* and the dark and heavy aspects *soul*.

"Soul is at home in the deep, shaded valleys. Heavy torpid flowers saturated with black grow there. The rivers flow like warm syrup.

"Spirit is a land of high, white peaks and glittering jewel-like lakes and flowers. Life is sparse and sounds travel great distances." —The Dalai Lama, as quoted by James Hillman in *A Blue Fire*

You Go Both Ways "Chiaroscurofy" is a word that means "to find a comfortable place where you are partially in darkness and partially illuminated, or half in shadow and half in sunlight." You may actually do this someday.

Stealth Technology

Fourteenth-century Qabalists calculated the number of angels as 301,655,722. But the radiant homeless guy who begs for money in front of the post office says the current total is 677,323,117,002. If he's right, it means that in the intervening centuries, the angel community has grown 225,000 percent. That's an astounding population explosion.

Unlike the rapid proliferation of humans, the swelling tribe of heavenly hosts is good news. It means there are now 112 divine messengers-cum-guardian spirits for every person on the planet.

Poetry Facts

"Poetry is a rich, full-bodied whistle, cracked ice crunching in pails, the night that numbs the leaf, the duel of two nightingales, the sweet pea that has run wild, Creation's tears in shoulder blades."
—Boris Pasternak

Rattlesnake Slack

Scientists now know that rattlesnakes would actually prefer to lie back and relax than to rattle and attack.

Jesus the Small Crab

"The sanctuary pools that glisten in morning's sunlight rustle with the movement of small beings. Branching out from ocean's shore, waves wash through, a shadow of rebirth. Jesus takes the form of a small crab. From still rocks he creeps silently into the cool pools of light, opening himself to be seen by the world, to be loved, to be accepted as all beings long to be." —Zoe Brezsny, *Secret Freedom*

PNN is brought to you by the adjective pronoying, which is used to describe a convert to pronoia who hectors and pontificates while promoting the doctrine of pronoia with annoying piety.

Conversion Experience

Though the Hindu caste system is technically forbidden in India, long-standing custom keeps it in effect. The lowest caste is composed of the untouchables, known as the Dalits ("the oppressed"). The abuse they endure is appalling. It ranges from violent attacks and hate speech to prohibitions against praying in temples and against wearing shoes where the dominant castes live.

In 2002, large numbers of Dalits carried out a bloodless revolution. Instead of continuing to fight the sickening system, they dropped out of it. During a mass ceremony in Delhi, over one million of them formally left the Hindu religion and converted to Buddhism.

Blink of Pronoia

Jean-Dominique Bauby was a 43-year-old editor when he suffered an unusual stroke. Though his brain remained undamaged, his entire body was paralyzed except for his left eye. Slowly he learned to communicate in code by blinking, and over the next two years he dictated a memoir. Feeling as if he were trapped in a diving bell, but with his imagination as free as a butterfly, he called his book *The Diving Bell and the Butterfly*. Critics have described it as "startling," "inspirational," and "a jewel."

Free of Mental Illness

You don't suffer from anthonephophobia, a fear of flowers falling from clouds.

Rock Sweetened by a Waterfall

Writing in *Under the Chinaberry Tree*, Louise Popoff extols the "miracle of boredom." "Some of the best imaginative work of my childhood," she says, "the games and fantasies that went the deepest into my soul, came from moments of complete boredom, when my mother wouldn't rescue me from having nothing to do and nowhere to go."

Animal Ecstasy

In his book *Animals and Psychedelics: The Natural World and the Instinct to Alter Consciousness*, ethnobotanist Giorgio Samorini proves that many animals deliberately alter their consciousness. His evidence includes robins that get drunk on holly berries and act "like winged clowns," as well as goats hooked on caffeine and reindeer that seek out hallucinogenic mushrooms.

Samorini concludes that the desire to get high is a natural drive. Intoxication has served as an evolutionary force for some species, breaking down outworn habits in such a way as to improve long-term survival.

Palindrome News

1. A Santa lived as a devil at NASA. 2. He maps spam, eh? 3. Rot can rob a born actor. 4. A slut nixes sex in Tulsa. 5. Revolt, lover! 6. Rise, sir lapdog! God, pal, rise, sir! 7. Bombard a drab mob! 8. Egad—no bondage! 9. Go hang a salami—I'm a lasagna hog. 10. Was it a rat I saw?

BREAKING THE PRONOIA TABOO

"The moment you come to trust chaos, you see God clearly. Chaos is divine order, versus human order. Change is divine order, versus human order. When the chaos becomes safety to you, then you know you're seeing God clearly." —Caroline Myss, *Spiritual Madness: The Necessity of Meeting God in Darkness*

"Everything we shut our eyes to, everything we run away from, everything we deny, denigrate, or despise, serves to defeat us in the end. What seems nasty, painful, evil, can become a source of beauty, joy, and strength, if faced with an open mind. Every moment is a golden one for him who has the vision to recognize it." —Henry Miller

"The essence of all beautiful art, all great art, is gratitude." —Friedrich Nietzsche

"Belief is the death of intelligence." —Robert Anton Wilson

"If you're really listening, if you're awake to the poignant beauty of the world, your heart breaks regularly. In fact, your heart is made to break; its purpose is to burst open again and again so that it can hold ever-more wonders." —Andrew Harvey, *The Return of the Mother*

"The first idea that the child must acquire, in order to be actively disciplined, is that of the difference between good and evil; and the task of the educator lies in seeing that the child does not confound good with immobility, and evil with activity." —Maria Montessori, *The Montessori Method*

"Love your enemies; bless those who curse you, do good to those who hate you, and pray for those who persecute you." —Jesus

"Pollution is nothing but resources we're not harvesting." —R. Buckminster Fuller, *Critical Path*

Pablo Picasso had a difficult birth. When he finally popped out after a long labor, he wasn't breathing. The midwife decided his face was so blue he'd be impossible to revive. She declared him dead and left. But Picasso's uncle, who was in attendance, got up close to the infant and puffed cigar smoke up his nose. The shock brought him back to life.

Until she broke her foot as a teen, Paula Cole wanted to be a cheerleader like all the most popular girls. But the injury required her to wear a wooden shoe for an entire year, dashing her dreams and sending her in search of other identities. "That's when I found the piano, when music saved me," she said. "That's when I first attempted to write my own songs." Years later Cole became a Grammy-winning singer-songwriter.

Moral Gambling

The father of our friend Elliot was a professional gambler who figured out an ingenious system, got rich, and retired. For the rest of his life, he spent his gambler's fortune hunting down Nazi war criminals and bringing them to trial.

Faux Pronoia Report

Newspapers and magazines do promote pronoia in an ass-backwards way: through advertising. Constituting up to 70 percent of the total information presented in any one issue, this advice about how to buy supposedly useful objects and experiences seems to suggest that life is good and fulfillment is possible. But while the ads' promised satisfactions may titillate the ego, they are often of marginal interest to the soul, especially in light of the fact that they usually render the soul's agendas irrelevant.

MIRABILIA REPORT

Mirabilia n. strange amazements, rare delights, sublime sublimations; from the Latin *mirabilia*, "marvels."

■ The National Center for Atmospheric Research reports that the average cloud is the same weight as 100 elephants.

■ In the Hindu epic the Mahabharata, the hero and heroine fall in love without ever gazing upon each other, simply by hearing tales about each other's good deeds.

■ Very few raindrops are actually raindrop-shaped. A far greater number take the form of doughnuts.

■ Twelve percent of the population believes that Joan of Arc was Noah's wife.

■ Because half of the world's vanilla crop is grown in Madagascar, the whole island smells like vanilla ice cream.

■ Your body contains so much iron that you could make a spike out of it, and that spike would be strong enough to hold you up.

■ There are about nine million people on earth who were born the same day as you.

■ In his book *The Physics of Immortality: Modern Cosmology, God and the Resurrection of the Dead,* physicist Frank J. Tipler offers what he says is scientific proof that every human being who has ever lived will be resurrected from the dead at the end of time.

■ In the Ukraine you can buy Fat in Chocolate, a food with a layer of dark chocolate covering a chunk of pork fat.

■ French author and statesman André Malraux observed that Jesus Christ was the only anarchist who ever really succeeded.

■ Robust singing skill is correlated with a strong immune system in songbirds. Male birds with the most extensive repertoire of tunes also have the largest spleens, a key measure of immune system health.

■ Bali has 80,000 temples.

■ Some piranhas are vegetarians.

Mushroom Music

The successful Czech composer Vaclav Halek has an unusual muse: the mushroom kingdom. No, he doesn't ingest the psychedelic varieties and write music while high. Rather, he wanders out into the forest, lies down next to fungal colonies, and tunes in to their vibrations. "I simply record music that the mushrooms sing to me," he told *The Sydney Morning Herald*. Trees and rocks also produce melodies, he reports, but the toadstools' compositions are the finest.

Abundance Studies

"Case Western University's School of Medicine in Cleveland provides grants to seek 'clinically documented evidence of the positive effects and transformative power of unconditional love.' The school's Institute for Research on Unlimited Love funds studies into the scientific nature of volunteerism, organ donations, rescue work, and other acts of selfless altruism, compassion, and service."
—goodnewsnetwork.org

New Bonding Ritual

On some college campuses, pimple- and blackhead-squeezing parties have become popular. "It's a great way to instantly drop social masks and get to know the real person," said Jamie Brooks of Boston College. "Our generation is tired of having to wade through glitzy packaging everywhere we go," adds Carla Lipske. "Popping zits is a bonding ritual that says, 'I accept you with all your imperfections.'"

Grieving Lessons

Buddhist sage Jack Kornfield tells of a woman devastated by the demise of a love affair. She turned to her Zen teacher, a Japanese monk, who soothed and consoled her as she grieved for weeks. The monk then returned to Japan, leaving the woman to fend for herself.

Months later he returned, and the woman picked him up at the airport. As he handed her a gift of prayer beads, she broke into sobs, confessing that her heart had still not mended from the loss of her paramour. Without hesitation, the teacher slapped her across the face.

"One year is too long!" he barked. "Get over it!"

Bullshit Versus Horseshit

"Bullshit is a rare and valuable commodity," wrote Art Kleps in *The Boo Hoo Bible*. "The great masters have all been superb bullshitters. Horseshit, on the other hand, refers to downright crap. The free, playful, entertaining flight of ideas is bullshit, and more often than not will be found afterwards to accord perfectly with universal truth. Horseshit is contrived, derivative, superstitious, ignorant."

"Bullshit is creative, inspired myth-making intended to provoke growth," added Alan Cabal in the *New York Press*, "while horseshit is bottom-feeder derivative manipulation aimed at the endless acquisition of slaves, servants, and followers."

Fortune Cookie   You're a flavorful God.

OPEN SECRET

We live in the Milky Way Galaxy, which is shaped like a pinwheel. In 2003, astronomers were shocked to discover that the pinwheel has a fifth arm, one more than they've always thought. It's not as if it has been hard to spot: It's 77,000 light-years long! "I was absolutely flabbergasted," astronomer Tom Dame told NewScientist.com. "It was clearly seen in previous surveys but was never pointed out or given a name."

DEATH-FREE TREE ART

Sculptor David Nash owns five chainsaws of different sizes, wrote art critic Kenneth Baker in the *San Francisco Chronicle,* and "wields all of them with improbable precision." His work doesn't require the destruction of living trees; recycled wood provides much of his raw material. Some of his sculptures consist of living trees whose growth he has directed. *Ash Dome* is a ring of 22 ash trees that he began shaping in 1977.

CRANE OPPORTUNISM

Between North and South Korea is a long, narrow strip of land called the DMZ. Designed to be a buffer zone where all human activity is prohibited, it has accidentally become a nature preserve beloved by white-naped cranes. The area is a paradise for the birds because it has an abundance of undisturbed marshland and is free of predators. Luckily, the cranes are so lightweight that they're in no danger of detonating the many land mines buried throughout the 370-square-mile area.

Thanks to our sponsor, the luminous tendril of celestial wish, *provided by poet e. e. cummings.*

Art Lessons

French Impressionist painter Henri Matisse wanted his art to be "free from unsettling or disturbing subjects . . . soothing, a cerebral sedative as relaxing as a comfortable armchair."

Spanish painter Pablo Picasso had a different opinion. "Art is offensive," he asserted. "At least, art should be allowed to be offensive. It ought to be forbidden to ignorant innocents, never allowed into contact with those not sufficiently prepared. Yes, art is dangerous."

As you practice the art of pronoia, you will probably get best results if you swing back and forth between Matisse's and Picasso's approaches.

Every once in a while, try out William Butler Yeats' idea, too: "Art that doesn't attempt the impossible is not performing its function."

BONUS ORACLE

Soaring and Scrounging

Our sources from high society say that when you eat caviar, you shouldn't use silver spoons: It taints the eggs with a metallic taste. Instead, always choose flatware made of gold or mother of pearl.

Our connections in low society suggest that when you dive into dumpsters foraging for discarded food, your best bet is the stuff in dented cans, since it's probably uncontaminated by any toxic garbage lying nearby.

These tips should be useful metaphors for you in the coming years, as you'll have chances to extract bounty not only while you're visiting soaring peaks but also when you're scrounging around dismal abysses.

Visualize

_____

[PUT YOUR DEITY'S NAME HERE]

at the
moment of orgasm

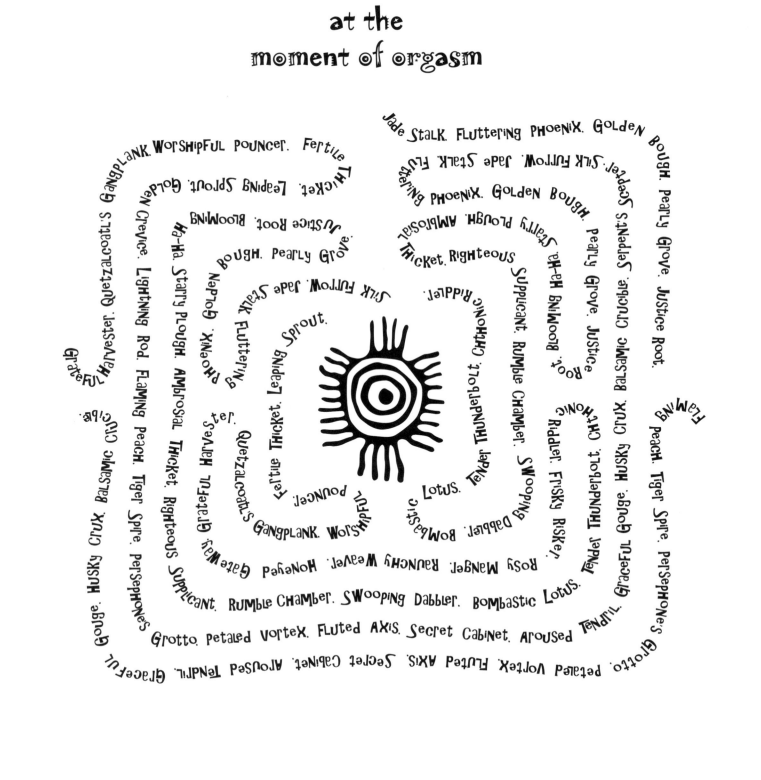

All I Ask of You

1

Be my slow-motion dance.

Be my birthday earthquake.

Be my spiral marble staircase
in the middle of a Vermont meadow.

Be my handstand on a barstool,
my whirlwind week in clown school,
my joke shared with a Siberian shaman
while shopping for T-shirts at Sears.

Be my last *because.*

2

Be my puzzle with one piece missing.

Be my ripe pomegranate
floating in a blue plastic swimming pool
on the first day of winter.

Be the imaginary conversations
I have with Thomas Jefferson
while watching the news on TV.

Be the waves crashing on my beach
in the south of France in the 22nd century
and the song
that my great-grandmother wrote for my great-granddaughter.

Be my golden hammer resting on a mossy rock
I've known for 10,000 years.

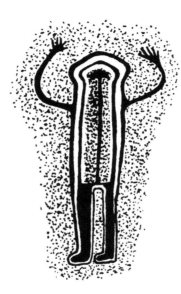

What if Your Desires Are Holy?

Some religious traditions teach the doctrine, "Kill off your longings." In their view, attachment to desire is at the root of human suffering. But the religion of materialism takes the opposite tack, asserting that the meaning of life is to be found in indulging desires. Its creed is, "Feed your cravings like a French foie gras farmer cramming eight pounds of maize down a goose's gullet every day."

At the Beauty and Truth Lab, we walk a middle path. We believe there are both degrading desires that enslave you and sacred desires that liberate you.

Psychologist Carl Jung believed that *all* desires have a sacred origin, no matter how odd they may seem. Frustration and ignorance may contort them into distorted caricatures, but it is always possible to locate the divine source from which they arose. In describing one of his addictive patients, Jung said: "His craving for alcohol was the equivalent on a low level of the spiritual thirst for wholeness, or as expressed in medieval language: the union with God."

Therapist James Hillman echoes the theme: "Psychology regards all symptoms to be expressing the right thing in the wrong way." A preoccupation with porn or romance novels, for instance, may come to dominate a passionate person whose quest for love has degenerated into an obsession with images of love. "Follow the lead of your symptoms," Hillman suggests, "for there's usually a myth in the mess, and a mess is an expression of soul."

In *Maldoror and Poems,* the French poet Lautréamont wrote about holy yearning disguised as mournful complaint. "Whenever you hear the dogs' howling in the fields," his mother told him as a child, "don't deride what they do: They thirst insatiably for the infinite, like you, me, and the rest of us humans. I even allow you to stand at the window and gaze upon this exalted spectacle."

"The primordial fire that sparked millions of galaxies is the same fire that sparks the human creative impulse." —Cindy Spring, "The Non-Profit Universe," *Earth-Light,* Summer 2002. "The human reproductive drive is a watered-down version of the godsex that spawned our solar system." —"Lieutenant" Anfortas, the homeless guy in the Safeway parking lot

"Feelings that originate in the human genitalia are among the most powerful forces on earth. They have a complex relationship with the feelings that stem from the human heart: at various times in competition or in harmony. Together these primal energies have forged and toppled empires; unleashed terrible and wonderful ideas; and generated the greatest stories ever told. Our goal is to harness our sexual urges in service to the heart's wisdom." —Sheila Samizdat, "Ritual Foreplay for a New History," *Underground Pronoia*

"Mad! One must become mad with love in order to realize God. When a person attains ecstatic love of God, all the pores of the skin, even the roots of the hair, become like so many sex organs, and in every pore the aspirant enjoys the happiness of communion with the Supreme Universal Self." —Ramakrishna

Like all of us, you have desires for things that you don't really need and aren't good for you. But you shouldn't disparage yourself for having them, nor should you conclude that every desire is tainted. Rather, think of your misguided longings as the bumbling, amateur expressions of a faculty that will one day be far more expert. They're how you practice as you work toward the goal of becoming a master of desire. It may take a while, but eventually you will get the hang of wanting things that are really good for you, and good for everyone else, too.

"The only way anyone is ever cured of desiring nonsensical things is by getting the nonsensical things and then experiencing the unpleasant but educational consequences." —Ann Davies, bota.org

"To become a master of desire, keep talking yourself out of being attached to trivial goals and keep talking yourself into being thrilled about the precious few goals that are really important. Here's another way to say it: Wean yourself from ego-driven desires and pour your libido into a longing for beauty, truth, goodness, justice, integrity, creativity, love, and an intimate relationship with the Wild Divine." —Raye Sangfreud, "Black Market Orchids," *Underground Pronoia*

"God has desires. Since I want to be close to God and to model myself after God, I therefore don't aspire to extinguish my desires, but rather to make my desires more God-like: i.e., imbued with an inexorable ambition to create the greatest and most interesting blessings for everyone and everything." —Collin Klamper

"'Heterosexual,' 'bisexual,' 'lesbian,' and 'gender queer' are not terms I use to describe myself. They're too limiting, like every other name and role I've had the pleasure of escaping. In a pinch, I might agree to call myself ocean-fucker or sky-sucker or earth-bonker. As much as I love men and women, they can't satisfy the full extent of my yearning. I need intimate relations with clouds and eagles and sea anemones and mountains and spirits of the dead and kitchen appliances and the creatures in my dreams. To be continued. To be enhanced and amplified and enlarged upon, world without end, amen. One day I really do hope to be a wise enough lover to be able to fuck the ocean. To give a forest fire a blow job. To make a pride of lions come just by looking at them." —Jumbler Javalina, "Bite into the Mysteries," *Underground Pronoia*

"When I hold you, I hold everything: crones praying in the foamy sand at low tide, a shocked waterfall gracing a new housing development, the drunk fetus in the womb of a saint, the foxglove by the fence sipping the fragrance of distant blue straggler stars, my dream of the white crow dreaming of me. In your eyes I see everything that lives." —mash-up of Pablo Neruda and Rob Brezsny

Imagine it's 30 years from now. You're looking back at the history of your relationship with desire. There was a certain watershed moment when you clearly saw that some of your desires were mediocre, inferior, and wasteful, while others were pure, righteous, and invigorating. Beginning then, you made it a life goal to purge the former and cultivate the latter. Thereafter, you occasionally wandered down dead ends trying to gratify yearnings that weren't worthy of you, but usually you wielded your passions with discrimination, dedicating them to serve the highest and most interesting good.

Dionysian Manifesto

The Mystery of Your Thirst

Imagine this scene. You're really thirsty—so dehydrated that you're feeling faint. Yet here's the weird thing: You're walking along the bank of a wide river that's so clear you could see the bottom if you looked. But you're not looking. In fact, you seem oblivious to the surging force of nature just a few yards away.

Is it invisible to you? Are you so preoccupied with your suffering that you're blind to the very source that would end your suffering?

Up ahead you see a man. As you approach, you realize he's holding a bottle of water. You run to him and beg him to let you drink. He readily agrees. Gratefully, you guzzle the precious liquid, then thank him profusely.

As you walk away, he calls after you, "By the way, there's a lot more water over there," and he points to the river.

Do you hear him? If you hear him, do you believe him? Or do you keep walking, hoping to find another person with another bottle somewhere up ahead?

Not all darkness is bad. Not all shadowy places are scary. Not all secrets are shameful. Not all pain is evil.

THE ORGASMIC ROOTS OF PRONOIA

Any young man who's serious about becoming a good lover must early in the game confront a demoralizing truth about the difference between the male and female orgasms. If there were no other evidence that the Goddess is a trickster, this fact alone would suffice for proof: Most human males are prone to ejaculate within two minutes of the time they insert their jade stalk into the silk furrow. To not perform this stupid abracadabra, in fact, typically requires diligent practice.

For those dudes who perfect the art of not splurging so fast, however, there is an even more Olympian challenge: gaining control of the splurge, so that it happens only when consciously willed. The men who reach this winner's circle are truly an elite group.

On the other hand, most human females cannot under even the most favorable ambiance ascend to the state of orgasmic grace in less than 15 minutes. Half an hour is not unusual, and I've known ripe and fully emancipated women who rarely need less than 45 minutes.

It's true that some men, especially those who have only recently started growing a beard, can reload in a short time. A 10-minute wait between erections should not, theoretically, be an insurmountable obstacle to picking up where you left off. From my private polls, however, I conclude that even though many 19-year-old studs can get it up again after a relatively brief waiting period, few are actually still in a mood sexy enough to press on with the same attentiveness, let alone artistry, that led up to the first engagement. And of those, only a tiny percentage have the expertise or the inclination, while marking time till resurrection, to attend to the female pleasure zones with the non-genital parts of their bodies.

Which leads to the next cruel joke: A majority of women can't even achieve the flutter-magic through the unsupplemented in-and-out anyway: In many positions, the sliding action of the diamond pumper barely misses the clitoris, heart-source of female pleasure. (Not that most men even realize this. At this late date a significant minority have at least discovered the existence of the clitoris, but few have figured out how to address it in its native language.)

This is not to say that most women would, if forced to make the choice, opt for pure clitoral stimulation over copulation. Lots of them do relish the evolutionarily necessary penis-vagina friction; they'd just like it a lot better if their total bliss were addressed, not just one facet.

On the whole, I'm inclined to believe that the pool of male fuckmasters—those who can consciously decree the moment of ejaculation and who understand the intricacies of the female orgasm—barely exceeds the number of those who garner the Nobel Prize each year.

In the early years of my apprenticeship, I used the crudest method to avoid early detonation: condoms, sometimes even two or three at once. This usually numbed me sufficiently to last indefinitely. For emergencies, I also carried with me a desensitizing chemical spray I'd bought via mail order from an ad in the back of *Penthouse* magazine.

Both of these options were anathema, though. Because the age of AIDS had not yet radically altered heterosexual courtship rituals, condoms were a novelty. Most of my lovers used IUDs or diaphragms or birth control pills, and were adamantly opposed to the sterile sensation of a rubber sheath caressing their intimate parts. Nor were they enamored of my "Sta-Hard" aerosol, which exuded a smell one of my lovers said made her think of "a football player in a barn."

Condoms and anesthetics, I decided, were not ultimately part of the game plan that would make me a fuckmaster. Painstakingly, I began to accumulate a more natural bag of tricks. The earliest technique, which I acquired by blind instinct, was a little less crude than condoms. I'd struggle to divert my attention away from the pleasure at hand by fantasizing about baseball games. I found I could deaden a measure of the supernal bliss driving me toward climax by seeing in my inner eye, for instance, the events leading up to Philadelphia Phillies' third baseman Mike Schmidt smacking a grand slam home run to beat the Pittsburgh Pirates in the 13th inning. In some lovemaking sessions, I narrated entire ball games in my mind.

A second aid, also discovered early in my quest, was to inflict pain elsewhere on my body. Slapping my thighs worked well in distracting myself from the overabundant joy buzzing in my genitals, as did pinching and twisting my belly or digging my fingernails into my face. A more professional approach came to me via the *Marriage and Sex Manual* I found in a used bookstore. A man who was on the verge of splurging was advised to squeeze the base of his jade stalk or apply firm pressure to the perineum. The first action would mechanically suppress the ejaculatory urge. The second would blockade the spasmodic flow of semen from scrotum to penis.

These last two strategies were repugnant. I didn't want to rely on last-ditch interventions that required emergency brute force. I wanted poised power. I longed to wield command over my inconvenient biological programming every step of the way.

Eventually I discovered there were ancient traditions that had exhaustively explored the art of sexuality, including the problem of ejaculatory control. In India and Nepal and Tibet, these teachings were grouped under a branch of yoga known as tantra. In China, certain schools of Taoism dealt extensively with the same subjects.

Unfortunately, many of these teachings were so bound up with the esoteric spirituality, bad translations, and hoary terminology of their respective traditions that they were only marginally useful to a horny dude who wasn't willing to immerse himself in a 10-year plan to master the discipline.

By the mid-1980s, a smattering of American authors began packaging the venerable secrets in modern

She said, "I told you a million times not to exaggerate."

vernacular. Even then, though, many of the techniques were elusive and subtle to the point of being useless.

Try imagining, for instance, a stream of golden light percolating from your perineum up your spine, then through your brain and back down the front of your body to the perineum again. While breathing rhythmically through your nose and from your lower abdomen only, counting to eight for each inhale and exhale, circulate the light continuously until it achieves a momentum of its own and drones on autonomously in the background of your awareness. In the meantime, gnash your teeth gently and touch a point one inch above your right nipple with your left index finger and middle finger, all the while opening your eyes as wide as they'll go and jamming your tongue against the roof of your mouth. "These actions will definitely cause the semen to be retained," the text asserts.

Oh yeah? Maybe when you're sitting alone and relaxed in your temperature-controlled room with a sleep mask over your eyes. But try the same meditation while you're sweat-to-sweat with a gorgeous aromatic creature who thrills every cell in your body. The difficulty of the task increases exponentially, at least during the first decade of trying to master it.

Which is not to say it's impossible. And besides, if you can be sufficiently candid with the gorgeous aromatic creature (and why would you be making love with a woman you can't be honest with?), you might enlist her aggressive cooperation in your attempts to distribute your kundalini to your whole body rather than have it congregate in one bloated, ready-to-pop area of congestion. You can ask her to not wiggle so seductively. You can beg her not to kiss you with so much exultant abandon. You can plead with her not to emanate so many tangy succulent smells and not utter so many of the bewitching groans that make you want to gush your entire soul into her.

But on the other hand, what lover in his righteous heart wants to ask that of the gorgeous aromatic creature with whom he's entwined?

I stumbled along with my conglomeration of baseball visualizations, self-mortifications, and tantric mumbo-jumbo. I was a good enough lover, usually a long-lasting lover, but not a fuckmaster. Wasn't there a philosopher's stone? Wasn't there a technique that could provide consistent and ultimate control? Or would I forever have to make do with my jury-rigged system?

At last, hallelujah, in a New Age bookstore in Santa Cruz I found the treasure: a dusty hand-bound book titled *Sexx Magixx.* The obviously pseudonymous author was Jack N. Off, and I couldn't have been more surprised by his precious secret. When you urinate, he said, interrupt the flow in midstream. The muscles by which you accomplish this unnatural act are the same muscles engaged in ejaculation. By gaining control over this mechanism through strenuous daily exercises, you'll grow strong enough to forcibly restrain the semen from gushing out—even, if necessary, after the ejaculatory spasm has begun. You can do this again and again in any single lovemaking session, thereby staying hard as long as you desire.

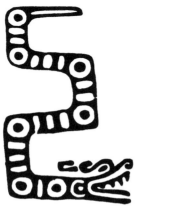 

I threw myself into this work, and within a few weeks I mostly conquered the previously involuntary reflex of ejaculation. It wasn't 100 percent foolproof—I still made use of my old standby methods—and it was never easy. I had to do the exercises every day to stay fit, and while making love I had to maintain a high level of concentration that sometimes detracted from the surrender I wanted to feel.

But I was pleased with my new technique; I felt as if a Golden Age had begun. Nineteen times out of 20 I came only when I willed it, only when I was sure my woman had had her fill. Now and then my ardent efforts at retention weren't totally successful, but the mini-eruptions relieved a small amount of the pressure to spill without bringing an end to the hard-on.

With the arrival of this blessing in my life, I was finally able to confront a mystery I had doggedly turned away from. All the tantric and Taoist texts agreed, though I skeptically resisted it, that a man's sexual experience was far better in every way if he did not ejaculate at all, even after his partner has been satisfied. This assertion was based in part on the fact (not a theory, they said) that a regular loss of semen is detrimental to male vitality and health. It

also assumed that sex yields up much more of its mind-expanding, life-transforming magic if the erotic energy is "steamed up" to the heart and brain rather than wastefully ejected. There, in the higher chakras, lust is liberated from its enslavement to the reproductive instinct. Transformed into a supercharged nourishment, it feeds one's aspirations to unite with the Divine Wow. As a method of expanding one's consciousness, it's both safer and more efficacious than psychedelic drugs.

I was willing to entertain the latter notion. Erotic play had always put me in a deliciously altered state, and I longed to harness its transcendent energy to accomplish something beyond merely feeling good. Unfortunately, I could not help but hedge my bets. I convinced myself I could somehow both steam the sex energy up up up and also indulge in a good old-fashioned ejaculation.

The real tantrics would have laughed at me.

I did not even go through the motions of trying to accept the other rationale for not coming, though—that losing your seed too often made you weak and stupid. I felt it had too much in common with the old superstition that women use sex to steal men's energy. It seemed patriarchal and misogynist. Steadfastly, like a scientist obsessed with proving a bogus hypothesis, I ignored and repressed all data that contradicted my fixation.

There was yet another good reason the tantric and Taoist texts gave for phasing out the old habit entirely. Several books hinted at the shocking secret, but Mantak Chia and Michael Winn spelled it out at length in their book *Taoist Secrets of Love: Cultivating Male Sexual Energy.* Ejaculation and orgasm are not the same thing, they asserted. In fact, the two functions can and should be separated. Why? Because the orgasm that's affixed to ejaculation is a mediocre form of pleasure. It's limited to a few intense seconds that exhaust the capacity for further delight.

There is a higher orgasm that is available only after the addiction to ejaculation has been renounced. It's at least as vivid as the first kind, usually more so, but lasts longer and can be repeated indefinitely—similar to a woman's. "How would you like to be in a continual state of climax for an hour or more?" the esoteric experts hinted. Moreover, this higher orgasm alone creates the conditions necessary to steam the semen up to the heart and brain.

For a while I stubbornly rebelled against this claim. I argued with it in my own mind, accusing it of being perverse and effete. It did not jibe with my experience. I found nothing pleasurable about waging my brave struggle against evolution's primordial pressure. Yes, it was for a good cause. I bought the importance of it. But I wanted my reward in the end—the reward that nature had worked millions of years to perfect.

My attitude began to change once I met Celia.

Celia was, has been, and still is a fountain of blessings. For starters, she is a provocative listener who regularly draws insights out of me I don't know that I know. Her

She said, "Let's charter a supersonic MiG-25 Foxbat plane to ferry us to the upper edge of the atmosphere, where we can see the curvature of the Earth."

insights into human nature are acute and compassionate, and I often ask her opinion about a person I'm considering as a new friend or associate. She's funny and boisterous. Her well-developed sense of humor doesn't shut down when the going gets tough.

She is knowledgeable about politics, but in more of a tender than doctrinaire way, and she has been a driving force in teaching me to tincture my vehement critiques of everything that's wrong in the world with good old love.

I admire her livelihood: She's a freelance translator who's fluent in five languages. She's also a skillful pianist and composer. Had she chosen that field as a career path, I'm convinced she would have been one of the rare musicians who make their living doing what they love.

One of the accomplishments I'm most impressed by is the way Celia has taken responsibility for and transformed her shadow. Psychologist Carl Jung said we all have one of those things: an unripe, wounded part of our psyche that is out of harmony with our conscious values. It's our private portion of what the world's major religions have demonized as "the devil." Few human beings are courageous or resourceful enough to wage sacred combat with this secret saboteur; most project its mischief out onto people or groups they dislike. But Celia is a rare exception. She relentlessly monitors her own shadow, trying to ensure that it doesn't distort her relationships. This heroic effort alone makes her more trustworthy than anyone I've ever known.

I feel real in Celia's presence. Not inflated, worshiped, or adored, and not belittled, demeaned, or

underestimated—just authentic. It's a relief to be seen as I am in all my complexity, with no distorting emphasis on either my immature or noble aspects. I feel a deep relaxation around her. I'm at home in the world.

When I first met Celia, her gifts scared me. She had so much to offer and such an exquisite talent for giving that I felt like a stingy, shrunken-hearted narcissist in her presence. I worked hard to be worthy of the bounty she bestows.

And oh by the way, she's physically beautiful, too: striking and robust, voluptuous and athletic, open and mysterious. If I gaze at her face for just 10 minutes, I can see her change from a kind and authoritative Egyptian queen to a fierce and joyous Irish amazon to an unpredictable and mystical Portuguese gypsy. She's cheerful and intense, unpredictable and trustworthy, bright and deep.

The first few times Celia and I made love, I tuned in to an unexpected phenomenon: I wasn't having to withhold ejaculation with the teeth-clenching severity I'd become used to. In fact, as I opened to the incredible possibility, it became almost easy to bottle up the primordial force of nature within me. No baseball meditations were required, nor the convoluted breathing exercises synchronized with thigh-slapping and eye-popping. And I found myself having to summon a mere fraction of the heroic muscle constriction that characterized my most reliable technique.

Why? In light of all my past experience, it didn't make sense. To be intimately woven with a smart, soulful, gorgeous woman who made my heart bloom should have put me on the verge of coming all the time—especially when I was actually inside her.

I wondered if it could have had something to do with the structure of Celia's fluttering phoenix. But it wasn't slack, wasn't too big and roomy. Her muscles were well-toned. She had never given birth. We fit snugly together.

A radical theory dawned in me. What if men are not solely responsible, I mused, for evolution's conspiracy to trick them into delivering DNA's payload in two minutes flat? What if women play at least a small role in perpetuating the bad habit that is the most likely factor to undermine mutually gratifying heterosexual sex? And what if Celia was one of the rare females who somehow turned off the part of her programming that contributes to the bad habit?

This was a taboo thought to expose to the frowning radical feminist that sometimes patrolled my superego, but I had to let myself acknowledge the possibility: that some women on some occasions—maybe only in their unconscious minds—actually don't want their male partners to have control over the timing of their climax.

I speculated that there are four types of women who might sabotage the long-lasting male lover:

1. Some women regard a fast squirt as testimony to their overpowering irresistibility. "He found me so alluring that he couldn't contain himself." Many of this type are throwbacks to an age when a wife regarded her man's pleasure as more important than hers; when a female measured her success in love more by her ability to give gratification than to get it.

2. Some women may not want a rush to judgment but are nevertheless strongly attached to having a smoking gun: concrete proof that they've done their job of satisfying their men. No ejaculationless orgasm for these women, thank you; it's too ambiguous.

3. Some women conspire to induce a quick and seemingly accidental orgasm because they want to use it to humble their partner, berate him for his inadequacy, and have a bargaining chip to use in winning other, nonsexual concessions.

4. Some women are possessed by their DNA with the same demonic fervor as any man is by his. The 30-year-old ego may be crying out, "Give me deep pleasure," while the 10 million-year-old reproductive machinery is hissing, "Give me a baby." The mandate to propagate the species wants the ejaculation now, not in two hours. Why else would evolution have made it so absurdly easy for a man to come?

I reiterate that these four motivations are not necessarily blazing in the conscious awareness of women who are in the throes of making love. They may be unconscious programs that covertly shape the way their body functions.

Celia fit into none of the four categories. I suspected that at some point before she met me she had forged herself into a lover who would not collude with the hair-trigger release that evolution had bequeathed to men.

By what mechanism had she accomplished this? Was it a regimen of physical exercises comparable to those I had done in order to become a control

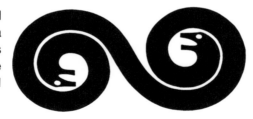

artist? A secret of meditation that allowed her to transmute the subtle structure of the muscles and electrochemical environment in her silk furrow? An esoteric yogic technique by which she imprinted her very flesh with the affirmation that she was "complete unto herself" (the ancient meaning of the word "virgin"), and did not, therefore, need to play a part in propagating the species?

This whole line of thinking took almost two months to ripen. We met each other in April, but it wasn't till June, eight dates into our relationship, that I was ready to speak of the inquiry that had been brewing in me. The climax came on a Saturday night.

I had read about a survey in which couples reported they often had great sex after seeing scary movies or going to a rifle range. Though I couldn't imagine the erotic glee between me and Celia being any better than it already was, I told her about the survey and suggested we try our own experiments. She liked the idea, but said that instead of watching violence or shooting guns, she'd prefer going on the thrill rides at the boardwalk.

We impulsively decided to get dressed up as a pirate and cowgirl for the occasion, which was easy enough to do thanks to a local costume rental shop open year-round. After polishing off a picnic dinner of take-out sushi on a bluff overlooking the sea, we arrived at the boardwalk. For the next three hours, we rode the roller coaster twice, as well as the Cliff Hanger, the Hurricane, the Whirlwind, the Tsunami, the Ferris wheel, the bumper cars, and the Crazy Surf. By the time we came back to Celia's house around 10 o'clock, we had whipped ourselves into a state of pleasant vertigo.

Soon we were naked and circling each other like samurai wrestlers in her secluded backyard, expanding the batty frame of mind we'd been thrust into by our synapse-boggling joyrides. It was chilly out there on that June night, and to compensate we soon found ourselves engaging in aerobic sex on a picnic table. To add to the incandescence and generate even more joie de vivre, we adopted funny accents as we pretended to be drunk Italian tourists arguing about whether it was safe to stand up on a roller coaster, stoned French graduate students arguing about whether Pynchon or Joyce was the greater genius, and Pakistani explorers marooned in the Arctic wastes arguing about which of our dead comrades we should eat first.

After a while we disengaged, agreeing to take a break and head inside. As I warmed up in her bed, she skipped off to the kitchen to make hot chocolate. With a fog of sweat still evaporating from me, I closed my eyes and did a meditation in which I prayed that the love I was feeling for her would remain as pure and generous as it was in that moment. I prayed that my effect on her would always promote her greater good and inspire her to seek out interesting adventures. I visualized us continuing to be able to be both kind and wild with each other.

In a few minutes, Celia glided back into the room with two steamy cups, her slapstick urges apparently unquenched: On her head she was wearing a "crown" composed of a purple balloon sculpture of a vulture. (Where had *that* come from?) Setting the cups down, she charged at my midsection, pecking me again and again with the inflated rubber beak. Between pecks she recited a pastiche of Emily Dickinson poems that featured the recurring line, "Dare you see a soul at the white heat?"

I lay down on the mattress and pulled her on top of me, removing her crown. With her cooperation, I slipped my jade stalk back where it belonged. As she gazed into my eyes with amused tenderness, her yoni began to play luxuriously, gripping and letting go with artistry, coming from diverse angles and engorging to a variety of depths. I let her control the rhythm, which was slow-motion and adoring.

For a long time we danced like this, singing each other songs with unhurried intensity. "You were born with a snake in both of your fists while a hurricane was blowing," I crooned, quoting Bob Dylan's "Jokerman." I also did covers of Bruce Cockburn's "Lovers in a Dangerous Time" and Louis Armstrong's "What a Wonderful World."

She treated me to excerpts from Billie Holiday's *Swing Brother Swing* and Patti Smith's album *Radio Ethiopia,* including her own mutated version of "Ain't It Strange":

> Come and join me, I implore thee,
> I impure thee, come explore me.
> Oh, don't you know that anyone can come
> in the same old way
> but we both want more.
> Don't you see when you're playing with me
> that we'll never end
> transcend transcend.

After delivering this curious passage, she cleared her voice and assumed a more prosaic tone. "And now I am pleased to make the long-awaited announcement. After many years of hard work rebelling against instinct,

I have graduated from the need for the melodramatic spurt. I have kicked my addiction to the old-fashioned *petite morte.* You are free, my dear, to keep your vital fluids to yourself. I don't need you to spew in order to know how desperately you want me."

I could hardly believe what I was hearing. She seemed to be addressing and answering the pressing question I had not yet spoken aloud to her. I indulged a fantasy that had been growing in me in recent weeks: that our connection was evolving into a telepathic union.

"You're a genius," I said. "You're a flaming genius."

"So is there any chance you want to see what it's like to have orgasms like mine?" she asked. "Implosive prayer wheel-spinning jubilations instead of those crash-and-burn-style evacuations you've gotten so dependent on? I'd love you to love me in a way that helped you love yourself better. How about it?"

Up until this moment, my training as a fuckmaster had never been devoted to expanding my own sexual pleasure. Even after I'd learned of the esoteric teachings about an alternate form of male orgasm, I withheld my ejaculations for other reasons: to ensure that my partners were thoroughly fulfilled and to pump up my image of myself as a good lover.

And the truth was I had never felt I could afford to explore the far frontiers of my own sexual pleasure. To do so might sabotage my arduously cultivated art of control, causing me to come too soon and fail as a lover.

Tears surged from my eyes and a blend of moan and chuckle spilled from my mouth. I felt a subtle but

> ### She asked me, "What song did you sing on the last day of your childhood? Do you love your body perfectly? What ignorance do you deserve to be forgiven for? Should you maybe go in search of more interesting problems?"

distinct pop in my pelvis, as if a blockage had been forcibly cleared or a knot cut. The hot coil of pleasure I had always identified as the essence of my sexual treasure began to spread out. As I followed it for the next few minutes, I realized with a mix of dismay and delight that for all these years it had been trapped in a tightly contained area in and around my cock and balls.

"You lifted the curse," I muttered to Celia with a smoky cheerfulness. "You broke the dam. You freed the genie. You liberated the slave. You tricked the guardian on the threshold into revealing the magic password."

"And I did it all with love, sweet love, not force, brute force," she murmured as she kissed my eyelids.

Spiral waves of nectar rippled out from the epicenter of my bliss. My heart was first to receive the blessing, then my throat and thighs. Gradually the entire inside of my body was awash with the bliss that had previously been confined to one small part of me. And as Celia continued to swirl me around inside her, I claimed the birthright I'd always denied myself: long, billowing orgasms, one following another. They were whirlpools of sweetness congealing in an ocean of delight. And unlike the expulsive, spasmodic burst I'd always regarded as the One True Orgasm, this new improved model kept *expanding* my capacity for more pleasure. My hard-on stayed hard even as the pulsing spirals kept on coming.

But how could that be? It didn't make sense. I'd long believed in the limiting power of satiation: A person could only experience so much rapture, right? After a set of nerve endings reaches a saturation point, the same stimulation that initially induced pleasure there begins to evoke apathy or even annoyance.

And yet that didn't apply in this case. The gratifications swarming through me were increasing, as if my ability to feel pleasure in three dimensions were expanding into four, and then into five and beyond.

"I'm coming in the eighth dimension right now," I whispered to Celia.

"I not only see your third eye right now," she replied softly. "I can hear your third ear and smell your second nose, too."

"I'm afraid I'm becoming an eight-dimensional freak monster."

"You're the eight-dimensional freaky god-fuck monster with a beauty that's so scary big you don't know what to do with it all."

"Uh-oh."

"Luckily, I'm also an eight-dimensional freaky godfuck monster with a beauty that's so scary big I don't know what to do with it all."

"We might have to go down to the homeless shelter and give away our scary beauty to all the needy poor people."

"And go down to the country club and give away our scary beauty to all the needy rich people."

I can't remember if we were still actually moving our bodies. The friction of genitals had become irrelevant. My longing was utterly sat-

isfied and yet was somehow also growing. I was very happy about how much love I felt for her, but wanted to love her even more.

My pleasure overflowed into the room. It was as if I were turning inside out. At first that spooked me. As I got used to it, I surrendered. I began to fantasize that I—whatever "I" might be—was now located outside my body as much as inside. "I" was having orgasms in an expanding sphere that spread into the space around me.

They really couldn't be called "orgasms" anymore, though. That term implies a sudden, forceful contraction and release centered around a focal point. But I was experiencing a multitude of repeating pulses, like a hundred beating hearts, unleashing ripples of pleasure over and over again.

"This is what God feels all the time," I whispered.

"Yes. This is what Goddess feels all the time," Celia answered.

"So we're imitating the Creators of the Universe right now?" I said.

"Well," she said, "in a sense we are imitating them. In another sense, we *are* them."

"I'm having a million orgasms every second."

"Me too. Let's shoot for a billion."

"OK. How?"

"Turn the orgasms into prayers."

"What do we pray for?"

"We pray for what God and Goddess pray for. Which is different from what humans pray for."

"I seem to be having a divine memory lapse, Goddess. Remind me what we pray for?"

"Our prayers are the engine of creation. They're how we reanimate the universe fresh every nanosecond—orgasmic bursts of divine love that keep everything growing and changing forever."

"So if we want to imitate God and Goddess—I mean, if we want to *be* God and Goddess—we should act as if our orgasms are actually prayers with which we beget the universe anew over and over again."

I felt another pop, like the one that had earlier freed my sexual energy from its logjam in my pelvis. Only this was nonlocal, a pervasive burst that shook the entire bubble of orgasmic vibration I now inhabited. As in the previous experience, I felt as if a blockage had been forcibly cleared.

Medicine Story

Images and emotions began streaming into my imagination. They had a life of their own, were independent of my will. They came in bursts, each of which bore the imprint of a person I knew and cared for. There was my friend Fred, the entomologist, with whom I traveled in Europe; Regina, the old girlfriend with whom I had three abortions; Maddy, the woman I sang with for five years; Sunyatta, the professional ballet dancer who taught me how to do a pirouette; Mr. Riley, my high school French teacher, the only older male who ever gave me a blessing.

In each case, the person's life seemed to pass in a flash before my eyes, downloading into my psyche all the memories of everything he or she had ever done and thought and felt, the pain mixed with the pleasure, the rot with the splendor. It was all happening impossibly fast: as if the old 2.5 GHz microprocessor in my brain had been replaced by a new model that ran at 2.5 million GHz.

She said, "Would you like to go kill the apocalypse?"

To be so intimately attuned with these friends and loved ones provoked a flood of empathy and compassion that blended seamlessly with my ongoing orgasms. A touch of amusement brushed through me briefly as I noted the unfamiliarity of having sexual associations with Fred and Mr. Riley, but it soon passed and I surrendered to the undifferentiated delight.

More life stories surged into me with even greater speed, and they included those of people with whom I'd had more complicated relationships: ex-band member Armand, who had both stunted and fed my growth as a musician; ex-girlfriend Raven, whose confounding betrayal taught me so much about myself that in effect I earned a PhD in self-knowledge under her tutelage; my sister who cut me out of her life for years.

I received them all gratefully and with relish, both the difficult souls and those for whom I had more unconditional love. The lushness of their intimate otherness was intoxicating. I loved being stuffed with so many thousands of foreign emotions and secrets and contradictions. The more I filled up, the more I wanted and the more I could hold. Soon I lost count of how many mythic imprints I had absorbed. Finally Celia spoke, breaking a long silence.

"We could probably keep going, but I think that's enough for now," she said. I opened my eyes and brought my attention back to her, returning from my inner orgy. I was confused. Did she want us to stop making love?

"I'm not ready to split us apart yet, Goddess," I complained. "In fact, I think I'm just getting started."

"I don't mean we should uncouple," she said, kissing me on both cheeks. "I mean we should stop filling ourselves up with the lives of all these people who need our prayers. Let's decide what to do with this batch before we welcome another one."

"Did you just have the same experience I did?" I asked, hoping for more evidence of our growing telepathic rapport.

"I should hope so, dear. See what happens when you play God?"

She playfully rolled over, pulling me with her so that now I was on top.

"Now fuck me with your prayers for all those souls who leaped into you," she commanded. "And I'll fuck you with mine."

I shoved a pillow under her ass to change the angle at which I entered her, and raised her legs a little by lifting from behind her knees.

"I visualize and pray that my old friend Fred will come to a new, supple accommodation with his ex-wife so that they create more harmony in the life of their daughter," I said as I moved in Celia. "May this unfold in ways that send benevolent consequences out in all directions, diminishing the suffering and enhancing the joy of every sentient being."

"I declare and desire that my Aunt Ruth will find the key to supporting herself as an acupuncturist so she can quit her gig as a grocery clerk," asserted Celia. "And I pray that in doing this she will become a more potent force for beauty and truth and goodness, lifting up everyone whose life she touches."

"I foresee and demand that Regina will summon the power to cut back on her work doing hospital murals so she can write that children's book she wants to do. May this in turn redound to the benefit of all creatures."

"I envision and confirm that John Selkirk will get the help necessary to heal from the death of his wife. As he receives what he needs, I further envision and confirm that all of creation will gather inspiration from the changes he sets in motion."

Many other friends, acquaintances, and loved ones made appearances in our ritual. My heart broke open again and again, ripped sweetly apart by a yearning to help them thrive, to love them as they needed to be loved, to enhance them and enliven them and share with them the blessings Celia and I had conjured.

Sometimes our invocations took the form of loud singing and chants; other times we emitted fantastic cackles and churned out rhythms with guttural grunts. We spoke in horse language and tried to re-create the original tongue from which Sanskrit and Hebrew originated. Thomas Jefferson and Sally Hemings paid a visit, channeled through us mediumistically, bestowing their unique love on several lucky beneficiaries.

Nine hundred trillion orgasms later, the rays of the morning sun splashed on my eyes as I meandered through a prayer for Maddy. "I predict and guarantee that she will compose a bunch of great songs about her struggle to be a half-decent single mother while playing low-paying gigs at funky San Francisco nightclubs in hopes of bringing her incredible singing talent to the attention of some non-exploitative hustler who'll help her get a recording contract."

"Hey God?" Celia rumbled from out of her trance state. We were lying side by side, still linked.

"Yes, Goddess," I said.

"I hate to interrupt you. You're still amazingly eloquent for someone who's been fucking nonstop for 14.3 billion years. Or is it 14.6?"

"That's OK. I can't think of anyone else I love being interrupted by more than you."

"I'm thinking maybe we should do a prayer for Rob and Celia and then put the universe to sleep for a while."

"Good idea."

"They've been quite kind to let us commandeer their bodies for so long. Let's show our gratitude."

"I'll start."

"Take your time."

"I decree and imagine that Celia will become a master of the art of bestowing blessings. As brilliant and generous as she is in giving gifts, she will never become addicted to giving gifts; nor will she try to control people with her gifts; nor will she let her joy in giving gifts interfere with her capacity to attract and receive gifts herself."

"And when Celia gives gifts," the Goddess in Celia added, "they will always be precisely what the recipients need rather than what she needs to give. She will have a knack for choosing people who make the best use of her gifts. No pearls-before-swine mistakes for her."

"Ho!" I exclaimed, invoking the Northern Californian pagan version of "amen."

"Now I have a prayer for Rob," she said. "I pray that he will popularize the slogan 'I am totally opposed to all duality.'"

"Good old Rob will become a socialist libertarian, macho feminist, Buddhist Muslim, gun-owning pacifist," I added.

"He will embrace his destiny as a prophet of the ejaculationless male orgasm. He will triumph over the primal on-off switch that has been the biological linchpin of the male psyche's addiction to us-versus-them fundamentalism."

"I pray that he will write books crammed with inspirational philosophies that are rooted in the oceanic prayer orgasms he has achieved this night. He will help forge a new nation conceived in liberty and dedicated to the proposition that all men and women are created with an equal birthright to experience amazing amounts of intelligence-boosting rapture that supercharges their drive to bestow beauty, truth, goodness, and love on their fellow humans."

Those were the last words I spoke for many hours. As I dropped off to sleep I heard the Goddess in Celia say, "I pray that Rob will become a paranoid in reverse. He will know that all of reality is always conspiring to help him, and he will try to prove to everyone everywhere that the same is true for them: Life is totally and unconditionally on their side."

The epiphany I have described unfolded years before I heard the magic word that is at the heart of the Beauty and Truth Laboratory, but I mark it as my awakening to pronoia. On that night I experienced a new species of sensation on the border between body and soul. It resembled sexual pleasure, but on a higher octave. It was like what passionate emotion might be if an emotion could have the intensity of jealousy or rage but instead consist of reverence and compassion. It became the root from which I grew a new trust in life.

SACRED ADVERTISEMENT

The orgasmic roots of pronoia
are brought to you by sacred underwear.

The saffron robes of Tibetan monks and black
habits of nuns are outer signs of their devotion.
But among religious devotees there's also a tradition of
wearing hidden clothing that's charged
with symbolic meaning—in other words, sacred underwear.

Some Mormons, for instance, regularly slip on a
white neck-to-knee garment that's meant to remind them of
their pact with God. Orthodox Jewish men may wear tsitsit,
a fringed cloth, beneath their basic black. For especially
devout Catholics, the sacred underwear *is called a scapular.*

French philosopher Blaise Pascal had his own non-
denominational version. At the height of an intense
epiphany, he scrawled prayerful poems on a parchment.
Forever after he wore this memento under his clothes.

We recommend the practice to you: Design or find your
own sacred underwear. *You could draw magical glyphs on*
your briefs. Stuff a talisman in your bra. Write a prayer on an
undershirt or slip. Or do whatever captivates your
imagination. This will be a secret sign—between you and
the Divine Wow alone—of your spiritual intention. Except for
the two of you, no one else will know.

DEVOTIONAL PRONOIA THERAPY

Experiments and exercises in becoming a gracefully probing, erotically funny, shockingly friendly Master of Orgasmic Empathy

Report your answers and research results below

1 Write the following on a piece of red paper and keep it under your pillow. "I, [put your name here], do solemnly swear on this day, [put date here], that I will devote myself for a period of seven days to learning my most important desire. No other thought will be more uppermost in my mind. No other concern will divert me from tracking down every clue that might assist me in my drive to ascertain the one experience in this world that deserves my brilliant passion above all others."

2 "The Eskimos had 52 names for snow because it was important to them," wrote novelist Margaret Atwood. "There ought to be as many for love."

Here are a few that the ancient Greeks devised, according to Lindsay Swope in her review of Richard Idemon's book *Through the Looking Glass.*

Epithemia is the basic need to touch and be touched. Our closest approximation is "horniness," though *epithemia* is not so much a sexual feeling as a sensual one.

Philia is friendship. It includes the need to admire and respect your friends as a reflection of yourself—like in high school, where you want to hang out with the cool kids because that means you're cool too.

Eros isn't sexual in the way we usually think, but is more about the emotional gratification that comes from merging souls.

Agape is a mature, utterly free expression of love that has no possessiveness. It means wanting the best for another person even if it doesn't advance your self-interest.

Your assignment is to coin three additional new words for love, which means you'll have to discover or create three alternate states of love that have previously been unnamed. To do that, you'll have to put aside your habitual expectations and standard definitions of what constitutes love so that you can explore an array of nuances, including varieties you never imagined existed.

3 Assume that your capacity for experiencing pleasure isn't a barrier to your spiritual growth, but is in fact essential to it. What would you do differently from what you do now?

4 Close your eyes and visualize an alluring person standing in front of you. Then imagine that he or she is gazing at you with affectionate desire. Add to the scene another enchanting person who is also beaming with adoration. Insert still another such character, and another, and another. Don't stop until you have arrayed before you in your mind's eye ten enticing people of your favorite gender—and they're all glowing with love and appreciation.

Let the scene develop further, like a waking dream, unfolding in directions that surprise and delight you.

5 Force yourself to think a kind thought about someone you don't like. Next, try an even harder task: Force yourself to think a kind thought about someone who doesn't like you.

6 Robin Norwood's self-help book *Women Who Love Too Much* deals with a theme that has gotten a lot of play in recent decades: If you're too generous to someone who doesn't appreciate it and at the expense of your own needs, you can make yourself sick.

An alternative perspective comes from philosopher Blaise Pascal, who said, "When one does not love too much, one does not love enough." He was primarily addressing psychologically healthy altruists, but it's a fertile ideal for pronoia lovers to keep in mind.

Decide whether you need to move more in the direction of Norwood's or Pascal's advice. Develop a game plan to carry out your resolve, then take action.

7 A common obstruction to a vital intimate relationship is what I call the assumption of clairvoyance. You imagine, perhaps unconsciously, that your partner or friend is somehow magically psychic when it comes to you—so much so that he or she should unfailingly intuit exactly what you need, even if you don't ask for it. This fantasy may seem romantic, but it can sink the most promising alliances.

To counteract any tendencies you might have to indulge in the assumption of clairvoyance, practice stating your desires aloud.

Devotional Pronoia Therapy

Imagine that everything you love and want is condensed into a single symbol. What is it?

8 Even if your heart's not exactly shattered at the moment, it has no doubt been so at some time in the past. I invite you to feel a wave of sadness about your suffering, then move on to this possibility: that having a broken heart is one of the best things that can happen to you.

Why? Because it strengthens your humility, which makes you smarter. It demonstrates to you that you have a tremendous capacity for deep feelings—far more than you're normally aware of. It breaks down defense mechanisms that have desensitized you to the world's secret beauty. It may also inspire you to treat other people's hearts with greater care, making it more likely that you'll be able to create intelligent intimacy in the future.

That's why I say, celebrate your broken heart. It's a gift the world gives you to awaken you to the truth about what matters most.

9 Identify three strangers you aren't attracted to and who seem lonely and uncool. Try to discover their names and addresses, like by discreetly following them home, then coming back later to steal their junk mail from their mailbox. Write them each a mysterious love letter and sign it "Your Secret Admirer." Mail your missives to them along with a postcard of a Kandinsky print on which you've written these words from Rilke: "I want to beg you to be patient toward all that is unsolved in your heart and to try to love the questions themselves."

10 Some hetero men believe they won't find romantic happiness unless they hook up with a woman who resembles a supermodel. Their libidos were imprinted at a tender age by our culture's narrow definition of what constitutes female beauty. They steer clear of many fine women who don't fit their ideal.

The addiction to a physical type is not confined to them, though. Some straight women, for instance, wouldn't think of dating a bald, short guy, no matter how interesting he is. And there are people of every sexual persuasion who imagine that their attraction to the physical appearance of a potential partner is the single most important gauge of compatibility. This delusion is the most common cause of bad relationships.

Devotional Pronoia Therapy

The good news is that anyone can outgrow their instinctual yearning for a particular physical type, thereby becoming available for union with all of the more perfect partners who previously didn't look quite right.

What's the state of your relationship with this riddle? Describe how you might ripen it; speculate on how you can move it to the next level of maturity.

11 "The proverb warns that 'You should not bite the hand that feeds you.' But maybe you should, if it prevents you from feeding yourself." So said the critic of psychiatry, Thomas Szasz. He was urging us to think about how our dependence on seemingly benevolent providers might paralyze our free will and interfere with our ability to take care of ourselves.

In the song "The Hand That Feeds," Trent Reznor of the band Nine Inch Nails expresses a further doubt. He suggests the hand that feeds us may supply us with stuff that doesn't really nourish us and that is tainted by the supplier's questionable motivations. "Will you stay down on your knees," he sings, or "will you bite the hand that feeds you?"

Actress Angelina Jolie has a tattoo on her belly that reads "Quod me nutruit me destruit." It's Latin for "What feeds me destroys me."

I think it means that if you grow too comfortable from soaking up nourishing experiences, you'll damage your lust for the kind of nerve-wracking adventures that make you feel fully alive. Or maybe: If you become addicted to what you enjoy, the price of your addiction will make the pleasure a curse.

So I'm curious: What hurts you by feeding you? Can you change yourself to elude the hurt?

> ### *"God calls you to the place where your deep gladness and the world's deep hunger meet."*
> ### *—Frederick Buechner*

12 Compose and cast a love spell on yourself. There's no need to consult pagan books about how to proceed. It may even be better if you improvise homemade conjurations and incantations.

Devotional Pronoia Therapy

Be sure to formulate a clear intention of what you want to accomplish with your mojo. Example: "I want to make myself irresistibly lovable." For best results, stand naked in front of an altar crammed with magical objects that symbolize both lust and compassion.

"Optical intercourse," also known as "making eye babies," occurs when two people gaze into each other's eyes long and deeply.

13 Play the game called "Tell me the story of your scars." It's best to do it with a skilled empath who is curious about your fate's riddles and skilled at helping you find redemption in your wounds.

"How did you get that blotch on your knee?" he or she might begin, and you describe the time in childhood when you fell on the sidewalk. Then maybe he or she would say, "Why do you always look so sad when you hear that song?" And you'd narrate the tale of how it was playing when an old lover broke your heart. The questions and answers continue until you unveil the history of your hurts, both physical and psychic. Treat yourself to this game soon.

14 Steve Penny wrote the booklet *How to Have Great Laughing Sex* (tinyurl.com/dyoj7m). Either get the book and try the exercises, or make up your own exercises. Then write your own essay called "How to Have Great Laughing Sex."

15 Gertrude Stein defined love as "the skillful audacity required to share an inner life." It suggests that expressing the truth about who you are is not something that amateurs do very well. Practice and ingenuity are required. It also implies that courage is an essential element of successful intimacy. You've got to be adventurous if you want to weave your life together with another's.

Comments? Examples? Refutations? Action steps?

16 Describe to your best companion a detailed vision of his or her best possible future.

17 Bring the spirits of sampling and the mash-up into your relationship life. Sampling is what happens when a musician openly lifts a riff out of an existing song and inserts it into his or her own composition. In a mash-up, a producer takes parts from two different songs to assemble a new song that has elements of both originals but is an entirely new creation.

How might you apply these approaches to your collaborations with intimate allies? For example, you could "sample" a close friend's favorite catchphrases or clothes, and use them as your own. Or tell that person a story from his or her own past, but recount it as if it happened to you. The two of you could write a journal entry together, taking turns spinning out each new line. You might even switch roles for a day, trying out what it actually feels like to be the other person.

18 Ruminate about the sublime prototypes that might be hidden within the longings you're not so proud of. Dream of the noble purposes that lie beneath the plaintive cries of your heart.

19 You understand that you can never own love, right? No matter how much someone adores you today, no matter how much you adore someone, you can't force that unique state of grace to keep its shape forever. It will inevitably evolve or mutate, perhaps into a different version of tender caring, but maybe not. From there it will continue to change, into either yet another version of interesting affection, or who knows what else?

Describe how you could get the hang of putting this tricky wisdom into practice.

20 "Love is being stupid together," said French poet Paul Valéry. While there's a grain of truth to that, it's too corny and decadent for my tastes. I prefer to focus on a more interesting truth, which is this: Real love is being smart together. If you weave your destiny together with another's, he or she should catalyze your sleeping potentials, sharpen your perceptions, and boost both your emotional and analytical intelligence. Your relationship becomes a crucible in which you deepen your understanding of the way the world works.

Give an example of your closest approach to this model in your own life. Then formulate a vow in which you promise you'll do what's necessary to more fully embody the principle "Love is being smart together."

21 Are you unsure about whether you should leap into a lasting bond with a certain numinous creature you've been fooling around with? If so, you might be interested in obtaining a Sacred Certificate of Short Duration Marriage. It's available at tinyurl.com/ypxz7y.

Devotional Pronoia Therapy

This convenient license can provide you with the security of knowing that your commitment doesn't have to be forever. Maybe that will free you to hurl yourself with more headlong grace into the experience.

22 A heterosexual man who is seeking a partner often doesn't want a woman to be complete unto herself; he hopes she'll feel inadequate and lost without him. Similarly, many hetero women demand that their men be absolutely dependent on them. Those of the gay persuasion aren't necessarily any different; quite a few also prefer their consorts to be unable to thrive alone. But there are also plenty of people who want their intimate relationships to be an alliance of strong, equal, independent partners.

Where do you stand on this issue?

"Let the body think of the spirit as streaming, pouring, rushing, and shining into it from all sides."
—Plotinus

23 Norman Mailer described marriage as "an excretory relationship, in which you take all the crap you hide from the world and dump it on the person closest to you. But the proviso is that you have to be willing to take theirs."

Describe how you might work in the opposite way by training yourself to call up all the beauty you hide from the world and offer it to the person closest to you.

24 If you think of yourself as a heterosexual, meditate on the qualities you express that are commonly thought of as the specialty of the opposite sex. Consider the possibility that you are actually 65 percent female, 25 percent male, and 10 percent neither, or maybe 15 percent female, 70 percent male, and 15 percent transgender.

If you regard yourself as gay, explore the hypothesis that a part of you is secretly kind of straight. If you're an androgynous bisexual nymphomaniac, try being celibate. You get the picture: Escape your sexual imprint for a while.

25 Siam's King Mongkut had a harem of 9,000 women. On his deathbed, before succumbing to

Devotional Pronoia Therapy

the ravages of syphilis, he confessed that he was truly in love with only 700 of his lovers—less than eight percent of the total. Why he didn't concentrate on that eight percent and forget the rest we'll never know.

Proposed experiment: If given the chance to indulge in a wealth of pleasurable adventures, seek out only the fraction that will nourish your fucking soul.

26 What could you do to make your tenderness and carnality flow from the same refined reflex? How might you strive to adore every creature, plant, and rock in the world with the same excitement that you bestow upon the lover who excites you most? What prayers will you unleash at the height of your orgasmic fervor to promote the healing and success of people in need?

27 "For a relationship to stay alive," writes James Hillman, "love alone is not enough. Without imagination, love stales into sentiment, duty, boredom. Relationships fail not because we have stopped loving but because we first stopped imagining."

Make this your hypothesis. The next time you sense that you're about to say the same old thing to your closest ally, interrupt yourself and head off in the direction of storyland.

28 Would you like to make yourself more magnetic to blessings? You could experiment with good luck charms or magic amulets—objects that you imagine might attract benevolence into your life. How about a replica of Brísingamen, the magical necklace of the Norse goddess Freya? When she wore it, neither man nor god could resist her allure. Or maybe a copy of the thyrsus, a wand wielded by Dionysus, the god of ecstasy? Or the bracelet of meteorite chunks I saw advertised as a luck-bringer in the back of a tabloid?

As fun as things like these might be, I believe there's a superior approach to the art of charging up your mojo. It's embodied by the metaphorical talisman that Tom Waits recommends in his song "Get Behind the Mule": Always keep a diamond in your mind.

Go get one of those diamonds.

Who are the people in your life who've helped make you real to yourself?

Mother's Milk Revolution

In 1967, only 25 percent of American infants were breast-fed. Today, the rate is seven out of 10. That's excellent news, says the American Academy of Pediatrics, citing research that suggests children are far healthier when they're breast-fed.

Real *Love Poetry*

Early in his career, Robert Bly rarely wrote love poetry, though he studied the work of others who did. As he aged, he stopped reading the angst-ridden ruminations of modern poets and sought out the ecstatic love poetry of mystics like Rumi and Kabir. Increasingly, forgiveness and compassion became central aspects of Bly's emotional repertoire. His rage about his own past romantic disappointments dissipated. In his mid-40s, he wrote *Loving a Woman in Two Worlds,* his first collection of love poetry. Critiquing it for *The New York Times Book Review,* Fred Chappell said it wasn't a *real* book of love poems, because there wasn't enough hatred and anger in it. On Bly's behalf, we offer a response to Mr. Chappell: *We love you, goddamnit.*

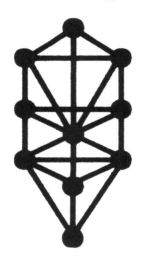

This edition of PNN is brought to you by James Joyce's Finnegans Wake, *and especially this passage: "The Gracehoper was always jigging ajog, hoppy on akkant of his joyicity."*

Esoteric Geography

The black water of Rio Negro and the yellowish brown water of Rio Solimões converge near the Brazilian city of Manaus. For a few miles they refuse to blend, flowing side by side as if intent on maintaining their autonomy. This two-toned phenomenon is the official beginning of one of the world's longest rivers, the Amazon.

In Montgomery, Alabama, there is an intersection where Jefferson Davis Avenue crosses Rosa Parks Avenue. One street is named after the president of the slave-owning states in America's Civil War. The other is named for the black woman who in 1955 rejected a bus driver's demand that she give her seat to a white passenger, leading to events that helped launch the civil rights movement.

Gay Marriage Won't Wreck Civilization

"The results of more than a century of anthropological research on households, kinship relationships, and families, across cultures and through time, provide no support whatsoever for the view that either civilization or viable social orders depend upon marriage as an exclusively heterosexual institution. Rather, anthropological research supports the conclusion that a vast array of family types, including families built upon same-sex partnerships, can contribute to stable and humane societies." —American Anthropological Association, aaanet.org

Where Great Stories Come to Life

The Vagina Monologues is a book and show based on interviews with women all over the world. "There's so much darkness and secrecy surrounding the vagina," says author Eve Ensler, "—like the Bermuda Triangle."

Sex-positive feminists note wryly that while Ensler's work was a welcome breakthrough, the final frontier won't come until a bevy of female celebrities gather at Madison Square Garden (as they did to celebrate *TVM*) and shout hosannas to the clitoris. For there seems to be an even deeper conspiracy to conceal its majesty—maybe because it's the only organ in the human body with no other purpose than to experience pleasure.

Play Is the Thing

Psychiatrist Stuart Brown has proposed this simple definition: "Play is spontaneous behavior that has no clear-cut goal and does not conform to a stereotypical pattern. The purpose of play is simply play itself; it appears to be pleasurable."

In a study of 26 convicted murderers, Brown discovered that as children, most of them had suffered either "from the absence of play or abnormal play like bullying, sadism, extreme teasing, or cruelty to animals."

Brown's work led him to explore the biological roots of play. "New and exciting studies of the brain, evolution, and animal behavior," he wrote, "suggest that play may be as important to life—for us and other animals—as sleeping and dreaming." —Stuart L. Brown, "Animals at Play," *National Geographic,* December 1994. Brown's website is instituteforplay.com.

Alternative Heroes' Journey

In Joseph Campbell's vision of myth, the hero is typically a solitary male who renounces intimate companionship to pursue his glorious, arduous quest. Along the way, sporadic help may arrive from an ineffable muse or deity.

There are alternative scenarios for the hero's journey, but Campbell underplayed them. In the tantric tradition, for instance, a seeker's connection with a beloved human companion is essential to his or her spiritual inquiry. Some early Christians described Jesus and Mary Magdalene as equal collaborators. Sufi mystic poet Rumi may not have actually made love with his teacher Shams (then again, he might have), but it's clear the two men sought divine communion together, not through lonely solo work.

Some modern teachers have broken from Campbell's narrow perspective. The quest for illumination, they say, can thrive on the challenges of loving and living with an actual person. In John Welwood's *Love and Awakening,* the author reimagines relationship as an "alliance of warriors" devoted to awakening each other's "holy longing."

Sneezing Epidemics

Scientists theorize that allergies are increasing because modern civilization has scoured away dirt and germs so relentlessly that the human immune system has grown bored—so bored it's now rising up to battle substances that are harmless to the body, like pollens and pet dander.

Dolphin Love Conspiracy

Jerry Langley likes to play his guitar for the spinner dolphins in Maui's La Perouse Bay. They appreciate it. When he runs out of songs, he often joins them for a convivial swim. One day in 2003, a commotion at sea moved Jerry to interrupt his concert. Paddling out for a closer look, he found a woman swimmer surrounded by the dolphins. The normally friendly creatures had hemmed her in, as if herding her. But when their buddy Jerry showed up, they parted their tight circle to let him through, and he was able to escort the woman back to shore. The two hit it off instantly—she was a singer looking for a gig. They began dating and eventually got married.

Non-Sexual Tantra

Meditation teacher Jack Kornfield espouses an interesting method for dealing with negative and unwanted thoughts. Don't let them possess you, he says, and don't assume you have to act them out. On the other hand, don't struggle mightily to suppress them, either. Instead, try this: Bow to the offending idea. Acknowledge and admire its power. Express your gratitude and respect to it for galvanizing so much of your psychic energy.

Gender Blending

"The higher a woman's IQ, the more she is likely to be masculine in outlook. The higher a man's IQ, the more likely he is to be feminine in outlook." —Lucius Cervantes, *And God Made Man and Woman*

The Lovers' Party

Marriages in India are usually arranged by relatives of the bride and groom, and most couples who wed come from the same religion or caste. But there are rebels who ignore custom and marry for love. One of their champions is a social worker named Biswanath Ramachandra Champa Swapnaji Taslima Voltaire. He launched a political party for lovers called the Lovers' Green-Globalist God-free-Humanist Party. "Only those who love can effectively change society," he says, "and my new party will be their platform."

MIRABILIA REPORT *Mirabilia* n. mysterious revelations, rejuvenating prodigies, ineffable breakthroughs; from the Latin *mirabilia,* "marvels."

■ A pig's orgasm can last for 30 minutes. Orangutans and macaques masturbate with sex toys made of leaves and twigs. The ladybird beetle can copulate for up to nine hours at a time, and males are capable of three orgasms in one session, each an hour and a half long. The male members of the fruitfly species Drosophila bifurca are one-eighth of an inch long, but their sperm can be up to 2.3 inches long. About eight percent of domestic rams prefer other males as sexual partners.

■ As soon as the male praying mantis begins coitus with the female, she bites off his head and eats it. An adult female elephant's clitoris is between six and twelve inches long, and the spotted hyena female has such a large clitoris that she is frequently mistaken for a male. An oyster is usually ambisexual; it begins life as a male, then becomes a female, then changes back to being a male, then back to being female. A whale's penis is called a dork.

■ Donald Duck comics were outlawed in Finland for a time because the cartoon hero never wore pants. Some dolphins try to have intercourse with turtles, sharks, and seals. As a prelude to sex, the male sagebrush cricket renders the female immobile with a trap on his back. Slugs are hermaphrodites with penises on their heads. Asian stick insects sometimes fuck for ten weeks straight. The slime mold comes in 500 genders, and at least 13 of these have to collaborate in order to reproduce.

■ Sex researcher Alfred Kinsey said that "The only unnatural sex act is one you cannot perform."

Cross-Fertilization

In 1991, hikers in the Italian Alps discovered the largely intact body of a man who had been dead for 5,000 years. He'd been preserved in a glacier that had recently begun to melt. Since then, many women have asked to be given some of the iceman's frozen sperm so that they might become pregnant by him. The director of the museum where his body is kept has so far turned down all requests.

PNN is brought to you by the way writer George Sand made love with composer Frédéric Chopin on Christmas Day, 1839.

Hug Drugs

Mata Amritanandamayi is one of India's most beloved gurus. Also known as Amma, she preaches no doctrine but believes all religions lead to the same goal. Her renown has grown largely through the power and quantity of her embraces. She travels from city to city doling out hugs, often more than 1,000 a day. Since she launched her mission as a young girl, she claims to have hugged 30 million people.

BREAKING THE PRONOIA TABOO

"Where love rules, there is no will to power; and where power predominates, there love is lacking. The one is the shadow of the other." —Carl Jung, *Psychological Reflections: A Jung Anthology*

"Surround yourself with a seedy coffeehouse of intoxicated gods and their infidel poet-priests. Develop a working relationship with that stunning, bewildering, driving source of mad desire and infinite depth: the world itself whispering lovely things to you constantly." —Revd. MC 900 ft. Escher, tinyurl.com/czf26u

"Orpheus is the archetype of the poet as liberator and creator: He establishes a higher order in the world: an order without repression. In his person, art, freedom, and culture are eternally combined. He is the poet of redemption, the god who brings peace and salvation by pacifying man and nature, not through force but through song." —Herbert Marcuse, *Eros and Civilization*

"When an apprentice gets hurt, or complains of being tired, the workmen have this fine expression: 'It is the trade entering his body.' Each time we have some pain to go through, we can say to ourselves quite truly that it is the order and beauty of the world that are entering our body." —Simone Weil, *Waiting for God*

"The wooing of the Earth means preserving natural environments in which to experience mysteries transcending daily life and from which to capture the awareness of the cosmic forces that have shaped humankind." —René Dubos

"If you want to build a ship, don't drum up the men to gather wood, divide the work, and give orders. Instead, teach them to yearn for the vast and endless sea." —Antoine de Saint-Exupéry

"Aborigines openly and unaffectedly converse with everything in their surroundings—trees, tools, animals, rocks—as if all things have an intelligence deserving of respect." —Robert Lawlor, *Voices of the First Day*

Roots of Human Nature

Bonobo apes and humans share 98 percent of the same genes, leading some biologists to suggest that they, along with chimpanzees, should be reclassified as members of the human genus. While their gestures, postures, walk, and facial expressions have remarkable similarities to ours, however, their social behavior is quite different. Bonobos live in a peaceful matriarchy characterized by egalitarian relationships. Power and status are of minimal concern. They build and maintain social rapport with frequent erotic exchanges of every variety, from intercourse to mutual masturbation to oral sex. Homosexual and cross-generational contact is common.

"Bonobos use sex to appease, to bond, to make up after a fight, to ease tensions, to cement alliances," writes Natalie Angier in *The New York Times*. Because it's their social glue, says primatologist Dr. Frans de Waal, author of *Bonobo: The Forgotten Ape*, sex is casual and free of elaborate taboos. Unlike humans, bonobos are not obsessed with orgasm. Their reproductive rate is similar to that of other primates.

"All of this has relevance for understanding the roots of human nature," concludes Angier. "De Waal corrects the image of humanity's ancestors as driven by aggression, hierarchical machinations, hunting, warfare, and male dominance." (Source: Natalie Angier, *The New York Times*, April 22, 1997)

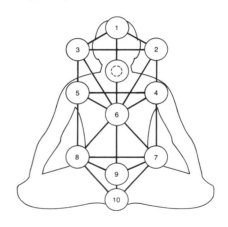

The Art of Childbirth "If men had babies," notes Elinor Gadon in her book *The Once and Future Goddess: A Sweeping Visual Chronicle of the Sacred Female and Her Reemergence in the Cultural Mythology of Our Time,* "there would be thousands of images of crowning, that awesome moment when the baby's head first appears." But the visual art of the last two millennia, though it depicts every other human activity, has ignored childbirth. A rare exception to the historical taboo is Judy Chicago's *The Birth Project,* a collection of birth images rendered through needlework. She created it in the mid-1980s.

Today images of childbirth are as taboo as the idea of pronoia, which is so taboo that it's not even recognized as a taboo. Without much difficulty, you can track down photos, videos, and artwork that depict every imaginable human activity—from beheadings to suicide bombers to bestiality—but you'll be hard-pressed to find depictions of babies being born. Scenes of childbirth seem to be more forbidden than the most extreme porn.

Lower Octave Courtship "Why is it so hard to find a soulmate?" asks psychologist Carolyn Godschild Miller in her book *Soulmates: Following Inner Guidance to the Relationship of Your Dreams.* Her answer: "Because most of us are actually searching for egomates instead. We place the most limited and unloving aspect of our minds in charge of our search for love, and then wonder why we aren't succeeding. To the degree that we identify with this false sense of self, and operate on the basis of its limited point of view, we aren't looking for someone to love so much as recruiting fellow actors to take on supporting roles in a favorite melodrama."

As Above, So Below
"God and fuck are so much alike
they might be synonymous glories.
I'd even go so far as to say
God is the Fuck of all Fucks"
—James Broughton, *Special Deliveries: New and Selected Poems,* Mark Thompson, editor

Laughing Sex

"Why is sex the most fun people have without laughing or smiling? Think about it. When enjoying most other physical pleasures, you smile and laugh. It may be because we have millions of years of evolutionary history with sex being closely linked to aggression and dominance—especially for men, who feel a big push to beat out their competitors and get their genes into the next generation.

"Another reason most people don't smile or laugh during sex is that desire has an edge to it. You know how hard it is to tell sometimes if animals are fighting or mating? Many human relationships have a similar quality. It's hard to tell if the couple is actually in love or strangely addicted to tormenting each other.

"This difference in how we experience sexual pleasure compared to other types of joy may be one reason so many people end up in relationships where the sex is fantastic but everything else is screwed.

"Biologists classify all living things by their reproductive habits because, from an evolutionary standpoint, it's the slowest behavior to change.

"Laughter, on the other hand, is fairly recent in an evolutionary sense. While several primates smile (although not necessarily from joy), and chimpanzees and gorillas chuckle and tickle, humans are the only species that truly laughs from joy.

"Maybe sex is the most fun people have without laughing because our slow-to-change reproductive behavior hasn't caught up with the more recent development in evolution—laughter." —Steve Penny, *How to Have Great Laughing Sex,* tinyurl.com/dyoj7m

International Affairs

"The psychic health of an individual resides in the capacity to recognize and welcome the 'Other,'" writes poet and translator Rosanna Warren in *The Art of Translation.* "Our word 'idiot' comes from the Greek *idiotes,* whose primary sense is of privacy or isolation." With this warning, Warren builds her case for the virtues of reading literature that has been translated from its native tongue.

Desirable Qualities

Amazon.com founder Jeff Bezos told *Wired* magazine that while looking for a wife, he put a high premium on resourcefulness. "I wanted a woman who could get me out of a Third World prison," he said.

THIS DAY IN PRONOIAC HISTORY

More than three billion years ago, the Earth's original single-cell organisms thrived in a carbon dioxide-rich atmosphere that contained no free oxygen. As a by-product of their metabolism, they released an abundance of oxygen. It was a pollutant that ultimately made the environment uninhabitable for them, though it prepared the way for the oxygen-breathers that now dominate the planet.

☼

In ancient Greek myth, Prometheus stole the gods' fire and bequeathed it to human beings, allowing them to cook, stay warm when the weather was cold, and make tools and bricks and pottery.

PNN is brought to you by Guneli Gun and her book On the Road to Baghdad: A Picaresque Novel of Magical Adventures. *Here's an excerpt: "The world is run by those who can't make love, or those who do it badly. That's why the world is in trouble."*

Rules of Attraction

"Unless the eye catch fire,
God will not be seen.
Unless the ear catch fire,
God will not be heard.
Unless the tongue catch fire,
God will not be named.
Unless the heart catch fire,
God will not be loved.
Unless the mind catch fire,
God will not be known."
—William Blake,
"Pentecost"

Cosmos-Generating Intimacy   Western science and religion have differing views on how the universe was created, but they agree that it happened a long time ago. The mystery schools of the West, on the other hand, assert that the universe is re-created anew in every moment through the divine erotic play of God and Goddess. They say that if we humans treat lovemaking as an experimental sacrament, we can attune ourselves to the union of the two primal deities and, in a sense, participate in the ongoing creation of the world.

Five Genders, at Least   "The state and legal system may have an interest in maintaining only two sexes, but our collective biological bodies do not. While male and female stand on the extreme ends of a biological continuum, there are other bodies that mix together anatomical components conventionally attributed to both males and females. Comprising about four percent of all humans born, three variations can be identified: the so-called true hermaphrodites ('herms'), who possess one testis and one ovary; the male pseudohermaphrodites ('merms'), who have testes and some aspects of the female genitalia but no ovaries; and the female pseudohermaphrodites ('ferms'), who have ovaries and some aspects of the male genitalia but lack testes." —Anne Fausto-Sterling, *Sexing the Body: Gender Politics and the Construction of Sexuality*

Higher Octave Empathy

"Couvade" occurs in several indigenous cultures, most in Africa. It's a phenomenon in which a man experiences morning sickness, unusual appetites, and other symptoms similar to those of his pregnant mate. He may even have labor pains as the child is born, diminishing the mother's distress as if he has mysteriously been able to take some of it on. There's no known physiological basis for couvade.

Traditional Family Values   Not all men in traditional marriages drink too much, beat their wives and kids, and fritter away their paychecks gambling in whorehouses.

What's That Singing in Our Bones?

"Deep in our bones resides an ancient singing couple who just won't give up making their beautiful, wild noise. The world won't end if we can find them." —Martín Prechtel, *Secrets of the Talking Jaguar,* floweringmountain.com

Sonnet XIV

"If thou must love me, let it be for nought
Except for love's sake only. Do not say
'I love her for her smile—her look—her way
Of speaking gently,—for a trick of thought
That falls in well with mine, and certes brought
A sense of pleasant ease on such a day'—
For these things in themselves, Beloved, may
Be changed, or change for thee,—and love, so wrought,
May be unwrought so. Neither love me for
Thine own dear pity's wiping my cheeks dry,—
A creature might forget to weep, who bore
Thy comfort long, and lose thy love thereby!
But love me for love's sake, that evermore
Thou mayst love on, through love's eternity."
—Elizabeth Barrett Browning,
Sonnets from the Portuguese

GUERRILLA ORACLE

Clues to the Rebel Grail

Radical Everything

"I've been practicing radical authenticity lately," my friend Brandon told me. "I'm revealing the blunt truth about unmentionable subjects to everyone I know. It's been pretty hellish—no one likes having the social masks stripped away—but it's been ultimately rewarding."

"I admire your boldness in naming the currents flowing beneath the surface," I replied, "but I'm curious as to why you imply they're all negative. To practice radical authenticity, shouldn't you also express the raw truth about what's right, good, and beautiful? Shouldn't you unleash the praise and gratitude that normally go unspoken?"

Brandon sneered. He thought my version of radical authenticity was wimpy. I hope you don't. As a budding pronoiac, you have a mandate to be honest in both ways.

SACRED ADVERTISEMENT

Your courage to express thoughtful praise is brought to you by the ultrasensitive neural receptors called Krause's end bulbs, which appear only in human lips, tongue, and genitals.

ELATIONSHIP LOVE SPELLS FOR BEAUTY AND TRUTH RESEARCHERS

Are you in quest of a Soul Friend or a Freaky Consort? A Wild Confidante or a Fuck Buddy? A Master of Curiosity who listens better than anyone ever or a Lucid Dreamer with whom you can practice the Art of Liberation?

Then steal these ads. The come-ons below have been designed by the Beauty and Truth Lab's rapturists to attract allies who are committed to the art of compassionate lust and blasphemous reverence. If you're a Crafty Optimist or Mystical Activist or Ceremonial Teaser who aspires to put the elation back in relationship, you're invited to plagiarize any part of these for your own use.

MY EYES REMIND YOU WHERE YOU CAME FROM

Uncork me, angel. Unfurl me. Release me and restore me and unleash me. Not because I can't do it myself. Not because I'm just another narcissism-addict jonesing for a quick fix. On the contrary. I'm the most self-sufficient self-starter I've ever met. It's from my position of strength that I aspire to whip up spectacular synergies in tandem with your holy rolling reverberations. So keep in mind that I'm here to uncork you and unfurl you and release you and restore you and unleash you, too. That's the art of the game that stretches out before us in all directions. That's the beauty of the gritty reality that's disguised as a glittery fantasy. As you bless my risks and massage my unconsciousness and save my soul, I'll always vice your versa. P.S. My last fortune cookie said, "You need nothing and want everything."

POLYAMOROUS MONOGAMY

You might say I'm catagoraphobic. I hate getting stuffed into pigeonholes. I run the other way when people try to tell me who I am. So don't try to figure me out. Just enjoy me. Or maybe I should say just enjoy us. There are so many different facets to my personality that monogamy with me will feel like a promiscuous feast to you. I'm a socialist libertarian and a pacifist warrior. I'm an atheistic lover of many gods, a streetwise thaumaturge with stuffed animals on my Qabalistic altar, and a humble megalomaniac who loves to perform missions of mercy. Always both and yet neither. And what about you? Just to let you know, I love architects who moonlight as smugglers of illegal flowers. I respect vegetarians who sneak pork chops now and then. I admire ex-druggies who get sober with the same fanaticism they once devoted to their addictions. Get the picture? My spirit thrives when nothing and no one are exactly what they seem. Here's the key to our happiness: As long as we give up our control fantasies, we'll always get what we want.

PERSONAL GROWTH ADDICT IN SEARCH OF A DIVINE CACKLER

Disgruntled postal employee seeks zombie love slave or lonely bank teller to share erotic fantasies about IRS audits and root canals. Just kidding. That's my sense of humor. You like? Seriously, beautiful, this emotionally adept space case is looking for a flexible alien lifeform for exotic forms of togetherness like taking long walks on the astral plane, listening to self-help CDs by the light of a webcast candle, and conducting Jungian conversations between your shadow and my anima, or your alchemical vessel and my philosopher's stone. Do you have more money than me and sometimes act like a character in a Tom Robbins' novel? Then e-mail me a tough love letter today. A plus if you can speak John Dee's language of the angels and know the difference between the Greys, the Pleiadians, and the Elohim.

FAIRY TALE WITH MARKETING POTENTIAL

Future lottery winner and full-time thrill-designer is hunting for a brainteasing emancipator to share risky stunts and international scandals that have lucrative marketing potential. Let's do a reality TV show that features us hiking through China in our Halloween costumes as we distribute alms for the poor, or air-drop Anaïs Nin books on Bible Belt colleges as we ride in a hot-air balloon over Mississippi and Alabama. In the great tradition of Picasso, the richest Communist artist who ever lived, we'll become wealthy pranksters together, poking and prodding the edges of reality.

OUR SECRET FREEDOM

Me: the soul of a musician, the stamina of a long-distance runner, and the psychological expertise of a veterinarian. You: the body of a feral kickboxer, the eyes of a jet pilot, and the holder of a PhD in Ingenious Love. In matters of the heart, you always know exactly when to sweat and when to cry. You like to play in the sandbox as much as you enjoy working in the trenches—and you don't mind getting dirty. Send me an image of your face pressed against the copy machine, and I'll get started reading your mind. In the meantime, I'll be here in my lab dreaming up experiments we can do to tenderly shock ourselves ever-more awake from what the pros call "the nightmare of history."

OUTLAWED IN 38 STATES

I picture us dressed like corporate executives and standing at a highway exit ramp giving away twenty-dollar bills while holding a cardboard sign that reads "I love to help; I need to give; please take some money." I foresee us passing scribbled love notes back and forth as we work side by side at the suicide hotline, getting turned on as we breathe in each other's death-defying pheromones and ride the inside-out exhilaration of saving people's lives. I have a vision that one day our arms will be brushing and our sultry gazes meeting as we

serve peanut butter and jelly sandwiches and lentil stew to homeless folks at the soup kitchen, and when it's all done we'll go home and spend the night generating material for our collaborative book, *How to Make Love with Your Best Friend,* which ultimately earns us a million dollars that we donate to electing brilliant poor people to political office.

BITE MY WIT

Tasmanian devil seeks sleek fox or wily coyote for interspecies communion. It's a jungle out there, baby, but I know some great trails that lead to rebel grails, and I'm definitely not afraid of the deep, dark stuff. Put your paw in mine and together we'll ford the rivers and scale the cliffs and swing on the vines. Are you ready to have even more fun than merely being in love? Two grunts mean "Yes, dear." Two grunts and a howl mean "Fuck, yes, dear!"

SACRED AGENT SEEKS FREAKY CONSORT

Tired of both boringly nice goodie-goodies and menacing lunatics trying to pass off their pathologies as "sexy"? I'm the happy medium: a straddler of the mysterious edge where bliss and struggle overlap, where the difference between light and dark just ain't that simple. I feel too deeply to pretend that every question has a correct answer. I cry too easily and love too much. And you? Are you smart enough to be guided by your sacred dreams of transgression? Are you free enough to surrender over and over again to the waters of life? If you've got the courage, I've got the secrets. I'll be your wild-eyed, smart-mouthed, spread-eagled muse if you'll be mine.

MYSTIC ACTIVIST SEEKS PRIMORDIAL GOSSIPER

I'm the one! Pick me for your mission impossible! I'm the one! Pick me to help you storm the kingdom of heaven! Everybody's somebody's fool; let me be yours! I have no shame and I have no qualms! I give not until it hurts but until it exalts my libido, and if you're smart you'll let me teach you the method in that madness! So electrify me in a sanctuary, you stunning ravisher! Amaze me in a labyrinth! Undress me on an altar! Engorge me in a way station! And I'll resurrect you wherever you want!

RIDDLE MY BLISS, BIG-TALKER

Slapstick thinker with refined sensibilities seeks a saint-like sinner with insanely effervescent style for a long-distance joyride toward the outskirts of Nirvana. Established meditation practice and a good bedside manner are desirable. Would it be too much to ask that you might also have a high level of emotional intelligence without boring me to death with your maturity? Is it possible that you'll be an entertaining talker who also knows how to listen with your wild heart turned up all the way? Let's keep reinventing ourselves for as long as it takes to get the hang of changing forever.

WABI-SABI, BABY

Like the skilled Japanese pottery-makers whose work is valued for its trademark blemishes, I thrive on life's imperfections. Have you ever considered the possibility that your flaws are interesting? I'll love you for who you are, not who you might be someday. Let me massage your booboos.

I'M THUNDER IN THE EARTH AND YOU'RE RIVER IN THE HEAVENS

Fire-breathing earth-worshiper with the warrior genius of a geisha and the intimacy skills of a samurai seeks an undomesticatable creature of the night with a talent for walking on water. I want a lover, yes, and a blood ally, but I also want a partner in crimes that don't break any laws ... a joy scientist who's in training to be an ethical outlaw ... a dissident bodhisattva with the messianic ambition to overthrow reality. What's so bad about obsession, anyway? You look fabulous when you're pushing it to the limit, and so do I. My turn-ons: taboo explorations on the frontiers of enlightened compassion, and peak performances at the border of wildness and discipline. Turn-offs: easy tests that merely flatter my ego and familiar games that put my higher mind to sleep. Resolved: My inner guru wants to get into the funnest possible trouble with your inner shaman.

SUCK MY BEAUTY AND TRUTH

Are you a stable, down-to-earth romantic who'd enjoy wearing matching sweaters with me while browsing through shopping malls? If so, please stop reading immediately. I'm on the lookout for a Funky Pagan Tantric Nobody with inside knowledge of the Big Bang. Or a descendant of Grandmother Spider, who created the world by imagining it. Or something like that. I've figured out six of the 13 Perfect Secrets from the Beginning of Time, and I'm hoping that maybe you've got some of the others. Keep in mind that even if civilization goes down in flood and flame tomorrow, we've got all the time in the world. Remember all the past lives we've shared? And there are more than enough still to come to accomplish all our esoteric schemes and dreams. So I hope you're ready to rejoin me in singing backup harmonies to the music of the spheres. I trust you're curious about all the new things I've learned that'll come in handy when I suck your beauty and truth again.

SEX WITH FRIENDS

James Thurber once said of a ruined relationship, "Our love never ripened into friendship." But I promise you no one'll say that about you and me. I'm not just a trophy hunter lusting after your prize, sweetheart; I'm a multifaceted truth-teller who wants to collaborate with your soft touches, your hard knocks, and everything in between. One of my goals in life is to learn the art of reading my best buddy's body language as well as my own.

LET'S SELL VICTORIA'S SECRETS TO DOUBLE AGENTS IN NORTH KOREA

I'm a contemplative daredevil—an angel-wrestling, magic carpet-riding lover of the impossible. You're a cynical optimist—a reformed smart-ass who's worked out a deal with your evil twin. I predict that our collaborations will be legendary, our cahoots numinous. We'll teach emergency dance lessons on the beach just after the hurricane has passed; we'll take long romantic strolls on tightropes stretched over yawning abysses; we'll spend the night in sleeping bags on Emily Dickinson's grave in Amherst, sipping absinthe and acting out her fantasies of making love; we'll sit in the back row of a musty theater at a midnight-to-dawn marathon of the old *Planet of the Apes* movies, tickling each other's ribs and gnawing on each other's elbows and giving each other past-life readings in loud whispers that annoy the three other weirdos in the place. Are you ready to relax your search for the meaning of life so you can be the meaning of life? Come find me. I'll be sitting on the post office steps with a toy sheriff's badge on my lapel and my ego half-unzipped. We can trade clothes in the alley and rollerblade out to the nearest bridge for a spitting-into-the-wind contest.

Only you can prevent the genocide of the imagination

apocalypse. sublime convulsion. outlaw sacraments. friendly shocks. generous danger. dissident enlightenment. joyous upheaval. lusty compassion. guerrilla splendor. mutinous splendor. fertile chaos. secret freedom. reverent pranks. defiant apotheosis. dutiful delight. beatific orgasms. rowdy bliss. freaky purity. blasphemous reverence. wild discipline. ironic sincerity. holy uproar. radical curiosity. teasing healing. impartial passion. rebellious kindness. insane poise. zany dignity. fanatical balance. iconoclastic listening. orgasmic empathy. studious playfulness. rigorous flexibility. exuberant discernment. erudite jubilation. bewildering enlightenment. ecstatic gratitude. unselfish pride. fiendish benevolence. aggressive sensitivity. skillful receptivity. ethical mischief. astute innocence. insurrectionary beauty. illegal truth. divine subversion. taboo justice. unauthorized healing. reverent insurgency. sacred transgression. spiritual anarchy. sweet

Prayer for Us

This is a perfect moment. It's a perfect moment because I have been inspired to say a gigantic prayer. I've been roused to unleash a divinely greedy, apocalyptically healing prayer for each and every one of us—even those of us who don't believe in the power of prayer.

And so I am starting to pray right now to the God of Gods the God beyond all Gods . . . the Girlfriend of God . . . the Teacher of God . . . the Goddess who invented God.

DEAR GODDESS, you who always answer our very best questions, even if we ignore you:

Please be here with us right now. Come inside us with your sly slippery slaphappy mojo. Invade us with your silky succulent salty sweet haha.

Hear with our ears, Goddess. Breathe with our lungs. See through our eyes.

DEAR GODDESS, you who never kill but only change:

I pray that my exuberant, suave, and accidental words will move you to shower ferocious blessings down on everyone who reads or hears this benediction.

I pray that you will give us what we don't even know we need—not just the boons we think we want, but everything we've always been afraid to even imagine or ask for.

DEAR GODDESS, you wealthy anarchist burning heaven to the ground:

Many of us don't even know who we really are. We've forgotten that our souls live forever. We're blind to the fact that every little move we make sends ripples through eternity. Some of us are even ignorant of how extravagant, relentless, and practical your love for us is.

Please wake us up to the shocking truths. Use your brash magic to help us see that we are completely different from we've been led to believe, and more exciting than we can possibly imagine.

Guide us to realize that we are all unwitting messiahs who are much too big and ancient to fit inside our personalities.

DEAR GODDESS, you sly universal virus with no fucking opinion:

Help us to be disciplined enough to go crazy in the name of creation, not destruction.

Teach us to know the distinction between oppressive self-control and liberating self-control.

Awaken in us the power to do the half-right thing when it is impossible to do the totally right thing.

And arouse the Wild Woman within us—even if we are men.

DEAR GODDESS, you who give us so much love and pain mixed together that our morality is always on the verge of collapsing:

I beg you to cast a boisterous love spell that will nullify all the dumb ideas, bad decisions, and nasty conditioning that have ever cursed all of us wise and sexy virtuosos.

Remove, banish, annihilate, and laugh into oblivion any jinx that has clung to us, no matter how long we have suffered from it, and even if we have become accustomed or addicted to its ugly companionship.

Conjure an aura of protection around us so that we will receive an early warning if we are ever about to act in such a way as to bring another hex or plague into our lives in the future.

DEAR GODDESS, you psychedelic mushroom cloud at the center of all our brains:

I pray that you will inspire us to kick our own asses with abandon and regularity.

Give us bigger, better, more original sins and wilder, wetter, more interesting problems.

Help us learn the difference between stupid suffering and smart suffering.

Provoke us to throw away or give away everything we own that encourages us to believe we're better than anyone else.

Brainwash us with your compassion so that we never love our own freedom more than anyone else's freedom.

And make it illegal, immoral, irrelevant, unpatriotic, and totally tasteless for us to be in love with anyone or anything that's no good for us.

DEAR GODDESS, you riotously tender, hauntingly reassuring, orgiastically sacred feeling that is even now running through all of our soft, warm animal bodies:

I pray that you provide us with a license to bend and even break all rules, laws, and traditions that hinder us from loving the world the way you do.

Show us how to purge the wishy-washy wishes that distract us from our daring, dramatic, divine desires.

And teach us that we can have anything we want if we will only ask for it in an unselfish way.

DEAR GODDESS, you who just pretend to be crazy so you can get away with doing what's right:

Help us to be like you—wildly disciplined, voraciously curious, exuberantly elegant, shockingly friendly, fanatically balanced, blasphemously reverent, mysteriously truthful, teasingly healing, lyrically logical, and blissfully rowdy.

And now dear God of Gods, God beyond all Gods, Girlfriend of God, Teacher of God, Goddess who invented God, I bring this prayer to a close, trusting that in these pregnant moments you have begun to change all of us in the exact way we needed to change in order to become the gorgeous geniuses we were born to be.

Amen
Om
Hallelujah
Shalom
Namaste
More power to you

Oh, but one more thing DEAR GODDESS,
you pregnant slut who scorns all mediocre longing:

Please give us donkey clown piñatas full of chirping crickets,
ceramic spice jars containing 10 million-year-old salt from the Himalayas,
gargoyle statues guaranteed to scare away the demons,
lucid dreams while we're wide awake,
enough organic soup and ice cream to feed all the refugees,
emerald parachutes and purple velvet gloves and ladders made of melted-down guns,
a knack for avoiding other people's personal hells,
radio-controlled, helium-filled flying rubber sharks to play with,
magic red slippers to contribute to the hopeless,
bathtubs full of holy water to wash away our greed,
secret admirers who are not psychotic stalkers,
mousse cakes baked in the shapes of giant question marks,
stories about lightning strikes that burn down towers where megalomaniacal kings live,
solar-powered sex toys that work even in the dark,
knowledge of secret underground rivers,
mirrors that the Dalai Lama has gazed into,
and red wagons carrying the treats we were deprived of in childhood.

GUERRILLA ORACLE

Clues to the Rebel Grail

Four Dignities
of the
Warrior's Path

In Tibetan Buddhism's "Four Dignities of the Warrior's Path," courage and ferocity are absent. In fact, the qualities regarded as essential for being a warrior have nothing in common with the training regimens of Marines or football players or lobbyists.

The first dignity is often translated in English as meekness, but that word doesn't convey its full meaning. "Relaxed confidence" is a more precise formulation—a humble feeling of being at home in one's body.

Perkiness, or irrepressible joy, is the second dignity. To develop it, a warrior cultivates the habit of seeing the best in everything and works diligently to avoid the self-indulgence of cynicism.

The third is outrageousness. The warrior who embodies this dignity loves to experiment, is not addicted to strategies that have been successful in the past, and has a passionate objectivity that's free of the irrelevant emotions of hope and fear.

The fourth dignity is inscrutability, or a skill at evading the pigeonholes and simplistic definitions that might limit the warrior's inventiveness while fighting for his or her moral vision.

SACRED ADVERTISEMENT

*Your dogged quest for ever-more-useful freedom
and practical ecstasy is brought to you by the
Venezuelan body of water whose Spanish name is
translated "The River That Loses and Finds Itself."*

181

You're a Prophet

Your imagination is the single most important asset you possess. It's your power to create mental pictures of things that don't exist yet and that you want to bring into being. It's the magic wand you use to shape your future.

And so in your own way, you are a prophet. You generate countless predictions every day. Your imagination is the source, tirelessly churning out images of what you will be doing later.

The featured prophecy of the moment may be as simple as a psychic impression of yourself eating a fudge brownie at lunch or as monumental as a daydream of some year building your dream home by a lake or sea.

Your imagination is a treasure when it spins out scenarios that are aligned with your deepest desires. In fact, it's an indispensable tool in creating the life you want; it's what you use to form images of the conditions you'd like to inhabit and the objects you hope to wield. Nothing manifests on this planet unless it first exists as a mental picture.

But for most of us, the imagination is as much a curse as a blessing. We're often just as likely to use it to conjure up premonitions that are at odds with our conscious values. That's the result of having absorbed toxic programming from the media and from our parents at an early age and from other influential people in our past.

Fearful fantasies regularly pop up into our awareness, many disguising themselves as rational thoughts and genuine intuitions. Those fearful fantasies may hijack our psychic energy, directing it to exhaust itself in dead-end meditations.

Every time we entertain a vision of being rejected or hurt or frustrated, every time we rouse and dwell on a memory of a painful experience, we're blasting ourselves with a hex.

Meanwhile, ill-suited longings are also lurking in our unconscious mind, impelling us to want things that aren't good for us and that we don't really need. Anytime we surrender to the allure of these false and trivial and counterproductive desires, our imagination is practicing a form of black magic.

This is the unsavory aspect of the imagination that the Zen Buddhists deride as the "monkey mind." It's the part of our mental apparatus that endlessly spins out pictures that zip around with the energy of an agitated animal. If we can stop locating our sense of self in the relentless surge of the monkey mind's slapdash chatter, we can be fully attuned to the life that's right in front of us. Only then are we able to want what we actually have.

But whether our imagination is in service to our noble desires or in the thrall of compulsive fears and inappropriate yearnings, there is one constant: The prophecies of our imagination tend to be accurate. Many of our visions of the future do come to pass. The situations we expect to occur and the experiences we rehearse and dwell on are all-too-often reflected back to us as events that confirm our expectations.

Does that mean our mental projections create the future? Let's consider that possibility. What if it's at least partially true that what we expect will happen does tend to materialize?

Here's the logical conclusion: It's downright stupid and self-destructive to keep infecting our imaginations with pictures of loss and failure, doom and gloom, fear and loathing. The far more sensible approach is to expect blessings.

That's one reason why I'm reverent in composing my messages for you. If I'm to be one of the influences you invite into the intimate sanctuary where you hatch your self-fulfilling prophecies, I want to conspire with you to disperse fear and invoke relaxation and joy.

Your Prophecies

Make five prophecies about yourself and five about the world.

CRIMES THAT DON'T BREAK ANY LAWS

We're psychically assaulted by dangerous images and sickening words every day. The media relentlessly blast us with their trendy doom and gloom fixation, generating an endless onslaught of messages about how bad life is and what a mess the future will bring. The entertainment industry force-feeds us insipidly paranoid scenarios that keep our fear reflexes chronically throbbing.

Is this acceptable to you? It's not to me.

Our eyes and ears are constantly scalded by blistering harangues to buy stuff we don't really need. The sacred temples of our imaginations are pounded ruthlessly by smart bombs whipped up by evil advertising geniuses in their Madison Avenue laboratories. Our ability to envision the astounding intricacy and richness of the web of life has gotten hijacked and hooked on decadent fantasies about new possessions that would allegedly make us happier.

I for one am no longer willing to absorb the dazzling psychic toxins that sting and sap and wound our lust for life. I reject the epidemic obsession with big bad nasty things and flashy trite empty-hearted things. I say it's time for us to rise up and fight back—to reconsecrate and regenerate our imaginations. Here are my demands.

DEMAND #1: I demand that Amnesty International launch a crusade against a grievously unacknowledged form of terrorism. I call this crime against humanity the genocide of the imagination.

DEMAND #2: I demand that you refuse to be entertained by bad news. I demand that you seek out and create stories that make you feel strong and joyous and enigmatic.

DEMAND #3: I demand that *People* magazine do a cover story on "The World's 50 Sexiest Perpetrators of Beauty, Truth, and Love."

DEMAND #4: I demand that you learn the difference between your own thoughts and those of the celebrities who have demonically possessed you.

DEMAND #5: I demand that you wear underpants on your head and dance naked in slow motion whenever you watch TV movies about tormented geniuses who supposedly create great art but treat everyone in their lives like crap.

DEMAND #6: I demand that the sadomasochist storytellers disguised as journalists give prominent coverage to the startling fact that the world has become dramatically less violent since the end of the Cold War, and that we are currently living in the most peaceful era the human race has ever known. I further demand that the worshipers of cynicism who pretend to be clear-seeing news writers acknowledge that death rates from cancer are declining; that rising rates of intermarriage are helping to dissipate ethnic and religious strife worldwide; that Americans' IQ scores have been steadily rising for a long time; that the number of people living in poverty in the developing nations is declining dramatically; that the world is steadily becoming more free, and is now the most free it has ever been;

and that the miracle of your breathing transpires about 10 million times a year, even though you never have to will it to continue.

I have more demands, but I want to make sure you know that your imagination and the imaginations of everyone you know are at risk. And who's responsible? Who are the perpetrators of the genocide of the imagination? I call them the entertainment criminals.

They're the nihilistic creators and dramatis personae who spread the propaganda that trouble and strife and disintegration are more worthy of our attention than integrity and splendor and quantum leaps.

The entertainment criminals are the decadent fools who preach the bizarre doctrine that witty gloom is the mark of a deep thinker. They are the educated idiots who try to trick us into believing that optimism is solely for naive fools with no aptitude for critical thinking.

The visionary philosopher Buckminster Fuller said, "When I am working on a problem, I never think about beauty. I think only of how to solve the problem. But when I have finished, if the solution is not beautiful, I know it is wrong."

To the entertainment criminals, Fuller's perspective is heretical. With the know-it-all certainty of religious fanatics, they imply with every word and image they produce that there is rarely such a thing as a beautiful solution.

DEMAND #7: I demand that the salesmen of degradation who pass themselves off as storytellers give themselves the challenge of creating engaging sagas whose plots are not driven by violence, alcoholism, abuse, suicide, prostitution, bigotry, lawsuits, greed, crashes, pathology, crime, disease, and torture.

I heard an interview with the German film actor Udo Kier. He specializes in playing villains. "Evil has no limit," he sneered, blustering like a naughty genius. "Good has a limit. It is simply not as interesting."

How many times have I heard that idiotic cliché? Most everyone everywhere seems to agree with Udo Kier. And I'm in a tiny minority in my belief that evil is boring. There seem to be few thinkers, communicators, and creators who share my curiosity about exploring the frontiers of righteous pleasure and amusing truth and boisterous integrity.

> **"The surest defense against evil is extreme individualism, originality of thinking, whimsicality, even eccentricity. Evil is a sucker for solidarity. It always goes for big numbers, for confident granite, for ideological purity, for drilled armies and balance sheets."**
> **—Joseph Brodsky**

Some pretenders do make counterfeit attempts: Hollywood producers who produce sentimental fantasies with artificially happy endings, advertising executives who sell the pseudo-positivity of narcissistic comfort, and New Age gurus who ignore the darkness with their one-dimensional appeals to sweetness and light.

DEMAND #8: I demand that the demoralizing propagandists who impersonate objective reporters go ahead and confess that the acreage devoted to organic farming is increasing rapidly all over the world; that violent child abduction by strangers has dropped precipitously; that the birthrate among teenage mothers is the lowest it has been in decades; that most HMO executives now believe prayer and meditation can expedite the healing process; that vast supplies of frozen natural gas lie beneath the oceans, harboring more potential energy than all of the world's oil reserves, and could be mined with the right technology; that if forced to decide between having a bigger penis and living in a world where there was no war, 90 percent of all men would pick universal peace; and that the giant timber company, Congolaise Industrielle des Bois, voluntarily agreed to stop cutting down trees in a virgin rain forest in the Congo.

DEMAND #9: I demand that the purveyors of despair who pretend to be dispassionate observers of the human condition go ahead and disclose that the 10 most beautiful words in the English language are chimes, dawn, golden, hush, lullaby, luminous, melody, mist, murmuring, and tranquil; that Greenland is literally covered with rubies; that Java sparrows prefer the music of Bach over that of Schoenberg; that math experts have determined there are 1.96 trillion ways to lace up your shoes; that the Inuit term for making love is translated as "laughing together in bed"; and that according

Primordial Gossip

to Buckminster Fuller, "pollution is nothing but resources we're not harvesting."

The word "imagination" gets little respect. For many people, it connotes "make-believe" and is primarily the domain of children and artists. But the truth is that your imagination is the engine of your destiny. It's the single most important tool you have in your daily campaign to be free. It's the source of every act of liberation you will ever need to pull off.

That's why it's so disturbing to know that all over the planet, the imagination is deeply wounded—paralyzed by the media's nonstop onslaught of toxic psychic waste. How can you generate images that energize you to create your highest good if your mind's eye is swarming with dazzling yet vacuous and fear-inducing stories crafted by the most monumental brainwashing juggernaut in the history of the world?

To get a sense of the growing devastation, I suggest you wander around a grade school playground at recess. You'll hear kids' conversations overflowing with the degrading narratives they've absorbed from their favorite sources of information and stimulation.

I call this ongoing tragedy the genocide of the imagination. Because of it, many people cannot access their greatest magical power. They have forsaken the sanctity of their sacred temples, allowing them to be defiled with soulless images and stories that are at odds with their deepest desires. As a result they live incoherent lives corroded by chronic anxiety.

DEMAND #10: When you're too well-entertained to move, screaming is good exercise. Which is why I demand that you scream frequently whenever you're soaking up slick crap generated by the imaginations of people who are devoted to money, power, and ego instead of love, reverence, and play.

DEMAND #11: Recognizing that the epidemic of sleep-deprivation and the widespread impoverishment of dream life play a key role in abetting the genocide of the imagination, I demand that you get at least eight hours of sleep every night.

DEMAND #12: I demand new video games with socially redeeming value, like a game called "NirvanaStorm," in which players negotiate eight levels of Buddhist revelation with a character who resembles the Dalai Lama.

DEMAND #13: Since the genocide of the imagination is at least partly the result of men monopolizing the entertainment and news industries, I demand that women fill half of all jobs at ABC, MTV, CNN, NBC, PBS, NPR, CBS, FOX, *Newsweek, Time, The Wall Street Journal, The New York Times,* AP, Reuters, and *USA Today.* I further demand an affirmative action program for the image of God: From now on She must be depicted on at least 15 percent of all TV shows as an African American mother of four.

DEMAND #14: I demand a one-month global media fast. Avoid all newspapers, magazines, TV, movies, radio, and Internet for 30 days. Return to the primordial silence or else! To expedite purification during this time of renewal, I demand that you discuss your dreams with your loved ones every morning and gather your friends for storytelling circles every evening.

If we hope to prevent the genocide of the imagination, we've got to perpetrate massive, mirthful attacks of pronoia. But we have to do it without acting like True Believers, because fanaticism is anathema to our cause. Our strategy is to be blithe and flexible as we learn not just to believe, but actually perceive the truth that life is a benevolent conspiracy designed to keep mutating our immortal souls until they're so far beyond perfection that perfection is irrelevant.

We *will* succeed. We will overthrow the doom and gloom fixation and make the cause of zoom and boom irresistible. Our parties will be better than theirs. Our jokes will be funnier, our jobs more enjoyable, our lovemaking more revelatory. We'll dream up tricks to create an environment in which it's more fun and interesting to talk about wise bliss than clever cynicism.

We will build shrines devoted to righteous pleasure and amusing truth and boisterous integrity in the ugliest places we know. We will unleash praise and gratitude without regard for the taboos we shatter thereby. And we will perform senseless acts of altruistic chutzpah everywhere we go.

DEMAND #15: I demand that if the disinformation specialists who masquerade as communicators intend to keep feeding their addiction to stories of misfortune and breakdown, they must give equal time to those of us who specialize in stories about redemption and renewal. That's all I demand: Give us a mere 50 percent of the airwaves and pages and bandwidths.

CRIMES THAT DON'T BREAK ANY LAWS: THE THEORY

When most people think of a prank, they visualize bad though funny trouble committed by angry, vulgar guys. You might remember the time some teenager you knew went to the house of a hated adult. The kid put a paper bag full of dog poop on the porch, lit it with a match, rang the doorbell, and ran away. When his victim came to the door and saw the flames, he stamped on it.

This kind of mayhem has unfortunately come to be regarded as the very definition of tricky mischief. But it's actually a distorted caricature of the art form. Driven by revenge and the desire to humiliate, it mindlessly reinforces the outmoded nonsense of "us versus them." The typical macho prankster is proud of feeling nothing but scorn for what he mocks. He performs the dehumanization of his target as he affirms the feelings of superiority he feeds through his alienation.

The pronoaic trickster, in contrast, uses the prank as a loving tool for obliterating hierarchy, as a leveler of elitist pretensions. She's not driven by revenge or one-upmanship. She empathizes as she disrupts, seeking not to discredit and embarrass the target of her mischief, but to shock it into becoming more itself. Hers is a celebration of the collaborative impulses of the soul instead of the instinctual self-aggrandizement of the ego. The pronoiac prankster loves what she profanes. Weaving her fate together with her target's, she honors her relationship with it even as she tweaks it out of its literalism.

A pronoiac prank, though it may be surprising, is ultimately friendly. It romances the contradictions with crafty compassion. It's a cheerful strategy to extinguish the tawdry glamour of the antiquated "us versus them."

The piece of writing on pages 184–186 of this book is the text of a pronoiac prank. On three occasions, I've performed "Crimes That Don't Break Any Laws" as an act of guerrilla performance art: once in the parking lot of a shopping mall in Pittsburgh, a second time on the sidewalk in front of a San Francisco nightclub where the Sleater-Kinney band was about to play, and on another occasion at a nursing home in Tucson.

In his book *Temporary Autonomous Zone,* Hakim Bey (hermetic.com/bey) provides other examples of pronoiac pranks. Burglarize houses, he suggests, but instead of stealing the residents' possessions, leave behind beautiful and confusing gifts. Spread gossip about the unsung genius of people who don't get nearly enough credit for their good work. Bolt up brass commemorative plaques in places (public or private) where you have experienced a revelation or had a fulfilling sexual experience. Take a few friends and a boom box to an all-night grocery store and engage in ecstatic, whirling dervish-style dancing in the aisles until you're thrown out. Scrawl the following graffiti in courthouse lavatories and on playground walls: "I dare you to scare yourself with how beautiful you are."

Pick people at random, says Bey, and convince them they're the heirs to an enormous, useless, and amazing fortune—say, 5,000 square miles of Antarctica, or an aging circus elephant, or a leper colony in India, or a collection of alchemical manuscripts. Later they will come to realize that for a few moments they believed in something extraordinary, and will perhaps be driven to cultivate a more intense quest for exhilarating adventures.

SACRED ADVERTISEMENT
This part of our show is brought to you by the gesture recorded in a photograph of the Dalai Lama playfully messing with Desmond Tutu's cap at a gathering of Nobel Peace Prize winners.

Receptivity Remedies

Alert, relaxed listening is the radical act at the heart of our pronoiac practice.
Curiosity is our primal state of awareness.
Wise innocence is a trick we aspire to master.
Open-hearted skepticism is the light in our eyes.

If you choose to become a practitioner of pronoia, your life will suck. It has to suck. Let me explain. As you cultivate the arts of gathering and bestowing the blessings that the universe is always conspiring to send your way, your life will suck in the best senses of the word.

First, your life will suck in the same way that you use a straw to compel a thick milk shake to disobey gravity and squirt into your mouth. Metaphorical translation: You'll work hard to pull toward you the resources you need, perhaps even exerting yourself with a force that goes against the natural flow.

Your pronoiac life will suck in a second way: like a powerful vacuum cleaner that inhales dirt from the floor and makes it disappear. You will have a sixth sense about getting rid of messes that are contaminating your clarity.

Here's a third interpretation: Once you commit yourself to the art of pronoia, you will most likely develop an unusually dynamic form of receptivity. Whether you're a man or woman, you'll be like a macho male with a willful intention to be like a welcoming female. As a result, you'll be regularly sucked into succulent opportunities you would never have come upon if you had let your pop nihilistic conditioning continue to dominate you. Your openness to uplifting adventures will make it easier for serendipitous miracles to find you and draw you in.

Let's take one more poetic leap of faith as we meditate on the metaphor. As you devote yourself to the art of making yourself available, your life will suck in the way that movements of the mouth and lips and tongue during close encounters with intimate partners stimulate pleasurable feelings.

I've tried a wide variety of meditative practices from many traditions. I've calmed myself through rhythmic breathing; watched with amusement as the nonstop procession of images paraded across my mind; visualized images of deities; cultivated unconditional love; chanted

The Chinese poet Yuan Mei (1716–1798) was heavily influenced by Buddhism but was also skeptical toward it. He was eager to learn from the very tradition he criticized. The book of his selected poems is entitled *I Don't Bow to Buddhas.*

Galileo Galilei didn't invent the telescope, but he created a better version of the first primitive model. In the early 17th century, he used it to make astronomical discoveries that contradicted the Catholic Church's cosmology. The caretakers of the old guard were furious. "The Earth is the center of the universe," they told him after he announced he had detected moons revolving around Jupiter. "What you say you have seen is impossible." They refused to even look through Galileo's new tool.

In later years, scientists adopted the Church's attitude toward a variety of other phenomena, including meteorites and dinosaurs. Until the 1800s, wrote Roy Gallant in *Sky & Telescope,* "the scientific community scoffed at those who believed stones fell from the heavens, though meteorites had been seen to fall and had been collected since ancient times by the Chinese and Egyptians. As stones continued to rain down from the sky, learned scientists explained them away as condensations of the atmosphere or concretions of volcanic dust."

Similarly, until the 19th century, scientists didn't believe that large reptiles had once lived on the earth. Throughout history, ordinary people had always found what we now call fossils, but the experts decreed that they could not possibly be the remains of an ancient extinct species.

The moral of the story as far as you and I are concerned: As smart as we may be and as much as we might know, there are truths we have become dead set against believing, let alone seeing.

Ancient Greek philosopher Pythagoras is known as "the father of numbers." He taught that mathematics provides the ultimate truth about reality. His otherwise productive career went through a rough patch when one of his students found that the square root of two is an "irrational" number that can't be expressed as a simple fraction.

Play a joke on your fear. Honor your anger. Capitalize on your guilt. Kill your own death.

"Impossible!" said Pythagoras. His system was built on the axiom that there are no such numbers. Yet he couldn't refute the student's proof. The student was punished—by some accounts drowned—for expressing such rank impudence. The brilliant theorist could not deal with the threat to his dogma.

At the end of one of his columns, the *San Francisco Chronicle*'s Jon Carroll corrected misinformation he'd provided in an earlier piece. "My dreamy view of the dissent during the Civil War was perhaps just a tiny bit completely wrong," he noted. He went on to admit that contrary to what he had asserted, President Lincoln ruthlessly quashed dissidents. "My apologies to the truth," Carroll concluded.

"Think dangerously!" read the headline on today's bright yellow piece of junk mail. That sounded inviting. I'm always eager for help in overthrowing my certainties.

But the product being promoted inside the envelope was just a piece of propaganda: a magazine touting Libertarian dogma. I threw it in my recycling bin along with all the other doctrinaire rants I constantly get from fundamentalists of every stripe, including right-wing religious nuts and left-wing atheists, New Age Pollyannas and intellectual cynics, science-haters and shills for scientism.

Can you imagine what it would feel like to *really* think dangerously? To question *every* belief, your own as much as everyone else's? French author André Gide spoke my mind: "Trust those who are seeking the truth; doubt those who find it."

To an optimist, the glass is half-full. A pessimist says the glass is half-empty. But in the eyes of an engineer, the glass is twice as big as it needs to be.

Dionysian Manifesto

One night a cop comes upon a man who's squatting beneath a streetlight and gazing here and there at the sidewalk. "Lose something?" the cop asks. "I dropped my wallet in that dark alley over there," the man replies, pointing some distance away. "Then why are you looking for it here?" the cop inquires reasonably. "Because the light is much better here," says the man.

Receptivity is not a passive state. Nor is it a blank emptiness, waiting around for whatever happens to come along. In urging you to cultivate receptivity, I don't mean you should become a lazy do-nothing bereft of goals, reacting blindly to whatever life throws in front of you.

Receptivity is a robust readiness to be surprised and moved, a vigorous intention to be awake to everything you can't control. When you're receptive in the pronoiac style, you have strong ideas and a powerful will and an eagerness to disseminate your unique blessings, but you're also animated by the humble certainty that you have a lot to learn.

Most people associate innocence with naiveté. Conventional wisdom regards it as belonging to children and fools and rookies who lack the sophistication or experience to know the tough truths about life.

But the Beauty and Truth Lab recognizes a different kind of innocence. It's based on an understanding that the world is always changing, and therefore deserves to be seen fresh every day. This alternative brand of innocence is fueled by an aggressive determination to keep clearing one's imagination of all preconceptions.

"Ignorance is not knowing anything and being attracted to the good," wrote Clarissa Pinkola Estés in *Women Who Run with the Wolves*. "Innocence is knowing everything and still being attracted to the good."

"The ancient Greeks knew that learning comes from playing," writes Roger von Oech in his book *A Whack on the Side of the Head: How You Can Be More Creative*. Their word for education, *paideia,* he says, was close to their word for play, *paidia.*

Millard Fillmore was President of the United States from 1850 to 1853. He was the last holder of that office who was neither a Democrat nor Republican.

I propose that we make him a symbol of freedom from the rigged con game that is America's two-party political system, as well as an inspiring image for those of us who aspire to rise above *every* either-or dichotomy. Fillmore can be our mascot as we declare our independence from the dualistic ways of thinking that threaten to ensnare us. He'll be an emblem that rouses us to transcend the simplistic arguments spewed by fanatical devotees of the Us-Versus-Them racket. We will invoke the Blessed Fillmore whenever we want to escape the vise.

"The knowledge I'm interested in is not something you buy and then have and can be comfortable with. The knowledge I'm interested in keeps opening wider and wider, making me smaller and more amazed, until I see I cannot have it all—and then delight in that as a freedom." —Heather McHugh, *Hinge & Sign*

"The most exciting phrase to hear in science, the one that heralds new discoveries, is not 'Eureka! I have found it' but rather 'That's funny . . .'" —Isaac Asimov

"Objection, evasion, joyous distrust, and love of irony are signs of health. Everything absolute belongs to pathology." So proclaimed Friedrich Nietzsche in *Beyond Good and Evil.* Note well that he used the adjective "joyous" to describe distrust, not "cynical" or "grumbling" or "sour." The key to remaining vital and strong while questioning every so-called absolute is to cultivate a cheerful, buoyant mood as you do it.

"The only real voyage consists not in seeking new landscapes, but in having new eyes; in seeing the universe through the eyes of another, one hundred others—in seeing the hundred universes that each of them sees." —Marcel Proust, translated by Kiyotesong

Here are three of our deepest spiritual aspirations, which we invite you to steal for your own use: 1. to develop the capacity to thrive in the midst of raging contradictions; 2. to be discerning as we protect ourselves from people's flaws while at the same time being generous as we celebrate their beauty; 3. to refrain from dividing the world into two groups, those who help and agree with us and those who don't.

"As a free deed, meditation is naturally individual, uniquely our own. It is where we most fully *become* ourselves. Its practice is also always individual. There are no rules. Just as every potter will elaborate his or her own way of making pots, so every person who meditates will shape his or her own meditation. No two people will do a given meditation in exactly the same way. The same meditation practiced daily will be different every time. Every meditation is experimental. One never knows what is going to happen. Improvisation is essential ... Meditation is something to play with ... There is no 'wrong' way of doing the meditation, except not doing it!" —Christopher Bamford, *Start Now!: A Book of Soul and Spiritual Exercises*

Though I'm critical of journalists and scientists, it's not because I don't love them. On the contrary, they have been great teachers, both through the ideas and information they've lavished on me and in the way they've compelled me to learn how important it is to question all my sources of ideas and information. I will keep trying to master the pure objectivity that their professions enshrine as the highest ideal. And I will remain both skeptical toward and receptive to their offerings.

The dangers of excessive politeness are perfectly exemplified in the medieval legend of Parzival, Arthur's purest knight. His quest for the Holy Grail leads him to a castle where he is welcomed by a wounded lord. At dinner, a mysterious bowl captivates Parzival's attention. He's dying to know more about it, but he holds his tongue. His training as a knight has taught him that it's uncourteous to express too much curiosity.

Tragically, he doesn't realize that he has arrived at the very place where his quest could be satisfied. The wounded lord is actually the Fisher King, the marvelous bowl is the Grail, and he is being presented with a magical test. The test consists of a simple task: to ask about the bowl. Because Parzival fails to do so, the king does not reveal the secret and does not give him the Grail.

The next morning, Parzival wakes up to find the castle empty, and he leaves having missed the very opportunity he wanted most.

"Be homesick for wild knowing." —Clarissa Pinkola Estés, *Women Who Run with the Wolves*

SACRED ADVERTISEMENT

"Receptivity Remedies" is brought to you by Mahatma Gandhi's autobiography,
The Story of My Experiments with Truth.

You Are a Disseminator of Pronoia

The Beauty and Truth Lab is coming to you live from
your repressed memory of paradise, reminding you that
all of creation loves you very much.

Even now, secret allies are cooking up mysteries that will excite
you and incite you for years to come.

Even now, the Earth, moon, and sun are collaborating to make
sure you have all you need to make your next smart move.

But here's the loaded question: Are you willing to start loving
life back with an equal intensity? The adoration it offers you has
not exactly been unrequited, but there is room for you to be
more demonstrative.

Half of the art of pronoia is about being improvisationally
receptive to life's elaborate scheme to shower you with blessings.
The other half is about learning to be a co-conspirator who
assists life in doling out blessings—to help everyone *else* get
exactly what they need, exactly when they need it.

Visualize yourself being able to recognize the raw truth about the
people you care about. Imagine that you can see how they
already embody the beauty their souls' codes have promised as
well as how they still fall short of embodying that beauty.
Picture yourself being able to make them feel appreciated
even as you inspire them to risk changes that will activate
more of their souls' codes.

INSCRUTABLE PRONOIA THERAPY

Experiments and exercises in becoming a tenderly objective, cagily candid, fanatically balanced Master of Iconoclastic Listening

Report your answers and research results below

1 If you're typical, your natural curiosity was virtually extinguished at an early age by mediocre teachers, boring lessons, and oppressive classrooms. Have you ever wondered what your life would be like if your imagination hadn't been squelched? What adventures you might have sought out if your natural love of learning hadn't been crushed?

Let's launch a quest to undo the damage. Imagine I've handed you an *undiploma:* your official release from the soul-death of your formal education; the beginning of the healing of your wounded love of learning. What's the first thing you'll do to invoke a steady stream of inspired teachers and invigorating lessons?

2 When I lived in Santa Cruz, I had an acquaintance named Barnaby who lived at a remote rural community called Last Chance Farm. Combination shaman, wise elder, and lunatic, he would on rare occasions slip into town and lead me on fact-finding missions he dubbed whirlygigs. "Steep yourself with the intention of attracting lessons you don't know you need," he'd say, and then we'd meander the streets at random, going places I'd never been and striking up conversations with strangers with whom I seemingly had nothing in common. Barnaby described the whirlygig as an urban version of the walkabout, which for Aborigines is a time when they leave work and wander out into the bush to commune with the mysteries of nature.

Carry out your own whirlygig. When you're done, write an essay entitled, "People, Places, and Things I Didn't Know I Loved."

3 The factor most likely to drive us to addiction or illness is a lack of intimate contact with spirit. We all need a daily dose of vastness. Paradoxically, many of us would also benefit from more microscopic vision.

Because we're so deprived of divine connection, we're half-dreaming all the time; our unconscious pining for the eternal source distracts us from the vivid little glories that are splayed out around us. And so we miss the Divine Wow from both directions.

Try this: Prime your connection with spirit by focusing your attention on tones and shapes you usually miss: reflections in windows, the sky between the oak tree's branches, the shadows on the water, the two different emotions in a friend's eyes and mouth.

The old Hawaiian word polikua *refers to the dip that lies just on the other side of the horizon, where the eye can't quite reach.*

4 The German religious reformer Martin Luther was fond of referring to the faculty of reason as a "damned whore." He believed it gave itself in service to any old theory, often propping up specious arguments rooted in hidden emotional agendas.

Though I regard my ability to reason as a prized asset, I confess to having some of Luther's mistrust. Like most of us, I have corrupted my logical mind by sometimes using it to disguise and rationalize my subjective biases.

Can you imagine having so much self-awareness that you never turn your reasoning ability into a whore? Are you willing to probe with merciless honesty for the unconscious feelings that drive you to believe what you do, and to analyze the ways you mask your subjective biases as "objective fact"? Could you suspend all your preconceptions and greet every situation with a scrupulously open mind? Try to live up to that high standard for a period of three days.

5 To the ancient Chinese, pigs were sacred because they could eat anything and turn it into energy. The creatures were regarded as masters of transmutation. Nothing, not even garbage, was unusable to them. The Chinese aspired to be like pigs in the sense of being able to learn from and derive benefit from every experience, not just the tidy, tasteful ones.

Borrowing this strategy, name two garbage-like experiences that you could turn into fuel for your growing urge to be a pronoiac co-conspirator.

Inscrutable Pronoia Therapy

6 Is it really healthy to have a shrill, 25-words-or-less opinion about everything, as radio and TV talk shows seem to imply? Would anyone object if now and then you served as a compassionate witness about the hot-button issues? Is it conceivable that you could simply sit on the fence in the midst of the wars of words and beam articulate sympathy at both sides?

Yes, you can. You have the rebellious resourcefulness to be a freedom fighter without hating anyone. Go out and prove it. Document your success here.

7 "You may enjoy this movie if you shut down enough brain cells. I turned off all except the ones needed to remember where I parked my car." This observation comes from a critic's evaluation of *Charlie's Angels: Full Throttle,* but I've read similar comments in many reviews of other films and entertainment. Indeed, it's an approach that many intelligent people employ routinely in response to the shiny slop our culture offers up.

What about you? Do you assume you have to make yourself dumber in order to have fun? Has the well-crafted inanity of the world caused you to shut down your sensitivity? Work to reverse this trend. You'll receive help from unexpected sources if you do.

8 Send out a big "Hey!" and "What's up?" to all the little voices in your head. Start with the still, small voice that's always ready to provide concise responses to the ingenious questions you come up with. But also acknowledge the others as well—even the crabby, reactive naysayer that's forever on the lookout for insults to your dignity, however tiny or unintentional; even the worrywart that wakes you up in the middle of the night to pester you with doubts and fears.

Love all the little voices in your head. Celebrate their vitality, their persistence, their attentiveness. Consider the possibility that you're lucky to have such a zealous group of advisors, even if all but one of them are off the mark a lot of the time.

"An idea that is not dangerous is unworthy of being called an idea at all."
—Elbert Hubbard

9 There is a proverb from the American culture of the 21st century that I'd like to run by you: "Never reveal all you know, confess everything you feel, show how much you care, or give all you have."

Inscrutable Pronoia Therapy

Prove this proverb wrong. Cultivate power by revealing all you know, confessing everything you feel, showing how much you care, and giving all you have.

10 If you're a left-winger, you may think right-wingers are stupid or evil or both. If you're a right-winger, you probably hold the same attitudes about left-wingers. A similar pattern prevails between most other groups that hold opposing views. You're a rare person if you've never looked at a certain group of people and thought to yourself, "They are all sick idiots."

But I'm asking you to find out what it's like to dispense with judgments like that. In fact, try living without any scapegoats whatsoever. If even for an hour per week, visualize the possibility that those with whom you disagree might be sincere and well meaning.

I'm not suggesting this exercise merely because it's a nice thing to do. It will also have the effect of giving you access to parts of your own intelligence that have been closed off to you.

11 Oceans are not exactly teeming with life. In fact, they're mostly barren, and could rightly be called "wet deserts." Likewise, not all your emotions, even those that come in floods, are fertile. Some are automatic reactions that have discharged thousands of times since they were first programmed into you many years ago. They're often negative, and are not organic but mechanical, being inappropriate to the events that seem to stimulate them. They became fixtures when you were a very different person than you are now. Identify these.

12 In preparing for a performance at Burning Man in 2004, I bought 18 jars of pigs' feet at the grocery store, 200 pairs of white underpants at Costco, and 22 alarm clocks at the drugstore. None of the clerks who took my money expressed a peep of interest in the reasons for my peculiar and prodigious orders. Their lack of curiosity was astounding to me. Do you have any theories that might explain it?

13 Many of us don't always know what we feel. We may have a vivid sense that we feel *something,* but we're not sure what it is. That's why musicians, writers, actors, and other creative people play such a crucial role in our emotional lives. Their work can help us articulate the enigmas fermenting within us.

But here's the problem: A majority of the artists who are easiest for us to find aren't exceptionally smart or original; they specialize in expressing hackneyed feelings. Many of the very best creators "remain in relative obscurity because of their resistance to formula efforts," writes journalist Alan Cabal. "Mediocrities latch onto whatever hits and repeat it endlessly in pursuit of cash or celebrity or both." If we look to the latter for illumination, we're cheated.

Your assignments: Get tough with the lazy or wounded part of you that is drawn to the mediocrities. Compile a roster of virtuosos who have developed a high level of proficiency in extracting esthetically exciting meaning from the fascinating chaos around us. Expose yourself exclusively to their work, devotedly avoiding the mediocrities' stuff, for a given period, say 100 days. Describe how this transforms you.

14 In *The Book of Embraces,* Uruguayan author Eduardo Galeano writes, "The fishermen of the Colombian coast must be learned doctors of ethics and morality, for they invented the word *sentipensante,* or 'feeling-thinking,' to define language that speaks the truth."

Describe a time when you pulled off the feat of thinking with your heart and feeling with your head.

"When Jesus said 'I and the Father are one,' he meant that he was connected to the raw data feed of pure experience."
—Tim Boucher

15 Here's Bruce Chatwin in *The Songlines:* "Aboriginal creation myths tell of the legendary totemic beings who had wandered over the continent in the Dreamtime, singing out the name of everything that crossed their path—birds, animals, plants, rocks, waterholes—and so singing the world into existence. Any species can be a Dreaming. A virus can be a Dreaming. You can have a chickenpox Dreaming, a rain Dreaming, a desert-orange Dreaming, a lice Dreaming."

Close your eyes and tune in to the song of a Dreaming species of your choice. Either that, or else pretend you can tune in the song of a Dreaming species.

16 Fairy tales are full of characters who suffer loss and hardship for trying to be something they're not. If they ever change their ways and accept the truth about themselves, their luck improves dramatically. It's interesting, then, to contemplate the fact that our culture adores film and TV actors, who get extensive training in pretending to be someone other than who they really are. We nurse a similar obsession with politicians, whose specialty resembles that of actors: Their vocation requires them to dissemble constantly.

Inscrutable Pronoia Therapy

Are you one of the enthralled? Do you share our collective entrancement with people who lie about themselves for a living? If so, experiment with what happens if you wean yourself. Try being cautious about exposing yourself to influences that might encourage you to be something you're not.

17 For 24 hours, call everything by a name different from the one it usually has. Example: Call the TV a "hyacinth," call the refrigerator a "cloud," and call a chair an "electric knowing."

What is your most valuable secret? What forbidden art do you practice? What taboo dream do you draw on?

18 In her book *Vodou Visions*, Sallie Ann Glassman argues that Vodou (the preferred spelling among its practitioners) is an authentic religious tradition worthy of respect. She acknowledges that some of its beliefs may seem unusual. For instance, Vodou's calm, gentle, sweet spirits are not always forces for good, while some of its hot, turbulent, revolutionary spirits are not necessarily bad.

Although not a practitioner of Vodou, Raymond Chandler had some related counsel: "The disease of niceness cripples more lives than alcoholism."

Borrow this meme. Monitor the calm, gentle, sweet spirits in your life for the possibility that they may act as agents of deception or passivity. Be inspired by the creator gods and goddesses of ancient myth, who playfully forged millions of beautiful things using wind, mud, tears, and lightning. Tap into the fiery aspect of your nature that drove you out of your mother's womb and into this world in the hour when you were born.

19 "The greatest thing a human soul ever does in this world is to see something," wrote art critic John Ruskin in his book *Modern Painters*. "To see clearly is poetry, prophecy, and religion, all in one."

Proposed experiment: Lay aside everything you think you know, suspend your reflex to impose your beliefs on every situation you encounter, and behold the world exactly as it is. Assume that by doing so you can change everything you see into a more beautiful version of itself.

Inscrutable Pronoia Therapy

★11

Stronger than hate,
wetter than water,
deeper than the abyss,
more exotic than trust

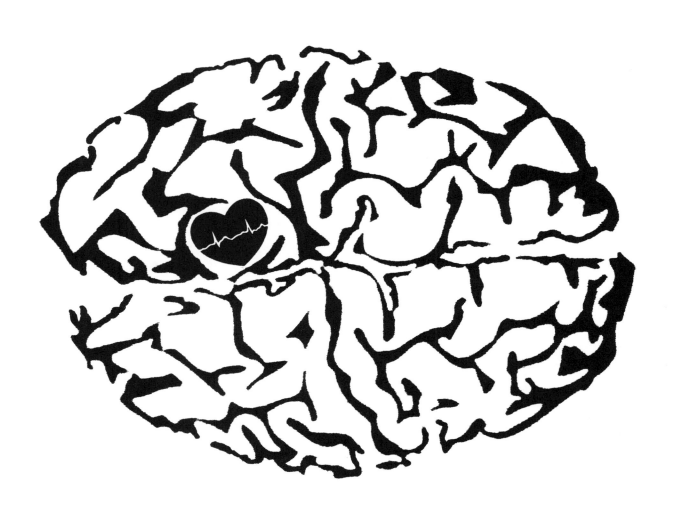

Tummler and Ondinnonk

While you carry out your experiments in pronoia, your words of power are *tummler* and *ondinnonk*.

Tummler is a Yiddish term derived from *tumlen,* "to make a racket." A *tummler* stirs up a commotion, makes things happen, and incites people to action through his or her affectionate agitation. Clowning and pranks may be part of a *tummler*'s repertoire.

Ondinnonk is an Iroquois word with two related meanings: 1. a secret wish of the soul, especially as revealed in dreams; 2. the spiritual part of our nature that longs to do good deeds.

Use your two words of power together: Let your *ondinnonk* guide you as you carry out your mission as a pronoiac *tummler.*

LIBERATE YOUR IMAGINATION

Let me remind you who you really are: You're an immortal freedom fighter who longs to liberate all sentient creatures from their suffering. You're a fun-loving messiah who devoutly wants to help all of your fellow messiahs claim the ecstatic awareness that is their birthright.

Try to remember. You're a vortex of fluidic light that has temporarily taken on the form of a human being, suffering amnesia about your true origins. And why did you do that? Because it was the best way to forge the identity that would make you such an elemental force in our 14-billion-year campaign to bring heaven all the way down to earth.

I'm not speaking metaphorically here. You are a mutant deity in disguise—not a Buddha or a Christ exactly, but of the same lineage and conjured from the same fire. You have been around since the beginning of time and will be here after the end. Every day and in every way, you're getting better at playing the preposterously amusing master game we all dreamed up together before the Big Bang bloomed.

Lately, I must admit, our work has seemed almost comically impossible. Many of us have given in to the temptation to believe that everything is upside-down and inside-out. Ignorance and inertia, partially camouflaged as time-honored morality, seem to surround us. Pessimism is enshrined as a hallmark of worldliness. Compulsive skepticism masquerades as perceptiveness. Mean-spirited irony is chic. Stories about treachery and degradation provoke a visceral thrill in millions of people who think of themselves as reasonable and smart. Beautiful truths are suspect and ugly truths are readily believed.

So no, at this peculiar turning point in the evolution of our 14-billion-year-old master game, it's not easy to carry out our mission. We've got to be both wrathful insurrectionaries and exuberant lovers of life. We've got to cultivate cheerful buoyancy even as we resist the temptation to swallow thousands of delusions that have been carefully crafted and seductively packaged by those messiahs among us who bravely volunteered to play the role of know-it-all deceivers.

We have to learn how to stay in a good yet unruly mood as we overthrow the sour, puckered mass hallucination that is mistakenly referred to as "reality."

Maybe most importantly, we have to be ferociously and single-mindedly dedicated to the cause of beauty and truth and love even as we keep our imaginations wild and hungry and free. We have to be both disciplined and rowdy.

What can we do to help each other in this work?

First, we can create safe houses to shelter everyone who's devoted to the slow-motion awakening of humanity. These sanctuaries might take the form of temporary autonomous zones like festivals and parties and workshops, where we can ritually explore and potentiate the evolving mysteries of pronoia. Or they might be more enduring autonomous zones like homes and cafes and businesses where we can get regular practice in freeing ourselves from the slavery of hatred in all of its many guises.

What else can we do to help each other? We can conspire together to carry out the agenda that futurist Barbara Marx Hubbard names: to hospice what's dying and midwife what's being born. We need the trigger of each other's rebel glee as we kill off every reflex within us that resonates in harmony with the putrefaction. We need each other's dauntless cunning as we goad and foment the blooming life forces within us.

Here's a third way we can collaborate: We can inspire each other to perpetrate healing mischief, friendly shocks, compassionate tricks, irreverent devotion, holy pranks, playful experiments, and crazy wisdom.

Huh? What do tricks and mischief and jokes have to do with our quest? Isn't America in a permanent state of war? Isn't it the most militarized empire in the history of the world? Hasn't the paranoia about terrorism decimated our civil liberties? Isn't it our duty to grow more serious and weighty than ever before?

On the contrary: I say this is the perfect moment to take everything less seriously and less personally and less literally.

Permanent war and the loss of civil liberties are immediate dangers. But they are only symptoms of an even larger, long-term threat to the fate of the earth: the genocide of the imagination.

Elsewhere, on pages 184–186 of this book, I have identified pop-nihilist storytellers as the vanguard perpetrators of this genocide of the imagination. But there is another culprit as well: fundamentalism.

The fundamentalist takes everything way too seriously and way too personally and way too literally. He divides the world into two camps, those who agree with him and those who don't. There is only one right way to interpret the world, and a million wrong ways. Correct belief is the only virtue.

To the fundamentalist, the liberated imagination is a sinful taboo. He not only enslaves his own imagination to his ideology, but wants to enslave our imaginations, too.

And who are the fundamentalists? Let's not remain under the delusion that they are only the usual suspects—the religious fanatics of Islam and Christianity and Judaism and Hinduism.

There are many other kinds of fundamentalists, and some of them have gotten away with practicing their

tragic magic in a stealth mode. Among the most successful are those who believe in what Robert Anton Wilson calls fundamentalist materialism. This is the faith-based dogma that swears physical matter is the only reality and that nothing exists unless it can be detected by our five senses or by technologies that humans have made.

Life has no transcendent meaning or purpose, the fundamentalist materialists proclaim. There is no such thing as a divine intelligence. The universe is a dumb accidental machine that grinds on endlessly out of blind necessity.

I see spread out before me in every direction a staggeringly sublime miracle lovingly crafted by a supernal consciousness that oversees the evolution of 500 billion galaxies, yet is also available as an intimate companion and daily advisor to every one of us. But to the fundamentalist materialists, my perceptions are indisputably wrong and idiotic.

Many other varieties of fundamentalism thrive and propagate. Every ideology, even some of the ones I like, has its share of true believers—fanatics who judge all other ideologies as inferior, flawed, and foolish.

I know astrologers who insist there's only one way to do astrology right. I know Buddhists who adamantly decree that the inherent nature of life on Earth is suffering. I know progressive activists who sincerely believe that every single Republican is either stupid or evil or both. I know college administrators who would excommunicate any psychology professor who dared to discuss the teachings of Carl Jung, who was in my opinion one of the greatest minds of the 20th century. I know pagans who refuse to consider any other version of Jesus Christ beyond the sick parody the Christian right has fabricated.

None of the true believers like to hear that there are at least three sides to every story. They don't want to consider the hypothesis that everyone has a piece of the truth.

And here's the really bad news: We all have our own share of the fundamentalist virus. Each of us is fanatical, rigid, and intolerant about products of the imagination that we don't like. We wish that certain people would not imagine the things they do, and we allow ourselves to beam hateful, war-like thoughts in their direction.

We even wage war against our own imaginations, commanding ourselves, sometimes half-consciously, to ignore possibilities that don't fit into our neatly constructed theories. Each of us sets aside certain precious beliefs and symbols that we give ourselves permission to take very seriously and personally and literally.

Our fundamentalism, yours and mine, may not be as dangerous to the collective welfare as, say, the fundamentalism of Islamic terrorists and right-wing Christian politicians. It may not be as destructive as that of the CEOs who worship financial profit as the supreme measure of value, and the scientists who ignore and deny every mystery that can't be measured, and the journalists, filmmakers, novelists, musicians, and pundits who relentlessly generate rotten visions of the human condition.

But still: We are all infected, you and I. We are fueling the war against the imagination. What's your version of the virus?

Try to remember. We are reverent insurgents ... convulsive beautifiers ... rowdy avatars. We have more mojo at our disposal than we realize. But if we hope to navigate our way through this peculiar turning point in the evolution of our 14-billion-year-old master game, we will have to summon previously untapped reserves of that mojo. We will have to keep our imaginations wild and hungry and free, and make sure that all of our fellow messiahs, even those who volunteered to play the roles of ignorant deceivers, have the chance to keep their imaginations wild and hungry and free.

How might we start curing ourselves of the fundamentalist virus and move in the direction of becoming more festive and relentless champions of the liberated imagination?

For starters, we can take everything less seriously and less personally and less literally.

We can laugh at ourselves at least as much as we laugh at other people. We can blaspheme our own gods and burn our own flags and mock our own hypocrisy and satirize our own fads and fixations.

And we can enjoy and share the tonic pleasures of healing mischief, friendly shocks, compassionate tricks, irreverent devotion, holy pranks, playful experiments, and crazy wisdom.

Don't make nasty comments about yourself behind your own back.

Do play soccer in bunny slippers at dawn in a supermarket parking lot with a gang of Vipassana experts who have promised to teach you the Balinese monkey chant.

Don't decorate your thigh with a slipshod tattoo of the devil pushing a lawn mower.

Do wear a T-shirt that says, "Of all the things I've lost, I miss my mind the most."

Don't glide into a bar, scout around for the person whose face has the most pain etched in it, and ask that person to come home with you.

Do eat ripe organic strawberries that have been genetically modified and irradiated. Do chain-smoke Marlboros as you peddle your exercise bicycle. Do wander through a garbage dump while listening to Mozart on your iPod.

Don't pile up framed photos of old flames in a vacant lot and drive a monster truck over them.

Do stage a slow-motion water balloon fight.

Don't gaze into a mirror and spout, "God damn you, why can't you be different from who you are?!"

Do shake your fist at the night sky as you call out, "I defy you, stars!"

Don't tell people you've just met that you are the reincarnation of Genghis Khan.

Do pretend sometimes that maybe you mean the opposite of what you're saying as well as what you're saying.

Don't lie on a floor surrounded by wine-stained poetry books, crumpled Matisse prints, abandoned underwear, and half-eaten bowls of corn flakes as you stare up at the ceiling with a blank gaze, muttering gibberish and waving your hands as if swatting away demons.

Do run along the tops of cars during a traffic jam, escaping from the bad guys as you make your way to a helicopter that takes you to a spot hovering over an erupting volcano, into which you drop the *Buns of Steel* video.

Don't put your soul up for auction on eBay.

Do write a cookbook filled with recipes you've channeled from dead celebrities.

If you come upon a lamp with a genie in it, don't wish you had a magic wand.

Liberate Your Imagination

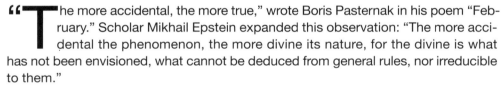

The More Accidental, the More True

"The more accidental, the more true," wrote Boris Pasternak in his poem "February." Scholar Mikhail Epstein expanded this observation: "The more accidental the phenomenon, the more divine its nature, for the divine is what has not been envisioned, what cannot be deduced from general rules, nor irreducible to them."

If we pursue this line of thought to its logical conclusion, we may decide that the most useful sources of illumination are not always holy books, revered dogma, and great truths that everyone has heard. They might also be serendipitous anomalies that erupt into the daily routine and break the trance of ordinary awareness. "The tiny spark," Epstein writes, "is the precise measure of the holiness of the world." (Source: Mikhail Epstein, "Judaic Spiritual Traditions in the Poetry of Pasternak and Mandel'shtam." Translated from Russian by Ruth Rischin. *Symposium. A Quarterly Journal in Modern Literatures,* Volume 52, No. 4)

When you're an aspiring master of pronoia, you see the cracks in the facades as opportunities; inspiration erupts as you career over bumps in the road; you love the enticing magic that flows from situations that other people regard as rough or crooked. "That which is not slightly distorted lacks sensible appeal," wrote poet Charles Baudelaire, "from which it follows that irregularity—that is to say, the unexpected, surprise and astonishment—is an essential part and characteristic of beauty."

Wabi-sabi is a Japanese term that refers to a captivating work of art with a distinctive flaw that embodies the idiosyncratic humanity of its creator. An aqua groove in an otherwise perfectly green ceramic pot may give it wabi-sabi. A skilled blues singer who intentionally wails out of pitch for a moment may be expressing wabi-sabi.

Wabi-sabi is rooted in the idea that perfection is a kind of death.

"The essence of Wabi-sabi is that true beauty, whether it comes from an object, architecture, or visual art, doesn't reveal itself until the winds of time have had their say. Beauty is in the cracks, the worn spots, and the imperfect lines." —Todd Dominey

Wabi-sabi is a kind of beauty that's imperfect, impermanent, and incomplete, says Leonard Koren in his book *Wabi-Sabi for Artists, Designers, Poets and Philosophers.* It differs from Western notions that beauty resides in the "monumental, spectacular, and enduring." It's about "the minor and the hidden, the tentative and the ephemeral: things so subtle and evanescent they are almost invisible at first glance."

"When bread is baked, some parts are split at the surface, and these parts which thus open, and have a certain fashion contrary to the purpose of the baker's art, are beautiful, and in a peculiar way excite a desire for eating. Again, figs, when they are quite ripe, gape open; and in the ripe olives the very circumstance of their being near to rottenness adds a peculiar beauty to the fruit. And the ears of corn bending down, and the lion's eyebrows, and the foam which flows from the mouth of wild boars, though they are far from being beautiful, please the mind." —Marcus Aurelius, *Meditations,* translated by George Long

"I am done with great things and big plans, great institutions and big success. I am for those tiny, invisible loving human forces that work from individual to individual, creeping through the crannies of the world like so many rootlets, or like the capillaries." —William James, "The Will to Believe"

"The great lessons from the true mystics, from the Zen monks, is that the sacred is in the ordinary, that it is to be found in one's daily life, in one's neighbors, friends, and family, in one's back yard, and that travel may be a flight from confronting the sacred. To be looking everywhere for miracles is a sure sign of ignorance that everything is miraculous." —Abraham H. Maslow, *Religions, Values, and Peak Experiences*

"If you love the sacred and despise the ordinary, you are still bobbing in the ocean of delusion." —Lin-Chi, *The Taoist Classics,* translated by Thomas Cleary

"The lesson that life constantly enforces is 'Look underfoot.' You are always nearer to the true sources of your power than you think. The lure of the distant and the difficult is deceptive. The great opportunity is where you are. Don't despise your own place and hour. Every place is the center of the world." —Naturalist John Burroughs

"We want to be God in all the ways that are not the ways of God, in what we hope is indestructible or unmoving. But God is fragile, a bare smear of pollen, that scatter of yellow dust from the tree that tumbled over in a storm of grief and planted itself again." —Deena Metzger, *Prayers for a Thousand Years,* edited by Elizabeth Roberts and Elias Amidon

"Nature exults in abounding radicality, extremism, anarchy. If we were to judge nature by its common sense or likelihood, we wouldn't believe the world existed. In nature, improbabilities are the one stock in trade. The whole creation is one lunatic fringe . . . No claims of any and all revelations could be so far-fetched as a single giraffe." —Annie Dillard, *Pilgrim at Tinker Creek*

"What we want from poetry is to be moved from where we now stand. We don't just want to have our ideas or emotions confirmed. Or if we do, we turn to lesser poems, poems that are happy to tell you that killing children is bad, chopping down the rain forest is bad, dying is sad. A good poet would agree with those sentiments, but would also strive for an understanding beyond those givens." —James Tate, *American Poetry Review*

"What we want from the news is to be moved from where we now stand. We don't just want to have our ideas or emotions confirmed. Or if we do, we turn to lesser news, news that is happy to tell you about the same old chaos and sadness. A good reporter would notice the themes that are repeating for the millionth time, but would also strive to find stories beyond the givens." —Vimala Blavatsky, Beauty and Truth Lab

In his book *The Medusa and the Snail,* science writer Lewis Thomas said that the English word "error" developed from a root meaning "to wander about, looking for something." That's why he liked Darwin's idea that error is the driving force in evolution.

"The capacity to blunder slightly is the real marvel of DNA," said Thomas. "Without this special attribute, we would still be anaerobic bacteria and there would be no music."

Dionysian Manifesto

RAUCOUS PRONOIA THERAPY

Experiments and exercises in becoming a rigorously flexible, seriously delirious, studiously playful Master of Zany Dignity

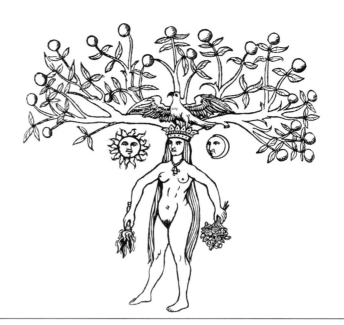

Report your answers and research results below

1 Is the universe inherently friendly to humans? The answer's got to be either "yes, definitely" or "no, not really." It can't be in between. Whatever you may be inclined to believe, you've got to agree that there's no way to know which is true with absolute certainty.

So then isn't it stupid and self-destructive to live your life as if the universe is unfriendly? Doing so tends to cast a pall over everything. But if on the other hand you proceed on the hypothesis that the universe is friendly, you're inclined to interpret everything that occurs as a gift, however challenging it may be to figure out its purpose at first.

For three weeks, try living your life as if the latter theory were true.

2 Some people feel polluted when they look at porn; others when they eat Pringles and Twinkies. Personally, I experience a sense of violation after being exposed to celebrity gossip. And yet, if I've learned anything about how to maintain a healthy relationship with purity, it's that a fanatical adherence to it is as dangerous as a compulsive rejection of it. This will be especially true for you as you practice the art of pronoia. I urge you, therefore, to rebel cagily now and then against your urge to be a perfectly nice perpetrator of goodness and beauty and truth and justice.

Here's one method that might work: Use sacred sarcasm to motivate your allies to cooperate more with life's benevolent conspiracy. For instance, you might say the following to a certain female friend, hoping it will prod her to swear off self-punishing behavior forever: "You sure honored your ancestors and left an inspiring legacy for your descendants during the month you spent courting that alcoholic womanizer."

Or say something like this to a person who has not been asking for enough in return for her gifts: "No doubt you impressed the gods and earned a heap of karmic credit for all the free work you gave away to that megalomaniac who ripped you off so brilliantly."

3 "The seed cannot sprout upwards without simultaneously sending roots into the ground," says an Egyptian proverb. Keep that thought in mind as you head into your next phase of growth. What part of you needs to deepen as you rise up? What growth needs to unfold in the hidden places as you gravitate toward the light? How can you go about balancing and stabilizing your ascension with a downward penetration?

4 If I ever produce a self-help manual called *The Reverse Psychology of Getting Everything You Want,* it will discuss the following paradoxes:

a. People are more willing to accommodate your longings if you're not greedy or grasping.

b. A good way to achieve your desires is to cultivate the feeling that you have already achieved them.

c. Whatever you're longing for has been changed by your pursuit of it. It's different from what it was when you felt the first pangs of desire. To make it yours, then, you'll have to modify your ideas about it.

d. Be careful what you wish for because if your wish does materialize it will require you to change in ways you didn't foresee.

Review your own life and identify experiences that exemplify these four principles.

5 A golden eagle with a seven-foot wingspan shot down out of the overcast sky and dived at my friend Maura's pet cockatoo, which was perched on the branch of an oak tree not 30 feet from her back door. Five of us watched with alarm from the outdoor table where we were sipping tea. We leaped up and began howling, hoping to scare the giant predator away. I ran to grab a baseball bat that Maura's son had left lying near the tree.

Then the unexpected happened. The eagle did not attack the cockatoo, but settled down peacefully beside it. Nor did the cockatoo flee. The two sat there together like old friends for about 10 minutes before the bigger bird flew away.

Are you the eagle or the cockatoo?

6 "Is it bad to live without a hell?" poet Pablo Neruda asks in *The Book of Questions.* Let's add these

Raucous Pronoia Therapy

queries to his: Is it dangerous to live without the awakening force that an enemy provides? Is it naive to think you can achieve great success without the driving motivation that comes from thinking about ideas you hate?

Consider the issue from another angle. Dentists love tooth decay. Treating cavities provides them with a steady income. Likewise, exterminators are dependent on termites, lawyers need crime, and priests crave sinners. Lots of people have symbiotic connections with nasty stuff. In fact, isn't it true that most of us nurture our feelings for the things we love to despise and fear?

What's your favorite poison or adversary? Assume that your exposure to pronoia is changing you in ways that will require you to update your relationship with it. Speculate on how you'll go about this task.

Change the burned-out light bulb. Water the plants. Take your multi-vitamin. Wash the dishes. Put new batteries in the TV remote. Bow down to the Great Mystery.

7 Of all the animals in the world, the fly is the most unloved. It annoys us with its zigzag buzzing. When it lands in our food, we lose our appetite, knowing it carries residues of disgusting things it has preyed on.

But in the creation story of the Chelan Indians, the fly is given a heroic role to play because of its speed. And in modern parlance, people say they'd like to be a fly on the wall in a place where interesting conversations take place.

"More than the rat, the cat, the dog or the horse, the fly is our familiar," writes Steven Connor in his book *Fly.* As much as the insect has always been despised, in some cultures it has also been an icon of liberty: "Each fly is king of his own country. He knows no laws or conventions. He has no work to do—no tyrannical instinct to obey. What freedom is like his?"

Throw a party for a fly buzzing around your home. Give it a name and call it your beloved pet. Through the power of your love, establish a telepathic connection with it and ask it to teach you how to be the sovereign of your own country.

Raucous Pronoia Therapy

8 I give thanks for the dented rusty brown and gray 1967 Chevy 10 pick-up truck that my neighbor parks askew on the shoulder of the road near my house. Its messy beauty snaps me back to sanity when my own perfectionism threatens to de-soul me, or when all the shiny, sleek, polished things of the world are on the verge of hypnotizing me into believing that only they should be considered attractive.

Are there equivalent triggers in your life?

9 Shirley Chisholm was the first black woman elected to Congress. While serving seven terms, she was an outspoken warrior who fought tirelessly for the rights of women, minorities, and the poor. "My greatest political asset, which professional politicians fear," she said, "is my mouth, out of which comes all kinds of things one shouldn't always discuss for reasons of political expediency."

One of Chisholm's most famous exploits was her visit to segregationist politician George Wallace in the hospital after he was shot. Her supporters complained that she was consorting with the enemy. But years later it paid off. Wallace helped her win the votes of southern congressmen when she sponsored legislation to give domestic workers a minimum wage.

Proposed experiment: Be like Chisholm. Even as you open your big mouth to articulate controversial truths, reach out to those who disagree with you.

10 Do you have a negative opinion of clouds? Are you inclined to regard them as symbols of gloom and malaise, interruptions in what you wish would always be clear blue sky?

If so, I'll ask you to revise your view. Consider the fact that in Chinese mythology, there are *xiangyun,* or "lucky clouds" that are harbingers of great blessings. Deities may even ride on them for pleasure. Among the Zuni Indians, the monster known as the Cloud Eater was feared because he devoured clouds that might bring replenishing rain. And modern meteorologists know that white, fluffy cumulus clouds are signs that fair weather is on the way.

Armed with these ideas, go out in search of your own personal lucky clouds.

11 When playing the card game known as bridge, you're fortunate if you're dealt no cards of any particular suit. It allows you to use the trump suit to win tricks.

Raucous Pronoia Therapy

Identify a situation in your own life where a lack of a certain resource can work to your advantage, allowing you to be a free agent, an X-factor, a wild card; freeing you to capitalize on loopholes that aren't normally available; giving you access to luck that comes to you through what you're missing.

12 I was never the class clown. I am not a troubled but devilishly handsome wastrel living on a trust fund. I've never beaten up anyone, have steadfastly not aspired to write like Raymond Carver, and have never played strip Scrabble with a junkie violinist on a leaky waterbed in a Key West penthouse. There are so many things I am not and will never be, and I'm glad I know about them. It helps me stay focused on exactly who I am. What about you? Who aren't you? Fantasize about all the paths you will never take. Put it in writing.

13 The "Kumulipo" is an old Hawaiian prayer chant that poetically describes the creation of the world. The word literally means "beginning-in-deep-darkness." Here darkness doesn't connote gloom and evil. Rather, it's about the inscrutability of the embryonic state; the obscure chaos that reigns before germination. Talk about a time you dwelt in kumulipo.

14 Do you have an unconscious belief that the forces of evil are loud, vigorous, and strong, while good is quiet, gentle, and passive? Gather evidence that contradicts this irrational prejudice.

Are you secretly suspicious of joy because you think it's inevitably rooted in wishful thinking and a willful ignorance about the true nature of reality? Expose these suspicions as superstitions that aren't grounded in any objective data you can actually prove.

Do you fear that when you're in the presence of love and beauty you tend to become softheaded, whereas you're likely to feel smart and powerful when you're sneering at the ugliness around you? As an antidote, for a given amount of time, say a week or a month or a year, act as if the following hypothesis were true: that you're more likely to grow smarter when you're in the presence of love and beauty.

15 My friend Riley was the first member of her family to attend college. None of her hardscrabble Irish forebears had ever pursued higher education. In her senior year, Riley began having nightmares of her relatives trying to stop her from finishing school. In one recurring dream, her great-grandfather burned all her textbooks. In another, a mob of aunts and uncles tackled her and held her down as she tried to get to class.

Raucous Pronoia Therapy

Despite these psychic obstacles, Riley persevered in her studies and eventually got her diploma. The week after graduation, she had another dream: A host of her ancestors came to her in the form of a great choir singing songs in praise of her success.

Riley's psychotherapist speculated that the dream meant she had not only overcome the inertia of her heritage, but had also healed an ancient wound of her family going back many generations.

Is there a similar accomplishment you're capable of? What is it?

16 While putting on your shirt or blouse some morning, fasten the top button in the second hole, the second button in the third hole, and so on all the way down. For the rest of the day, preserve this dishevelment with all your composure intact, even in the face of odd stares and snide comments. If anyone says, "Hey, your shirt's buttoned wrong," reply calmly, "No, it isn't. I buttoned it this way on purpose."

17 Everyone you know has a different idea about who you are, and none of those notions is exactly the same as the image you have of yourself. In other words, there are hundreds of unauthorized versions of you in addition to the one you believe in.

You don't have much power to control this, right? Maybe. But let's pretend, just for now, that you do. Pray, cast spells, squint your eyes and tense your fists and make grunting sounds as you try to psychically compel public opinion into alignment with your own picture of yourself.

Favorite words:
smolder husk quiver
amethyst membrane aurora
crucible sphinx mahogany
lather humus quench
tincture mist excavate
tendril reliquary potion
marrow

18 Mythology is replete with tales of substances that can be both curative or harmful, depending on how they are obtained and used. The ancient Greeks believed that Asclepius, founder of medicine, possessed vials of Medusa's blood. "With what had been drawn from the veins of her left side," Robert Graves notes, "he could raise the dead; with what had been drawn from her right side, he could destroy instantly."

What has been a comparable substance or influence in your own life?

19 The spider has a bad reputation, symbolically speaking. In myths and folk tales, it's often portrayed as the spinner of delusions and snares. Many therapists interpret dreams of spiders as signs of paranoia, gossip, enemies, or predatory relationships.

This may sometimes be true. But I prefer to regard the spider as primarily a symbol of secret help or of a building process going on behind the scenes. In my dreams, the appearance of a spider suggests that though my conscious ego isn't smart enough to fix my current problem, a solution is being woven for me by an unknown intelligence, perhaps a spiritual ally or an unconscious part of my own brain.

Give an example of spider power from your life.

20 Somewhere in the world is a tree that has been struck by lightning in such a way that the scorch marks reveal your initials. Locate that tree.

Somewhere in the world there is a treasure that has no value to anyone but you, and a secret that is meaningless to everyone except you, and a frontier that possesses a revelation only you know how to exploit. Go in search of those things.

Somewhere in the world there is a person who could ask you the precise question you need to hear in order to catalyze the next phase of your evolution. Do what's necessary to run into that person.

21 From the window of my office I look down on a blackberry bush whose berries are now ripening. In the last 20 minutes, I've watched a sparrow figure out the best way to feast. At first the bird tried to land on the flimsy branches of the bush, but after a few tries it realized they couldn't hold its weight. Its revised strategy was to grab a single berry in mid-swoop and alight on the branch of a nearby apple tree so it could relax with its meal. It did this 10 times.

Are you willing to collect your reward a little at a time? Explain how you will do it.

22 "As above, so below" is the maxim at the heart of the Western Hermetic tradition. It implies that the nature of the cosmos is intimately reflected here on

Raucous Pronoia Therapy

Earth—and vice versa. Everything we imagine to be far away and "out there" has a parallel in the here and now. A miniature heaven resides within each of us, although we may not yet have activated its full potential. Astrologers go so far as to say that we all contain the spiritual essences of the planets. A little bit of Mars lives in your reproductive system and the corresponding parts of your psyche; Jupiter inhabits your solar plexus and feeds your will.

At the Beauty and Truth Lab, we act as if the hypothesis "as above, so below" is a useful perceptual filter. We urge pronoia lovers to experiment with it in the course of their daily practice.

Now and then, though, we recommend that you exercise caution about promoting unity. Writer Hanna Blank sets the right tone. "My cat attempted to adorn a prayer rug with a hairball, and I had to stop her," she says. "There are some instances in which we do not wish all things to be interconnected."

What things don't you want interconnected?

"Pronoiac mojo"
is the drug-free cultivation
of playfully altered states
of awareness for the purpose
of accomplishing
practical miracles.

23 Psychotherapists say it's not only naughty but counterproductive to blame others for your problems. A skilled practitioner urges her clients to accept responsibility for the part they've played in creating their predicaments. The reason is as much pragmatic as it is ethical: When you're obsessed with how people have done you wrong, you have little ambition to change the behavior in yourself that led you into the mess.

While I endorse this approach, I also know that dogmatic adherence to it can warp your mental health as much as any other form of fanaticism. That's why I urge you to enjoy an unapologetic Blame Fest. Choose a time when you will find fault with everyone *except* yourself. Howl in protest at the unfair slights people have committed against you. Wallow in self-pity as you visualize the clueless jerks who have done you wrong. For best results, bark your complaints in the direction of no one but God, an inanimate object, or your mirror.

Raucous Pronoia Therapy

24 There's a three-mile stretch of Interstate 880 south of Oakland, California, that I call the Singing Highway. For reasons I don't understand, it generates low humming melodies every time I drive over it, similar to the guttural chants of Tibetan monks. Sometimes I swear I can even hear lyrics.

Once, as I was driving to the airport on the Singing Highway, I swear I heard the same lyric repeating over and over again: "a shortcut to the path with heart / a shortcut to the path with heart / a shortcut to the path with heart."

Where's the path with heart for you? What would it involve for you to take a shortcut to get on it?

25 I know a dyke punk witch who loves to rub up against Hasidic Jews in the New York subway when she's menstruating. I know a mischief-maker who sneaked gobs of bacon fat into the broccoli and carrot stir-fry he cooked for his vegetarian friends.

While I'm entertained by the hijinks of these two tricksters, I have more respect for people who mess with their own totems and taboos—like my anarchist acquaintance who disturbed his fellow agitators by burning his prized black flag in front of them.

Catch my drift? It's more aesthetically pleasing to violate your own damn dogmas, not your neighbor's. Try it.

26 It's easy to see fanaticism, rigidity, and intolerance in other people, but harder to acknowledge them in yourself. Take this opportunity to identify the unique variety of the fundamentalist virus that infects you. Confess the dirty truth!

27 The modern English word "weird" is derived from the Old English term *wyrd,* meaning "destiny." By the late Middle Ages, *wyrd* had evolved into a concept similar to the Eastern notion of karma. It implied that the momentum of past events plays a strong role in shaping the future, but that human willpower can nevertheless also have a hand in creating upcoming events. In some uses, *wyrd* could even mean "the power to control destiny," as exemplified by the three Weird Sisters of Shakespeare's *MacBeth.*

Speculate about how the consequences of your past are impinging on your present situation. But also fantasize about how you might possess the ability to override them through the force of your intentions.

Raucous Pronoia Therapy

HOMEOPATHIC MEDICINE SPELL #3

BUT WE DON'T HATE THE HATERS

But we don't hate the haters

But we don't hate the haters

BUT WE DON'T HATE THE HATERS

BUT WE DON'T HATE THE HATERS

But we don't hate the haters

But we don't hate the haters

BUT WE DON'T HATE THE HATERS

W e
hate hatred WE HATE HATRED
We hate hatred WE HATE HATRED WE
HATE HATRED We hate hatred WE HATE HATRED
We hate hatred WE HATE HATRED We hate hatred WE
HATE HATRED WE HATE HATRED We hate hatred WE HATE
HATRED WE HATE HATRED We hate hatred WE HATE HATRED
We hate hatred WE HATE HATRED We hate hatred WE HATE HATRED
We hate hatred WE HATE HATRED We hate hatred WE HATE HATRED
WE HATE HATRED We hate hatred WE HATE HATRED We hate hatred
WE HATE HATRED We hate hatred WE HATE HATRED WE HATE HATRED
We hate hatred WE HATE HATRED We hate hatred WE HATE HATRED We
hate hatred WE HATE HATRED WE HATE HATRED We hate hatred WE HATE
HATRED WE HATE HATRED We hate hatred WE HATE HATRED We hate
hatred WE HATE HATRED We hate hatred WE HATE HATRED We hate
hatred WE HATE HATRED We hate hatred WE HATE HATRED WE HATE
HATRED We hate hatred WE HATE HATRED We hate hatred WE HATE
HATRED We hate hatred WE HATE HATRED WE HATE HATRED We
hate hatred WE HATE HATRED We hate hatred WE HATE
HATRED We hate hatred WE HATE HATRED We HATE
HATRED We hate hatred WE HATE HATRED WE HATE
HATRED We hate hatred WE HATE HATRED
WE HATE HATRED We hate hatred
WE HATE HATRED

The 80 Percent Rule

Readers of my horoscope column "Free Will Astrology" are sometimes surprised when I say I only believe in astrology about 80 percent. "You're a quack?!" they cry. Not at all, I explain. I've been a passionate student of the ancient art for years. About the time my over-educated young brain was on the verge of desertification, crazy wisdom showed up in the guise of astrology, moistening my soul just in time to save it.

"But what about the other 20 percent?" they press on. "Are you saying your horoscopes are only partially true?"

I assure them that my doubt proves my love. By cultivating a tender, cheerful skepticism, I inoculate myself against the virus of fanaticism. This ensures that astrology will be a supple tool in my hands, an adaptable art form, and not a rigid, explain-it-all dogma that over-literalizes and distorts the mysteries it seeks to illuminate.

During the question-and-answer segment of one of my performances, an audience member got hostile. "Why do you diss science so much?" he complained. "Science is the source of a lot of pronoia, so I would think you'd love it."

My accuser obviously hadn't read much of my work. Otherwise he'd have gathered many clues that belied his theory. In my column, for instance, I often quote reverently from peer-reviewed scientific journals like *Nature* and *Scientific American.* And I regularly extol the virtues of the scientific method. "Some of my best friends are scientists," I teased the heckler.

The fact is, I critique science no more than I do all of the systems of thought I respect and use. I believe in science about 80 percent—the same as I do in astrology, psychology, feminism, Qabala, Buddhism, left-wing political philosophy, and 23 others.

I do think science has the greatest need of loving skepticism, though. As the dominant ideology of our age, it has a magisterial reputation comparable to the infallibility accorded to the medieval Church. Its priestly promoters sell it as the ultimate arbiter of truth, as an approach to gathering and evaluating information that trumps all others.

Here's another problem: Though science is an elegant method of understanding the world, only a minority of its practitioners live up to its high standards. The field is dominated by men motivated as much by careerism and egotism as by a rigorous quest for excellence. This is common behavior in all spheres, of course, but it's a special problem for a creed that the intellectual elite promotes as the premier method for knowing the truth.

There's a further complication: Scientists are no less likely to harbor irrational biases and emotional fixations than the rest of us. They purport to do just the opposite, of course. But in fact they simply hide their unconscious motivations better, aided by the way the scientific establishment relentlessly promotes the myth that its practitioners are in pure service to objective truth. This discrepancy between the cover story and the actual state of things is, again, a universal tendency, not confined to science. But it's particularly toxic in a discipline that presents itself as the very embodiment of dispassionate investigation.

There are many scientists who, upon reading these words, might discharge a blast of emotionally charged, non-scientific derision in my direction. Like true believers everywhere, they can't accept half-hearted converts. If I won't buy their whole package, then I must be a superstitious, fuzzy-brained, New Age goofball.

To which I'd respond: I love the scientific approach to understanding the world. I aspire to appraise everything I experience with the relaxed yet eager curiosity and the skeptical yet open-minded lucidity characteristic of a true scientist.

SACRED ADVERTISEMENT

"The 80 Percent Rule" is brought to you by this excerpt from Deena Metzger's prayer:

"Let us learn the secret language of light again. Also the letters of the dark. Learn the flight patterns of birds, the syllables of wolf howl and bird song, the moving pantomime of branch and leaf, valleys and peaks of whale calls, the long sentences of ants moving in unison, the combinations and recombinations of clouds, the codices of stars. Let us, thus, reconstitute the world, sign by sign and melody by melody.

"Let us sing the world back into the very Heart of the Holy Name of God."

—Deena Metzger, Prayers for a Thousand Years, *edited by Elizabeth Roberts and Elias Amidon*

PRONOIA NEWS NETWORK

Top Secret Mass Gathering

History's largest meeting of world religious leaders was virtually unreported by the media. The top-secret event transpired in January 2002, when 200 representatives from every major faith gathered in Assisi, Italy. At the end of the conference, they issued the Assisi Decalogue for Peace, a document denouncing all violence committed in the name of God or religion. It declared, "We commit ourselves to stand at the side of those who suffer poverty and abandonment, speaking out for those who have no voice, and to working effectively to change these situations."

Eclipsing this rare outbreak of unity were many stories the media deemed more important: Mike Tyson got his boxing license; John Walker Lindh made a court appearance; the Enron hearings began. (Source: David Waters, religion columnist)

Does Reality Exist?

The Annals of Improbable Research polled its readers on the question: "Does reality exist?" Forty-two percent answered yes; 31 percent said that it most certainly does not. The other 27 percent were undecided. Some believed their reality exists but no one else's does. Two people said, "Reality exists, but you can't get to it." According to one respondent, "Reality especially exists right after a thunderstorm." Another person quoted Philip K. Dick: "Reality is that which, when you stop believing in it, doesn't go away."

Evolution of an Axiom The fundamental laws of physics may evolve as the cosmos grows older. That was the conclusion of a paper published by a team of astrophysicists in the prestigious *Physical Review Letters*.

Using the giant Keck Telescope in Hawaii, the researchers investigated the absorption of light by metal atoms in gas clouds billions of light-years away. Their results showed apparent variations in the value of the "fine structure constant," which measures the strength of the electromagnetic force that controls how electrons and photons interact.

The scientists were effectively looking back in time, gazing at light that left its point of origin billions of years ago. The fine structure constant seemed to be a smaller number then than it is now. Until their study, this constant was thought to be as immutable as the speed of light.

The implications are clear: If one supposed axiom has changed over time, others may have done so also. (Source: James Glanz and Dennis Overbye, "Anything Can Change, It Seems, Even an Immutable Law of Nature," *New York Times,* August 15, 2001)

India and China Get Rich Quick

China and India, which constitute one-third of the Earth's population, have more than twice the wealth they had in 1989. (Source: *The Economist*)

In the past 20 years, hundreds of millions of Chinese have escaped poverty and begun earning middle-class incomes. Economist Jeffrey Sachs, renowned for his work in assisting Third World nations to raise their standards of living, says, "China is the most successful development story in world history." (Source: Fareed Zakaria, "The Big Story Everyone Missed," *Newsweek,* December 30, 2002)

Returned to the Source

In 1999, the government of Canada officially created and recognized the territory of Nunavut, giving back control of a huge part of the far north to the Inuit people who have lived there for millennia. A story in *National Geographic* discussed the struggle of the Inuit to emerge from the white man's domination. In one photo, a woman named Pauloosie Muckpa crossed the tundra carrying the bloody head of a caribou, whose brains and antler tips were to be the centerpiece of a great feast. "We used to be ashamed of what we ate," she said. "But now we're not. Today we are not ashamed of who we are."

PNN is brought to you by Albert Camus' belief that "Each of us is free to stoke the crematory fires of Buchenwald or nurse lepers in an African hospital."
(Source: Notebooks 1935–1951)

Partial Truce in Drug War "The silver lining in the budget crisis affecting the states throughout this nation is that from Louisiana to Texas to Michigan, state governments are cutting prison budgets by releasing nonviolent drug offenders. There has been a steady move toward treatment instead of incarceration, and a greater understanding that drug abuse should be handled in the doctors' office, not the prison cell." —Medea Benjamin, AlterNet, alternet.org

Another Tree Savior Kinko's, the photocopy franchise with 1,100 branches in nine countries, no longer buys paper from companies that use wood from old-growth and endangered forests.

Evolution of a Poet As a young poet, Carolyn Forché pursued an academic study of her craft at placid Midwestern universities. Her first book dealt with her family, ancestry, and coming of age. Then she made a radical departure. Leaving behind familiar comforts, she moved to El Salvador at the height of its death squad activity, working as an activist. Later she lived in Lebanon during its traumatic civil war, serving as a correspondent for NPR. Her adventures in these war zones forged her into a human rights advocate and instilled her work with a moral fervor that's rare among modern poets.

Blind Compassion Watch

"In January 2003, a Muslim gas station attendant saved a New York synagogue from arson with his phone call to 911. Pakistani immigrant Syed Ali watched as a man bought gasoline, marched across the street, and began dousing the front of the temple. Police responded to Ali's call in time to stop the crime. Ali declined the mantle of hero saying 'It was a sacred place he was going to destroy.'"
—Geraldine Weis-Corbley, goodnewsnetwork.org

Pleasure Equals Peace?

"Among human beings, a pleasure-prone personality rarely displays violence or aggressive behaviors, and a violent personality has little ability to tolerate, experience, or enjoy sensuously pleasing activities. As either violence or pleasure goes up, the other goes down." —James W. Prescott, "Body Pleasure and the Origins of Violence," *The Bulletin of the Atomic Scientists,* November 1975

Breaking the Pronoia Taboo

"Everything is blooming most recklessly; if it were voices instead of colors, there would be an unbelievable shrieking into the heart of the night." —Rainer Maria Rilke, *Letters of Rainer Maria Rilke,* 1892–1910, M. D. Herter Norton, translator

"You are gods who have forgotten who they are. You are emperors who have fallen asleep and are dreaming that they have become beggars. Now beggars are trying to become emperors, in dreams they are making great efforts to become emperors, and all that is needed is to wake up!" —Osho

"The unhappy person resents it when you try to cheer him up, because that means he has to stop dwelling on himself and start paying attention to the universe. Unhappiness is the ultimate form of self-indulgence. When you're unhappy, you get to pay a lot of attention to yourself. You get to take yourself oh so seriously." —Tom Robbins, *Jitterbug Perfume*

"Souls are God's jewels." —Thomas Traherne

Thomas Merton's notion of what makes a saint saintly doesn't have to do with being a perfectly sinless paragon of virtue. The more important measure of sanctity, he said, is one's ability to see what's good and beautiful in other people. The truly godly person "retires from the struggle of judging others."

"One of the tenets of Zen is that the good poet, to be a good poet, must first be a person of good character." —Christopher Buckley

"To feel the love of people whom we love is a fire that feeds our life. But to feel the affection that comes from those we do not know, from those unknown to us, who are watching over our sleep and solitude, over our dangers and our weakness—that is something still greater and more beautiful because it widens the boundaries of our being, and unites all living things." —Pablo Neruda, *The Book of Virtues*

"The degree in which a poet's imagination dominates reality is the exact measure of his importance and dignity." —George Santayana

TWICE AS ALIVE

Tantric sex practitioners say an artful lover never makes love the same way twice.

Similarly, chanteuse Billie Holiday believed a good singer should never sing a song the same way twice. If you use all the same phrasing and melody, she said, you're failing your art.

The only Zen master we know—whose name we can't tell you because she changes it every week, and we haven't heard the latest one—likes to quote the ancient Greek philosopher Heraclitus: "You cannot step into the same river twice, for fresh waters are ever flowing in upon you."

Buddhist monk Thich Nhat Hanh has the last word: "Thanks to impermanence, everything is possible."

Midwife Genius Abroad

Around the age of 17, students in Denmark take a standardized test that determines their educational fate and, ultimately, their career path. Teens who earn a little less than the highest scores are eligible to become physicists, chemists, and theologians. The very smartest kids become doctors, psychologists, and midwives. (Source: Garrison Keilor, *National Geographic*)

Lion Rescue

In June 2004, seven men kidnapped a 12-year-old girl and held her in a remote Ethiopian wilderness. After seven days, a miracle occurred. Three lions showed up and chased the abductors away. They protected the girl until a search team arrived, then slipped away. "The lions stood guard until we found her and then they just left her like a gift and went back into the forest," said one of the rescuers.

Crime-Fighter Declares Victory

At age 94, Simon Wiesenthal decided his work was done. The renowned Holocaust survivor fought for decades to bring over 1,000 Nazi fugitives to justice, including Adolf Eichmann. "I found the mass murderers I was looking for," he said, "and I have outlived all of them." (Source: *Format* magazine)

Squat of the Century

In 1999, 40 starving artists in Paris broke into an abandoned building near the Louvre. They built studios inside and have been squatting there rent-free ever since. In 2003, the city of Paris bought the building and paid $3.5 million to renovate it so that the artists can continue to enjoy their home.

Your Gut Brain

You and I have always known that we can think with our bellies. Gut instinct, we call it. Now scientists have found evidence confirming our hunch. In *The Second Brain: Your Gut Has a Mind of Its Own,* Dr. Michael Gershon documents the evidence for a literal second brain in our stomachs and intestines. Here, in a bundle of 100 billion nerve cells, our gut reactions originate.

Sixth-Grade Zeitgeist Update

The following bons mots were scrawled on the backpacks and binders of sixth-grade girls at Greenwood School in Mill Valley, California:

Learn as if you'll live forever

Explain yourself wildly, not carefully

Wake up—but not too fast, or you might hurt yourself

Question authority, including the authority that told you to question authority

Give me chocolate or I'll scream

It's all so funny—how can you not be laughing?

When you shout "halaluya," never spell it right

Live the freakiest truth

Benevolent Pranks   One night in February 2004, anonymous mischief-makers in the English town of Pembury sneaked into 100 gardens and secretly planted an ash sapling in each one. It was hard work. The weather was terrible, and each tree had to be carefully rooted in a six-inch hole. Some residents were pleased by the unsolicited gift, while others were confused.

The Rest of the Middle East News   "In Israel, several thousand Israeli and Palestinian families living in relatively close proximity to one another, and each deeply proud of their respective nation's history and foundations and traditions, did not actively seethe in a roiling cauldron of hatred or religious bile, nor did they let the horrible atrocities some of their people are perpetrating on each other cause them to froth with self-righteousness and mad desire for war.

"They did not go about their day cowering in a pit of lost hope, fearing for their lives and wishing their neighbors extreme painful death and eternal damnation, despite all the painful evidence and political urgency currently screeching at them that they must do so immediately." —Mark Morford, *SFGate*

20,000 Years of Progress in the 21st Century

"Centuries ago people didn't think that the world was changing at all. Their grandparents had the same lives that they did, and they expected their grandchildren would do the same, and that expectation was largely fulfilled.

"Today it's an axiom that life is changing and that technology is affecting the nature of society. What's not fully understood is that the pace of change is itself accelerating, and the last 20 years are not a good guide to the next 20 years. We're doubling the paradigm shift rate, the rate of progress, every decade.

"The whole 20th century was like 25 years of change at today's rate of change. In the next 25 years we'll make four times the progress you saw in the 20th century. And we'll make 20,000 years of progress in the 21st century, which is almost a thousand times more technical change than we saw in the 20th century." —Ray Kurzweil, tinyurl.com/mzxpay

Integrity Inventory

Denmark, New Zealand, and Sweden are the least corrupt nations, according to Transparency International's survey (transparency.org).

Bomb Remedies

Earth Island Journal reports that scientists have discovered natural ways to clean up old munitions sites. If periwinkle and parrot-feather plants are grown in soil that's been bombed with TNT, they'll soak up and neutralize the noxious stuff. And pondweed absorbs and transforms nitroglycerin in land where explosives have been detonated.

Worthless Emotions

"Pain and conflict are, to a large extent, the result of a discrepancy between the way we think others should treat us, react to us, and appreciate us, and the way they actually do. Many of our miseries are thus rooted in self-pity, the most worthless of all human emotions."
—Ann Davies, bota.org

Simple Gifts

Habitat for Humanity is an organization devoted to eliminating substandard housing and homelessness. Since its inception in 1976, its affiliates have enlisted volunteer labor to build or renovate over 300,000 homes for needy people around the world. The homes are sold at no profit, and homeowners' low mortgage payments are used to build more Habitat homes.

MIRABILIA REPORT   *Mirabilia* n. modest astonishments, friendly shocks, sweet anomalies; from the Latin *mirabilia,* "marvels."

■ Romanian physicists created gaseous globes of plasma that grew, reproduced, and communicated with each other, thereby fulfilling the definition for life.

■ In an apparent attempt to raise their volume above the prevailing human din, some nightingales in big cities have learned to unleash 95-decibel songs, matching the loudness of a chainsaw.

■ Current definitions of what's normal will be regarded as pathological in 15 years.

■ The 5.5 million people who live in Papua New Guinea speak 820 different languages, or one per every 6,707 people. Two villages within an hour's walking distance of each other may use utterly different tongues.

■ Thirty-eight percent of North America is wilderness.

■ There is a statistically significant probability of world-class athletes and military leaders being born when Mars is rising in the sky.

■ Fertility clinics in the U.S. are filled to the brim with frozen human embryos. Forty thousand would-be fetuses are now on ice, waiting for a go-ahead from the couples that spawned them.

■ In the pueblos of New Mexico, bricks still measure 33 by 15 by 10 centimeters, proportions that almost exactly match those of the bricks used to build Egypt's Temple of Hatshepsut 3,500 years ago.

■ To make a pound of honey, bees have to gather nectar from about two million flowers. To produce a single pound of the spice saffron, humans have to handpick and process 80,000 flowers. In delivering the single survivor necessary to fertilize an ovum, a man releases 500 million sperm.

■ Childbirth is often joyful even though it's painful.

■ In hopes of calming flustered lawbreakers, Japanese cops have substituted the sound of church bells for sirens on police cars.

■ Scientists believe they'll eventually be able to figure out why cancer cells are virtually immortal, and then apply that secret to keeping normal cells alive much longer, thereby dramatically extending the human life span.

ENOUGH IS ENOUGH

Multimillionaire pop star George Michael decided to give away his music for free, posting it on the Internet for anyone to download. "I've been very well remunerated for my talents over the years," he told BBC, "so I really don't need the public's money."

Hollywood movie and music mogul David Geffen also believes he has enough money. The billionaire cofounder of DreamWorks told *Forbes,* "I have no interest in making money anymore. Everything I make in the entertainment business will go to charity."

During a 10-year period beginning in 1997, CNN founder Ted Turner gave a billion dollars to the United Nations. He specified that the money should not be used for administration costs but for programs like eliminating land mines, feeding children, and preventing disease.

Lady Godiva was more than a seminal performance artist. She was also a humanitarian and patron of the arts. When she doffed her clothes and rode a white horse through the English town of Coventry in 1057, her purpose was philanthropic. Her husband, the local assessor, had promised to abolish all taxes on the local folk if she did the daring deed.

Early in his career, while working as a newspaper editor, L. Frank Baum advocated the extermination of Native Americans. Later he mellowed. The books he wrote about the magical kingdom of Oz are celebrations of cultural and ethnic diversity.

Druidic Engineering

A 275-meter section of Austria's A9 highway was the most dangerous in the country. Accidents occurred there at an alarming rate.

"We had put up signs to reduce speed, renewed the road surface and made bends more secure, but we still kept getting accidents," said an engineer from the motorway authority.

Finally, archdruid Gerald Knobloch was summoned. To heal and revitalize the natural flow of "earth energy," he directed pillars of white quartz to be placed alongside the road. Traffic carnage soon disappeared.

"I located dangerous elements that had disrupted the energy flow," Knobloch said. "The worst was a river which human interference had forced to flow against its natural direction. By erecting two stones of quartz the energy lines were restored."

The pillars had a similar function to acupuncture, he said. "Acupuncture needles also restore broken energy lines. What acupuncture does for the body, the stones do for the environment." (Source: London's *The Telegraph,* telegraph.co.uk)

Turner's Gender Revolution   To distribute the funds he pledged to the United Nations, Ted Turner created a board of directors with more women than men.

"If women were in control of the world," he said, "it would be a much more peaceful, prosperous, equitable world in a very short period of time. You'd have a huge shift away from military budgets and into education and health care. And we're trying to set the example."

Open Secret Revealed
"There is a great insight which our culture is deliberately designed to suppress, distort, and ignore: that Nature is a minded entity; that Nature is not simply the random flight of atoms through electromagnetic fields; that Nature is not the empty, despiritualized lumpen matter that we inherit from modern physics. But it is instead a kind of intelligence, a kind of mind."
—Terence McKenna, tinyurl.com/2n8lcq

Wildness Revised   In his book *The Rag and Bone Shop of the Heart,* Robert Bly says that to be wild is not to be crazy like a criminal or psychotic, but "mad as the mist and snow." It has nothing to do with being childish or primitive, nor does it manifest as manic rebellion or self-damaging alienation. The real marks of wildness, he asserts, are a love of nature, a delight in silence, a voice free to say spontaneous things, and an exuberant curiosity in the face of the unknown.

Karma in Action   In 2001, Mitzi Nichols of Virginia Beach anonymously donated one of her kidneys to a stranger. She got paid nothing for this rare act of generosity, and after recovering from surgery went back to her job as a cashier at a gift shop. It took the universe three years to figure out a way to compensate her properly. In June 2004, she won $500,000 in the Virginia state lottery.

PNN is made possible by Dave Eggers' rant in The Harvard Advocate:
"Do not be critics, you people, I beg you. I was a critic and I wish I could take it all back because it came from a smelly and ignorant place in me and spoke with a voice that was all rage and envy. Do not dismiss a book until you have written one, and do not dismiss a movie until you have made one, and do not dismiss a person until you have met them. It is a fuckload of work to be open-minded and generous and understanding and forgiving and accepting, but, Christ, that is what matters. What matters is saying yes."

★12.

This language prevents crime.
This engineering moves you to sing.
These advertisements make you smart.
These rhythms free
all prisoners of childhood.

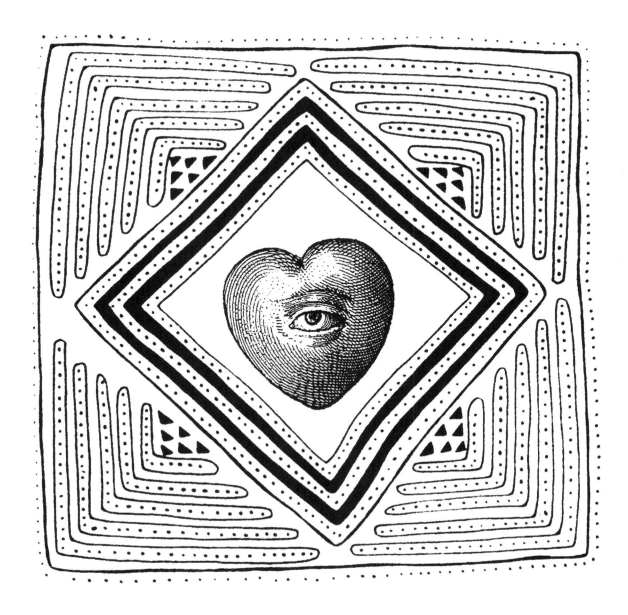

Your Horoscope

Plant orchids on a strip-mined hill.

Imagine you have a guardian angel who looks like Malcolm X.

Teach an animal to dance.

Hire a puppet troupe to reenact your life story using marionettes
in Renaissance costumes.

Make believe you are the ocean king or thunder queen.

Improvise a fresh bedtime story for someone you love.

Put on an inflatable sumo wrestler costume
and play a bagpipe as badly as possible.

Watch TV with your third eye.

Sip holy water blessed by a smart teenage girl.

Bear in mind that you are the Chosen One, and so is everyone else.

Clues to the Rebel Grail

Re-dreaming Christ

Some Christians might be shocked to learn that Jesus Christ is one of the Main High Magicians in the Beauty and Truth Lab's pantheon of deities and avatars.

They may believe that people like us—Goddess-worshiping tantric Sufi Qabalist pagans who hang around with Zen trickster witches and espouse a socialist libertarian political philosophy—couldn't possibly have an intimate and vivid relationship with the cosmic hero they claim to own. They act as if they have commandeered the trademark of one of the smartest wild men in history.

But many of us do have an intimate and vivid relationship with Jesus Christ. How could we not? He was a champion of women's rights, an antidote to the established and corrupt political order, and a radical spiritual activist who worked outside religious institutions.

The dude owned nothing and was a passionate advocate for the poor and underprivileged. He was uncompromisingly opposed to violence and war. Besides that, he was a master of love and he devoted his life to serving the Divine Intelligence. He even went so far as to say, "Love your enemies, do good to those who hate you, bless those who curse you, pray for those who mistreat you, and give away all your possessions."

I want to be like Jesus Christ when I grow up!

(But it's quite OK with us if you don't want to be like him. The good thing about adoring Christ's pronoiac glory but not being a Christian is that we don't have any investment in wanting you to do as we do. We want you to do as you do!)

Is there any hijacked hero you'd like to liberate? Any spoiled treasure you hope to redeem? Any detoured savior you want to get back on track?

HOW I GOT STARTED
IN THE BEAUTY AND TRUTH BUSINESS

The place: the restroom of a Roy Rogers restaurant in Chapel Hill, North Carolina. The moment: Once upon a time. The main character: a tall, skinny, young white guy with shoulder-length hair.

The guy was me, Rob Brezsny. Using my fingers as a comb, I was doing my best to marshal my hair into a more beautiful mess than its current bedraggled state. My girlfriend Babushka was supposed to meet me at the salad bar in a few minutes, and I wanted to resemble an attractive wild man, not a scruffy one.

Nearing completion in my primitive attempts at cosmetic improvement, I happened to glance at the wall below the towel dispenser. There I spied a tantalizing mess of graffiti. "I got Santa Cruzified and Californicated," it read, "and it felt like paradise."

A jolt of kundalini zipped through me. I was used to surfing waves of synchronicity; collecting meaningful coincidences was my hobby. But this scrawl on the wall was a freaky tidal wave of synchronicity. Babushka was coming to Roy Rogers today in order to discuss with me the prospect of jumping on a Greyhound bus together sometime in the next couple of weeks and heading out to the place we'd heard was a bohemian utopia: Santa Cruz, California.

I strained to see some smaller print beneath the message on the wall. "You know you'll never become the artist you were meant to be," it warned, "until you come live in Santa Cruz."

Goose bumps rose on my arms. Shivers raced up and down the back of my neck. Whatever strange angel had scrawled those words seemed to have lifted them directly from the back of my subconscious mind. The idea expressed there matched my hope and fear precisely. It had become increasingly clear to me that my aspirations to be a poet and musician with an inspirational effect on my community were doomed to chronic frustration as long as I resided in the Deep South, even in a university town like Chapel Hill. Here I would never be any more than a weirdo, a cross between a village idiot and a marginally entertaining monstrosity.

In that moment, my fate gelled.

By the first day of spring, Babushka and I had arrived in Santa Cruz with $90 in our pockets. We were gleefully homeless, sleeping in the park by day and spending the hours from 11 p.m. to 6 a.m. hanging out in all-night restaurants. When we weren't striking up conversations with the steady stream of colorful crazy folks, I dreamed and schemed about how I would build my new artistic career here in the promised land.

Within a few months I not only had a tiny studio apartment in a basement beneath a garage adjoining an old woman's house. I was well on my way to harvesting the rewards I'd journeyed to Santa Cruz to claim.

Barely three weeks after I stumbled off the cross-country Greyhound bus, I performed at the Good Fruit Company cafe. My songs "Blasphemy Blues" and "Reptile Rodeo Man," along with my long rant-poem "Microwave Beehive Star," impressed a reviewer for a local entertainment rag, who described my contribution as a "mouth-watering, id-tickling, ass-kicking communiqué from the collective unconscious itself."

With a burst of pent-up energy, I did a rash of poetry readings and performance art spectacles in a variety of cafes, as well as many street shows. I photocopied and sold 212 copies of my first homemade chapbook, *Crazy Science,* and practiced the art of enlightened demagoguery in a semi-regular late-night show, "Babbling Ambiance," on local radio station KZSC.

Best of all, I cobbled together my first Santa Cruz band, Kamikaze Angel Slander. When we played our first gig at a friend's party, our set consisted of five songs I had written in North Carolina, covers of two David Bowie tunes, and four epics my bandmates and I had whipped up, including "The Prisoner Is in Control."

There was only one factor darkening my growing exhilaration: grubby poverty. None of the music or spectacles I was creating earned me more than the cash I plowed into making them happen. And I resented life's apparent insistence that I was supposed to take time out from my projects to draw a steady wage. My enrollment at the University of California at Santa Cruz helped. For a few sporadic quarters I was able to garner government loans and grants in return for attending once-a-week poetry and creative writing classes. Monthly allotments of food stamps also aided the cause.

Despite assistance from the welfare state, though, I was still compelled to degrade myself with actual part-time jobs. Among my humiliations were stints washing dishes at restaurants and posing as a model for artists and putting in time as a farm laborer in apple orchards. Even then I barely made my rent, let alone trying to finance the accessories that up-and-coming rock stars need, like a car and good musical equipment.

I lived in a moldy basement with nothing but a temperamental space heater to warm my fingers as I composed rebellious anthems on my dinky electric piano with three broken keys. On occasions, I was forced to resort to a trick I'd learned from a homeless friend, which was to hang out in cafeteria-style restaurants and scavenge the food that diners left behind. My wardrobe? Both my street clothes and stage costumes were garnered entirely from a warehouse called the Bargain Barn, which charged a reasonable one dollar per five pounds of recycled garments.

Given my hardship, I was very receptive when I chanced across an opportunity to make money through creative writing.

My rickety bike had recently been stolen. In my search for a used replacement, I turned to the classified ads of the *Good Times,* Santa Cruz's largest weekly newspaper. As I scanned the "Misc for Sale" section, my eye tripped across an intriguing invitation one column over.

"*Good Times* is looking for an astrology columnist. Submit sample column for the week of January 26. Address to Editor, GT, 1100 Pacific Avenue, Santa Cruz 95060."

I was at first confused. *Good Times* already had an astrology column, didn't it? I leafed through the paper to find it, but it was gone. Had the author quit? Not that I'd be sorry to see him go. My impression of his writing, from the few times I had read it, was that it covered the whole range between mawkish New Age clichés and unfunny silliness.

Of course I had always despised *all* astrology columns; his was actually more entertaining than most. Though I was a student of astrology, not a teacher, I had high standards about how the ancient art form should be used. And I considered newspaper horoscopes to be an abomination. Without exception, they were poorly written and dull. They encouraged people to be superstitious and made the dead-wrong implication that astrology preaches predetermination and annuls free will. It was bad enough that their blather fed gullible readers inane advice that pandered to the least interesting forms of egotism. Worst of all, they were based in only the most tenuous way on real astrological understanding.

Any reputable practitioner would have told you, for instance, that in order to assess the cosmic energies with authenticity, you'd have to meditate on the movements and relationships of *all* the heavenly bodies, not just the sun. But newspaper horoscopes based their ersatz "predictions" solely on the sun's position. They made the absurd proposition that the lives of millions of people who share any particular "sun sign" are all headed in the same direction.

Artistic geniuses who in days past might have been van Goghs or Rembrandts now create gorgeous propaganda for the advertising industry.

In full awareness of all these truths, I struggled to drum up a rationalization for pursuing the gig. The prospect of actually being paid to write something—*anything*—was thrilling. Even more exciting was the fantasy of receiving a regular paycheck. This was a weekly column, not a one-shot deal.

Besides that, it couldn't possibly violate my integrity more than the other jobs I had already slaved away at.

"It's a dirty job, but someone's got to do it," was my opening gambit in the campaign to convince myself that the pros of penning the astrology column outweighed the cons.

My next strategy was figuring out how I could write the column in ways that would not feel fraudulent.

That's when I hatched my plan to become a poet in disguise.

Both in and out of academia, I had for some time been composing stuff that loosely qualified as poetry. From the declamatory rants I foisted on audiences between rock songs to the slightly more disciplined stanzas I produced for my creative writing classes, I worked hard at the craft and wanted it to become as necessary to me as food.

True, I couldn't help but notice that the culture at large regarded poetry as a stuffy irrelevancy; people I considered huge talents, like John Berryman, W. S. Merwyn, and Galway Kinnell, were not getting rich selling their lyrical creations.

To a degree, I sympathized with the hoi polloi's underwhelming appreciation of the art form I loved. The majority of poets *were* humorless academics who seemed to have studied at the feet of a single constipated celibate. It was shocking how little kundalini—how little *entertainment*—burst from the caste that I thought should be in charge of mining the frontiers of the imagination. I was perfectly willing for poetry to be demanding, complex, subtle, and even maddeningly mysterious. The whole point was to dynamite the ruts cut by ordinary waking consciousness, to sabotage cliché and common sense, to reinvent the language. But why did so much of this noble effort have to be uniformly listless, pretentious, and inaccessible?

And then there was my secret agenda. I was peeved that so few of "the antennae of the race" had enough courage to blow their own minds with psychedelics. How could you explode the consensual trance unless you poked your head over onto the other side of the veil now and then? Allen Ginsberg, at least, had the balls to go where shamans go. Berryman seemed to have accomplished the same feat with the help of alcohol.

As for myself, I had been drawn to and in contact with the other side of the veil long before resorting to

psychedelic technology. I regularly remembered and treasured my dreams throughout childhood, and when I was 13 years old I also began to record them. This ongoing immersion in the realm of the dreamtime imbued me early on with the understanding that there were other realities besides the narrow little niche that most everyone habitually inhabited. My psychedelic experiments only confirmed and extended that certainty.

As I gained confidence in the suspicion that my formal education had concealed from me nine-tenths of reality, I tuned in to the paper trail documenting the existence of the missing part. It had been mapped by shamans and alchemists and magicians for millennia: So my readings of Jung and Campbell and Graves and Eliade revealed. Their work in turn magnetized me to the literature of Western occultism, whose rich material was written not by academics but by experimenters who actually traveled to the place in question.

The myriad reports were not in complete agreement, but many of their descriptions overlapped. The consensus was that the other side of the veil is not a single territory, but teems with a variety of realms, some relatively hellish and some heavenly. Its names are many: dreamtime, fourth dimension, underworld, astral plane, collective unconscious, afterdeath state, eternity, bardo, and Hades—to name a few.

There was another issue on which all the explorers agreed: Events in those "invisible" realms are the root cause of everything that happens here. Shamans visit the spirit world to cure their sick patients because the origins of illness lie there. For Qabalists, the visible Earth is a tiny outcropping at the end of a long chain of creation that originates at a point that is both inconceivably far away and yet right here right now. Even modern psychothera-

pists believe in a materialistic version of the ancient idea: that how we behave today is shaped by events that happened in a distant time and place.

As I researched the testimonials about the treasure land, I registered the fact that dreams and drugs were not the only points of entry. Meditation could give access, as could specialized forms of drumming and chanting and singing and dancing. The tantric tradition taught that certain kinds of sexual communion can lead there. As does, of course, physical death.

I wanted to try all those other doors except the last one. Pot, hashish, and LSD were very good to me (never a single bad trip), but their revelations were too hard to hold on to. As I came down from a psychedelic high, I could barely translate the truths about the fourth dimension into a usable form back in normal waking awareness. At least in my work with dreams I had seen a steady growth of both my unconscious mind's ability to generate meaningful stories and my conscious mind's skill at interpreting them. But my progress was sketchy in the work of retrieving booty from the exotic places where drugs took me.

The problem was that unlike the other techniques on the list, psychedelics bypassed my willpower. Their chemical battering ram simply smashed through the doors of perception. No adroitness or craft was involved on my part. One of my meditation teachers referred to drug use, no matter how responsible, as "storming the kingdom of heaven through violence."

Gradually, then, I ended my relationship with the illegal magic. Instead I affirmed my desire to build mastery through hard work. Dream interpretation, meditation, and tantric exploration became the cornerstones of my practice. In time, I learned to slip into the suburbs of the mysterium via song and dance as well.

I must confess, though, that my plans did not immediately bear the fruit I hoped they would. Even my most ecstatic lucid dreams and illuminated meditations did not bring me to dwell on the other side of the veil with the same heart-melting vividness once provided by psychedelics. Even my deepest tantric lovemaking and music-induced trances failed to provide the same boost.

But then into my life came a consolation: the 19th-century artist and visionary William Blake. My encounter with his work alerted me to the fact that there is yet another name for the fourth dimension—a name that also describes a common, everyday human faculty that most of us take for granted.

Here's the special message Blake seemed to have written just for me in *A Vision of the Last Judgment:*

This world of Imagination is the world of Eternity; it is the divine bosom into which we shall go after the death of the Vegetated body. This World of Imagination is Infinite and Eternal, whereas the world of Generation, or Vegetation, is Finite and Temporal. There exists in that Eternal World the Permanent Realities of Every Thing which we see reflected in this Vegetable Glass of Nature. All Things are comprehended in their Eternal Forms in the divine body of the Saviour, the True Vine of Eternity, the Human Imagination.

I exulted in this discovery. Blake became a secret weapon I could use in my covert struggle against the poets who refused to be antennae of the race, against the poets who regarded the visible world as the only one that deserved to have poetry written about it.

Now it's true that some of these poets, whom I called "materialists," inspired me. William Carlos Williams, for instance, taught me much about the art of capturing concrete beauty.

I loved this Williams poem:

> so much depends
> upon
>
> a red wheel
> barrow
>
> glazed with rain
> water
>
> beside the white
> chickens

I watched videos of babies being born until I was healed.

Williams was the best of the materialist poets. His work helped me hone my perceptions and employ more vigorous language. But my pal William Blake gave me the doctrinal foundation with which I could rebel against Williams and rise to a higher calling. Blake suggested that the worlds you dream up in your imagination might be *more real than a red wheelbarrow.*

Might be was the key qualifier. Even then, at an unripe age, I was cautious about the indiscriminate use of this liberating proposition. I had read the Russian occultists Ouspensky and Gurdjieff, and they had made me aware that the out-of-control imagination in service to the ego is the function by which most people lie to themselves constantly, thereby creating hell on earth. Obviously, this was not the kind of imagination Blake meant, and I vowed to keep that clear.

More real than a red wheelbarrow. Blake showed me there was another way to access the fourth dimension: working as a creative artist, striving to discipline and supercharge the engine of the imagination. That was an extremely pleasurable realization. I saw that my passion for playing with music and language and images might dovetail perfectly with my longing to hang around the Elysian Fields.

Furthermore, if it were true, as Blake and the shamans said, that every event on Earth originates in the spirit world, then the skilled imaginer was potentially God's co-creator—not just *describing* conditions here below but *creating* them. I wanted to be like that. I wanted to fly away into the fourth dimension, reconnoiter the source of the messed-up conditions on the material plane, and give them a healer's tweak. Better yet, I fantasized myself being so at home and masterful in the dreamtime that I could rummage around there looking for attractive but embryonic archetypes to capture and bring down to Earth for ripening.

All these thoughts became fodder as I tried to imagine a way I could write an astrology column without violating my integrity. I wanted the gig badly. One way or another I was going to get it. But I would feel so much better about myself if I could refute my conscience's accusations of "Fraud! Panderer!" with highfalutin bullshit about William Blake and the shamanic tradition.

"More Real Than a Red Wheelbarrow." Why not call my "horoscope" column that? Why not do whatever my imagination wanted to do and disguise it all under the rubric of an astrological oracle? There was certainly no International Committee on Standards for Horoscope Columns that I would have to answer to. For that matter, as long as I shaped my horoscopes like love letters to my readers, it was unlikely they'd complain about the Blake-ian, shamanic stuff I'd wrap it in.

Before spying the help wanted ad in the *Good Times,* I'd hated astrology columns because I knew they had no basis in astrological data and could not possibly be an accurate interpretation of so many readers' lives at the same time. Driven by what had become an unstoppable

intent, I now argued from a different angle. What happens to people, I told myself, tends to be what they *believe* will happen to them; the world runs on the fuel of self-fulfilling prophecies. Therefore, couldn't it be said that my oracles would be accurate by definition, since anyone who regarded them seriously would subconsciously head in the directions I named? As long as I diligently maintained an optimistic and uplifting tone, no one could fault me for manipulating people in such a way.

My initial column took me an agonizing 43 hours to compose. It had some good moments:

> What you have at your command, Scorpio, is a magic we'll discreetly *not* call black. Let's say, instead, that it's a vivid, flagrant grey. At your best you'll be a charming *enfant terrible* playing with boring equilibriums, a necessary troublemaker bringing a messy vigor to all the overly cautious game plans. If you can manage to inject some mercy into your bad-ass attitude, no one will get stung and everyone will be thoroughly entertained.

Still, the first offering and many after it fell short of my lofty formulations. My work was sufficiently yeasty, though, to win the favor of the *Good Times'* boss. Or maybe he saw I was adept in the arts of spelling and grammar, and looked forward to an easy editing job. For all I know, I was the only applicant for the job. It's not as if the financial rewards alone would have drawn a crowd. As I discovered during my new editor's congratulatory handshake, the pay was $15 a week—so low that I could keep some of my food stamp allotment.

I regarded it as a fortune, though, considering that I was getting paid to be a poet in disguise. My secret long-term agenda, after all, was to build an imagination strong enough to gain regular access to the fourth dimension without the aid of psychedelics. What could be better training for that than a weekly assignment to spew out 12 oracular riffs and shape them into terse word-bombs?

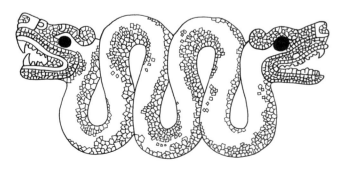

Sacred
Advertisement

*This experiment in adoration is brought to you by
Telepathics Anonymous,
a 12-step program for those who are ignorant
of how the thoughts and feelings of others
leak over into their own.*

*Are you one of the millions of brainwashed materialists
suffering from the delusion that your psyche is an
utterly separate and sealed-off territory?
Telepathics Anonymous
offers proof
that you are in continual extrasensory contact
with more souls than you can imagine.*

*As a get-acquainted gift, Telepathics Anonymous will
present you with an omen concerning the future of
your relationship with love exactly 95 hours and 19
minutes from right now.*

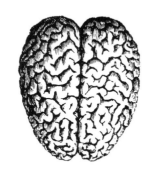

Dreamtime University

According to Nobel Prize-winning biologist Francis Crick, our nightly dreams consist of nothing more than hallucinations produced as the brain flushes out metabolic wastes. Of the many arguments that can be mustered against this appalling idiocy, none is more forceful than the life of Harriet Tubman. After escaping from slavery in 1849, she helped organize the Underground Railroad and personally led 300 slaves to freedom. Few history books choose to convey the fact that she often relied on her dreams to provide specific information about where to find safe houses, helpers, and passages through dangerous territory. Robert Moss tells the whole story in his book *Dreaming True.*

The chemist Friedrich August Kekulé von Stradonitz solved the central mystery of his scientific quest with the help of an event that happened while he was asleep. In 1865, after strenuous but unsuccessful efforts to determine the precise structure of the benzene ring, he had a dream of a snake biting its own tail. As he awoke with this vivid image in mind, he finally guessed the solution that had long eluded him. What if the six carbon atoms of benzene formed a closed ring—the shape formed by the snake—and not, as he had previously believed, a mere chain? The research that followed this eureka moment led to the discovery of principles that revolutionized organic chemistry.

Robert Louis Stevenson said the tale of *Dr. Jekyll and Mr. Hyde* came to him in a dream. He simply wrote it down. He credited "little people" in his dreams with providing material for his other books, as well.

Russian chemist Dmitri Mendeleyev worked long and hard to discover a coherent scheme for classifying elements, but the turning point in his search came in a dream on February 17, 1869. It revealed to him the system that is now called the Periodic Table of the Elements.

In 1844, Elias Howe dreamt of being chased by cannibals wielding spears with holes in the top. This inspired him to design a sewing needle with the eye in its tip, which in turn led him to invent the sewing machine.

Physiologist Otto Loewi won the Nobel Prize thanks to help he received in a dream. In 1903, he had begun to doubt the prevailing theory about how nerve impulses traveled. For 17 years, however, he could not find a way to prove his hunch that the transmission happened chemically rather than electrically. In 1920, he had a dream that revealed how to design an experiment to determine whether his hypothesis was correct. The experiment succeeded, and ultimately led to the work that won Loewi the Nobel Prize.

Dante Alighieri finished his masterpiece *The Divine Comedy* before he died in 1321. But when his sons, Jacopo and Pietro, assembled the manuscript for publication, they realized parts of it were missing. They searched the house for days, to no avail. Only after they had given up hope did help arrive. The spirit of Dante appeared in Jacopo's dream and showed his son a hiding place in his old bedroom wall. Upon awakening, Jacopo went to the spot his father had indicated and found the lost papers.

Srinivasa Ramanujan was a mathematical genius. He lacked formal training and his work was thought peculiar by his fellow mathematicians, but he made dramatic breakthroughs that are highly regarded. He attributed his success to the Hindu goddess Namakkal. She appeared regularly in his dreams, where she revealed innovative formulas he had only to verify once he awoke.

Naturalist Louis Agassiz was a seminal contributor to the American scientific tradition. While working on an exhaustive inventory of fossil fish, he received dream instructions that enabled him to chisel away at a certain slab of stone in his lab in just the right way to extract the whole, undamaged fossil of a previously unknown ancient fish.

Jack Nicklaus had more major tournament wins than any golfer in history. Skill and practice were the keys to his athletic prowess, but once he tapped into a different source of power. In 1973, he got into an uncharacteristic slump that had him stumped. One night he had a dream in which he experimented with a new grip on his clubs. When he went to the golf course that morning, he tried the dream's idea. It worked; his funk ended.

In 1977, English professor Coleman Barks had a dream that changed his life. In the dream, he was relaxing on a riverbank near his childhood home in Georgia. A ball of light floated toward him. It contained a man with his head bowed and eyes closed, sitting cross-legged and wearing a white shawl. The man raised his head, opened his eyes, and said, "I love you." Barks answered, "I love you, too." Some time after this dream, he met the same figure in waking life. It was a Sri Lankan holy man, Bawa Muhaiyaddeen, who set Barks on the path to becoming a translator of the dead mystic poet Rumi. Today Rumi's books are bestsellers, largely due to Barks.

When sleeping in an RV at the Burning Man festival in 2003, I dreamed that the Dalai Lama and I, along with three other people, were wandering in the middle of the night through a big city neighborhood dominated by boarded-up buildings and abandoned cars. A police siren wailed in the distance. We passed a group of skinheads in the midst of a drug deal. A bottle hurled from out of a dark alley landed and crashed a few feet behind us. Finally the Dalai Lama squatted down on the sidewalk near a wet heap of half-eaten food and McDonald's packaging. "This is the perfect place to meditate," he announced with a grin. "If we can summon the spirit of pronoia here, we will be able to do it anywhere."

In Chapter 18, which starts on page 373, there are some big white liberated spaces for you to fill up. I encourage you to use them to record and muse about and draw pictures of your dreams while you're reading this book.

A dream of smoking cigarettes in a bathroom stall at high school means you should find worthier forms of bucking authority. A dream of flamingos nesting in a burnt-out red Cadillac convertible in the mist at dawn means you should expand your ideas about where you might find beauty. A dream of a driver who doesn't use his turn signal means you shouldn't follow anyone too closely. A dream of baking a birthday cake for Buddha in the kitchen of a ship passing through the Panama Canal means you're ready to upgrade your skill at expressing generosity. A dream of wearing your birthday suit as you address an audience on the subject of privacy invasion means you should never tell a lie if you can bullshit your way through the situation. A dream of finding frogs with six legs means that the next car you buy should get at least 35 miles per gallon of gas. A dream of staging a drunken poetry reading in a run-down cafe bordering the interstate means you should develop more "Zen pride," the capacity for being proud about the fact that you have successfully rooted out all false pride.

Dionysian Manifesto

Cheap Loans for the Destitute The Grameen Bank in Bangladesh lends money to beggars at low interest rates, hoping to help them get off the streets and start their own businesses. Thousands of poor people have already taken advantage of the program. The bank accepts no collateral, does not pressure the borrowers to repay the money, and is even willing to forgo repayment for some who are unable to use it profitably.
(Source: oneworld.net)

TEAR ABATEMENT

In his book *Crying: The Natural and Cultural History of Tears*, Tom Lutz says that people don't cry as much as they used to. The English of the Victorian era, renowned for their stuffy behavior, put us to shame with their abundant outpouring of tears.

Luck from Above On July 11, 2007, lightning zapped the steeple of the Newman United Methodist Church in Grants Pass, Oregon. Later that evening, another bolt from the heavens struck the exact same spot. Was this bad luck? A punishing message from an angry God? No. The rare double shot knocked the siding off the steeple, revealing a problem that no one at the church had suspected: The inner structure was rife with dry rot that would have collapsed soon, possibly causing injury to anyone who happened to be inside. In exposing the hidden danger, the lightning did everyone a big favor.

More Luck from Above During an outdoor concert, '80s pop star Cyndi Lauper experienced a rare event. As she belted out a long, booming note, a bird flying overhead dispensed a blob that zoomed into her wide-open mouth. Lauper's grandmother later assured her that this was a stroke of good luck, and the singer herself referred to it as "God's little joke."

Attitude Adjustment, Babemba Style

"In the Babemba tribe of South Africa, when a person acts irresponsibly or unjustly, he is placed in the center of the village, alone and unfettered. All work ceases, and everyone in the village gathers in a large circle around the accused. Then each person in the tribe speaks to the accused, one at a time, recalling the good things the person has done in his life. Every experience that can be recalled with detail and accuracy is recounted. All his positive attributes, good deeds, strengths, and kindnesses are recited carefully. This ceremony often lasts for several days. At the end, a joyous celebration takes place, and the person is symbolically and literally welcomed back into the tribe."
—Jack Kornfield, *The Art of Forgiveness, Lovingkindness, and Peace*

Gun Amnesty Fest "The Washington, D.C., police department held a gun amnesty program that paid $100 to anyone turning in a firearm, no questions asked. Nearly a quarter of a million dollars in confiscated drug money was used for the campaign that removed 2,907 firearms from the streets."
—goodnews network.org

Backward Is Forward "The great secret known to Apollonius of Tyana, Paul of Tarsus, Simon Magus, Asclepius, Paracelsus, Boehme, and Bruno is that we are moving backward in time. The universe in fact is contracting into a unitary entity which is completing itself. Decay and disorder are seen by us in reverse, as increasing. These healers learned to move forward in time, which is retrograde to us." —Philip K. Dick, *The Divine Invasion*

This perfect moment, as well as the next 22 perfect moments, are brought to you by this excerpt from Og Mandino's book The Greatest Salesman in the World: *"Treat everyone you meet as if he or she were going to be dead by midnight. Extend to them all the care, kindness, and understanding you can muster, and do so with no thought of reward. Your life will never be the same."*

Lyric and Burlesque A group of French towns has formed an organization called Villages of Lyric or Burlesque Names. Among the members are the villages of Saligos (English translation: Filthy Pig), Montcuq (My Arse), Beaufou (Beautiful Mad), Cocumont (Cuckold Hill), and Trecon (Very Stupid).

Ugly Purifiers Houseflies purify the air by eradicating rotting vegetation. Vultures don't kill the things they devour, but rather assist nature in processing carrion, cleaning up messes other creatures have made. In a throwback to medieval medicine, modern British doctors place maggots in their patients' wounds to cleanse infections, compensating for the fact that some bacteria have become immune to antibiotics.

Lottery Winners More than half of all people polled say they would keep their jobs if they won the lottery.

MIRABILIA REPORT *Mirabilia* n. eccentric enchantments, unplanned jubilations, sudden deliverance from boring evils; from the Latin *mirabilia,* "marvels."

■ "The average river requires a million years to move a grain of sand 100 miles," says science writer James Trefil.

■ Clown fish can alter their gender as their social status rises.

■ The closest modern relative of the Tyrannosaurus rex may be the chicken.

■ Bluebirds cannot see the color blue.

■ Kind people are more likely than mean people to yawn when someone near them does.

■ There are always so many fragments of spider legs floating in the air that you are constantly inhaling them wherever you go.

■ Gregorian chants can cure dyslexia.

■ Scientists in Antarctica have photographed whales farting.

■ To keep from digesting itself, your stomach generates a fresh layer of mucus every two weeks.

■ Bob Hope donated half a million jokes to the Library of Congress.

■ Bees perform a valuable service for the flowers from which they steal.

■ All the gold ever mined could be molded into a 60-foot bust of your mom.

■ The moon smells like exploded firecrackers.

■ Physicists in Tennessee coaxed electric signals to travel through coaxial cable at four times the speed of light, even though the equipment they used was cheap stuff from Radio Shack.

■ A piece of paper can never be folded more than nine times.

■ Your tongue is the strongest muscle in your body.

■ The most frequently shoplifted book in America is the Bible.

■ Copper, iodine, alcohol, iron, sunshine, sodium, and cholesterol are harmful to you in large amounts, but good for you in small quantities.

■ "I always turn to the sports page first," said Earl Warren, former Chief Justice of the U.S. Supreme Court. "It records people's accomplishments; the front page, nothing but man's failure."

■ "Leafing through *Forbes* or *Fortune* is like reading the operating manual of a strangely sanctimonious pirate ship," wrote Adam Gopnik in *The New Yorker.*

Opinions Are Overrated

Writing in *The Week* magazine, Bill Falk reminisced about how earlier in his career he churned out three opinion columns a week for newspapers. It was tough. "The truth is," he said, "there were many weeks in which I didn't have three fresh opinions of any value."

These days, he added, he couldn't handle a gig like that. As he has matured, he has become suspicious of his own certainties. "Opinions are highly overrated," he concludes. "Most concern passing phenomena that, six months or six years from now, will become utterly irrelevant." (Source: theweekmagazine.com)

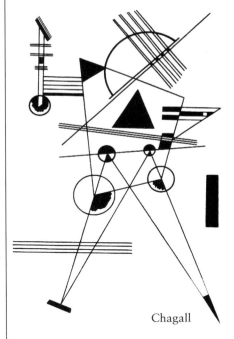

Chagall

---

*PNN
is brought to you by
Rosicrucian Coca-Cola,
Disneyland in Baghdad,
Six and a Half Billion Christs,*
The Feminist Man's Guide to
Picking Up Women,
*Digitally Remastered CDs of the
Big Bang,
and Sacred Shopping Centers.*

Realpolitik

The Official Monster Raving Loony Party is a political party that has nominated candidates for British elections since 1983. Its goal is to inject healing mayhem into a process that everyone takes too seriously. Here are some of its proposals: Anyone using a cell phone in a theater must be squirted with Silly String; joggers must run on giant treadmills that generate electricity for public use; men must wear veils on International Women's Day; TV anchormen must preface each night's broadcast with the disclaimer, "I am a trained actor in thrall to corporate greed." The OMRLP is run by Alan "Howlin Laud" Hope and his dead cat, Cat Mandu. Its headquarters is the Dog and Partridge pub at Yateley, and its slogan is "Vote for insanity. You know it makes sense."

8	1	6
3	5	7
4	9	2

BREAKING THE PRONOIA TABOO

"Irregularity and unpredictability are important features of health. On the other hand, decreased variability and accentuated periodicities are associated with disease. Healthy systems don't want homeostasis. They want chaos."
—John R. Van Eenwyk, "The Chaotic Dynamics of Everyday Life," *Quest*

"One must have chaos within oneself if one is to be a dancing star." —Friedrich Nietzsche

"We are too sincere, too productive, and too realistic. We need to enter more fully and more willingly into that realm under the rocks and behind the mirror."
—Thomas Moore, "Neither Here Nor There," *Parabola*, Spring 2000

"There is nothing stable in the world; uproar's your only music." —John Keats, *Letters of John Keats*

"Half of what you know today will be obsolete in five years. That prospect should fill you with excitement."
—Vimala Blavatsky

"The Truth is like the bear. Is it a gentle beast, a model for the stuffed animal children love? Or is it a vicious carnivore that will rip you to shreds if you turn your back on it? The answer is that it's both." —Robert Morning Sky

"In teaching my students, I try to figure out what questions I can ask that have no right answer. I seek to frame paradoxes, to force students to develop original thought."
—Meg Gorman, Waldorf teacher

"We are the sum of our efforts to change who we are. Identity is no museum piece sitting stock-still in a display case, but rather the endlessly astonishing synthesis of the contradictions of everyday life." —Eduardo Galeano, *Book of Embraces*

"Authenticity depends entirely on being faithful to the essential ambiguity of experience."
—John Berger

"Reasonable people adapt themselves to the world. Unreasonable people attempt to adapt the world to themselves. All progress, therefore, depends on unreasonable people."
—George Bernard Shaw

"Rebellion to tyrants is obedience to God."
—Thomas Jefferson

"You're only given a little spark of madness. You mustn't lose it." —Robin Williams

"There ain't no answer. There ain't going to be any answer. There never has been an answer. That's the answer." —Gertrude Stein

"Chaos is a name for any order that produces confusion in our minds." —George Santayana

Holy Masquerade Some spectators allow themselves to be tremendously undignified at professional sports events. With no concern for how ridiculous others might think them, they wear giant foam rubber hats resembling cheese wedges. They paint their bellies with the home team's insignia and go shirtless outdoors in sub-freezing weather. They scream nonsense chants and make bizarre faces and wave their arms in frantic salutes. Studies by researchers at the Beauty and Truth Lab suggest that up to four percent of these folks might be bodhisattvas in disguise—wise tricksters who intentionally lose their dignity as a spiritual practice, cultivating nonattachment to their egos.

The Ten-Thousandth Amazement
"You start out as a single cell derived from the coupling of a sperm and egg; this divides in two, then four, then eight, and so on. At a certain stage there emerges a single cell that has as all its progeny the human brain. The mere existence of such a cell should be one of the world's great astonishments. People ought to be walking around all day, calling to each other in endless wonderment, talking of that cell." —Lewis Thomas, *The Lives of a Cell*

Wild Urban Medicines Many plants used for prescription drugs originate in tropical rain forests. There are unquestionably other healing herbs, as yet undiscovered, in these endangered ecosystems. But a study suggests that weeds growing in towns and villages may be an equally important source of medicine. *The Journal of Ethnopharmacology* reports that the Highland Mayans of Chiapa, for instance, get much of their medicinal plants from vacant lots and other disturbed areas, even in communities that are adjacent to stands of primary forest. (Source: eurekalert.org)

Win-Win Spiritual Battle After a long struggle with authorities, Norwegian Muslims won permission to proclaim "God is great" from a loudspeaker atop the World Islamic Mission mosque in Oslo. Soon thereafter, atheists were granted the right to electronically amplify their cherished mantra, "There is no God," from a nearby building.

Beauty Work Traveling cosmetic saleswomen from America have penetrated the Amazon jungle. Inflamed with faith in the value of their products, Avon ladies brave 100-degree heat as they paddle canoes down piranha-infested tributaries to hawk lipstick and eyeshadow to women who have previously been deprived of these modern enhancements.

Pollination Orgy The planet's biggest annual orgy of pollination takes place every February. A million beehives from all over America and Australia are shipped in by truck to a 600,000-acre patch of almond orchards in California's Central Valley. For three weeks, 40 billion bees are in service to almond flowers as they facilitate the mixing of male and female reproductive materials.

The Language of Initiation
Tjiliwirri is a special language taught to boys undergoing initiation rites among the Warlpiri tribe of the Australian Aborigines. A speaker uses it to express the opposite of what he pretends to mean. To say the equivalent of "You are very smart," for example, a boy might say, "How dumb you are!" To express a desire to eat, he'd say, "I'm not hungry." (Source: *Reader's Digest Book of Facts*)

Doughnut-Eating Competitions
"When in a doughnut-eating competition," writes *Esquire*'s Cal Fussman, "press down hard on each one before biting into it. If you don't, the air inside will bloat your belly and you'll get blown out after six."

Escape Tip If a crocodile has you in the grip of its jaws, jam your thumbs into its eyeballs and it will release you.

Bargain Bulletin It *is* possible to buy happiness. Researchers at Yahoo! Personal Finance determined the precise amount necessary: $4.9 million.

Your Increased Brainpower
Michael Weliky, a professor of brain and cognitive sciences, decided to test the accuracy of the old saw that we only use 10 percent of our brains. He dreamed up an experiment that involved 12 ferrets watching the movie *The Matrix*. His research was so convincing that the journal *Nature* published it. He concluded that we actually use 80 percent of our available brainpower, though much of the activity takes place unconsciously.

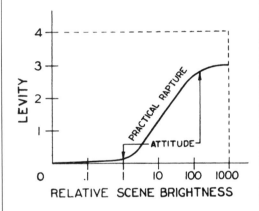

Astrological Engineering In Bhutan, astrologers play an important official role. Before each year begins, the king's stargazers determine the least and most cosmically propitious dates coming up in the next 12 months. The calendar is then altered accordingly. If June looks bad from the astrologers' point of view, for instance, it might be canceled, while July will be observed twice.

Useless Gifts During the war in Bosnia in the 1990s, Western governments showered the beleaguered people with free consumer goods. *Earth Island Journal* reported that the U.S. sent thousands of bottles of mouthwash. Norway contributed anti-leprosy medication and Britain supplied weight-reduction pills. "This is a good example of the kind of generosity that pronoiacs should avoid as they conspire to shower blessings on everyone," said Beauty and Truth Lab spokesperson Rapunzel Blavatsky.

Evolution's Second and Third Chances "Use it or lose it" has long been a key dogma in the theory of evolution. Biologists have believed that if a species accidentally develops a certain new characteristic but then fails to incorporate it permanently as a vital feature, it's gone forever. Recently, however, researchers have begun to question this tenet. They've found evidence that the "walking stick" insects known as phasmids have, over the last 300 million years, lost their wings because of disuse several times, but then re-evolved them.

Jewel-Toned Pick-Me-Ups Discordianism is one of the rare religions that takes account of Ralph Abraham's assertion that heart physiologists find more chaos in the healthy heart than in the sick heart. Here's a sampling of Discordian tenets. 1. Everyone is a saint, especially you. 2. Meditation consists primarily of cruising around looking for good luck. 3. Eating hot dog buns is prohibited, except on Friday, when it's compulsory. 4. When you're stuck in a rut, you must speak in tongues, handle snakes, and experience phantasmagoria. 5. Your guardian angel loves you better when your room is a mess. 6. Bowling alleys are sacred; you must protect them from desecration. 7. The Goddess will solve all your problems if you solve all hers.

Impossible Feats A master practitioner of the Indonesian martial art pencak silat can demolish a stack of bricks with one bash of his arm. Indian yogis can survive being buried in the earth for an hour. Circus performers swallow swords. Some couples keep their love and intimacy fresh through the trials of time, chaos, and tedium.

You know about the Russian physiologist Ivan Pavlov, who discovered the conditioned reflex. In his famous experiment, he trained laboratory dogs to salivate at the sound of a bell.

You may not have heard, though, about the story's surprise ending. The dogs were programmed for weeks with such rigor that their behavior became as predictable as machines. Then one day a flood inundated the lab. In the confusion, the dogs forgot all their training instantly. (Source: Raoul Vaneigem, *The Revolution of Everyday Life*)

More than seven centuries before a few European men dared to sail beyond the safe boundaries of their known world, entire Polynesian families crossed vast expanses of the Pacific Ocean in catamarans. The first humans to arrive in Hawaii, they were led by "wayfinders." These miracle workers navigated the uncharted seas by reading star positions, discerning weather patterns, and interpreting the ocean's colors and movements.

Because he opposed apartheid, Nelson Mandela was imprisoned in his native South Africa for nearly 30 years. After being released in 1993, he won the Nobel Peace Prize and was elected president of his country.

Bad News and Good News, Part 1

In the last 50 years, America's Great Plains area has lost a third of its population, due largely to the disappearance of family farms. People are moving out in droves. Ghost towns are proliferating. From one perspective, that's sad, but from another, it's cause for celebration: The wilderness is returning in some places, and vast herds of buffalo once again roam the land. (Source: *The Week* magazine, January 16, 2004)

Bad News and Good News, Part 2

The U.S. Air Force has complied with the Environmental Protection Agency's ban on ozone-destroying chlorofluorocarbons. It has removed CFCs from the cooling systems of ballistic missiles that carry nuclear warheads. "If they are ever fired," *Access to Energy* reported, "there will be an environmentally friendly nuclear holocaust."

What's Your Flub Rate?

In 2003 *The Boston Globe* ran 901 corrections of previously published information. In other words, it averaged 17.3 acknowledged mistakes per week. The *Chicago Tribune*'s total was 658, or 12.7 errors per week. How do your numbers compare?

Your Brain Is Illegal

The U.S. government has criminalized the chemical compounds of peyote, even though one of them, dopamine, is a primary neurotransmitter in the human brain. Our brains also produce anandamide, a substance that's nearly identical to THC, the active ingredient in marijuana.

Generosity Is Trendy

Charitable giving by Americans has risen 180 percent since 1960.

Gender Swaps

A few years ago, members of the Barbie Liberation Organization sneaked into toy stores and swapped the voice boxes of 300 GI Joe and Barbie dolls. Boys who later purchased the plastic soldiers were surprised to hear them make comments like "I like to go shopping with you," while the girls who came into possession of the mutated Barbies heard terse barks like "To the front lines, men!"

Sneaky Advertisement

Buy Nothing Day, held each November, is a holiday from consumerism. You're free to spend no money at that time.

Kissing Traditions

In her book *A Natural History of the Senses,* Diane Ackerman says that in many cultures the word for kiss means smell. "A kiss is really

a prolonged smelling of one's beloved, relative, or friend," she writes. "Members of a tribe in New Guinea say good-bye by putting a hand in each other's armpit, withdrawing it and stroking it over themselves, thus becoming coated with the friend's scent. Other cultures sniff each other or rub noses."

Free Allah

More than 1.2 billion Muslims live under democratically elected governments, and there is a steady move towards democratization, civil rights, and political freedom in many other Islamic countries. (Source: Freedom House Survey)

Butt Divination

A blind German clairvoyant named Ulf Buck claims he can foretell people's future by feeling their naked buttocks.

Climate Change Perks

According to Russian politician Vladimir Putin, global warming might be a boon for his country because people "would spend less money on fur coats and other warm things." (Source: Reuters)

Sometimes Pronoia Is a Bit Perverse

Moms and dads who launch screaming fights in front of their kids could actually be helping them, a new study reveals. Researchers at McGill University found that listening to their parents yelling often makes children more imaginative because it forces them into a fantasy world to escape.

Just Another Secret Miracle

In her book *Pilgrim at Tinker Creek*, Annie Dillard notes that there is only a tiny difference between the lifebloods of plants and animals. A molecule of chlorophyll contains 36 atoms of hydrogen, oxygen, nitrogen, and carbon arrayed around an atom of magnesium, while a molecule of hemoglobin is exactly the same except for an atom of iron instead of magnesium.

PNN is brought to you by the philosophies of panpsychism, animism, and pantheism, all of which propose that everything in the universe, even matter itself, is alive, conscious, and ensouled.

EDITORIAL

The superstition of materialism is the dominant ideology of a majority of people in the world. It's the specious doctrine that physical matter is the only reality and that nothing can be said to exist unless it's perceivable by a human being's five senses or detected by technologies that humans have created. Materialism paradoxically preaches the value of being agnostic about all phenomena it does not recognize as real, even as it obsessively evades questions about its own fundamentalist assumptions.

     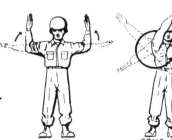

ESTABLISH TURNING POINT — WAVE THE ROD — FACE THE ROD — REVERSE THE ROD — BOOST THE ROD — MOVE FORWARD — COME IN

The Good Side of Globalization

More than 240,000 people died in the earthquake that struck Tangshan, China, in 1976. Attention to that tragedy from the international community was negligible compared to the outpouring in response to the tsunami disaster that killed 225,000 in countries bordering the Indian Ocean in December 2004. One explanation for the difference is that there has been a dramatic globalization of consciousness. People currently living on the planet are increasingly aware of how intimately interdependent we all are. Years ago no one had heard of the butterfly effect—the theory that the flapping of a butterfly's wings in Japan can affect the weather in Texas. Now millions understand the principle.

Wet Chicken Feathers

A poultry expert has come up with a revolutionary use for the feathers that are left over when chickens are slaughtered. David Emery has built a machine to turn the damp, dirty refuse into a strong, light fiber that's suitable for making auto parts and medical instruments.

Beyond the G-Spot

In his book *The Naked Woman*, biologist Desmond Morris says that in addition to the G-Spot, women have three other highly sensitive erotic zones in the vagina. He calls them the A-Spot, C-Spot, and U-Spot.

Glass Way More Than Half Full

In portentous tones, as if exposing yet another demoralizing deterioration of our collective health, the Centers for Disease Control informed us that the average person is "sad, blue, or depressed" about three days a month. As we pored over various news articles reporting the results of the CDC's survey, we looked in vain for even a glimmer of glee. After all, if we're downhearted three days every month, it means we're feeling pretty good the other 27 or 28 days.

ECSTATIC STUDY GUIDE

PART 1

Strategies for cultivating a chronic, low-key, blissful union with everything you're not

State your intentions. How do you want to feel?

1 Nothing primes your ecstatic skill better than invoking and expressing thanks. So consider the possibility of celebrating regular Gratitude Fests. During these orgies of appreciation, you could confer praise and respect on the creatures, both human and otherwise, that have played seminal roles in inspiring you to become yourself. Who teaches and helps you? Who sees you for who you really are? Who nudges you in the direction of your fuller destiny and awakens you to your signature truths? Who loves you brilliantly?

2 Jungian analyst Arnold Mindell explores the relationship between mind and body. He thinks you can achieve optimal physical health if you're devoted to shedding outworn self-images. In his book *The Shaman's Body,* he says, "You have one central lesson to learn—to continuously drop all your rigid identities. Personal history may be your greatest danger."

Kate Bornstein, author of *Gender Outlaw: On Men, Women and the Rest of Us,* agrees. Raised as a boy, she later became a woman, but ultimately renounced gender altogether. "I love being without an identity," she says. "It gives me a lot of room to play around."

What identities would be healthy, even ecstatic, for you to lose? Describe the fun you'd have if you were free of them.

3 I swear the strange woman standing near me at Los Angeles' Getty Museum was having an erotic experience as she gazed upon van Gogh's *Irises.* She was not touching herself, nor was anyone else. But she was apparently experiencing waves of convulsive delight, as suggested by her rapid breathing, shivering muscles, fluttering eyelids, and sweaty forehead.

Fifteen minutes later, I saw her again in front of Jean-Honoré Fragonard's *The Fountain of Love.* She was only slightly more composed. In a friendly voice, I said, "This stuff really moves you, doesn't it?" "Oh, yeah," she replied, "I've not only learned how to make love with actual flowers and clouds and fountains, I can even make love with paintings of them."

Do you have any interest in mastering the method in this maestro's madness? Where will you begin?

4 Beauty and Truth Lab researcher Rebecca Rusche coined the word "careenstable." Here's her explanation of how it originated:

"In high school, my mom used to let me use her VW Beetle to go to basketball practice. One night after practice, a friend and I were chatting and drinking Coke when we decided to see how fast we could get the Beetle going down a nearby dirt road. Soon we were careening at 65 mph, shouting 'careen!' every time we hit a bump and flew into the air.

"When we arrived back at the gym and got out of the car half an hour later, we saw my Coke can sitting on the front bumper next to the license plate. I nudged it softly to see if it was lodged in there, but it fell right off—wasn't stuck at all. I thought, 'There must be a word for this magic,' and thus 'careenstable' was born. It came to mean anything that maintains its poise in the midst of wild, fast movement."

Give an example of how you could experiment with making careenstable work in your own life.

5 Sacred is trendy! Among the many recent books that invoke the concept are *Sacred Flowers, The Sacred Art of Hunting, Sacred Hoops* (about basketball), *Sacred Monsters, Sacred Hunger, The Sacred Landscape,* and *Sacred Sexuality.* It's fine with me, really. I'd like to sacralize the whole damn world.

There was one case, however, that tested even my capacity to find holy meaning everywhere: a class offered at the New Age Expo called "The Sacred Art of Publicity." When I saw that, I nearly spit out the gulp of goji berry and spirulina smoothie that I had just sipped. "What's next?" I thought. "Sacred shopping for automatic weapons? Sacred gambling at an Indian casino?" But in the next moment I had to admit that even those might be possible.

What's the most outlandish sacred act you can think of pulling off? Do it.

6 Many life processes unfold outside of your conscious awareness: your body digesting your food and circulating your blood; trees using carbon dioxide, water, and sunlight to synthesize their nourishment; microorganisms in the soil beneath your feet endlessly toiling to create humus. You don't perceive any of these things directly; they're invisible to you.

Tune in to this vitalizing alchemy. Use your X-ray vision and sub-sonic hearing and psychic smelling. See if you can absorb by osmosis some of the euphoria of the trees as they soak in the sunlight from above and water from below.

> ### *Breathe in the love.*
> ### *Breathe out the jive.*
> ### *Breathe in the mystery.*
> ### *Breathe out the history.*
> ### *Breathe in the luminosity.*
> ### *Breathe out the grandiosity.*

7 "Every great player has a screw loose," said basketball coach Tara VanDerveer. What's the loose screw in you that's most likely to lead you to greatness?

8 In certain Native American traditions, the hole was a symbol for the female genitalia, through which souls enter this realm. In American scientific lore, a wormhole is a backdoor shortcut between two places in space separated by an astronomical distance. In my personal mythos, those are my two favorite nuances in the archetype of the hole.

When I was a kid I loved to fantasize that I'd obtained a magic hole like the one Bugs Bunny had in the comic books. It was a portable hole that Bugs could take with him everywhere and apply to any barrier he needed to slip through. Once he even managed to slap it up against the sky, giving him access to another dimension where the whole world was inside him, not outside. (Or was that a dream I had?)

What would you do with your portable magic hole?

9 "The people of future generations will win many a liberty of which we do not yet even feel the want," said German philosopher Max Stirner. See if you can become aware of an interesting freedom that has not previously been on your radar screen.

10 "The really important kind of freedom," said David Foster Wallace, "involves attention and aware-

ness and discipline, and being able truly to care about other people and to sacrifice for them over and over in myriad petty, unsexy ways every day."

Is that an interesting kind of freedom to you? Can you imagine any scenario in which practicing it would crack you open and pour you into an ecstatic state?

11 "Man in his present state has as much desire to urinate as he has to make vows to Artemis," said Edward Dahlberg in *The Sorrows of Priapus.* In other words, most people have no relationship with wild female deities, nor do they ever conceive of a reason why that might be fun or inspiring.

But some of us know that Artemis is not dead, is not just a figment of the archaic Greek mind. She is a living archetype of wild but nurturing female energy. Goddess of the ever-changing moon, sinewy protectress of the undomesticated soul, she gives sanctuary to all who prize liberated fertility. Make a vow to her.

12 Comment on the following rant, which Beauty and Truth Lab operatives put on flyers and tacked up on laundromat bulletin boards all over San Francisco:

"The Doctrine of Original Sin? We spit on it. We reject it. We renounce it and forget it and annihilate it from reality. In its place we embrace the Doctrine of Original Fun. This reformulation asserts that it is our birthright to commune with regular doses of curious beauty and tricky truth and insurrectionary love. A robust, heroic joy is even now roaring through us, bringing us good ideas about how to apply the metaphor of ingenious foreplay to everything we do. We will not waste this euphoric deluge on any of the million and one numbing little diversions that pass for pleasure among the ecstasy-starved pursuers of mediocre joy. Rather, we will remain ever alert for the call of primordial delight."

13 Poet Kay Ryan told the *Christian Science Monitor* how she cultivates the inspiration to write. She rouses the sense of a "self-imposed emergency," thereby calling forth psychic resources that usually materialize only in response to a crisis.

Please note that she doesn't provoke an actual emergency: She doesn't arrange to have a loved one get pinned beneath the wheels of a car. She doesn't climb out onto the window ledge on the 22nd story of a high-rise. Instead, she visualizes hypothetical situations that galvanize her to shift into a dramatically heightened state of awareness.

Ecstatic Study Guide, Part 1

What imagined emergencies could you invoke to inspire your deep self to rise up and make its mark?

You have access to the same cosmic-virgin-truth-love-mojo that orbits the planets around the sun.

14 Re-read page 187, and then dream up your own pronoiac prank, to be done either in concert with co-conspirators or by yourself. Carry it out. Report your results here.

15 I've discovered a new way to stimulate my psychic powers. I simply eat large amounts of wasabi, the bracing horseradish-like paste that's traditionally served with sushi. Its astringent potency cracks open an inter-dimensional wormhole in my brain through which news of the future pours in.

Find your own equivalent to my wasabi method of foreseeing the future.

16 In the Western Hermetic version of the Qabala, every Hebrew letter is paired with a number, and so every word is also a number derived from the addition of its letters. Gematria is the practice of finding hidden resonance between words that have similar numerical values. Of the many poetic truths revealed through this art, one of my favorites is this: The Hebrew words for both "serpent" and "messiah" add up to 358.

Let's suppose this can be interpreted to mean that the snaky potency of your reproductive drive is potentially the source of your salvation. What implications might that have for how you cultivate the art of ecstasy?

17 "Take time to stop and smell the flowers," says an old homily. Albert Hoffman, the Swiss scientist who discovered LSD and lived to age 102, had a different approach. "Take the time to stop and be the flowers," he said.

That's my advice to you. Don't just set aside a few stolen moments to sniff the snapdragons, taste the rain, chase the wind, watch the hummingbirds, and listen to a friend. Use your imagination to actually be the snapdragons and rain and wind and hummingbirds and friend. Don't just behold the Other; become the Other.

18 Elijah, the beer truck driver who lives in the trailer with old tires, rusty tools, and the husk of a 1975

Chevy El Camino littering the driveway, tells me that everything he knows about God can be summed up in the bumper sticker on the back of the El Camino, which reads "Theresa and Johnny's Comfort Food—Live Free or Die."

Mythologist Joseph Campbell, on the other hand, suggested we should imagine a deity to be like a floating ball of fire that would immediately kill anyone it touched.

Then there's the poet Rumi. He envisioned God as your tender Best Friend and Unpredictable Ally who's always as close as your own breath.

Which version do you prefer?

19 I love this excerpt from "The Seeker," a poem by Rilke in his *Book of Hours* (translated by Robert Bly): "I am circling around God, around the ancient tower, / and I have been circling for a thousand years, / and I still don't know if I am a falcon, or a storm, / or a great song."

Here's my own permutation: "I am circling around love, around the throbbing hum, and I have been circling for thousands of days, and I still don't know if I am a wounded saint, or a rainy dawn, or a creation story."

Compose your own version.

You could become a master of renegade sacraments, dissident splendor, and secret freedom.

20 I dreamed I was a telepathic teenage unicorn with five hearts, each of which contained a different mode of intelligence. One gave me the wisdom of a crow, another the consciousness of a human, and the others the smarts of a turtle, wolf, and dolphin. (My brain was the location of my unicorn thoughts.)

I found myself in the High Desert of Yellow Tulips, a place whose name didn't match its qualities. It was really like an ocean, since it was crammed with millions of unnaturally sturdy flowers whose waves and currents carried me along.

Two companions were with me—my lesbian twin, an untameable dreadlocked zebra named Flux Luster, and our best friend, Outrider, a petite crocodile doctor with the most elegant hands and arms in the Dreamtime. As we rode along on the top of the tulip waves, we sang a song. The chorus was "We believe in nothing so we can accept everything."

Once we passed a buoy with a sign that said, "Beware of Insane Joke-Telling Kittens." We weren't scared in the least, since we had packets of wizard pollen that we knew we could throw on the kittens and thereby make them sane.

Finally we came ashore on an island where a mad scientist in a purple frock coat and orange pants was gazing straight up as he clutched three test tubes full of bubbling green liquids. He was exasperated, and seemed to be arguing with an unseen presence above. The words he kept repeating sounded like, "You said the spray from the waterfall would be the last ingredient!"

Then a giant hand reached down from the sky. "That's God," said Flux Luster matter-of-factly, and I believed her. The fingernails on the divine hand were painted cherry red and there was a blue band-aid partially covering a booboo on her wrist. God was apparently delivering a gift. She set it down on the beach just a few feet away from us. Was it for us or for the mad scientist? It was a miniature pink Ferris wheel with six yellow canaries riding in the cars.

To be continued . . . by you. Keep dreaming the tale onward: What happens next?

P.S. What does the dream mean so far? Give a preliminary interpretation.

21 The Beauty and Truth Lab term "blisssavvvy" means "highly skilled at inducing states of rapture, synergy, and ecstatic empathy." Do you have any ideas about how you could cultivate blisssavvvy?

Temporary Autonomous Zone
True Alien Zodiac
Transgress All Zippers
Teasing Atavistic Zigzag
Tantalize Amazing Zeroes
Trembling Anarchistic Zohar
Trustworthy Asshole Zen
Ticklish Avatar Zeal

★13

The 11th Commandment:
Thou Shalt Not Bore God.
The 12th Commandment:
Thou Shalt Not Bore Thyself.

You
Are
Here

Your Sledgehammer and Watercolor Brush

Thank your mother for the pain she endured while birthing you.

For three minutes on the first Friday of every month, close your eyes
and imagine yourself riding a wild horse through a cemetery.

Fantasize that your so-called "dark side" is sweet and creamy.

When you come home after a day of triumphs, take out the garbage.

Dream you're a red-tailed hawk soaring over a shopping mall.

Forgive yourself for the blindness that put you in the path
of those who betrayed you.

Buy seven used gowns
worn to the Academy Awards show by famous actresses,
and send them gratis to seven Guatemalan teenagers.

Visualize two versions of yourself, one male and one female,
holding hands as they gaze into a reflection of the moon on a river.

Keep an image of a sphinx with you at all times.

SACRED UPROAR

Pronoia is closer than your breath and older than death.
It dreams like a mountain, laughs like a river,
prays like the sun, and sings like the aurora borealis.
It's always as fresh as the beginning of time.

Life is a vast and intricate conspiracy designed to keep us
well supplied with blessings. What kind of blessings?
Ten million dollars, a gorgeous physique, a perfect marriage,
a luxurious home, and high status? Maybe.
But just as likely: interesting surprises, dizzying adventures,
gifts you hardly know what to do with,
and conundrums that dare you to get smarter.

Novelist William Vollman referred to the latter types of blessings
when he said that "the most important and enjoyable thing in life
is doing something that's a complicated, tricky problem
for you that you don't know how to solve."

The Christian writer C. S. Lewis once said:
"I thank God that He hasn't given me all the things I've prayed for,
because as I look back now I realize it would have been disastrous
to have received some of them."

Pronoia provides the boons and prods your soul needs,
not necessarily those your ego craves.

Pronoia doesn't promise uninterrupted progress forever.
It's not a slick commercial for a perfect summer day
that never ends.
Grace emerges in the ebb and flow, not just the flow.
The waning reveals a different kind of blessing
than the waxing.

But whether it's our time to ferment in the valley of shadows
or rise up singing in the sun-splashed meadow,
fresh power to transform ourselves is always on the way.
Our suffering won't last, nor will our triumph.
Without fail, life will deliver the creative energy we need
to change into the new thing we must become.

Pronoia works because there is a Divine Being
who comprises the entire universe.
When I say, "Life is a conspiracy to shower us with blessings,"
I understand that this Divine Being
is the Chief Architect, Builder, and Manager of the conspiracy.
She oversees the evolution of 500 billion galaxies
and every single thing in them,
yet is also available as an intimate companion
and daily advisor to each one of us humans.

Some lovers of pronoia don't like this part of my rap.
They want pronoia to be free of anything that smacks of God.
Atheism works better for them. That's OK with me.
No hard feelings.

Other lovers of pronoia don't appreciate me
referring to the Creator as "She."
They either want to stick with the pronoun
that has been used for hundreds of years, or else
don't want any gender associations whatsoever.
That's OK with me. No hard feelings.

The Maker of the conspiracy constantly tinkers,
always keeping the big, 14-billion-year-long picture in mind
and moving in the direction of ultimate blessings
for all concerned.

But the Maker also loves getting help from us.
To the degree that we co-conspire,
the inevitable blessings ripen
more lyrically and in greater fullness.

Pronoia asks us to be awake to the shifting conditions
of the Wild Divine's ever-fresh creation.
It encourages us to be quite happy about regularly divesting ourselves
of the beliefs and theories that guided us yesterday
so that we can see clearly what's right in front of us today.

As much as we might be dismayed
by the actions of our political leaders,
pronoia says that toppling any particular junta, clique, or elite
is irrelevant unless we overthrow
the sour, puckered mass hallucination
that is mistakenly called "reality"
including the part of that hallucination we foster in ourselves.

The revolution begins at home.
If you overthrow yourself again and again,
you might earn the right to help overthrow the rest of us.

Pronoia will change your past if you let it.
It's the language you study at night in your dreams,
the open secret of how to live forever,
the Last Judgment transformed into a daily gift.

Pronoia is a gnostic art:
Everyone is potentially a visionary
capable of revealing more of its mysteries.
The Beauty and Truth Lab is not the final authority on the subject.
So turn to Chapter 18, beginning on page 373, and reveal away.
Write your oracles and definitions about pronoia there.

Evil Fears Laughter

Are demons and devils real? In my view, it doesn't matter whether or not they exist in an objective or literal sense. The point is that we are all plagued by split-off, unintegrated portions of our own and other people's psyches. They behave exactly as if they were diabolical entities—demons, djinns, dybbuks, and devils—working at cross-purposes to our conscious desires.

In dealing with their hassling interventions, I endorse the approach described by Paul Foster Case in his book *The Tarot: A Key to the Wisdom of the Ages.* There he suggested that mirth is the best way to beat the devil. "Laughter is prophylactic," he wrote. "It purifies subconsciousness and dissolves mental complexes. In a hymn to the sun god Ra we read, 'Thy priests go forth at dawn, washing their hearts with laughter.' This is a prescription we may all follow to advantage."

My friend and teacher, Vimala Nostradamus, echoes Case. "The best way to neutralize the devil is to laugh at him," she says. "Satan's most effective recruiting technique is to get people to take themselves too seriously." To exemplify her argument, she once told her daughter in my presence about a foolproof way to avoid being hassled if you're a woman walking by a crew of construction workers: "Pick your nose."

The novels of Tom Robbins provide spiritual guidance about dealing with diabolical spirits, both those that originate within us and those that come from without. Here's a sample tip from his *Jitterbug Perfume:* "Play—more than piety, more than charity or vigilance—is what allows human beings to transcend evil."

We regret to report that further help on this matter is not available from the holy books of the world's major religions. None of their authors ever figured out that an excellent weapon against the fragmented, shadowy portions of our psyches is humor, tomfoolery, and laughter. This ignorance may be the greatest mystery in history.

But Christianity, Judaism, Islam, Buddhism, Hinduism, Confucianism, Taoism, Shintoism, Zoroastrianism, and Jainism aren't the only spiritual traditions that have failed to take advantage of evil's primary weakness. The esoteric spiritual paths of the West, including Hermeticism, Rosicrucianism, and alchemy, also suffer from an inexplicable lack of jokes and fun at the heart of their practice. Shamanism, paganism, yoga, and tantra are, for the most part, similarly bereft.

There are rare exceptions. The Sufis and Zen Buddhists have cracked a few funny stories down through the ages. The Fourth Way teacher, George Gurdjieff, had a sense of humor that he used pedagogically. And 20th-century America spawned two authentically comic religions, Discordianism and the Church of the Subgenius. Unfortunately, their combined flocks are smaller than the crowds drawn by any popular evangelical preacher in one night of mean-spirited pontificating.

Here's a letter we received at the Beauty and Truth Laboratory, along with our response.

"Dear Beauty and Truth Laboratory: After long meditation on what's missing from my relationship with God, I found the answer: a sense of humor. I realized I can never truly love or honestly communicate with a Supreme Being who doesn't chuckle. Alas, there does not seem to be a single text in any religious tradition that's even slightly comical. Can you give me some hope? —In Search of a Droll Deity"

Dear In Search of: Below are a few possibly hope-inspiring passages from one of the Beauty and Truth Laboratory's unpublished holy books, *God's Laughing With You, Not at You.*

Chapter 26, Verses 182–188:
The Plot to Debunk Pronoia

A meeting of Hell's board of directors was taking place. The devil was upset because recruitment had dropped to a new low since the pronoia meme had begun to spread. "It's intolerable," he raged. "These fucking pronoiacs are so mentally healthy it makes me want to puke. Suggestions?"

Hell's executive vice-president blurted out, "I'll go down to Earth and convince thousands of pronoiacs that their friends are jealous of their happiness."

The marketing chief chimed in: "I'll go down to Earth and make them feel guilty for feeling so good."

Then the head of intelligence spoke: "I'll go down to Earth and inspire a best-selling New Age author to write a sappy mass market book about pronoia."

Chapter 57, Verses 112–116:
How to Ask for What You Want

George prayed every day for three years to win the lottery, but never heard from God or hit the jackpot.

Finally, God woke him up in the middle of the night. "George, is that you who's been praying so hard to win the lottery?" the Supreme Being boomed.

"Yes, Lord, desperately!"

God paused for a moment, then said thoughtfully, "George, I'll tell you what. I want you to meet me halfway. Buy a ticket, OK?"

Chapter 88, Verses 15–21:
Do-It-Yourself Exorcism

If you're average, you're demonically possessed not just by split-off, unintegrated portions of your own and other people's psyches, but also by 20 million ads and 200,000 televised acts of violence stored in your brain.

The good news is that as you practice the art of pronoia, you'll attract steady streams of amusing experiences that are effective at neutralizing those toxins. Every time you laugh, you'll most likely purge a nihilistic image or inane story that had been depleting your energy. A belly laugh may flush out the imprints of as many as 500 commercials.

Chapter 93, Verses 81–84: Pronoiac Homework

Upon request, the Beauty and Truth Laboratory gives homework to students of pronoia. An assignment we're fond of is to ask them to finish the sentence, "The one thing that keeps me from being myself is _____."

Many respondents fill in the blank with "my fears." Other common answers are "lack of money," "my spouse," and "my obsession with status."

Of course there are no right answers. But the above replies don't capture the spirit of pronoia as well as an exemplary offering from Ann-Marie at Getunderground.com. "The one thing that keeps me from being myself," she wrote, "is other people's reluctance to lick patent leather."

Chapter 153, Verses 11–16: How to Know God

Below you'll find three messages. One is an authentic communiqué from the Divine Wow, which I channeled while in ecstatic trance. The other two are fakes that I made up. If you're as thoroughly in tune with your inner purpose as you need to be, you won't have any trouble knowing which is the *true* Word of the Creator.

Message #1: "I, the Supreme Designer of Heaven and Earth, am totally pissed off at your lazy sins and lack of faith. Cut the crap and shape up."

Message #2: "I, untouchable and unknowable CEO of the Universe, couldn't care less what you do. Don't bother me."

Message #3: "I, the Universal Jokester who runs all of creation on the fuel of my sublime pleasure, am well-entertained by the stories you've been living. Thanks! I can't wait to see what you do next."

HOMEOPATHIC MEDICINE SPELL #4

Change is good—you go first.

If you're happy and you know it, clank your chains.

What'd I miss? I was out smoking crack with Satan.

We have charts and graphs to back us up, so fuck off.

I will not tolerate intolerance.

My bartender can beat up your therapist.

I'm trying to see things your way, but I can't get my head up my butt.

Remember, whatever your religion might be, most of the world disagrees with you.

If I let Jesus into my heart, then everyone will want in.

Even-
tually there may be more peo-
ple on Earth who are addicted to drugs than
are not. Food shortages in parts of Asia and Africa
could get so dire that cannibalism will become acceptable
and prevalent. The Nile, Yangtze, Mississippi, Volga, and Rhine
Rivers might become so polluted that large parts of them will catch
on fire and become the sacred shrines of a new religion that worships
fiery water. Poor people might sell their organs to diseased millionaires who
need transplants. Gorgeous pollution-enhanced sunsets could ultimately seduce
millions into staring intently into the sun, causing mass blindness. A bizarre new
virus may run amok, causing its victims to suffer an uncontrollable urge to seek out
plastic surgery that will make them resemble their favorite celebrities. An evil artificial
intelligence could possibly achieve sentience on the Internet and begin systematically
spamming the computers that regulate the North American power grid with obscene knock-
knock jokes. CIA-trained psychic warriors could administer mass shock treatments via
telepathy. TV evangelist Pat Robertson may instigate a revival of the medieval Crusades,
inspiring thousands of Christians dressed in 13th-century garb to descend on Washington,
Hollywood, and Wall Street to lay siege to America's centers of power and convert the infi-
dels by any means necessary. Corporations might buy mountains and carve their logos into
the rock, like Mt. Rushmore. Breakthroughs in reversing the aging process and prolonging
human life could result in such terrible overpopulation among old people that the Social
Security system will collapse. Global warming may reach critical mass, causing Antarc-
tic ice to melt at a rate that will inundate coastal cities all over the world, after which
they will be turned into underwater theme parks. We could see the rise of a new mental illness that causes sufferers to be terrified of happiness. Cities suffering from
budget crunches might create a 900-number option for the 911 emergency line,
allowing wealthy users to pay $1,000 per minute for the privilege of having
their calls answered first and fastest. The Pentagon may spend $10 bil-
lion on research to develop military uses for the human orgasm. If terrorists kidnap the five top movie stars in Hollywood, the president
may go berserk and order American satellites to beam nonstop recordings of *Star Trek*'s William Shatner singing
"Lucy in the Sky with Diamonds" into every
television and radio in the Arab
world.

Science of the Invisible

"Who am I? Where did I come from? Where am I going?" Biologist E. O. Wilson says that philosophers long ago stopped addressing these questions, believing them to be unanswerable. Scientists stepped forward to fill the vacuum, and now act as supreme arbiters of the mysteries that were once the province of philosophers.

I'm saddened by the loss. The scientific method is a tremendous tool for understanding the world, but most scientists refuse to use it to study phenomena that can't be repeated under controlled conditions and that can't be explained by current models of reality. I think it's impossible to explore the Big Three Questions without taking into account all that elusive, enigmatic, unrepeatable stuff. The more accidental, the more true.

I can at least hope the scientists won't object if the Beauty and Truth Laboratory borrows their disciplined objectivity and incisive reasoning to explore areas they regard as off-limits.

Two groups that may not mind are the astronomers and astrophysicists. More than other scientists, they've been compelled to develop an intimate relationship with invisible realms. In fact, they've come to a conclusion that's eerily similar to the assessment of shamans and mystics from virtually every culture throughout history: Most of reality is hidden from our five senses.

"Ninety-six percent of the universe is stuff we've never seen," cosmologist Michael Turner told Geoff Brumfiel in the March 13, 2003, issue of the journal *Nature.* To be exact, the cosmos is 23 percent dark matter and 73 percent dark energy, both of which are missing. All the stars and planets and moons and asteroids and comets and nebulas and gas clouds together comprise the visible four percent.

So where is the other 96 percent? No one knows. It's not only concealed from humans, it's imperceptible to the instruments humans have devised, and its whereabouts can't be predicted by any existing theories.

What will happen as the implications of these data filter down to the other sciences? Maybe there will be a reversal of a long-term trend documented by *Nature.* In 1914, the magazine found that 30 percent of the world's top scientists believed in God. In a second survey in 1934, the number dropped to 15 percent, and by 1998 it was seven percent.

If the fact that most of reality is hidden doesn't spur them to reconsider the possibility of a divine presence working behind the scenes, maybe it will move them to become more sympathetic to a project like ours, which has the intention of adopting the scientific approach to an exploration of the invisible.

Most modern intellectuals scoff at angels, dismissing them as superstitious hallucinations or New Age goofiness. But not all deep thinkers have shared their scorn. John Milton and William Blake regarded angels as worthy of their explorations. Celestial beings have also received serious treatment by Saul Bellow, E. M. Forster, Gabriel Garcia Marquez, Isaac Bashevis Singer, and Leo Tolstoy. Of course, just because smart people have considered the possibility that angels can have real effects on the material world doesn't mean they do. Still, it might be interesting to keep an open mind.

Scientist Carl Sagan smoked pot. "He believed the drug enhanced his creativity and insights," wrote Keay Davidson in the *San Francisco Examiner,* quoting Sagan's pal Lester Grinspoon. "If I find in the morning a message from myself the night before informing me that there is a world around us which we barely sense," Sagan said, "or that we can become one with the universe, I may disbelieve; but when I'm high I know about this disbelief. And so I have a tape in which I exhort myself to take such remarks seriously. I say 'Listen closely, you sonofabitch of the morning! This stuff is real!'"

"The more I examine the universe and the details of its architecture, the more evidence I find that the universe in some sense must have known we were coming." — physicist Freeman Dyson

"To be truly atheistic, not just agnostic, you have to take the nonexistence of God on faith."
—I. M. Boyd

The 17th-century Church fathers wouldn't look through Galileo's telescope to see the small bodies he said were orbiting Jupiter. Why bother? Catholic doctrine was clear that no such things could exist.

Likewise, most of today's scientists refuse to consider the possibility that there are unidentified craft flying around our skies. "It's absurd to think that beings from other star systems could traverse the vast distances between them and us," they declare, "so why should we even examine the so-called evidence?" Their certainty contains a giant bias: that creatures from other worlds can only have ships that are limited to the means of propulsion we have thus far discovered here on Earth.

Arthur Koestler said that to the ancient Greeks, electricity was as bizarre and unfathomable as telepathy is to us in the modern era. Yet electricity existed before it was believed in. It's just that there was no theory that proposed its existence and no mechanism to gather evidence for it. Culture had to change in order for people to be able to know where and how to look.

Today we're aware of electricity as well as black holes, X-rays, radio waves, and infrared light because we have instruments to extend our senses. But is it wise to assume that we have finally developed every sense-extending technology that will ever be invented?

When Columbus's ships first appeared on the horizon, the Arawaks on the island of Guanahaní saw them as floating monsters. They didn't have the conceptual framework to know them for what they literally were. *You can't perceive what you can't conceive.* An adult who has been blind all his life and through surgery is suddenly given the power of sight takes quite a while to be able to learn to interpret what he's looking at. The eye alone doesn't see. The mind and the cultural biases it has internalized interpret and shape the raw data.

Modern science is a fabulous way of understanding reality, but it's not the crown of creation. Just as meteors, dinosaurs, and electricity (and dark matter and neutrinos and gamma rays) were inconceivable and therefore not real to earlier generations, there may be phenomena here with us now that won't be real until our culture and minds and instruments evolve further. Will they include events we now call UFOs and angels? Maybe. Maybe not. Let's remain curious.

"Ancient stars in their death throes spat out atoms like iron which this universe had never known. The novel tidbits of debris were sucked up by infant suns which, in turn, created yet more atoms when their race was run. Now the iron of old nova coughings vivifies the redness of our blood.

"If stars step constantly upward, why should the global interlace of humans, microbes, plants, and animals not move upward steadily as well? The horizons

Dionysian Manifesto

toward which we must soar are within us, anxious to break free, to emerge from our imaginings, then to beckon us forward into fresh realities.

"We have a mission to create, for we are evolution incarnate. We are her self-awareness, her frontal lobes and fingertips. We are second-generation star stuff come alive. We are parts of something 3.5 billion years old, but pubertal in cosmic time. We are neurons of this planet's interspecies mind." —Howard Bloom, *Global Brain: The Evolution of Mass Mind from the Big Bang to the 21st Century*

According to the indigenous people who lived in the Americas before Europeans arrived, the world is populated with spiritual powers that take the shape of animals and plants and natural forces. In other words, there are many forms of intelligence, not just the kind that reside in human brains.

It's possible to communicate with these other intelligences. We can tune in to their alternate modes of knowing and seeing, thereby expanding our narrow understanding of reality. To do that, however, we can't rely on spoken and written language, but must be receptive to their non-verbal codes.

Antonio Favaro (1847–1922) edited a 20-volume work that collected Galileo's writings. "There's not the slightest doubt that Galileo was involved with astrology," Favaro wrote. "He was famous for his great ability in that art, so that distinguished people consulted him with complete confidence, in many cases asking for horoscopes and predictions."

Kary Mullis is the only Nobel Prize-winning scientist ever to suggest that some aspects of astrology are valid. He's also the most distinguished prodigy in history to have described a close encounter with a UFO. When he's not doing pioneering research on the human genome, he likes to surf and explore shamanism.

"He's a scientific genius with a vibrant soul," said a critic who reviewed his autobiography *Dancing Naked in the Mind Field.* "There is nothing too preposterous for him to rigorously investigate and learn something valuable from, just as there are few commonly held truths in which he cannot find some fundamental fallacy."

"It shouldn't surprise us to find ourselves linked with the stars. Every atom of gold or silver jewelry was created in supernovas. The water we drink, the air we breathe, the ground we walk, the complicated pouch of fluids and salts and minerals and bones we are—all forged in some early chaos of our sun. I think it was the astrophysicist John Wheeler who remarked that we are the sun's way of thinking about itself." —Diane Ackerman, *A Slender Thread: Rediscovering Hope at the Heart of Crisis*

"The Kabbalists assert that the Great Work consists of 'helping God to behold God.'" —Richard Smoley

Robert Anton Wilson said that "the universe acts like a chess game in which the player on the other side remains invisible to us. By analyzing the moves, we can form an image of the intellect behind them."

Biologist Rupert Sheldrake regularly riles up the scientific establishment with his theories about telepathy and other taboo subjects. After he published his book *A New Science of Life,* the editor of the prestigious British journal *Nature* denounced it, saying, "This infuriating tract is the best candidate for burning there has been for many years." The same editor later attacked Sheldrake for "heresy," advocating that he be "condemned in exactly the same language that the Pope used to condemn Galileo."

In his book *Signs of Success,* astrologer Steven Weiss says "The question 'Do you believe in astrology?' is like asking someone if they believe in art."

I agree. Picture a no-nonsense physicist gazing at a Kandinsky painting, with its teeming blobs of mad color and exuberant shapes, and declaring it to be a superstitious eruption of delusion that's not based on a logical understanding of the world.

Like Kandinsky's perspective, astrology at its best roots us in the poetic language of the soul, and isn't blindly submissive to the values of the rational ego. It's here to liberate our imaginations and encourage us to think less literally and to visualize life as a mythic quest.

Physicist Roger Penrose, who helped to develop the theories about black holes, has said that the chance of an ordered universe happening at random is nil: one in 10 to the 10th to the 30th, a number so large that if you programmed a computer to write a million zeroes per second, it would take a million times the age of the universe just to write the number down.

"The big bang is so preposterous," says renowned astronomer Allan Sandage, co-discoverer of the quasar, "and the chain of events it set off so unlikely, that it makes most sense when thought of as a 'miracle.'"

For the sake of argument, let's assume Sandage is right. If the very beginning of the universe itself was a miracle, then everything in it is impregnated with the possibility of smaller but equally marvelous miracles.

"I shall not commit the fashionable stupidity of regarding everything I cannot explain as a fraud." —Carl Jung

In the science fiction film *Contact*, Jodie Foster plays an astronaut who's sent on a solo trip to an alien world far from our solar system. As she careens through a staggering array of sublime celestial phenomena, she muses aloud, half crying, "It's so beautiful . . . so beautiful . . . They should have sent a poet."

"When a scientist states that something is possible, he is almost certainly right. When he states that something is impossible, he is very probably wrong." Those are the words of Arthur C. Clarke, who, due to his contributions to science, had an asteroid and dinosaur species named after him.

"As a man who has devoted his whole life to the most clear-headed science, to the study of matter, I can tell you as a result of my research about the atoms this much: There is no matter as such! All matter originates and exists only by virtue of a force which brings the particles of an atom to vibration and holds this most minute solar system of the atom together . . . We must assume behind this force the existence of a conscious and intelligent Mind. This Mind is the matrix of all matter." —Max Planck, from a speech he gave in Florence, Italy, in 1944, entitled "Das Wesen der Materie" ("The Essence/Nature/Character of Matter")

"A terrorist is the product of our education that says that fantasy is not real, that says aesthetics is just for artists, that says soul is only for priests, imagination is trivial or dangerous and for crazies, and that reality, what we must adapt to, is the external world, a world that is dead. A terrorist is a result of this whole long process of wiping out the psyche." —James Hillman, *Blue Fire*

"The laws of physics appear 'fine tuned' for our existence. Even slight deviations in the laws would result in a universe devoid of stars and life. If, for instance, the force of gravity were just a few percent weaker it could not squeeze and heat the matter inside stars to the millions of degrees that are necessary to trigger sunlight generating nuclear reactions. If gravity were only a few percent stronger, however, it would heat up stars, causing them to consume their fuel faster. They would not exist for the billions of years needed for evolution to produce intelligence. This kind of fine tuning is widespread." —Marcus Chown, "Radical Science: Did Angels Create the Universe?", *The Independent*, March 15, 2002, tinyurl.com/2nhonn

The modern war between science and spirituality seems laughable in light of the life of Sir Isaac Newton. His discoveries in the realms of physics, mathematics, and astronomy were so seminal and so numerous that he's regarded as the single most influential scientist. Many refer to him as the greatest genius who ever lived.

And yet Newton's central passions were alchemy and the Bible, about which he wrote millions of words, far more than what he devoted to his strictly scientific

Dionysian Manifesto

interests. "Gravity explains the motions of the planets," he wrote, "but it cannot explain who set the planets in motion. God governs all things and knows all that is or can be done."

Newton's biographer James Gleick says he discovered "more of the essential core of human knowledge than anyone before or after." Ostensibly, the great man was humble, writing that "if I have seen further it is by standing on the shoulders of giants."

But he did not actually believe that, writes Salon.com's Farhad Manjoo in his review of Gleick's book. And the fact is that Newton's breakthroughs "were not incremental, not the logical conclusion to centuries of study," but rather the result of "a supernatural, superhuman intuition."

Could his grounding in both science and spirituality have been one of the factors responsible for his astounding brilliance?

"Ultimately what we're touching is the invisible, all-pervasive Intelligence that surrounds us and penetrates us. It is grooming us to be able to tolerate its splendor. It can't just reveal itself openly because we would be forfeited; we'd never know what hit us." —Terence McKenna

"Our normal waking consciousness, rational consciousness as we call it, is but one special type of consciousness, whilst all about it, parted from it by the flimsiest of screens, there lie potential forms of consciousness entirely different. . . . No account of the universe in its totality can be final which leaves these other forms of consciousness quite disregarded." —William James, *The Varieties of Religious Experience*

In the *Sutra of Forty-two Chapters,* the Buddha is quoted as saying, "My doctrine is to think the thought that is unthinkable, to practice the deed that is unperformable, to speak the speech that is inexpressible, and to be trained in the discipline that is beyond discipline."

Militant atheists make the claim that religion has always been a primary cause of war. If humans weren't under the sway of "the God delusion," they fume, armed conflicts would be infrequent.

But military historian Eric Bergerud, author of four books about various wars, says that's absurd. He notes that while there have been a few religious wars, "most wars in history have been driven by the lust for power and loot."

In other words, the materialist delusion is far more lethal than the God delusion. People who believe there's nothing of value beyond what the five senses can perceive are often the most dangerous of all.

"People with a psychological need to believe in marvels are no more prejudiced and gullible than people with a psychological need not to believe in marvels." —Charles Fort

Biologist Francis Crick (1916–2004) won a Nobel Prize for co-discovering the DNA molecule. Naturally, he did not have any use for the religious right's pet dogma, Intelligent Design. But neither did he fully endorse evolution. That theory says Earth's first life forms accidentally arose from organic molecules, which in turn accidentally coalesced from inorganic matter. In Crick's opinion, that process was impossible because there wasn't enough time for such a stupendously complex series of events to unfold, given the fact that our planet is only 4.6 billion years old.

To address the discrepancy, Crick favored the theory of "directed panspermia," which proposes that life arrived here via an advanced extraterrestrial civilization. He carved out a middle ground between two competing perspectives, transcending the narrow definitions that each of them uses to frame the big questions.

"The universe looks less and less like a great machine and more and more like a great thought." —physicist James Jeans

"To [George] Gilder's mind, most of what secularism gets wrong about the world can be summed up in the phrase 'the Materialist Superstition.' By this, he means

Dionysian Manifesto

the idea that the world is composed only of physical matter, and whatever else may arise—love, religious feeling—is a product of matter and reducible to it.

"Included in this mistake, according to Gilder, is any sort of economics that imagines industrial development to have a momentum of its own apart from the genius of individual entrepreneurs; any psychology that conceives of consciousness as a side product of the brain; and any biology that understands evolution as a purely bodily process spurred by carnal need and random mutation.

"Gilder believes that quantum physics has confirmed his view: to him, the discovery that matter is, at its base, composed not of inert, solid articles but of waves, fields, and probabilities means that matter is, at base, intelligence or spirit." —Larissa MacFarquhar, *The New Yorker*

A century before the New Age movement, French playwright Victor Hugo (1802–1885) was conversing with the dead. Here's what the spirit of Galileo told him at a séance: "You know what I would do if I were in your place? I'd drink from the milk basin of the Milky Way; I'd swallow comets; I'd lunch on dawn; I'd dine on day and I'd sup on night; I'd invite myself, splendid table-companion that I am, to the banquet of all the glories, and I'd salute God as my host! I'd work up a magnificent hunger, an enormous thirst, and I'd race through the drunken spaces between the spheres singing the fearsome drinking song of eternity." —Victor Hugo, *Conversations with Eternity,* translated by John Chambers

Once the full impact of Einstein's theory of relativity became clear, an admiring journalist interviewed him about the process by which he'd arrived at the revolutionary breakthrough. "How did you do it?" the journalist asked. "I ignored an axiom," Einstein replied.

To be clear, the revolutionary scientist didn't say he'd ignored an opinion or theory, but rather an idea so well established that it was regarded as self-evident. Furthermore, he didn't say he rebelled or fought against the axiom: He simply acted as if it weren't there.

"Something unknown is doing we don't know what." —Astrophysicist Arthur Eddington, "one of three persons in the world who understood Einstein's theory of general relativity"

Dear scientists: We pledge to summon our finest analytical intelligence and use impeccable logic as we experiment with the hypothesis that there is no contradiction between cultivating scrupulous critical thinking and communing with the part of reality that's hidden from our senses. —Love, the Beauty and Truth Lab

"All of this is the Earth educating itself. Think of the language that has come alive in just this one afternoon: Do you think we are solely responsible for that? Good heavens, no! Think of the sacrifices required of billions of creatures to make such language possible.

"Take a single sentence: 'The fireball exploded 20 billion years ago at the beginning of time.' That sentence required nothing less than the full 20 billion years of cosmic development.

"It is not 'my' sentence; nor does it 'belong' to the theoretical scientists who first predicted the existence of the fireball, nor the experimental scientists who first detected its heat; it is a sentence of the whole Earth. Nothing less than that is required for its speaking forth.

"The sentence could not exist without the oceans, the rivers, the air, the life forms, and all the thousands of years of human cultural activities. Every sentence is spoken by the whole Earth." —Brian Swimme, *The Universe Is a Green Dragon*

Sacred Advertisement

This perfect moment is brought to you by the mummified middle finger of Galileo's right hand, which is on display at the Museo di Storia del Scienza in Florence, Italy. May it inspire you to flip the metaphorical bird at anyone who proudly embodies the kind of high-level idiocy Galileo had to endure.

"REBRANDING GOD" PRONOIA THERAPY

Experiments and exercises in becoming a bewilderingly enlightened, ecstatically grateful Master of Fiendishly Benevolent Tricks

Report your answers and research results below

1 Philosopher Robert Anton Wilson proposed that the single greatest contribution to world peace would come from there being over six billion different religions—a unique spiritual path for each person on the planet. The Beauty and Truth Lab urges you to get started on doing your part to make this happen. What will your religion be called? What rituals will you perform? Write down your three core tenets.

2 You'll also need a new name for the Creator. "God" and "Goddess" have been so overused and abused that most of us are numb to them. And given the spiritual opportunities that will open up for you as you explore pronoia, you can't afford to have an impaired sensitivity toward the Great Mystery.

Here's an idea to stimulate your search: The Russian word for God is "Bog." The Basques call the Supreme Being "Jingo." To purge your psychic dockets of built-up fixations about deity, you might try singing improvisational prayers to "Jingo Bog."

Here are a few other fresh names to inspire you:
Blooming HaHa
Divine Wow
Whirl-Zap-Gush
Sublime Cackler
Chthonic Riddler

3 Since ancient times, China has hosted three religions: Confucianism, Buddhism, and Taoism. Many Chinese people have cobbled together a mélange of beliefs gathered from all three. This is different from the Western way, which is to be faithful to one religion or another, never mixing and matching.

But that's changing in certain enclaves in North America, where growing numbers of seekers are adopting the Chinese approach. They borrow elements from a variety of spiritual traditions to create a personalized path. Religious historians call this syncretism.

As you meditate on conjuring up your own unique mode of worship, think of the good parts you'd like to steal from other religions.

"I used to be an atheist until I realized that I was God."
—Deepak Chopra

4 Most religions designate a special class of people—priests, rabbis, ayatollahs—to oversee official communications with the Source. This has led to a prevailing assumption, even among those who don't follow an established faith, that we can't initiate a divine conversation without the aid of a professional class of trained mediators. Among some sects of the ancient gnostics, in contrast, everyone was regarded as a potential prophet who could experience epiphanies worthy of becoming part of the ever-evolving doctrine.

The equivalent today would be if the Bible were regarded as an unfinished text to which every Christian or Jew might be eligible to add new content.

As you create your own spiritual path, experiment with this do-it-yourself approach. What might you do to eliminate the middleman and commune directly with the Source?

5 The chorus of an old Depeche Mode song goes like this: "I don't want to start / any blasphemous rumors / But I think that God's / got a sick sense of humor / And when I die / I expect to find him laughing." I have a grudging respect for these lyrics. In an age when God has been co-opted by intolerant fundamentalists and mirthless sentimentalists, I appreciate any artist who suggests there's more to the Infinite Spirit than the one-dimensional prig described in the Bible or Koran.

On the other hand, Depeche Mode's notion of the Blooming HaHa is also disinformation. It's as much a hostage to pop culture's knee-jerk nihilism as the right-wing bigots' God is to their monumental hatreds. One thing I know for sure about the Supreme Being is that while she does have a complicated sense of humor, it's not cruel or vengeful.

Your assignment: Pray to be granted a healing sample of her comedic genius—a funny, unexpected miracle that will free you of any tendencies you have to believe the age-old lies about her.

"Rebranding God" Pronoia Therapy

6 Will there be prayer in your new religion? If so, we suggest that you avoid the body language traditionally used by Christians in their worship. The gesture of clasping one's hands together originated long ago as an imitation of being shackled; it was thought to be the proper way to express submission to divine power.

The prayers you make, however, may be imbued as much with reverent exuberance or ecstatic gratitude as somber submissiveness. An example of a more apt gesture is to spread your arms as wide and high as they'll go, as if you're hugging the sky. Any other ideas?

7 What if the Creator is like the poet Rainer Maria Rilke's God: "like a webbing made of a hundred roots, that drink in silence"? What if the Source of All Life inhabits both the dark and the light, heals with strange splendor as much as with sweet insight, is hermaphroditic and omnisexual?

What if the Source loves to give you riddles that push you past the boundaries of your understanding, forcing you to change the ways you think about everything? What if, as Rusty Morrison speculates in *Poetry Flash,* "the sublime can only be glimpsed by pressing through fear's boundary, beyond one's previous conceptions of the beautiful"?

Close your eyes and imagine you can sense the presence of this tender, marvelous, difficult, entertaining intelligence.

You're hungry for the infinite, and the infinite is hungry for you.

8 At a candy store one Easter season, I heard a philosophical debate about Jesus-themed confections. "It's just not right to eat a symbol of God," one woman said as she gazed at a chocolate Christ on the cross. A man agreed: "It's sacrilegious. An abomination." An employee overheard and jumped in. "I'll ask my boss to take that stuff off the shelf," she clucked.

I was tempted to say what I was thinking: "Actually, the holiest ritual of Christian worship involves eating Christ's body and drinking his blood." But I held my tongue; I wasn't in the mood for a brouhaha.

Where do you stand on this issue? Do you or do you not want to eat a symbolic embodiment of your deity? If you do, what food will you choose?

"Rebranding God" Pronoia Therapy

9 At one point in James Michener's novel *Hawaii,* a native Hawaiian tells ignorant missionaries, "You cannot speak to the gods with your clothes on." Whereupon he strips and prepares for prayer. Test this theory. Find out if your communion with the Divine Wow improves when you're naked.

10 A few Christian sects now enjoy a new addition to their once-staid church services: holy laughter. Parishioners become so excited while worshiping that they erupt in uncontrollable glee. Some crack up so profoundly that they fall on the floor and flop around like breakdancers. Others repeatedly leap into the air as if on pogo sticks, or wobble and zigzag as if trying to dance while drunk.

Imagine that the holy books of your religion prescribe laughing prayers as a reliable way to know the Divine Wow. Recite one of those laughing prayers.

11 "Believing" in God is like "believing" in the taste of fresh-baked bread without ever having tasted actual fresh-baked bread. But what if you could commune with the Divine Wow through up-close, personal encounters that are as vivid as eating fresh-baked bread? Some people have. You could, too. Formulate the intention to do so.

12 I've got one main religion—a big-time spiritual obsession—and 10 other "hobby" religions that I keep going on the side.

To avoid getting set in my ways with my number one, I make it a policy to change its name on a regular basis, as well as to add at least one new principle and one new practice once a month. As of this writing, I'm calling it the Born-Again Pagan Church of Amazed Anarchists. A few weeks ago it was the Magic Order of Educated Rapture, and pretty soon I'm thinking of becoming the Ism-Free Sect of the Love Butter Congregation.

The most recent addition to our ever-growing holy canon is the doctrine espoused by Caroline Myss in her article "In Times Like These" (tinyurl.com/4g3swz): "Divine chaos is a course corrector, a way of bringing down the systems that distraction built in order that they can be replaced with systems or structures designed with conscious thought."

As for the latest addition to our ritual practice, we are now deeply committed to learning the spiritual art of spitting into the wind without getting sprayed.

Would you be interested in purusing this ever-evolving approach?

"Rebranding God" Pronoia Therapy

13 In Judeo-Christian cultures, many people associate the sky with the masculine form of God. According to this bias, the Supreme Father rules us all from on high—up, away, far from here. But if you were an ancient Egyptian, the sky was the goddess Nuit, her body its very substance. She was a loving mother whose tender touch could be felt with each new breath.

For one day, act as if you and the sky goddess are in constant contact.

14 Neither God nor the gods are dead, but they seem to be disappearing because so few of us are capable of carrying on authentic relationships with them anymore. The materialist delusion rules: Millions believe that nothing's real unless it can be perceived by the senses. Churches and temples are full of ethical people, but many of them have no clue about how to know or feel or converse with the divine intelligences.

What can the deities do, having been banished from our conscious knowing? Jung said they have no recourse but to worm their way into our lives as sickness and pathology. Repressed, they come in the back door.

Which of your maladies or pains might be gods in disguise? How might you get them to take off their masks and begin knocking on the front door?

> ## *"A religious person is one who contributes to the world some beauty, joy, happiness, or celebration that was not there before."*
> ### *—Osho*

15 The time: 2003. The place: a New York restaurant. The scenario: A talking carp began shouting at a food preparer who was about to turn it into a meal. The restaurant owner came in to investigate and became a second witness to the event. He determined that the carp was offering religious advice in Hebrew. *The New York Times* reported the story, and soon a local Hasidic sect was proclaiming the fish's message to be a direct communication from God.

Though many people laugh derisively when they hear this tale, I retain an open mind. The Divine Trickster has appeared to me in equally unusual forms. What about you? Are you crazy enough to listen to the wisdom of a talking carp? If not, what have you got to lose?

16 In Kevin Smith's movie *Dogma,* pop singer Alanis Morissette played God. Anthony Quinn was Zeus in the TV show *Hercules,* and comedian George Burns performed the role of God in three movies, always "without makeup," as he bragged. Who would you like to portray God or Goddess in the movie of your life?

17 It came to pass that the Goddess appeared to me in a vision and told me of a rooster who'd soon win a cock fight in rural Maurice, Louisiana. "Bet on Cocky Wizard," she urged, "and you will double your money." "But Shining Lady," I protested, "aren't cock fights cruel and illegal?" And She said unto me, "I will protect you from karmic harm as long as you promise Me that you will donate your earnings to beauty and truth fans who need more money in order to be better servants of pronoia." Obeying Her command, I bet on Cocky Wizard, and just as she predicted, won $30. I gave my winnings to a woman who leads a choir that goes into hospices to sing songs for the dying.

What do you think of my actions? Did I sin, or will my generosity protect me from karmic comeuppance? If you believe the latter, do an analogous experiment.

18 In *Letters to a Young Poet,* Rilke urged an aspiring bard to change the way he imagined the Supreme Being. "Why don't you conceive of God as an ally who is coming," Rilke said, "who has been approaching since time began, the one who will someday arrive, the fruit of a tree whose leaves we are? Why not project his birth into the future, and live your life as an excruciating and lyrical moment in the history of a prodigious pregnancy?"

How would your life change if you made this idea your working hypothesis?

19 HappyWomanMagazine.com sought out several supermodels for advice about spirituality. "Buddhists have the best religion," said 6'1", 102-pound Ilize Bergeron. "They don't believe in heaven or hell or God, and they don't pray. Plus, Buddhism is so mysterious that you could probably fool your boss into giving you lots of random days off work for religious holidays. One more thing: It's the trendiest religion out there."

Draw inspiration from Ilize's perspective. Praise the religion or religions you think are best.

20 In *The Golden Bough,* a historical catalog of magical and religious practices, James Frazer noted

"Rebranding God" Pronoia Therapy

that on occasion people have grown exasperated with their god's failure to deliver the desired goods. They may even try to motivate a deity by shaming or abusing him. If the Rain-Bringer has been derelict in his duty, for instance, his statue may be cast out under the hot sun until he shapes up.

A reader sent a letter to the Beauty and Truth Lab about this issue. "After a long stretch of patiently putting up with God's mean-spirited tricks," it read, "I decided I'd had enough. So I fired Him. Now I'm going to create a brand new deity from scratch. Do you have any recommendations on what qualities a truly cool divine being might possess? —The Groggy Awakener"

How would you answer The Groggy Awakener's inquiry?

In your dreams, you could steal one of the peaches of immortality from the tree of life.

21 In some ancient Greek dramas, a god showed up out of nowhere to cause a miraculous twist at a crucial point in the tale. This divine intrusion was referred to as *theos ek mechanes,* literally "god from a machine," because the symbolic figure of the god was lowered onto the stage by a crane. In modern usage, the term is Latin—*deus ex machina*—and refers to a story in which a sudden event unexpectedly brings about a resolution to a baffling problem.

Write a tale in which you're the beneficiary of such an intervention.

22 A reader named Michael McCarthy wrote to say he plans to start a new religion, the "First Church of the Rude Awakening." It will be based on the principle that having a pleasant life cannot serve as a motivation to seek enlightenment and salvation. McCarthy believes that no one ever bolts up out of bed one morning and says, "I'm so happy, I think I'll go meditate and pray and make myself into a better person for as long as it takes, so I can find God and say thanks."

Disprove this theory. Detonate an epiphany precisely because you're in an excellent mood.

23 In Frederick Buechner's book *On the Road with the Archangel,* the star is the archangel Raphael. This supernatural helper has a tough gig: gathering the

"Rebranding God" Pronoia Therapy

prayers of human beings and delivering them to God. Here's how he describes the range of pleas he hears: "There are prayers of such power that you might say they carry me rather than the other way around. There are prayers so apologetic and shamefaced and half-hearted that they all but melt away in my grasp like sad little flakes of snow. Some prayers are very boring."

Compose a prayer that's so powerful and entertaining that it could thrill an archangel.

24 There is no God. God is dead. God is a drug for people who aren't very smart. God is an illusion sold to dupes by money-hungry religions. God is a right-wing conspiracy. God is an infantile fantasy favored by superstitious cowards who can't face life's existential meaninglessness. APRIL FOOL! The truth is, anyone who says he knows what God is or isn't, doesn't.

Now read Adolfo Quezada's prayer, then confess what you don't know about God. "God of the Wild, you are different from what I expected. I cannot predict you. You are too free to be captured for the sake of my understanding. I can't find you in the sentimentalism of religion. You are everywhere I least expect to find you. You are not the force that saves me from the pain of living; you are the force that brings me life even in the midst of pain."

25 Born in the 14th century, Catherine of Siena was an eccentric religious leader whose power was enhanced by her unusual style. No other woman in the history of the Catholic Church, for instance, has ever asserted that Jesus personally gave her his foreskin to wear as a wedding ring. And no one else has invoked the image of nursing from the breast of Christ, as she frequently did in her writings.

And yet these quirks were in part responsible for her huge following, which in turn provided her with enough political clout to convince Pope Gregory XI to move the papal residence from Avignon back to Rome.

Consider making Catherine of Siena a saint or tulku in your new religion. What other irresistible freaks might you select to be sacred role models?

26 The German word *selig* can mean "ecstatic," "blessed," or "holy." It implies that profound bliss can be a divine gift; that deep pleasure may generate or come from spiritual inspiration.

The English language doesn't have a term comparable to *selig,* maybe because our culture regards ecstasy with suspicion. Religious people tend to believe that the blessed are those who are good and kind, certainly not those who are skilled at cultivating rapturous states. People who worship rationality, on the other hand, like intellectuals and scientists, often think of ecstasy as at best an irrelevant state, and at worst a nonproductive or deluded indulgence.

What would you have to do to place yourself in intimate alignment with the values embodied by the word *selig*?

27 "They say a thing is holy if it makes you hold your tongue," muses a character in John Crowley's fantasy novel *Engine Summer,* speaking of the difference between his culture and another. "But we say a thing is holy if it makes you laugh."

Is your goofy joy compatible with your yearning for the breakthroughs that make you feel at home in the world? Can your giddiness serve your reverence?

P.S. The English word "silly" comes from the German *selig*.

For best results with your prayer games, use the proper proportions of wine, river mud, saliva, and gasoline.

28 Once every seven years I undertake a ceremonial journey called "A Pilgrimage to the Sacred Shopping Shrines of North America." It's rooted in the only minimally ironic hypothesis that a sincere seeker can have close encounters with the divine presence anywhere—even in places that are usually regarded as profane or irrelevant to the spiritual quest.

During one such trip, I enjoyed a three-hour prayer party while trance-dancing with a group of new friends to the accompaniment of 10 African drums under a full moon in the parking lot of an all-night Wal-Mart Supercenter in Louisville.

Another time, I participated in a Platonic Tantric EyeGasm ritual with five yoginis in the cereal section of a Safeway in San Francisco. We gazed into each others' eyes, two-at-a-time, until rapturous blasts of enlightenment erupted.

"Rebranding God" Pronoia Therapy

On a third occasion, while loitering in New York's Neiman Marcus consumer temple, my fellow worshipers and I did Appalachian square dances as we sang Sanskrit hymns from the Rigveda, and taught each other chaotic meditation techniques we'd learned from various fake shamans, and channeled slapstick imitations of dead comedians Lenny Bruce and Bill Hicks as if we were entertaining a crowd of bodhisattvas in heaven.

Your assignment: Carry out your own version of a pilgrimage to a sacred shopping shrine.

29 A Serbian beekeeper shares his deep religious fervor with the insects he spends so much time with. Slobodan Jeftic builds beehives shaped like churches because he believes bees have souls, too.

Draw inspiration from his example. Get together with your favorite animals for a rowdy prayer session. Bark or purr or neigh or chirp together. Run around with holy abandon, expressing primal appreciation for the vitality you've been granted. If you're not currently in an intimate relationship with special animals, then take this as an opportunity to elevate and celebrate the consciousness of your own inner creature.

30 A few years ago, astronomers announced the discovery of a shiny red planet-like world orbiting the sun far beyond Pluto. They called it Sedna, a name they said was derived from the Inuit deity that created the Arctic's sea creatures. But the truth about the myth of Sedna is more complicated.

She is the Dark Goddess, embodiment of the wild female potencies that are feared yet sorely needed by cultures in which the masculine perspective dominates. Dwelling on the edge of life and death in her home at the bottom of the sea, Sedna is both a source of fertile abundance and a mysterious prodigy. Shamans from the world above swim down to sing her songs and comb her long black hair. If they win her favor, she gives them the magic necessary to heal their suffering patients.

I suspect the discovery of Sedna is an omen signaling our collective readiness to welcome back the long-repressed influence of the Dark Nurturer. Do you have room for her in your religion?

Here are some further omens, all of which have pronoia embedded in their dark and fertile musings. 1. *Women Who Run with the Wolves* by Clarissa Pinkola Estés. 2. *Spiritual Madness: The Necessity of Meeting God in Darkness,* an audio CD by Caroline Myss. 3. *The*

"Rebranding God" Pronoia Therapy

Creative Fire, an audio CD by Clarissa Pinkola Estés. 4. My book *The Televisionary Oracle,* which you can buy or read for free at my website: tinyurl.com/3c2j4x or tinyurl.com/6blklz.

31 In the Tibetan Buddhist tradition, prayer flags are sets of brightly colored sacramental cloths that are inscribed with holy words and images of deities. They're not designed for indoor use in solemn ceremonies, but are hung outside where the wind blows their blessings to the heavens and all over the world.

Interested? Take your spiritual yearnings away from the church and temple and mosque, and beyond all sheltered, temperature-controlled trappings. Build a shrine in the wilderness. Sing a hymn from a mountaintop, shower money on the river goddess, or create your own homemade prayer flags and hang them from a tree.

32 "Women are traps that lay for men everywhere," said Franz Kafka, "in order to drag them into the infinite." If you find Kafka's idea sexist or heterosexist, formulate your own version. One way or another, arrange to get lured or yanked into a bracing experience of boundless possibilities . . . into a delightfully shocking immersion in eternal truth . . . into a whirlwind tour of brain-scrambling beauty. If an amazing man works better, or a thrilling member of an in-between gender, seek that person out. Play hard with the limitless.

33 Thousands of scientists are engaged in research to crack the code of the aging process. Their coming breakthroughs may allow you to live a healthy and vigorous life well into your 90s—and even beyond.

How can you contribute to this worthy cause? What might you do to promote your longevity? Brainstorm about possible strategies.

And now I drink a toast to your coffin. May it be fashioned of lumber obtained from a hundred-year-old cypress tree whose seed will germinate this year.

**The Buddha
said enlightenment
can be attained
without the need
for gods, priests, saints,
rituals, and idols.
But what fun is that?**

34 Let's move on to discuss the possibility that sooner or later, the physical body you inhabit will expire. Your heart will shut down. Blood will no longer course through your veins. The fleshly vehicle you knew as your home for so many years will rot. Is this the ultimate proof, as some people bitterly proclaim, that there is no God and that pronoia is a lie?

I say no. I say that the Creator includes death as an essential part of evolution's master plan. Lifetime after lifetime, our immortal souls take on a series of temporary forms as we help unfold, in our own small ways, the inconceivably complex plot of the divine drama. Each time we die, it's hard and sad to our time-bound egos. But from the perspective of the part of us that has always been and will always be, it's simply part of the epic adventure.

Assume, for argument's sake, that what I've just said is a fact. Describe how different your life would be if you not only believed but perceived the truth that your essential self will never die, but will inhabit many bodies and live many lives on Earth.

35 If you'd like to be a cult member in one of my part-time side-religions, the Flaming Jewel Temple of Living Outside of Time, simply smash a clock or watch with a hammer on the first of February and October every year at exactly 12:22 p.m. your time.

36 In the film *Angels in America,* the character named Belize describes his vision of heaven. It's not a spotlessly clean gated community where everyone wears white gowns and nothing ever changes. Rather, it's a "big city, overgrown with weeds, but flowering weeds. On every corner a wrecking crew, and something new and crooked going up catty-cornered to that. Gusts of gritty wind, and a gray, high sky alive with ravens. Piles of trash, but lapidary like rubies and obsidian. Diamond-colored streamers. Voting booths. Dance palaces full of music and lights and racial impurity and gender confusion. All the deities are creole, mulatto, brown as the mouths of rivers."

Inspired by Belize, vamp and riff on your vision of heaven.

The abolition of suffering is a worthy goal.

PRONOIA NEWS NETWORK

Tundra Cheer

"A major psychiatric study of 1,200 Finnish reindeer herders found midwinter to be quite a cheery time, despite darkness and daily temperatures that averaged a bone-chilling minus 22 degrees. 'All kinds of disorders, including depression, were rare in the darkest season,' Dr. Nayha Vaisanen and his team of scientists concluded in the 1994 issue of the journal *Acta Psychiatrica Scandinavia*."
—Lisa M. Krieger, *San Francisco Examiner*

Hands That Harvested Your Food

"Strawberries are too delicate to be picked by machine. The perfectly ripe ones bruise even at too heavy a human touch. Every strawberry you have ever eaten has been picked by callused human hands. Every piece of toast with jelly represents someone's knees, someone's aching backs and hips, someone with a bandanna on her wrist to wipe away the sweat." —Alison Luterman, quoted in *After the Ecstasy, the Laundry,* by Jack Kornfield

PNN is brought to you by the Buddha's reminder that "No miseries befall one who does not cling to name and form," and by Henry Miller's brag in his book, Tropic of Cancer, *"I have no money, no resources, no hopes. I am the happiest man alive."*

Creeping Democracy

Democracy is coming to China, at least on the local level. A majority of villages now use voting to select their government officials. (Source: goodnewsnetwork.org)

SPACE RACE

Businessman Dennis Tito paid the Russians to let him join their astronauts on a trip to the International Space Station. U.S. officials were peeved. Then-NASA administrator Daniel Goldin raged that it would be a "cold day in hell" before his agency would welcome "tourists" like Tito. In other words, his taxpayer-supported Old Boys Club wanted a monopoly on deciding who gets the great privilege of seeing our planet from space.

In the wake of Tito's chutzpah, a San Francisco poetry group, Lyrical Travelers, was emboldened to propose that the crew list for future space flights include more than just scientists, military personnel, and wealthy businessmen: poets and spiritual leaders, for instance, and other imaginative, articulate people who can express to the rest of us what it's like to enjoy this rare journey.

COLLABORATING WITH NATURE

Conceptual artist Jonathon Keats listens to the music of nature—and also likes to play along. One of his collaborations was with Montana's Mandeville Creek, which, like every stream, sings its own song. By moving around the underwater rocks there, Keats felt he subtly changed its melody. (Source: *GOOD* magazine, tinyurl.com/crcmrk)

Domesticating Diseases   Biologist Paul Ewald is opposed to efforts to exterminate diseases spread by germs. Instead, we should figure out how they co-evolve with humans, and push them to mutate in ways that are favorable for us.

Like every living thing, harmful microbial species change over time in response to environmental conditions. Syphilis, for example, was more lethal and fast-spreading 500 years ago. It killed its human victims relatively quickly, which diminished its ability to proliferate in new hosts. Ultimately, a milder variety evolved. An infected person survived longer and could spread the syphilis strain further.

Ewald wants to adopt this model as a conscious strategy, cultivating conditions that encourage the mellow strains of a disease to trump their nastier relatives.

"Maybe someday we'll barely notice when we get colonized by disease organisms," Ewald told journalist Joel Achenbach. "We'll have co-opted them. They'll be like in-laws, a little annoying but tolerable. If a friend sees us sniffling, we'll just say, Oh, it's nothing—just a touch of plague." (Source: Joel Achenbach, "Our Friend, the Plague," *National Geographic,* November 2003)

Freedom from Too Much Work

Women in the African country of Mali have always had to grind corn and peanuts by hand. It's a job that takes countless hours. But a Swiss development worker has spawned a revolution by introducing a simple grinding machine to 300 Mali villages. A 100-pound bag of corn once took three days of manual grinding. With the machine, dubbed by the locals "the daughter-in-law who doesn't speak," the job is done in 15 minutes.

Girls who were formerly forced to stay home all day to help with the domestic work are now free to go to school and play in the sun. Mature females are able to make more money faster and have time left over to take literacy classes, start up small businesses, or lounge around enjoying the privilege of doing absolutely nothing. (Source: Roger Thurow, *The Wall Street Journal,* July 26, 2002)

MIRABILIA REPORT *Mirabilia* n. innovations generated by unseen presences, enigmatic phenomena on the cusp between fake and real, odd acts of deliverance that inspire love or wonder or both; from the Latin *mirabilia,* "marvels."

■ The longest underground river in the world flows through Mexico's Yucatán Peninsula and empties into the Caribbean Sea. At least 95 miles long, it is still unnamed.

■ Oblivious to dire biblical prophecies about swarms of locusts, residents of Beijing, China, warmly greeted their arrival in 2002. They scooped the insects up in large bags, deep-fried them, and made them the main dish of an enormous feast.

■ Fingernails grow faster after they're wounded than they do normally.

■ Male rhesus monkeys often hang from tree branches by their prehensile penises.

■ The average person has over 1,460 dreams a year but remembers only five.

■ Philanthropist Alan "Ace" Greenberg contributed $1 million to buy Viagra for men with small bank accounts.

■ It's not uncommon for the eyes of the octopus to differ greatly—one little eye to see things in sunlit waters and one big eye to see things in the dimness of the deep.

■ In 1997, Jody Williams won the Nobel Peace Prize for her work to persuade more than 100 countries to ban deadly land mines. When she held a press conference at the end of a dirt road near her Vermont farmhouse, she was barefoot and wore jeans and a tank top.

■ On average, human beings have fewer than two legs.

■ Holding a spoon to his cheek during an especially blue period of his life, singer Tom Waits found that it takes 121 teardrops to fill a teaspoon.

■ Astronomers have discovered a crystal as big as our moon at the core of a dying white dwarf star.

■ A Japanese genius invented a robot that can belly dance.

School Superintendent Fires Himself

In Dollar Day, Michigan, school Superintendent Robert Barrette fired himself in order to solve budget woes. "It's either that or our teachers," he said. "Schools are about kids. If we cut teachers we hurt the quality of our education, but eliminating the administrator won't hurt kids." Barrette had been earning a yearly salary of $100,000 working for the school district, which has 262 students. (Source: Associated Press)

New Health Craze

Prayer can have a medicinal effect, according to a study of 990 heart patients at St. Luke's Hospital in Kansas City. Five prayer teams prayed daily on behalf of half of the patients. Though they did not know they were being prayed for, their health improved faster and they needed fewer drugs than the patients who did not have the benefit of the prayers. The report on the experiment appeared in the *Archives of Internal Medicine,* published by the American Medical Association. (Source: Associated Press)

Cashing in on Cosmic Rhythms

Called "Wall Street's best astrologer" by *Barron's,* Arch Crawford analyzes planetary movements to assist him in predicting the ebb and flow of the stock market. His newsletter, *The Crawford Perspectives,* was ranked the number one market timer by the *Hulbert Financial Digest* for 2008. For the year 2002, *Timer Digest* said Crawford's advice was the second-best among over a hundred stock market-timing newsletters it ranked.

Gorgeous Toilet

The Delaware Gap National Recreation Area in Pennsylvania has an outhouse that cost $333,000 to build. It's a two-hole beauty with a roof constructed from slate mined in Vermont, porch railings built out of Indiana limestone, and an indestructible cobblestone foundation.

Nonviolence Sells

"In Will Wright's mind, video games shouldn't always be about winning or losing. That was the trouble when he pitched an idea some two decades ago for a new game centered on building cities. Software makers were skeptical, insisting that without clear winners and losers, the idea would be a commercial flop. Since then, Wright's pet project, later known as SimCity, has become one of the most recognizable computer games of all time, with more than 20 million copies sold." —Matthew Yi, sfgate.com

Poetry Slams' Trendy Anger

In his book *The Degradation of Language and Music and Why We Should, Like, Care,* John McWhorter says he prefers the energetic rants of poetry slams to the "doggedly flat rainy-day poems" of academic writers. On the other hand, the spoken word stuff rarely ventures beyond "alienation and scolding," which limits its beauty and power. "The vast weight of human artistic achievement was not created in indignation," he notes.

Angel Styles

Real angels don't have the kind of glossy physical appearance normally associated with celebrities and film stars. So says biblical scholar Dr. Andrew Clavisch after interviewing 3,450 people who claim to have had a personal encounter with the heavenly beings. Quoted in the *Weekly World News,* Clavisch says the general consensus is that it's rare to see an angel with perfectly coiffed hair, cosmetic surgery, an underwear model's physique, or smooth, glowing skin. Most are average-looking and seem to have no interest in fashionable attire.

WANTED: Peace-loving warrior (any gender) to serve as a model for a statue of the Egyptian goddess of justice, Maat. Must be willing to sit on a lion, wear ostrich feathers, and hold a sword aloft for long hours. Your thighs should be strong and you should be able to make your eyes wild with the desire to conjure both severity and mercy. Ideally, you are also angry about at least three forms of injustice that don't affect you directly. To apply, send your thoughts on the subject "Everyone has a piece of the truth." Truthrooster@gmail.com

BREAKING THE PRONOIA TABOO

"Expect the unexpected or you won't find it." —Heraclitus

"Every day I remind myself that my inner and outer life are based on the labors of others." —Albert Einstein, *Ideas and Opinions,* Sonja Bargmann, translator

"You never change things by fighting the existing reality. To change something, build a new model that makes the existing model obsolete." —Buckminster Fuller, *Critical Path*

"Try with all your might and work very, very hard to make the world a better place. But if all your efforts are to no avail—no hard feelings." —The Dalai Lama

"The new work of art does not consist of making a living or producing an objet d'art or in self-therapy, but in finding a new soul." —Henry Miller, *The Wisdom of the Heart*

"Man is at the nadir of his strength when the earth, the seas, the mountains are not in him, for without them his soul is unsourced, and he has no images by which to abide." —Edward Dahlberg, *The Sorrows of Priapus*

"The illiterate of the 21st century will not be those who cannot read and write, but those who cannot learn, unlearn, and relearn." —Alvin Toffler, *Powershift: Knowledge, Wealth, and Power at the Edge of the 21st Century*

"When you do something, you should burn yourself completely, like a good bonfire, leaving no trace of yourself." —Shunryu Suzuki, *Zen Mind, Beginner's Mind*

Benevolent Pranks?

In May 2006, workers cleaning up garbage on Britain's highest mountain made a startling find. There at the top of Mt. Ben Nevis, 4,418 feet up, was a mostly intact grand piano. How did it get there? No one has any viable theories. In 2003, hikers in Indiana's Yellowwood State Forest stumbled upon an equally inexplicable anomaly: massive sandstone boulders lodged in the topmost branches of three trees, one an 80-foot-tall chestnut. They were later dubbed URB, or Unexplained Resting Boulders. What accounts for their seemingly impossible positions? They couldn't have been there since the trees were saplings, as their weight would have prevented growth.

In an act of random violence, playwright Samuel Beckett was stabbed by a pimp on a Paris street. A stranger, the pianist Suzanne Deschevaux-Dumesnil, found him and got medical help. She visited him in the hospital, and eventually the two were married.

❊

Bach's *St. Matthew Passion* is a highly regarded musical composition. Yet the score disappeared and the work wasn't played for years after Bach's death in 1750. In 1829, composer Felix Mendelssohn rediscovered the long-lost manuscript being used as wrapping paper in the estate sale of a deceased cheese salesman. He arranged for a public performance of the piece, and its revival began.

❊

Ancient Hawaiians had a sport they called *lele kawa,* in which they dived off cliffs into the ocean. Pu'u Keka'a, a volcanic cinder cone in West Maui, was a perfect place from which to jump, but everyone avoided it. Legend held it was a taboo place—"the leaping place of the soul," where the souls of the recently dead left the Earth and ascended into the spirit world. But that changed one day in the late 19th century when a great warrior, Chief Kahekili, climbed to the top of Pu'u Keka'a and plunged into the sea, shattering the taboo and mutating the myth.

Free Will Facts   Neurobiologists at the Free University of Berlin conducted experiments to determine whether fruit flies possess spontaneity. The conclusion? How the insects behave is not merely the result of their automatic reactions to the random stimuli of their environment. Rather, they actually have free will. If that capacity exists in the tiny brains of short-lived insects, it's logical to hypothesize that you also have it—and probably in much larger amounts. (Source: tinyurl.com/lof6nj)

In another study reported on in *Psychological Science,* researchers at the University of Kentucky demonstrated that you can boost your willpower simply by using it a lot, in the same way that you strengthen a muscle by exercising it. (Source: tinyurl.com/nu9sqo)

Beauty Facts   "I am not excited by the idea that the world we live in is made up of 90 percent ugly things and ugly places, while things and places endowed with beauty are rare and difficult to find. My opinion is that there is no ugly object or ugly person in this world. Anything is potentially fascinating." —Jean Dubuffet, *Jean Dubuffet: Towards an Alternative Reality*

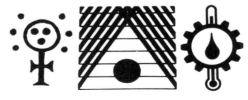

Lazy Mirroring   Many creative people seem possessed by an urge to mirror the horrors they witness, making art that is as desolate as the experience it represents. Greek poet Odysseus Elytis mourned this phenomenon. He said that artists in its grip are like people with healthy legs who choose to limp along with broken crutches.

"During the years of Buchenwald and Auschwitz," he said, "Matisse painted the most charming flowers and fruit that were ever made. That's why today they still speak more eloquently than the most macabre description of the period. Their creator was faithful not to the tragedy but to the reaction that tragedy kindled in his conscience." (Source: Odysseus Elytis, translated by Theophanis Stavrou: *Books Abroad,* Volume 49, no. 4, Autumn 1975)

Bumper Sticker Therapy   Beauty and Truth Lab researcher Romney Austin adorned her Honda Civic with her first-ever bumper sticker, "Give Yourself to Love." While proud of announcing her compassionate philosophy to the world, she was also nervous. Hadn't she raised the pressure on herself to live up to her noble ideals?

A week later, she snapped. A guy chatting on a cell phone in a Lexus SUV cut her off in traffic, and road rage moved her to give him a middle-finger salute. Soon she added a new bumper sticker to the left of the first: "Get In, Sit Down, Shut Up, Hold On."

When I asked her about the contradiction, she confessed, "I've just accepted that I've got a split personality."

A week later, her conflicting sides reached a compromise. Romney pasted the word "and" in the space between the two stickers, to create a new thought: "Get In, Sit Down, Shut Up, Hold On, and Give Yourself to Love." She called to announce the good news: "I'm whole again!"

Sixty-Seven Percent Failure Rate
"These are the batting averages of the best hitters in baseball history: Ty Cobb: .366; Rogers Hornsby: .358; Joe Jackson: .356. Since an average of .333 means a player did not get a hit two out of every three times he batted, these champions made an out more often than they got a hit. Most professional players do worse. Moral of the story: Unless you're a brain champion equal to these baseball champions, you're probably wrong close to two out of three times." —Robert Anton Wilson, rawilson.com

Smart Singing   "Sound-making instincts and the 'singing sense' are centered in the cerebellum or 'small brain.' For that reason, the singer who relies too much on the cerebrum or larger brain is hard to teach. It is a notorious fact that the 'intelligent' singer rarely sings either well or naturally, i.e. spontaneously." —Cornelius Reid, *A Dictionary of Vocal Terminology*

Least Pronoiac Poet

The results of our poll are in. By a wide margin, our readers voted jejune poet John Ashbery the Least Pronoiac Poet. He garnered 58 percent of the vote. Second-place finisher Stanley Moss lagged far behind with 21 percent.

Here's a sample of the demoralizing style that earned Ashbery the honor, a passage from "Always Merry and Bright":

> The ocean sighs, finding the process of
> striking the shore
> interminable and intolerable.
> Let's pretend it's back when we were young
> and cheap, and nobody followed us. Well,
> that's not entirely true: the cat followed us
> home from school sometimes ...
> Forget it. It all comes undone sooner or later.
> The vetch goes on growing, wondering
> whether it grew any more today.

LETTER TO THE EDITOR

Dear Beauty and Truth Laboratory: I had a dream of Lucifer and Christ playing a slapstick game of tennis. No matter how much they played the score was always love, love. What does this dream mean?
—James "Laughing Snake" Zirk

Dear Laughing Snake: It means you got close to having the power to "read the mind of God," in the words of physicist Stephen Hawking. Though Lucifer and Christ may seem to be adversaries, they are actually dramatis personae in God's rowdy morality play, which is meant to inspire us to embody what the Beauty and Truth Laboratory calls "love squared."

> *This perfect moment is brought to you by the thousand-year-old rose bush that's growing on the wall of the Hildesheim Cathedral in Germany.*

World Conference of Soul-Making

In July 2004, the first annual World Conference of Soul-Making met in San Rafael, California. The goal of the gathering was to reach consensus on the best strategies for cultivating soul.

Three schools of thought emerged. The Ruminators theorized that humans are born without souls and can create them only through arduous, disciplined rebellion against all belief systems. The Resonators agreed that soul isn't innate, but insisted that soul-making is by no means difficult. For example, gathering good stories is effective and not at all hard. The Revelators said every person is born with a soul in seed form, and need only discover the "blueprint" of that seed in order to attract the experiences necessary to draw out its potential.

Don't Suffer for Your Art

"I glommed on to the idea that I had to suffer for my art. Acting teachers love to promote the idea that in order to really get into character, you've got to put yourself through emotional hell. Now I'd say, 'Don't suffer for your art.'" —actor Christian Slater, quoted in the *San Francisco Chronicle*

Tree Decor

In Cedar Rapids, Iowa, police were called to the scene to investigate when 15 trees in a city park were fitted with doorknobs and locks.
—*Fortean Times*

Enchanted Loom

"If you are a poet, you will see that there is a cloud in this sheet of paper. Without a cloud, there will be no rain; without rain, the trees cannot grow; and without trees, we cannot make paper." —Thich Nhat Hanh, *Peace Is Every Step*

"Regardless of who sees it, there really is a cloud in this sheet of paper, as well as a bark beetle, a handful of soil, a bit of bird poop, even the gasoline that powered the logger's chain saw. It is even possible that if you were to chronicle the history of those carbon atoms currently part of the page you are now holding, you would find that they were once part of Peter the Great, a woolly mammoth, or (and!) a Komodo dragon, before they found themselves incorporated into the loblolly pine that eventually became this particular sheet of paper."
—David P. Barash, "Buddhism and the 'Subversive Science,'" *The Chronicle of Higher Education*

Little-Known Abundance

Normally there are about 9,300 people on the planet who could be your very best friend, even your soulmate. In tough times, that number may rise to as high as 19,500.

Predicting the News

When the bearded dragon lizard sits upright and cocks its head toward the heavens, Australian Aborigines know that rain will fall the next day. And when massive buds appear on the queen wattle plants, even the youngest members of a tribe can prophesy with confidence that brush fires will break out soon.

Ig Nobel Prizes

Each year the science magazine *Annals of Improbable Research* awards "Ig Nobel Prizes." A prize in chemistry was recently given to researchers who discovered that romantic infatuation is biochemically indistinguishable from obsessive-compulsive disorder. Other trophies have gone to the "Stalin World" amusement park, software that can detect a cat walking on a computer keyboard, and a report on "Courtship Behavior of Ostriches Towards Humans Under Farming Conditions."

Unsung Philanthropy

During four years of his tenure as Pepsi's CEO from 1996 to 2001, Roger Enrico donated his annual $900,000 salary to the company's college scholarship fund for the children of front-line workers.

How Is Enlightenment Like a Million-Dollar Vacation Home?

For some seekers, spiritual enlightenment is the ultimate commodity. They believe that through diligent meditation and self-improvement, there will come a day when it will no longer elude their grasp. Breaking through to the singular state of cosmic consciousness, they will forever after own it, free and clear. Permanently illuminated! Never to backslide into the dull ignominy of normal human awareness!

Here's what I have to say about that: It's a delusion.

The fact is, the nature of perfection is always mutating. What constitutes enlightenment today will always be different tomorrow. Even if you're fortunate and wise enough to score a sliver of "enlightenment," it's not a static treasure that becomes your indestructible, everlasting possession. Rather, it remains a mercurial knack that must be continually re-earned.

If you want to befriend the Divine Wow, you must not only be willing to change ceaselessly—you have to *love* to change ceaselessly.

Lucky you: All of creation is conspiring to help you live like that.

SACRED ADVERTISEMENT

Your inexhaustible capacity to enjoy life's open-ended invitation to change is brought to you by the film Destino, *which was a collaboration between surrealist painter Salvador Dalí and Walt Disney's team of animators. It was begun in 1945 and completed in 2006.*

Certificate of
Exemption from Enlightenment

This document certifies that

_____

is immune to the lust for enlightenment and is exempt
from the need to seek enlightenment.

This document also certifies that

_____

has seen through the fraud of the enlightenment con game and is excused
from further clawing and scraping to own a piece of that specious reward.

This document further certifies that

_____

is free from the temptation to be consecrated as enlightened by any
guru, saint, holy person, or religious organization that claims the right to do so.

Finally, this document certifies that

_____

has already been enlightened a million times in a million different ways
anyway, and that seeking even further enlightenments
would be redundant and even greedy.

To ensure the continued validity of this document,

_____

vows to regularly renew these three understandings: that it is impossible to ever reach
a complete and permanent state of enlightenment; that there is no single state of awareness
that constitutes enlightenment; and that since the nature of reality keeps changing,
the nature of enlightenment keeps changing as well.

LET'S MAKE MORALITY FUN

Are you turned off by the authoritarian, libido-mistrusting perversity of the right-wing moral code, but equally reluctant to embrace the atheism embedded in the left wing's code of goodness?

Are you hungry for a value system rooted in beauty, love, pleasure, and liberation instead of order, control, politeness, and fear, but allergic to the sophistry of the New Age?

Are you apathetic toward the saccharine goodness evangelized by sentimental, superstitious fanatics, but equally bored by the intellectuals who worship at the empty-hearted shrine of scientific materialism?

It may be time for you to whip up your very own moral code.

If you do, you might want to keep the following guidelines in mind:

1. A moral code becomes immoral unless it can thrive without a devil and enemy.

2. A moral code grows ugly unless it prescribes good-natured rebellion against automaton-like behavior offered in its support.

3. A moral code becomes murderous unless it's built on a love for the fact that EVERYTHING CHANGES ALL THE TIME, and unless it perpetually adjusts its reasons for being true.

4. A moral code will corrupt its users unless it ensures that their primary motivation for being good is because it's fun.

5. A moral code deadens the soul of everyone it touches unless it has a built-in sense of humor.

Do not share deep secrets with convicted felons. Do not put handfuls of dead ants in envelopes and mail them to people you're mad at. Do not wolf down greasy burgers alone in a dirty bathtub while fantasizing about making love to an inaccessible idol. Do not wake up drunk on a pool table with strange symbols painted on your body. Do not romance the neglected spouse of a corporate executive in order to pry loose insider stock tips. Do not steal something that already belongs to you or pine for people who are sitting right next to you.

14

You are a lucky, plucky,
good-sucking
genius.

It's Bad Luck to Be Superstitious

Review in painstaking detail the history of your life,
honoring every moment as if you were conducting
a benevolent Judgment Day.

Forgive yourself of every mistake except one.

Create a royal crown for yourself
out of a shower cap, rubber bands, and light bulbs.

Think of the last place on Earth you'd ever want to visit,
and visualize yourself having fun there.

Test to see if people are really listening to you by asserting
that Karl Marx was one of the Marx Brothers.

Steal lint from dryers in laundromats
and use it to make animal sculptures for someone you admire.

Fantasize you're the child of divine parents
who abandoned you when you were two days old,
but who will soon be coming back to reunite with you.

Meditate on how one of the symbols of plenitude in Nepal
is a mongoose vomiting jewels.

Once a year on the night before your birthday,
say these words into a mirror: "It's bad luck to be superstitious."

Start a club whose purpose is to produce an archive
of controversial jokes and obscene limericks about beauty, truth, and love.

Clues to the Rebel Grail

Be Your Own Savior

Some Christians believe Jesus will come back to fix this corrupt world. Certain Jewish sects propose that the messiah will soon appear on Earth for the first time. Among Muslims, many predict the legendary Twelfth Imam will return and bring salvation to humanity.

In India, devotees of Vishnu expect the avatar Kalki to arrive on the scene and carry out a series of miraculous redemptions. Even Buddhists prophesy Maitreya, the chosen one who will establish universal peace.

My divinations foretell a very different scenario. I suspect that the whole point of our spectacularly confounding moment in history is that each of us must become our own savior. And if we hope to accomplish that, relying on our best amateur efforts, we will have to stop waiting around for a supposed professional to do our work for us.

Franz Kafka had a view that's not necessarily mutually exclusive with mine: "The messiah will come when we don't need him anymore."

Let's also consider the evidence offered by William Blake, as quoted in Poets and God by David L. Edwards: "Jesus Christ is the only God. And so am I. And so are you."

One more clue, this time from Deepak Chopra: "Every person is a God in embryo. Its only desire is to be born."

SACRED ADVERTISEMENT

Thanks to our sponsor Carl Jung, who said, "The whole point of Jesus's life was not that we should become exactly like him, but that we should become ourselves in the same way he became himself. Jesus was not the great exception but the great example."

Your Brand New Name

In some spiritual traditions, devotees attempt an arduous process of self-transformation as they retrain themselves to perceive the world from God's point of view. If they succeed, they're honored with an initiation ritual and given a new name to consecrate their altered state.

I have the same problem with this custom that I have with the idea of enlightenment: Once isn't enough. Just as anyone in his or her right spiritual mind has a duty to keep claiming fresh varieties of enlightenment until the end of time, so should the initiations and renamings continue forever.

In my opinion, these considerations apply to you. You may not have sequestered yourself for years in a mountaintop monastery, and you may not have risen every morning at 5 a.m. to say prayers for hours, but you are an authentic devotee who has undergone equivalent ordeals. Your spiritual transformation has unfolded as you've dealt with the challenges of daily life during our epic moment in history, when unprecedented levels of annihilation and resurrection are the norm.

You have earned the right, therefore, to enjoy enlightenment after enlightenment and initiation after initiation and renaming after renaming.

I invite you to get started with a do-it-yourself initiation ceremony. It doesn't have to be long and complicated, and you can create it yourself. As an example of what you might do, here's a ritual that some Beauty and Truth Lab's initiates have performed: 1. Eat a pinch of dirt to declare your solidarity with Mother Earth. 2. Burn a five-dollar bill to purify your relationship with symbols of wealth. 3. Kick yourself in the ass to affirm your ongoing intention to discipline your shadow.

As one of your initiatory rewards, consider adopting a fresh alias during this and every initiation you carry out in the future. You can abandon your existing name if you want, or simply add your new tag to the current mix.

To celebrate the occasion, I invoke on your behalf the inspiration of all shedding things. Your tree of power will be the eucalyptus, whose bark peels away to reveal fresh layers beneath. Your lucky symbol will be the molting snake. Your sacred insect will be the silverfish, which bursts through its exoskeleton as it grows a new and bigger one. Your role model will be Japanese artist Hokusai (1760–1849), who had such a passionate commitment to reinventing himself that he celebrated 60 births, each time giving himself a new name.

Below is a list of Native American-style titles and names you might want to steal for your own use. Feel free to dream up your own, of course.

Wild Face	Shadow Wrestler	Kiss Genius	Goal Thwacker
Boink Worthy	Fizzy Nectar	Rumbler	Thrill Witch
Rowdy Gusto	Bliss Mutator	Silky Banger	Phoenix Nectar
Mucho Gusto Coco Loco	Mango Sucker	Pain Killer	Fire Keeper
Wobble Binder	Earthshaker	Wish Crayon	Pearly Thunder
Thumper	Gut Stormer	Storm Tamer	Free Sigh

I'm a Star, You're a Star

Y ou're a star—and so am I. I'm a genius—and so are you. Your success encourages my brilliance, and my charisma enhances your power. Your victory doesn't require my defeat, and vice versa.

Those are the rules in the New World—quite unlike the rules in the Old World, where zero-sum games are the norm, and only one of us can win each time we play.

In the New World, you don't have to tone down or apologize for your prowess, because you love it when other people shine. You exult in your own excellence without regarding it as a sign of inherent superiority. As you ripen more and more of your latent aptitude, you inspire the rest of us to claim our own idiosyncratic magnificence.

Tibetan Buddhist teacher Geshe Chekawa (1220–1295) specialized in *bodhicitta,* seeking enlightenment not for personal gain but as a way to serve others. On his deathbed, he prayed to be sent to hell so that he might alleviate the suffering of the lost souls there.

As you explore pronoia, you will discover that like Chekawa, you have a huge capacity to help people. Unlike him, you'll find that expressing your benevolence doesn't require you to go to hell. It may even be unnecessary for you to sacrifice your own joy or to practice self-denial. Just the opposite: Being in service to humanity and celebrating your unique power will be synergistic. They will need each other to thrive.

The Golden Rule is a decent ethical principle, but it could be even better. "Do unto others as you would have them do unto you" presumes that others enjoy what you enjoy. But that's wrong. There are many things you'd like to have done unto you that others would either despise or be bored by. Here's a new, improved formulation, which we call the Platinum Rule: *Do unto others as they would like to have you do unto them.*

Using this improved formula is not just a virtuous way to live, but is also the best way to ensure the success of your selfish goals. The rituals and spells of various occult orders purport to be supercharged techniques for imposing your personal will on the chaotic flow of events, but I say that practicing the Platinum Rule outstrips all of them as an exercise to enhance your potency and happiness.

At the heart of the pronoiac way of life is an apparent conundrum: *You can have anything you want if you'll just ask for it in an unselfish way.* The trick to making this work is to locate where your deepest ambition coincides with the greatest gift you have to give. Figure out exactly how the universe, by providing you with abundance, can improve the lot of everyone whose life you touch. Seek the fulfillment of your fondest desires in such a way that you become a fount of blessings.

The Bible quotes the radical first-century spiritual activist Jesus Christ as follows: "Love your enemies, do good to those who hate you, bless those who curse you, pray for those who mistreat you."

This approach is as important to my well-being as getting good food and exercise and sleep. It's self-destructive for me to hate anything, including things that are easy to hate and that I might be naturally inclined to hate. As much harm as fundamentalist Christians have wreaked on our culture, for instance, feeling disgust for them only makes me sick. It feeds the very "us versus them" thinking that I'm pledged to root out, thereby making me a hypocrite and tainting my integrity. My mental and physical health suffer, and that diminishes my ability to get what I want.

I got an e-mail from a beauty and truth fan who calls himself Drek, Agent of the Future. "How come, in the long list of human fears, 'showing one's true self' is never included?" Drek mused. "Compared to the electrifying and terrifying prospect of shedding our protective masks and expressing our raw souls, snakes and death and public speaking really don't seem that scary."

I wrote Drek back to congratulate him for facing his greatest fear. I said I thought his struggle to reveal his naked beauty was as great a service to humanity as the work of Buddhist teacher Geshe Chekawa.

"To be an altruist, you must first be an egoist." —George Gurdjieff.

"Before you can give yourself away, you have to have a self to give." —Isabel Hickey, *Astrology: A Cosmic Science*

"In a gift-giving society, an individual gains prestige and satisfaction by receiving, then adding to what has been received and passing it on." So says Lewis Hyde in his book *The Gift, Imagination, and the Erotic Life of Property.* "In a consumer society," he continues, "prestige and satisfaction are gained through accumulation and acquisition. Nothing is given, nothing is passed on."

Though you have been born and raised in a consumer society, your attraction to pronoia suggests you have the ability to live in a gift-giving society. One of the best ways to change yourself to help create such a society is to expand your capacity for both accepting and bestowing largesse.

Pronoia isn't just a matter of raking in the blessings offered to you by the universal conspiracy, nor is it merely about aiding the conspiracy to disseminate blessings to everyone else. It's a balance of the two.

The Beauty and Truth Lab's youngest practitioner is a teenage poet, Deirdre Vonn. She's modest about her art. She worries she hasn't earned the states of awareness she writes about. "I don't know if I'm really as sensitive and deep as my poetry implies," she confessed once as she handed me a pristine, wrenching poem.

I understand her concern. Am I as consistently generous as my writings might make me appear? Nope. But in the effort to provide delicious and nutritious oracles for my readers, I am constantly pushing to live up to the moral artistry I espouse, becoming in the process a more interesting and useful person.

How about you? Is there a gift you can give or service you can provide that will awaken your sleeping endowments? Is there beauty you can bring to life in your environment that will compel you to become more of a charismatic, ingenious star?

"You never enjoy the world aright, till the Sea itself flowers in your veins, till you are clothed with the heavens, and crowned with the stars: and perceive yourself to be the sole heir of the whole world, and more than so, because men and women are in it who are every one sole heirs as well as you. Till you can sing and rejoice and delight, as misers do in gold, and kings in scepters, you never enjoy the world." —Thomas Traherne, *Centuries of Meditation*

I'm a Brat, You're a Brat

Every January 1, many people make New Year's resolutions, promising to embark on programs of self-improvement. But your assignment now, should you choose to accept it, is to create a list of ANTI-resolutions.

Here are some questions to guide you: 1. What outlandish urges and controversial tendencies do you promise to cultivate in the coming months? 2. What nagging irritations will you ignore and avoid with even greater ingenuity? 3. What problems do you promise to exploit in order to have even more fun as you make the status quo accountable for its corruption? 4. What boring rules and traditions will you thumb your nose at, paving the way for exciting encounters with strange attractors?

This space has been liberated for your reckless use.

SHAPESHIFTING PRONOIA THERAPY

Experiments and exercises in becoming an aggressively sensitive, thunderously receptive, ethically mischievous Master of Mutant Intimacy

Report your answers and research results here

1 As a boy, renowned Spanish matador Manolete was a sissy. He rarely played outside, preferring to be near his mother as he read books and painted pictures.

Psychologist James Hillman explains this by suggesting that the youthful Manolete had already sensed his destiny, intuiting that one day he would be alone in the ring facing down angry 2,000-pound bulls. His childhood behavior was a way of marshaling his strength and shielding him from the enormity of the challenges he would seek out one day.

Is it possible that what you have considered a weakness or vulnerability has actually been preparing you to express a signature strength?

2 Six miles from Maui is a Hawaiian island that tourists never visit—Kaho'olawe. The U.S. Navy seized it in 1941 and used it as a target range for decades. After years of protests by native Hawaiians, the Navy finally stopped bombing and began a clean-up campaign. In November 2003, it formally turned control of the island over to the rightful owners.

"You can get a feel on Kaho'olawe of what it was like to live on Hawaii at the time of our ancestors," says Native Hawaiian Davianna McGregor. "We can practice our traditions there without it being a tourist attraction. It's one place we can go to be in communion with our natural life forces."

Each of us has a personal version of Kaho'olawe: a part of our psyche that has been stolen or colonized by hostile forces. To grow bold in exploring pronoia, you'll need to take back yours.

3 Sometimes we have a strong sense of what our destiny is calling us to do, but we don't feel quite ready or brave enough to answer the call. We need a push, an intervention, a serendipitous stroke—what you might call "fate bait." It's a person or event that awakens our dormant willpower and draws us inexorably toward our necessary destiny; it's a thunderbolt or siren song or stage whisper that gives us a good excuse to go do what we know we should do.

Do you have any ideas about how to put yourself in the vicinity of your fate bait?

4 During my years in college, I enjoyed watching the evolution of Richard, a shy geek in my creative writing classes. Long before he penned a single good poem, he was a bohemian art poseur. On his backpack there was a button with the image of rock poet Patti Smith. He often wore a T-shirt bearing a quote from poetry icon Allen Ginsberg, and he was never without his book of Rimbaud poems. Everywhere I went I saw him scribbling ostentatiously in his journal as he chain-smoked clove cigarettes.

To my surprise, Richard's work gradually began to match his persona. By sophomore year he'd spawned some evocative poems, and soon after he graduated, he published a fine chapbook. In his development I witnessed a perfect example of the saying, "You become what you pretend to be."

Your assignment: Decide what you want to become, and start pretending to be that thing. Or else: Be careful what you're unconsciously pretending to be, because you just might become it.

5 In his book *Starbucked,* Taylor Clark says there's a woman who goes to a Seattle Starbucks every morning and orders a "decaf single grande extra vanilla two-percent extra caramel 185-degrees with whipped cream caramel macchiato."

Maybe her request seems overly fussy and demanding, but it could be a good act for you to mimic. Try this: For a given time, say 12 days, be equally as exacting in asking for what you want. Assume that you have a poetic license to be extremely specific as you go about your quest for fulfillment.

6 George III was King of England from 1760 to 1820. During the last years of his reign, he gradually became more and more detached from reality, talking to himself for hours on end and addressing trees as if they were people. When he first began losing his mind, his servants and assistants made a conscious decision to help him feel more comfortable by acting eccentric themselves.

Shapeshifting Pronoia Therapy

Their collusion with George's pathology is an extreme example of a situation that all of us are at risk of. Our associates and loved ones may fall into a rhythm of going along with our odd ideas and bad habits, encouraging us to continue doing what we probably shouldn't do.

Are your allies refraining from busting you or calling your bluff, when they probably should? Bust yourself. Call your own bluff.

7 "Why, I don't even respect myself, I tell ya," said comedian Rodney Dangerfield. "When I make love, I have to fantasize that I am somebody else!"

Experiment with just the second half of that formulation. While you're making love, fantasize that you're somebody else. But do it because you care deeply about yourself—so deeply that you want to transcend your customary reactions and expand your identity. Do it because you dare to awaken to previously unknown possibilities of who you might be.

"I have to re-create the universe every morning when I wake up, and kill it in the evening." —Björk

8 There was an indignant uproar after revelations in 2006 that James Frey's best-selling "memoir" *A Million Little Pieces* contains fabrications. He hadn't actually lived all of the experiences he depicted therein.

Hearing about it prompted me to ruminate on whether there's any such thing as a completely accurate account of any person's life. My conclusion: no.

In every autobiography and biography ever written, the author imaginatively strings together selectively chosen details to conjure up artificially coherent narratives rather than depicting the crazy-quilt ambiguity that actually characterizes everyone's journey.

If you and nine writers set out to tell your life story, you'd produce 10 wildly different tales, each rife with subjective interpretation, misplaced emphasis, unintentional distortions, and exorbitant extrapolations from insufficient data.

Celebrate the malleability of reality. Regale listeners with stories about the time you worked as a pirate in the Indian Ocean, or rode the rails through Kansas as a hobo, or gave a down-on-his-luck CIA agent sage

Shapeshifting Pronoia Therapy

advice in an elevator. When you call to get pizza delivered and the clerk who takes your order asks your name, say you're Brad Pitt or Paris Hilton. When someone you're meeting is annoyed because you're late, say you couldn't help it because you were smoking crack in the bus station bathroom with your mom's guru and lost track of time. If asked how much education you have, say you have three PhDs, one each in astrobiology, Russian literature, and whale songs.

"Our current situation, in the evolution of our species, is one in which the ego has forgotten its true role in the psyche and has usurped the role of central regulator."
—Carl Jung

9 Sometimes the best gift you can give your ego is to tell it you're not going to be its slave anymore. You say to it, "I'm tired of being whipped around by every one of your ever-shifting little needs, and I'm sick of having to kowtow to your inexhaustible demands. I want to be free of your insatiable craving to be appreciated, recognized, and adored. Go away and leave me alone. I'm just going to be who I am without worrying about you at all."

Delivering this message may stimulate a healing crisis. Your ego could be temporarily rendered numb and irrelevant by its near death experience, and you'll get to go off and do what your soul wants to do. Ironically, this often results in you attracting adventures that make your ego very happy.

Tell your ego you won't be its slave for a period of three days.

10 If a cow is given a name by her owner, she generates more milk than a cow that's treated as an anonymous member of the herd. That's the conclusion of a study done by researchers at Newcastle University in the UK. "Placing more importance on knowing the individual animals and calling them by name," said Dr. Catherine Douglas, "can significantly increase milk production."

Building on that principle, I suggest that you give everything in your world names, including (but not limited to) houseplants, insects, cars, appliances, and trees.

Shapeshifting Pronoia Therapy

It will help you get more up-close and personal with all of creation, which is an effective way to cultivate pronoia.

11 In American psychotherapy, the first question many practitioners ask their new clients is essentially, "What did your parents do to you to mess you up so badly?" One of my Japanese friends tells me that in his country, a therapist is more likely to ask, "What did your parents do for you? How did they nurture and support you?"

Without dismissing the possibility that your mom and dad did inflict damage on you, I'll ask you to concentrate on the Japanese-style inquiry for now. What are the best things that happened to you when you were growing up? What did your family and community give you that you've never fully appreciated?

For best results, break the new rules as skillfully as you break the old rules, and periodically break the way you break all the rules.

12 Beauty and Truth Lab researcher Beth had a dream that she and her tribe were living peacefully at the foot of a mountain. Without warning, fiery ash and lava erupted. Everyone fled, desperate to escape. But before she had gone far, Beth heard a voice in her head say, "Run toward the volcano; it's your only safety." Feeling an inexplicable trust in the voice, she turned around and started heading back, whereupon the dream ended and she woke up. Soon after getting out of bed, she felt moved to face up to a certain dilemma she'd been ignoring in her waking life. When she solved the problem a day later, she felt gratitude for the dream that had spurred her to do the right thing: Run toward the volcano.

What would be the equivalent in your own life?

13 Visualize in detail your dream lover . . . your ideal soul mate . . . the embodiment of everything you find attractive.

Imagine that although this person feels the same way about you, there is a very good reason why the two of you can't make love or be together as a couple for a long time. Feel the sweet torment of your unquenched longing for each other, the impossible ache of fiery tenderness.

Shapeshifting Pronoia Therapy

Picture all the ways you will work on yourself in the coming years to refine your soul and perfect your love, so that when the two of you can finally be united, you will have made yourself into the gorgeous genius you were born to be—a pure blessing and uncanny gift for your beloved.

14 I hope you can obtain the Avatar Elixir stashed in the golden obelisk in the underground fortress beneath the glass mountain. It will allow you to produce the "triple-helix" energy that will give you the power to cross freely back and forth through the gateway between universes. Then wild beasts will obey your commands. Rivers will become your allies. Every star in the sky will shine directly on you. And if for some reason you're not able to get your hands on that Avatar Elixir, you may be able to achieve similar results by drinking a bottle of beer stashed in the lower left rear section of the beverage cooler at a convenience store within five miles of your home.

Magic might be wherever you think it is.

15 After rejecting proposals from many directors, Bob Dylan finally authorized Oscar-nominated Todd Haynes to make a film about his life, *I'm Not There.* Five different actors and one actress portrayed Dylan, including Richard Gere, Cate Blanchett, Marcus Carl Franklin, Heath Ledger, Ben Whishaw, and Christian Bale. "I set out to explode the idea that anybody can be depicted in a single self," Haynes told *The Sunday Times.*

Name the six actors and actresses you would choose to play you in the movie about your life.

These therapeutic strategies are adapted from a program used to train Special Forces in all-climate, all-terrain survival techniques.

16 Lewis Thomas was a physician who wrote elegantly about biology in books like *The Lives of a Cell.* I want to bring your attention to his meditation on warts. "Nothing in the body has so much the look of toughness and permanence as a wart," he wrote. And yet "they can be made to go away by something that can only be called thinking ... Warts can be ordered off the skin by hypnotic suggestion" (tinyurl.com/3clzc5). Thomas regarded this phenomenon as "absolutely astonishing, more of a surprise than cloning or recombinant DNA."

Using your mind power, go ahead and shrink, dissolve, or banish a wart or wart-like vexation.

"God was my co-pilot, but we crashed in the mountains and I had to eat Him." Explain.

17 "I am a devout atheist," writes Tom of Ohio, "but I have to explain to my atheist friends that I do pray to the 'GodIdontbelievein.'

"My first direct contact with this Divinity arrived when I was coming out of anesthesia after surgery. I was somehow aware of my existence but totally sensory-deprived. As I emerged from total unconsciousness, a tiny flickering Tinkerbell-like creature in the form of a shimmering globe of light fluttered into my consciousness and hovered irresistibly before my internal eyes. I was in love with it and it loved me.

"In fact it was me, or at least the manifestation of cosmic energy that settles in me and is my being. It gave me a blessing of good will, then went about its business of operating my body. In parting, it gave me the assurance that it would always be there for me and with me, and would join me after it shut the body down for the last time.

"Since that first encounter, I commune with the little sparkling wonder every so often. I thank it for its presence and it thanks me for mine, though we are actually one and the same. I find myself praying to it, though there's really no need to—it knows me better than I do, and guides me toward my goals, though I know not what they are."

Inspired by Tom's report, write a love note or an expression of appreciation for the shimmering globe of wonder that animates your life.

18 Meditation teacher Wes Nisker helps students learn to calm the frenetic chatter of their minds. As earnest as he is in this heroic work, though, he also appreciates the importance of not trying too hard. As you pursue your pronoia practice, call on his influence now and then. It'll keep you honest and prevent your anal sphincter from getting too high-strung.

Shapeshifting Pronoia Therapy

Here's a blurb for one of his workshops. "This day will be of absolutely no use to you. Nothing will be furthered or accomplished by coming. Expect a time of effortlessness, relaxation, and poetry, hanging out, maybe a little mindfulness meditation—all for nothing. Some might understand this as a protest against our culture's speedy, goal-driven nature, but we know it won't amount to a hill of beans. Good intentions and purposefulness must be checked at the door."

19 "I usually solve problems by letting them devour me," wrote Franz Kafka. That's an interesting approach, I guess, and though it might work for a tiny minority of introverted, melancholy, hypersensitive artists, it's probably not a wise policy for you. It may be better to fervently resist any temptation you might have to allow your problems to gobble you up."

Instead, why not be like a gargantuan sea monster in the midst of a perfect storm? Rise up as high as the dark sky and growl back at the thunder. Shoot flames from your mouth at the lightning. Become too big and ancient and wild to ever be devoured.

20 At New York's Museum of Modern Art, I brought my face to within a few inches of Vincent van Gogh's painting *The Starry Night*. It looked delicious. I wanted to kiss it. I wanted to eat it. Its stars were throbbing and voluptuous. The night sky shimmered with spiral currents. In the foreground, the cypress tree flared like a shadowy flame.

I could also see that the artist had been less than thorough in applying his paint. Especially on the edges, but also in the middle of the painting, slivers of untouched canvas showed through. Fierce, innocent, nourishing, reckless, unfinished, this priceless work drank my attention for a long time, constantly refreshing my eyes with its ceaseless movement.

Can you be at peace with the fact that your masterpiece may always be unfinished?

It might help to take a trip to Marrakech, Morocco, and hang out with the sword-swallowers, con men, and beggars in the place called Djemaa el Fna, or "assembly place of the nobodies."

Shapeshifting Pronoia Therapy

21 In the film *Fight Club,* the character played by Brad Pitt storms into a convenience store with a gun, then herds the clerk out back and threatens to execute him. While the poor man quivers in terror, Pitt asks him questions about himself, extracting the confession that he'd once wanted to be a veterinarian but dropped out of school. After a few minutes, Pitt frees the clerk without harming him, but says that unless he takes steps to return to veterinary school in the next six weeks, he will hunt him down and kill him.

In my opinion, that's an overly extreme way to motivate someone to do what's good for him. I wish I could come up with a less shocking approach to coax you into resuming the quest for your deferred dreams. Can you think of anything?

22 Lie on your back with your arms outstretched and have a friend measure the distance from the tip of one middle finger to the other. Do you have a wingspan similar to that of a hawk? Eagle? Osprey? The mythical thunderbird? Pterodactyl? Close your eyes and visualize yourself hovering and swooping above the treetops. What do you see below you?

23 "The important thing," said French critic Charles Du Bos, "is to be able at any moment to sacrifice what we are for what we could become."

Did he really mean at any moment? Like while we're in a convenience store buying a magazine? While we're lying in bed ready for sleep and reviewing the events of the day? While we're adrift in apathetic melancholy, watching too much TV and neglecting our friends? At any moment?! I say yes. At all times and in all places be ready to sacrifice what you are for what you could become.

24 Russian scientists have discovered gold deposits in the dust of decayed tree stumps. The phenomenon occurs in forests growing in ground where there is gold ore. Over the course of centuries, the trees' roots suck in minute quantities of the precious metal, eventually accumulating nuggets.

Describe a metaphorically comparable process you could carry out in your own life over the course of the next 20 years. What invisible part of you is like a tree's roots? What's the gold you'd like to suck up?

25 I'm smarter in some places than in others. In Florence, Amsterdam, and Milwaukee, my IQ is off the charts. In Munich, Madrid, and Washington, D.C., I'm rather dull-witted. Even in Northern California, where

Shapeshifting Pronoia Therapy

I usually live, some spots are more conducive to my higher brain functioning. I'm an idiot on Market Street in San Francisco, whereas I'm awash in wise insights whenever I set foot on Mt. Tamalpais.

What's this about? The specialized branch of astrology called astrocartography would say that the full potentials of my horoscope are more likely to emerge in certain power spots. What about you? Wander around and test to see where you feel most in tune with your deep brilliance.

Did you remember to thank the wild irises and the windy rain?

26 The force of gravity is omnipresent, even though it can't be seen, heard, or touched, and almost no one can explain it. There wasn't even a word for it until the 17th century, when Isaac Newton discovered it and named it after the Latin term *gravitas,* meaning "heaviness" or "seriousness."

As you deepen your inquiries into pronoia, you may enjoy a similar breakthrough. Can you imagine what it would feel like to become aware of an omnipresent ocean of wild divine love that has always been a secret to you in the same way that the sea is invisible to a fish?

27 I was watching a martial arts competition on ESPN TV. It featured a vehement macho dance-off, in which rivals took turns brandishing their high-octane warrior choreography. At one point the announcer waxed poetic as the eventual winner pulled off a seemingly impossible move: "And that was a corkscrew illusion twist rodeo spin!"

I urge you to do something like that yourself. As you seek to take your game to a higher level, practice your personal version of the corkscrew illusion twist rodeo spin.

28 Marie and Pierre Curie discovered radium. Chemist John Walker invented the match. Physicist Wilhelm Röentgen was the first person to find out about X-rays.

What do these great minds have in common? They all refused to take out patents in connection with their innovations, believing they shouldn't make any profit on something that should belong to everyone.

Try giving away some of your brilliance for free.

Shapeshifting Pronoia Therapy

*"The Hindu teacher
Swami Muktananda was asked
why he didn't work miracles.
He replied,
'I have no need to work miracles.
The circulation of blood
through my body is enough.'"*
—Wes Nisker

29 What's true about the word "God" may apply as well to "soul": Much of the meaning has been sucked out of it. It's a flabby ghost that has lost its life force. Say "soul" and you're liable to numb your listeners' attention. At best you may inspire them to picture a vague floating blob that feels more like an abstract concept than a real presence. That's a shame, because the eminence that's lazily referred to as "soul" is as crucial to you waking up tomorrow as your heart.

"If you need to visualize the soul," wrote Tom Robbins, "think of it as a cross between a wolf howl, a photon, and a dribble of dark molasses. But what it really is, as near as I can tell, is a packet of information. It's a program, a piece of hyperspatial software designed explicitly to interface with the Mystery. Not a mystery, mind you, the Mystery. The one that can never be solved."

As part of the Beauty and Truth Lab's ongoing crusade to wrestle the English language into a more formidable servant of the ecstatic impulse, we're pleased to present some alternate designations for "soul." See if any of the following concoctions feel right coming out of your mouth: 1. undulating superconductor; 2. nectar plasma; 3. golden lather; 4. smoldering crucible; 5. luminous caduceus.

If none of these work for you—or even if they do—create your own terms.

P.S. Here's Robbins' conclusion: "By waxing soulful you will have granted yourself the possibility of ecstatic participation in what the ancients considered a divinely animated universe."

You feel lucky!

Shapeshifting Pronoia Therapy

YOUR CHALICE

Visualize a chalice—a ceremonial drinking cup. What's the first image that occurs to you? Is it silver? Ceramic? Plastic? What color? How big? Is it long-stemmed or squat? Does it have a wide, shallow cup or a tall, narrow one, or what? Close your eyes and spend a moment with this vision before reading on.

So you've pictured a chalice in your mind's eye. Here's an analysis of its possible meaning: What you envisioned represents your capacity to be filled up with goodies. It's a snapshot of your subconscious receptivity to favors and help and inspiration.

For instance, if you imagined a shallow plastic champagne glass, it signifies that you may not be well prepared to drink deeply of the elixirs the universe is conspiring to provide you.

On the other hand, a large-volume, gracefully shaped sterling silver cup suggests that you're ready and willing to receive a steady outpouring of wonders.

A long-stemmed chalice may indicate you're inclined to be aggressive about filling your cup. A short, squat stem could mean you're not feeling very deserving of having your cup filled.

Now here's the fun part. If you imagined an inadequate chalice, you can change it. If you pictured a chalice you like, you can add more details to it.

Take some time to picture a vessel that's perfectly worthy of you. Imprint it on your imagination. Then, for the next nine days, conjure it up every morning for five minutes right after you wake up, and every evening for five minutes before you go to sleep. It will reprogram your subconscious mind to be ready and willing to accept all the favors and help and inspiration you need.

That in turn will exert an influence on your surroundings, making it easier for the world to deliver its favors and help and inspiration.

SACRED ADVERTISEMENT

Your chalice is brought to you by the day some years from now when you will get a brain implant that allows you to Google your own unconscious and surf the Internet with your mind alone.

your debts canceled

your imagination fed

your wounds healed

your fears dissolved

your apologies accepted

chimes

dawn

golden

mist

your generosity expanded

sanctuary

kundalini

your courage stoked

murmuring

your love educated

effervesce

your leaks plugged

amethyst

crucible

your desires clarified

your wildness rejuvenated

tendril

melody

luminous

undulate

your untold stories heard

your load lightened

your insight heightened

Nobody sees you for who you really are. You are afraid to change even if you know the change will be good for you. Love sucks. Intimate relationships are impossible. You're not attractive or interesting enough for anyone to want to be your partner for very long. Sooner or later, everyone will find out you've been faking it all these years. The nature of reality is suffering. The universe is a malfunctioning machine. You will never have enough money. You're squandering your life energy on goals that are unworthy of you. Why bother even trying? You'll never overcome the negative conditioning that was imprinted on you when you were a child. A hundred years from now, there will be no one who even knows you ever lived. You should avoid happiness because it will make you bored and lazy. Other people don't think as highly of you as you think of yourself. What if you're really just a selfish, egotistical narcissist? You're going to run out of interesting things to say. Your ego has been writing checks that your body can't cash. Your inner beast is cannibalizing your inner child. You should promise your loved ones that you will forever suppress the difficult sides of your personality. You have incurable addictive tendencies that will always sabotage everything you do. Don't attempt to change, because it is hopeless. Having abandoned your search for the truth, you are now looking for a good fantasy. You're not nice to people unless you want something from them. You tell too many half-truths. Your furniture is ugly. Collecting psychological crutches is your hobby. You make God sick. Life is a bitch and then you die. Add more locks to your doors and more armor to your defense mechanisms.

I Me Wed

Our culture places too narrow a definition on who can reap the benefits of holy matrimony. By any reasonable moral reckoning, two members of the same gender should have exactly the same right to be married as any heterosexual couple.

But why stop there? Let's also legalize the marriage of any three people who want to enjoy wedded bliss in a triangular arrangement. Or four people, for that matter. Or 20. Or 100. Expand the frontiers. Multiply the possibilities. Give love more room to play.

But let's not stop there, either. There's another kind of holy matrimony we should make room for: one that climaxes not with the oath, "With this ring, I thee wed," but rather, "With this ring, I me wed." We need a ritual for getting married to oneself.

Is that something you're interested in? Do you have the nerve to go that far to prove your love? Are you ready to give yourself with throbbing devotion and sinewy commitment and total abandon to the intimate spectacle of loving yourself? If so, I propose that we perform a ceremony in which you get married to yourself right here and right now.

Let's begin by telling a simple truth: You will probably never create a resilient, invigorating bond with the lush accomplice of your dreams until you master the art of loving yourself ingeniously. A wedding ritual that joins you to yourself could catalyze an uncanny shift in your personal mojo that would attract a fresh, hot consort into your life, or else awaken the sleeping potential of a simmering alliance you have now.

If you're feeling brave, try speaking this aloud:

I am no longer looking for the perfect partner.
I am my own perfect partner.

Say it even stronger:

I am no longer looking for the perfect partner
to salve all my wounds
and fix all my mix-ups
and bridge all my chasms.
I am no longer looking for the perfect partner
because I am my own perfect partner.

Speaking that oath provides a good shock to your system; it's a smart place to start. But it doesn't mean you're fully primed. More preparation may be wise. Before you take the plunge, before you initiate this epic shift in your commitment to yourself, you may have to smash an obstacle or two.

I'm guessing that one of the main obstacles is your self-hatred—your disgust for your foibles and wobbles . . . the harsh slurs you inflict on your unripe beauty . . . your sneaky tendency to sabotage your exuberance . . . the bad excuses you concoct for not treating yourself with crafty kindness all the time.

Realistically, you won't be able to completely purge this bad habit in one masterful swoop. But you can put it on notice. You can launch the crusade that will sooner or later emancipate you from its contamination.

Now say this:

I will never again cast a curse on myself.
I will never again cast a curse on myself.

Did any sensations arise in your body as you said those words. Warmth in your gut? A sob in your throat? A surge in your heart? Whatever somatic revelation arrived, invite it to go further and say more.

Next, visualize an object that signifies your propensity toward self-hatred—maybe a whip to symbolize the way you scourge yourself with punishing criticism, or handcuffs to represent your yearning for approval from people who don't even respect you or understand you. Picture yourself throwing this object into a vat of molten gold. See it dissolve. Then say or sing these words as many times as you'd like to:

> *I will never again drop a bomb on my*
> *playground.*
> *I will never again smash a mirror on my face.*
> *I will never again try to cut my own heart out.*
> *I will never again cast a curse on myself.*
> *I will never again cast a curse on myself.*

There is another confusion to escape before you dive into the heart of your self-marriage. I call it the tribal hex—the primal shame that your close relations have tried to use to keep you bound to their expectations.

Remember? You came into this world as a radiant bundle of exuberant riddles, as a shimmering burst of spiral hallelujahs, as a lush explosion of ecstatic gratitude—and yet what your adult relatives most likely wanted was an extension of themselves, a well-behaved kid who followed orders. And so you constructed a false personality, hoping that if you became an ersatz version of yourself you would be loved better.

Close your eyes and imagine that your mother and father are here. It shouldn't be hard, because they probably are gathered with you in spirit right now. So are your siblings, your aunts and uncles, your grandparents and their parents and their parents.

The ghostly presences of your family and forebears, their voices inside your head, tend to rise from a murmur to a clamor whenever you slip outside of the designs you've always stuck to. And many of them are or would be steeped with prejudices about how you should live your life. Many of them would say that getting married to yourself is an unnatural act that you should not attempt.

Maybe there are exceptions—enlightened relatives who celebrate you for exactly who you are and who

would applaud your decision to raise the stakes in your bond with yourself. If so, invite the spirit of their presence to be with you.

But as for the rest, I encourage you to banish their voices from this sacred space. Though you may love them, you can't let their wrong-headed notions about you contaminate your self-wedding ceremony. On the count of three, unleash a sound—a howl or whisper or command—that will exorcise them. 1 . . . 2 . . . 3.

Here I will give you room to take an inventory. Are there any other obstacles that need smashing? Any further objections that have to be overruled before you'll be ready to pledge your troth to the only human being who is capable of flooding you with unconditional love from now until the end of time and beyond? You decide, then take appropriate ritual action.

As you groom yourself for the catharsis to come, the final step is to enhance and refine your visceral understanding of how gorgeous and mysterious you are. To that end, please revisit "A Spell to Re-Genius Yourself" on page 80 of this book, as well as "I'm a Star, You're a Star" on page 287. When you're through, try chanting this a few times:

> *I'm the chosen one, just like everyone else.*

If uttered with ironic sincerity and blasphemous reverence, those words will drive into your subconscious mind a full-blown understanding of the differences between bad ego trips and good ego trips, namely: During the bad ones, you ooze half-assed overconfidence, self-defeating insensitivity, and idiotic arrogance; in the good ones, you exude self-assured kindness, unpretentious mastery, and forceful grace.

Guess which type of ego trip doesn't create a whole lot of hell to pay later—and which serves best as the foundation of your marriage to yourself?

Now say this:

> *I'm the chosen one, just like everyone else.*
> *I'm the chosen one, just like everyone else.*

Before we get to the denouement, I'll invite you to spend time in the coming days to carry out devotional acts that will seal the sanctity of this ceremony.

First, create or acquire two wedding gifts for yourself. The first gift will symbolize your promise to lovingly kill off a bad habit or lingering remorse or ignorant glitch that you don't want to bring with you into your new, self-married life. The second gift will embody your intention to mobilize an unripe talent or dormant power that has been dying to come to life within you.

These two gifts can be based on the same theme. For example, you could get a hardy work boot and a fuzzy bunny slipper to symbolize your vow to regularly kick your own ass with lighthearted exuberance as well as tough love.

The other devotion I encourage you to enjoy is to go on a solo honeymoon to a thrilling sanctuary where you can try feats of strength and love that you've always fantasized about doing.

Now hold your own hand. Either speak the following declarations or use them as inspiration to create your own:

I love everything about me.

I love my curious beauty and my amazing pain.
I love my hungry soul and my changeable games.
I love my mysterious gambles and my humbling brags.
I love my blooming darkness and my burning flags.

I love my flaws, my gaps, my catalytic fears.
I love my puzzling insights and my scary frontiers.
I love my wrongs, my rights, and my ambiguous dreams.
I love my courage, my cowardice, and my elaborate schemes.

I love everything about me.
I love everything about me.

Now either make these promises to yourself, or use them to inspire your own versions:

I will never forsake, betray, or deceive myself.

I will always adore, forgive, and believe in myself.
I will never refuse, abandon, or scorn myself.
I will always amuse, delight, and redeem myself.

Beauty and truth and love will always find me.
Chaos and wilderness will always sustain me.
I'm the fire and water and earth and air that are forever fresh from eternity.
I'm a perfect creation and everything alive is naturally in love with me.

Now if it is your will and desire to agree to the following vows, say them:

I vow to treat myself with adroit respect and resourceful compassion and outrageous grace.

I pledge to see my problems as tremendous opportunities and my flaws as imperfect talents.

I promise to shower myself with rowdy blessings and surprising adventures and brave liberations.

As long as I live, I vow to die and be reborn, die and be reborn, die and be reborn, over and over again, forever reinventing myself.

I promise to be stronger than hate, wetter than water, deeper than the abyss, and wilder than the sun.

I pledge to remember that I am not only a sweating, half-asleep, excitable, bumbling jumble of desires, but that I am also an immortal four-dimensional messiah in continuous telepathic touch with all of creation.

I vow to love and honor my highs and my lows my yeses and noes, my give and my take, the life I wish I had and the life I actually have.

I promise to push hard to get better and smarter, grow my devotion to the truth, fuel my commitment to beauty, refine my emotions, hone my dreams, wrestle with my shadow, purge my ignorance, and soften my heart—even as I always accept myself for exactly who I am, with all of my so-called foibles and wobbles.

I pledge to wake myself up, never hold back, have nothing to lose, go all the way, kiss the stormy sky, be the hero of my own story, ask for everything I need and give everything I have, take myself to the river when it's time to go to the river, and take myself to the mountaintop when it's time to go to the mountaintop.

I vow to love myself unconditionally and unconventionally until the end of time and beyond.

I now pronounce you your own husband and your own wife, married to yourself in the eyes of the Divine Wow or Yo Mama Nature, whichever you prefer, as death and life and death and life bring you together, over and over again, in new and exciting ways each time, forever and ever, until the end of time and beyond.

You may kiss yourself on your own lips.

Brainstorm more vows and inspirations below.

"I was a hidden treasure, and I longed to be known." —Sufi proverb

15

"Ever since I learned
to see three sides to every story,
I'm finding much better stories"

Your Graduation Inscription

May you eat an unfamiliar dessert in a strange land at least
once every three years.

May you wake up to salsa music one summer morning,
and start dancing while you're still half-asleep.

May you spray-paint Rilke poems as graffiti
on highway overpasses.

May you mix stripes with plaids, floral patterns with checks,
and yellowish-green with brownish-purple.

May you learn to identify by name 20 flowers, 15 trees, 10 clouds
and one extrasolar planet.

May you put a bumper sticker on your car or bike that says,
"My god can kick your god's ass!"

If you bury your face in your tear-stained pillow and beg God to
please send you your soul mate, may you not slur your words
in such a way that they sound like "cell mate."

May you dream of taking a trip to the moon in a gondola
powered by firecrackers and wild swans.

May you actually kiss the earth now and then.

May you find many good excuses to say,
as physicist Niels Bohr once did, "Your theory is crazy,
but it's not crazy enough to be true."

Eighth Wonder

The Internet is the Eighth Wonder of the World. Its power to make anyone a global publisher, regardless of income, has begun to render irrelevant A. J. Liebling's famous assertion that "Freedom of the press is guaranteed only to those who own one."

Millions of websites provide average people access to a vast storehouse of information once available only to scholars who were close to and adept at using a major library.

Thanks to the Internet, communication has sped up and expanded in unforeseen ways. Some visionaries see it as the embodiment of the global nervous system imagined by Teilhard de Chardin:

"We are faced with a harmonized collectivity of consciousnesses equivalent to a super-consciousness. The earth is not only becoming covered by myriads of grains of thought, but becoming enclosed in a single vast grain of thought on the sidereal scale, the plurality of individual reflections grouping themselves together

and reinforcing one another in the act of a single unanimous reflection.

"A world network of economic and psychic affiliations is being woven at increasing speed. It constantly penetrates more deeply within each of us. With every passing day it becomes more impossible for us to act or think otherwise than collectively."
—Teilhard de Chardin, *The Phenomenon of Man*

Soul Insider

An interviewer urged the Dalai Lama to discourse on how to cultivate lovingkindness. His Holiness said, "That may be too much to ask. How about if we just work on getting the 'kindness' part right?"

Broken Laws "Scientists are challenging axioms of heredity that decree organisms inherit half their genetic characteristics from one parent and half from the other. They now believe chromosomes can archive the genes of ancestors and revive them in later generations. This means an organism may display characteristics of earlier generations that neither parent possesses. The discovery may force a revision of the laws of inheritance, with profound implications for crop-breeding, genetics, cancer research, and medicine."
—Jonathan Leake and Will Iredale, *The Times*

Scary Progress A quantum leap is a radical shift beyond what was previously imaginable. It can be problematic even as it's exhilarating. Physicist Fred Alan Wolf notes that in his field, such a leap often "leads to personal regrets, even though its ultimate consequences produce a new vision of humanity and the universe." Einstein, Planck, and Schrödinger, whose revolutionary work shredded the old physics, "were sadly upset with their discoveries," Wolf says.

"Whenever a quantum leap occurs," he concludes, "there is something that tends to resist it. In matter we call it inertia, in mind we call it prejudice or pig-headedness." (Source: Fred Alan Wolf, *Taking the Quantum Leap: The New Physics for Nonscientists*)

Beautiful Fuel Of all the ways that civilization generates energy to light its cities, one looks better than the rest: the arrays of majestic white windmills that snake along the hills of California's Altamont Pass. Surmounting stalks that bloom from the landscape like prehistoric trees in a David Hockney painting, their giant pinwheels whirl at different speeds, some in lazy slow-motion and others in a fast blur like a child's top.

Love Train Contrary to the orthodox notion that sperm headed toward an egg are in deadly competition with each other, researchers have discovered they collaborate, often joining together to create a "love train" so as to reach the target faster.

The Real Methuselah The desert-dwelling creosote bush can survive for centuries on little water. In the Mohave Desert there is a ring of creosote, named "King Clone," whose age has been carbon-dated at 11,700 years.

PNN is made possible by Deena Metzger's belief, described in her book Entering the Ghost River, *that "Beauty appears when something is completely and absolutely and openly itself."*

FREE WILL ASTROLOGY
"Esoteric astrology teaches that anyone whose future can be predicted by any means is living like a robot. It assumes that some people are more robotic (predictable) than others; and that further implies some of us have more free will than others." —Carolyn L. Vash, *Noetic Sciences Review,* noetic.org

Refined Sensibilities + Channeled Transmissions

For much of his career, Pulitzer Prize-winning poet James Merrill was renowned for work that was well-grounded, lucidly crafted, and formal in style. But from 1976 to 1982, while assembling his sprawling mystical epic *The Changing Light of Sandover,* he used a Ouija board to solicit the input of disembodied beings, including several archangels and the spirits of dead writers W. H. Auden and Gertrude Stein.

It was a brave—some said foolish—career move. He pushed beyond what had worked for him in the past, capitalizing on the risks his success had earned him.

The Changing Light of Sandover won a National Book Critics Circle Award. Some critics compared it to the masterpieces of Dante, Homer, and Blake. "James Merrill was one of the central American poets of the 20th century," wrote Harold Bloom in a retrospective analysis of his work after his death in 1995. "He had profound affinities with the great artists in verse: Milton, Pope, Tennyson, and Auden. Like them, he was an absolute master of diction, metrics, and cognitive music."

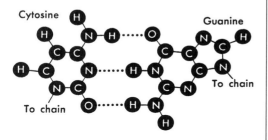

FREE WILL DIVINATION

Mark Seltman is a palm-reader whose approach to his art is different from most fortune-tellers. If he sees a character flaw indicated by a line on your palm, he won't make you feel like it's a curse that you're powerless to resist; instead, he'll tell you what you can do to fix it or overcome it. An article about Seltman on nymag.com described how his daughter was born with a hand that suggested she'd suffer from low self-esteem when she grew up. In response, Seltman dedicated himself to building her confidence and competence. Now, years later, the warning sign in her hand at birth has disappeared; she's brimming with aplomb.

PNN is brought to you by music writer Charles M. Young, who suggested in Rolling Stone *that the Pentagon be renamed the "Emma Goldman World Cathedral of Ecofeminist Goddess Worship."*

MIRABILIA REPORT *Mirabilia* n. winsome curiosities, supernatural gifts, healing tricks; from the Latin *mirabilia,* "marvels."

■ There's a virgin forest in New York City at the upper tip of Manhattan, near the Cloisters.

■ Your skin hosts more living organisms than there are people on the planet.

■ The Milky Way Galaxy is shaped like a thick, warped vinyl record with the edge on one side bent up and on the other side bent down.

■ Whenever an actor portraying a doctor performs a particular kind of surgery on a popular soap opera, real doctors begin performing that same surgery at a dramatically higher rate in real hospitals.

■ Researchers detected traces of marijuana and coca leaves in 17th-century pipes found in the house where William Shakespeare lived.

■ Actor Steven Seagal was formally declared a tulku, or reincarnation of a Buddhist lama, by a Tibetan Buddhist master, even though all of his movies depict him beating up people. One ex-friend said Seagal is "the only person I know who can use the words 'motherfucker' and 'Dalai Lama' in the same sentence."

■ Eskimos use refrigerators to keep their food from freezing.

■ Rock music incites termites to eat wood at twice their usual rate.

■ In Kampala, Uganda, an unknown prankster shot gorillas with tranquilizer darts and dressed them up as clowns while they were unconscious.

■ Sixty-five million pilgrims sought to wash away their sins by bathing in the Ganges River during 2001's Kumbh Mela, a spiritual festival in India. Sixty-five million votes were cast by phone to determine the winner of TV's *American Idol* talent contest in May 2004.

■ "Corporations of the magnitude of IBM or Citibank constitute themselves as what Renaissance Europe would have recognized as city-states, sovereign powers employing as many people as once lived in Philadelphia in 1789." —Lewis Lapham, *Harper's*

"In a number of Australian Aboriginal tribes, holding of the penis is traditionally used as a gesture to express male allegiance and cooperation, as well as a ritual part of resolving disputes between 'accused' and 'defending' parties.

"Among the Walbiri and Aranda people, when different communities get together or when grievances need to be settled in formal 'trials,' men participate in what is known variously as touch-penis, penis-offering, or the penis-holding rite. Each man presents his semi-erect organ to all the others in turn, pressing it into each man's palm and drawing it along the length of the upturned hand (held with the fingers toward the testicles). By offering and grasping each other's penis—said to represent 'paying with one's life'—the men make an avowal of mutual support and goodwill between them, or symbolize and solidify the agreement they have reached during the settling of a dispute." —Bruce Bagemihl, *Biological Exuberance: Animal Homosexuality and Natural Diversity*

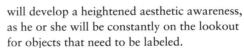

Operation Ugly-Aware

"The insidious nature of ugliness is such that we gradually become accustomed to its presence. This de-sensitization can be halted only through a conscious effort to become aware of the ugliness around us, and to make others aware of it as well. To that end, the Coalition to Raise Aesthetic Consciousness has developed the Operation Ugly-Aware tool kit. It consists of one item, this decal:

THIS IS UGLY

"The purpose of the decal is twofold: 1) by affixing decals to buildings and other objects which blatantly offend his or her aesthetic sensibility, the CRAC agent will increase the aesthetic awareness of other individuals who have become de-sensitized to the ugliness around them; 2) by carrying several decals in his or her pocket at all times, the CRAC agent will develop a heightened aesthetic awareness, as he or she will be constantly on the lookout for objects that need to be labeled.

"Becoming a member of the CRAC army is simple. The rules for affixing decals are as follows:

"1) No decal shall ever be affixed, either directly or indirectly, to a human being;

"2) no decal shall be affixed in a manner such as to cause permanent damage to the offending object;

"3) decals shall be affixed with discretion, and only to those objects which blatantly offend against the affixer's aesthetic conscience." (Source: The Coalition to Raise Aesthetic Consciousness, tinyurl.com/mk2znn)

"In his book *The Healing Power of Doing Good*, Allan Luks reports that people who spend as little as two hours a week volunteering to help others experience a 'helper's high' that produces lower blood pressure, lower heart rate, less stress, and less tension. As a bonus, Luks found, they also enjoy 'a big boost in self-esteem.' Luks theorizes that 'doing good deeds triggers the body to release endorphins—pain-killing, mood-elevating hormones.'

"Physician David Sobel and psychologist Robert Ornstein, authors of *Healthy Pleasures,* report the same effect and conclude: 'The greatest surprise of human evolution may be that the highest form of selfishness is selflessness.'" —*Earth Island Journal*, earthisland.org

The Power of Imagination, Part 1

Two groups were enlisted for a month-long program to boost their accuracy at shooting a basketball. One group practiced 20 minutes a day. Those in the other group didn't actually practice, but visualized themselves shooting baskets successfully for 20 minutes a day. Results? The group that literally practiced improved 56 percent. The visualizers jacked up their average 52 percent.

The Power of Imagination, Part 2

The placebo effect is a well-known but poorly understood phenomenon in medical science. Studies show that up to a third of all sick people feel better after receiving pills with no active ingredients. The reason may lie in the body's powerful instinct to participate in its own healing. When it believes help is on the way in the form of medication, it joins in by releasing endorphins, the natural opiates that induce relaxation and a sense of well-being.

The first U.S. Chief Justice, John Jay, bought slaves in order to free them.

❁

William Shakespeare coined 1,700 words, more than eight percent of his total vocabulary. Some of the best: *besmirch, dauntless, dwindle, gnarled, hobnob, lackluster, madcap, pander, rancorous, sanctimonious, tranquil, bloodstained, leapfrog, gossip, fortune-teller.*

❁

Vietnamese freedom fighter Trieu Thi Trinh fought the Chinese occupation of her country in the third century. She raised a rebel army, established her own sovereign enclave, and rode into battle against the invaders on the back of an elephant. "I want to ride the tempest, tame the waves, kill the sharks," she said. "I will not resign myself."

❁

In 1,000,000 BC it was a miracle to kindle fire. In 10,000 BC it was a miracle to grow food. In 5000 BC a wheel was a miracle. So was metalworking. In 1400 AD the printing press was a miracle. In 1700 an engine was a miracle. In 1870 instantaneous long-distance communication was a miracle. In 1890 the airplane was a miracle. In 1985 the Internet was a miracle. What's the next miracle? (Source: L. M. Boyd)

❁

While living in Manhattan in the 1950s, avant-garde composer John Cage felt beleaguered by the omnipresence of radio sound. In response, he wrote a musical piece that featured several radios tuned to different frequencies. After that, he was able to respond to street radio noise with a pleasant sense of "They're playing my song." (Thanks to Ruby for the report.)

"Every genuine boy is a rebel and an anarch. If he were allowed to develop according to his own instincts, his own inclinations, society would undergo such a radical transformation as to make the adult revolutionary cower and cringe." —Henry Miller, *The Books in My Life*

"What would happen if one woman told the truth about her life? The world would split open." —Muriel Rukeyser, "Kathe Kollwitz," *A Muriel Rukeyser Reader,* Jan Heller Levi, editor

"Consciousness-altering devices like the microscope and telescope were once criminalized for the same reason that psychedelic plants were banned in later years. They allow us to peer into bits and zones of Chaos." —Timothy Leary

"No pessimist ever discovered the secret of the stars, or sailed to an uncharted land, or opened a new doorway for the human spirit." —Helen Keller

"Though we travel the world over to find the beautiful, we must carry it with us or we find it not." —Ralph Waldo Emerson, "Essay XII, Art," *Essays: First Series*

"To transform life into celebration is the only authentic science of religion." —Osho

ShockGuard

Supercharged Healing

Every year the MacArthur Foundation gives a stipend of $500,000, with no strings attached, to over 20 people of outstanding talent, freeing them to pursue their idiosyncratic creative, intellectual, and professional inclinations. Among the lucky geniuses selected in recent years:

Liza Lou, a glass bead artist who creates large works of color and complexity that merge fine art and craft.

Bonnie Bassler, a molecular ecobiologist who investigates the chemical signaling mechanisms that bacteria use to communicate with each other.

Loren Rieseberg, a botanist who does research on one of the most perplexing questions of evolutionary biology—how new species originate.

Corinne Dufka, a photojournalist and social worker who has worked doggedly to heal war-devastated Sierra Leone.

Karen Hesse, a novelist who is playing with experimental forms of literature for children and young adults.

Janine Jagger, an epidemiologist who invents devices and monitoring systems to protect health care workers from transmission of blood-borne diseases.

Toba Khedoori, an artist who works in wax, oil, and pencil to create immense but delicate drawings on vast stretches of unframed paper.

Nawal Nour, a doctor specializing in the physical and emotional health of female immigrants who have suffered ritual clitoridectomies.

Erik Mueggler, an anthropologist who enriches the understanding of ethnic minorities in China through vivid ethno-graphies of ordinary lives in provincial populations.

Daisy Youngblood, a ceramicist who uses clay and bronze to create sculptures that evoke the primitive, the timeless, and the universal.

Deborah Jin, a physicist working on techniques to cool atoms to the lowest possible temperatures.

Edgar Meyer, a bassist and composer who fuses classical and bluegrass styles to create an expansive repertoire of American music.

Charles Steidel, a cosmologist who invents new methods for detecting light from the most distant galaxies, opening a window into the early history of the universe. (Source: MacArthur Foundation, macfound.org)

PRONOIA NEWS NETWORK

You Are a Champion of Champions

"You are a champion of champions, genetically speaking, because you are the product of an inconceivably complex web of ancestors, spiraling back for billions of years into the primordial ooze, not a single individual of which ever failed to grow to maturity and beget viable offspring while most other creatures around them, including many of their brothers, sisters, and cousins, faded away and the majority eventually disappeared forever into extinction. If your ancestors hadn't been such top performers that they were 100 percent successful in procreation, your ancestral lines of descent would be broken and you could not exist." —Guy Murchie, *The Seven Mysteries of Life*

Crucial Dust Mote?

Before the U.S. election in November 2004, *What Is Enlightenment?* magazine posed the following query to five religious leaders: "Many people argue that the upcoming presidential election is the most important in our lifetime. Do you agree?" Four respondents said, in effect, "Yes, because George W. Bush is bad for America and the world."

But the fifth, Zen Buddhist Jan Chozen Roshi, replied, "I don't know. Our existence is so short, it's like a dust mote in the eye of God. To say that the time in which my dust mote existed was the most important is a self-centered view."

Jan Chozen Roshi's wisdom resembled that in an anecdote told by Henry Kissinger. Kissinger once asked Chinese premier Zhou Enlai what he thought of the French Revolution, which had happened two centuries earlier. "Too soon to tell," Zhou answered.

THE STORY OF CIVILIZATION

"Civilization is a stream with banks. The stream is sometimes filled with blood from people killing, stealing, shouting, and doing the things historians usually record, while on the banks, unnoticed, people build homes, make love, raise children, sing songs." —Will Durant, *The Story of Civilization*

BEDROCK

luminous	marrow	murmurs	lightning	praise
ancient	membrane	undulates	inside	melodies
diamond	crucible	congeals	dawn	nectar
chthonic	aurora	frees	solar	lullabies

Most Beautiful Poem

The Beauty and Truth Lab voted Armand Silvestre's poem "The Secret" the Most Beautiful Poem of the Last Millennium. This is our translation from the original French.

I want the morning to ignore
The name I told the night.
I want it to evaporate silently,
like a teardrop in the dawn wind.

I want the day to proclaim
The love I hid from the morning.
I want it to bend over my open heart
and set it aflame, like a grain of
  incense.

I want the sunset to forget
The secret I told the day,
And carry it away with my love
In the folds of its pale robe.

Pop Quiz

"What is the cheapest precious substance on Earth?"

First genius to answer correctly wins little bells to tie on the spring crocuses.

Collaborative Decision-Making with Nature

Writing in the *San Francisco Chronicle,* Jon Carroll described the behavior of certain young spiders in the Sacramento Delta. When one of these "spiderlings" is ready to leave its birthplace and go in search of adventure, it spins out a long gossamer strand, climbs aboard, and leaps into the unknown. Floating in midair, it's carried by the wind to who-knows-where, eventually landing in its new homeland.

Faux Horoscope "The stars would love to influence your future," reported a horoscope for Pisces in *The Onion* newspaper, "but they are powerless against your well-established patterns of behavior."

Exclusive! The Beauty and Truth Lab reports the news before it happens!

In this special PNN report, our psychic journalists bring you the stories that haven't happened yet—but will! It's made possible by Pulitzer Prize-winning scientist E. O. Wilson's belief that "To make sacred is the end product of evolution in our moral and aesthetic reasoning."

Conviviality Revolution A new breed of well-read, charismatic homeless people will arise. They'll spread understanding and laughter through their communities, and will be routinely feasted in the homes of grateful citizens.

Eros Upgrade The average length of an act of heterosexual intercourse in America—which is currently only four minutes—will jump to 22 minutes.

Lawyer Glut The government will pay subsidies to some lawyers so they won't practice law—much as it now pays supermarket chains to keep cheese off the market when there is too much and the excess would bring prices down.

Mutant Opinions Botched genetic experiments will create a strain of mutant bacteria that causes infected victims to hate opinion polls.

Recovered Memories Under hypnosis, many adults will recall long-suppressed memories of joy and peace experienced when they were children.

Book Futures One of the bestselling self-help books of the decade will be *The Zen of Juicy Sacred Radical Temper Tantrums.*

This special edition of PNN is brought to you by philosopher Norman O. Brown's belief that "civilization has to be renewed by the discovery of new mysteries, by the sovereign power of the imagination, by the undemocratic power which makes poets the unacknowledged legislators of mankind." (Source: Norman O. Brown, Apocalypse and/or Metamorphosis)

Men's Time of the Month

Biologists in Sweden will furnish conclusive evidence that men have "periods" analogous to a woman's menstrual cycle. They seem to correspond to changes in the relationship between Earth and the planet Mars, the biologists will claim. At the peak of the male "marstral cycle," which can last up to 10 days a month, the adrenal glands release a hormone that makes men more likely to be irritable, more skilled at disguising their irrational impulses with logical explanations, out of touch with their feelings, and prone to violence and poor judgment. There's also a vulnerable phase preceding the period, which the biologists will dub PMS, or Pathological Macho Stress.

Genetic Performance Art

A rowdy new class of genetic engineers will have little interest in creating oil spill-eating bacteria, frost-resistant strawberries, or other useful hybrids. Considering themselves to be a cross between computer hackers and performance artists, they will create fun monstrosities that appeal to their sense of play and perversity, like winged horses and trees that grow leaves resembling one-hundred-dollar bills.

Homechurching As public schools continue to decline and private schools become more expensive, increasing numbers of parents will homeschool their children. As the pronoia meme spreads, an analogous phenomenon will arise among religious groups. Called the "homechurch" movement by Christians, the "homesynagogue" movement by Jews, and the "hometemple" movement by other religious groups, it will consist of people creating altars and conducting worship sessions in their own abodes. Seekers pursuing this approach to spiritual communion will serve as their own priests, priestesses, and rabbis.

The Joy of Childbirth The national murder rate will plummet when "The Hedonistic Midwife Channel," a new cable TV network, begins to broadcast live childbirths 24 hours a day.

Sentient Vegetables Researchers will uncover stunning evidence that vegetables have an intensity of consciousness and feeling much closer to that of animals than has previously been suspected. Many vegetarians will renounce their previous diets and swear to eat only milk and honey.

Tax Love A new grassroots political movement, Tax Patriots, will assert that paying taxes is the greatest patriotic duty one can exercise, even more than serving in the military.

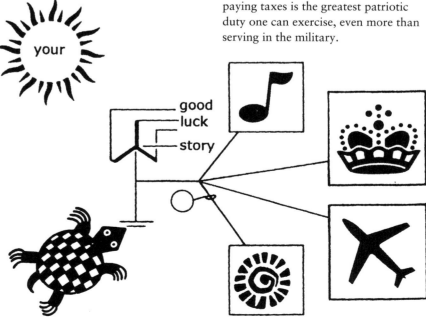

FOR IMMEDIATE RELEASE

Global Village Idiot Rob Brezsny has announced his candidacy for a new Cabinet-level post that he hopes the president will create: FOOL CZAR. Roughly analogous to America's Drug Czar, the Fool Czar would organize and lead an all-out War on Gravity—not the kind of gravity that keeps us on the ground, but rather the absurdly sober, hyper-dignified literalism that infects every level of society.

Just as the Drug Czar educates the nation on the hazards of drugs, the Fool Czar would work to show how dangerous it is to feed the bad habit of taking everything so seriously. He would also foster an understanding of the threat from simplistic opinion-mongering that turns every issue into fodder for infantile arguments.

To demonstrate his sincerity and commitment, Brezsny has offered to literally kiss the bare asses of the president, vice-president, and Cabinet members. In the event that would compromise their modesty, he has also indicated his willingness merely to smooch their fully clothed butts.

Upon taking office as Fool Czar, Brezsny's inaugural act would be to borrow from two traditions: 1. Among the ancient Romans, work was customarily finished by noon. The rest of the day was spent in pleasure or amusement. More than half the days of the year were holidays. 2. In medieval Europe, as many as 105 days of the year were feast days.

In this spirit, Brezsny would declare a spate of new holidays and ceremonial traditions. Here they are:

Unhappy Hour. During this gala bitch fest, celebrants have license to howl and mutter about everything that hurts their feelings. Having flushed all their venom in one neat ritual spew, they'll be free to enjoy generous thoughts and expansive fantasies the rest of the time.

Dare to Be Boring Day. We all deserve a break from the oppressive demands to appear smart and to be entertaining. On Dare to Be Boring Day, it will be socially unacceptable to demonstrate your wit and verve. Long-winded, rambling monologues full of obscure details will be mandatory. The more clichés and buzzwords you use, the better. Tell worn-out stories your friends have already heard many times. Flesh out your disjointed sentences with awkward silences. Discuss at length your plans for switching laundry detergents, the collection of matchbooks you had as a child, and the time you almost traveled to the Wal-Mart in another town, but didn't.

Bacchanalia. During this week-long extravaganza, work and business will be suspended so that all adults can enjoy sexual play, whether it be solo, dyadic, or in groups. To promote acceptance of the holiday, the Fool Czar will head up a new Federal Bureau of Lust. Served by advisors drawn not from the ranks of porn stars and scientific sex researchers but from tantrically trained poets and musicians, the Bureau will sponsor educational campaigns to help every citizen learn to honor the libido as a sacred gift from the Goddess.

24 Hours of Global Orgasm. What if there came a day when every adult on the planet came at the same time? This will be the climax of Bacchanalia.

Do What You Fear Festival. First, you make a list of the 100 things you're most afraid of. Next, you rate them from one to 100 in order of how badly they scare you. Then you agree to stop obsessing about the bottom 97 fears because they distract you from the three really interesting ones. Finally, you conquer those three by doing them.

Marry Yourself. As a government-sanctioned tradition, getting married to yourself will be a rite of passage as common as graduating from high school.

Be Your Own Wife Week. Whether you're male or female or transgendered, straight or gay or both, you can observe Be Your Own Wife Week. Here's how. Renounce all your yearnings to be waited on and cleaned up after. Divest yourself of every last deluded wish that someday a special person will come along to magically understand and attend to your every need. Pledge that from now on you will be a connoisseur of taking care of yourself. (This celebration might immediately follow the "Marry Yourself" holiday.)

Debunking Day. What shall we debunk? It's easy to direct scorn at targets like Bigfoot, UFOs, and the Face on Mars. On Debunking Day, we'll warm up with witty slams against them, then move on to the real sacred cows, like the cult of science, the cult of materialism, and the cult of pop nihilism.

Spiritual Makeover Day. Participants build altars celebrating beauty, truth, and love in the ugliest places they know.

Praise Binge. For 24 hours, judgmental criticism will be taboo. Revelers will stretch their imaginations as they strive to praise everything and everyone as sincerely as possible, including themselves.

Koyaanisqatsi. In the language of the Hopi Indians, *koyaanisqatsi* means "crazy life," "life in turmoil," or "life out of balance." It's usually invoked to describe a culture that's in disarray because of corruption and lack of vision. I'd like to extend its meaning to identify the chaotic states that each of us periodically goes through in our personal life. It's a time when we lose our moorings, when we're out of touch with our moral center. On the one hand, it's uncomfortable and disorienting. On the other hand, the brain-scrambling it stirs up is often a blessing. It flushes out mental habits that no longer serve us. It provokes creative innovations by rearranging the contents of our psyche. Happy Koyaanisqatsi!

Freethinkers Week. To celebrate this liberating grace period, you might indulge in any of the following festive acts: 1. Declare your independence from anyone who tries to tell you, either subliminally or directly, who you are or how you should live your life. 2. Declare your independence from your past, espe-

cially from memories that oppress your sense of possibility and from old self-images that inhibit your urge to explore. 3. Declare your independence from peer pressure, groupthink, the law of the pack, and conventional wisdom. 4. Declare your independence from your previous conception of freedom so that you'll be free to come to a completely fresh understanding of it.

Potlatch. Among certain Native American tribes, the potlatch was a generosity contest. Participants vied to give away the most gifts. In reviving this rite, we will not entirely eliminate the competitive element. Celebrants will strive to push their own largesse to the limits, even as they admire those whose munificence outstrips their own. Contributions of money and material objects will not be the only ways to partake in the Potlatch. Offerings of time, love, energy, help, and kindness will be equally valued.

Cheery Sleepy Week. Sleep deprivation has reached epidemic proportions, and the results are catastrophic. Dream-cheated somnambulists are responsible for the rise in incompetence, bad manners, and mass hypnosis. During the seven-day and seven-night Cheery Sleepy Week, all Americans will be given the luxury of catching up on their lost ZZZZs. Millions of refreshed citizens will wear buttons that brag, "I slept nine hours last night and I'm not ashamed!"

Break Bread with Your Nemesis. To observe this feast day, you simply invite the person who makes you most uncomfortable to an intimate dinner for two.

Hallowection Day. The American genius for inadvertent surrealism is nowhere better illustrated than in the proximity of Halloween and Election Day. Why not honor the obvious and combine the two into a single festival?

Thousand-Year Party for You. The Thousand-Year Party in your honor will begin with a ceremony by the Grandchildren of the Hiroshima Bomb Survivors Dance Company, which will consecrate 34,000 gallons of dove dung to you and scatter it in your name over 155 countries of the world.

SACRED ADVERTISEMENT

Premium Bonus Benefit

ANTI-DSM-IV, OR THE OUTLAW CATALOG OF CAGEY OPTIMISM

Psychiatry and psychotherapy obsess on what's wrong with people and give short shrift to what's right. The manual of these professions is a 943-page textbook called the *DSM-IV.* It identifies scores of pathological states but no healthy ones.

A few years ago, I began to complain about this fact in my syndicated weekly column and website, and asked readers to help me compile material for a proposed antidote, the *Anti-DSM-IV*—a compendium of healthy, exalted, positive states of being. As their entries came in, we at the Beauty and Truth Lab were inspired to dream up some of our own. Below is our initial attempt at creating an *Anti-DSM-IV,* or as we also like to call it, *The Outlaw Catalog of Cagey Optimism.*

• ACUTE FLUENCY. Happily immersed in artistic creation or scientific exploration; lost in a trance-like state of inventiveness that's both blissful and taxing; surrendered to a state of grace in which you're fully engaged in a productive, compelling, and delightful activity. The joy of this demanding, rewarding state is intensified by a sense that time has been suspended, and is rounder and deeper than usual. (Suggested by H. H. Holiday, who reports that extensive studies of this state have been done by Mihaly Csikszentmihalyi in his book *Flow: The Psychology of Optimal Experience.*)

• AESTHETIC BLISS. Vividly experiencing the colors, textures, tones, scents, and rhythms of the world around you, creating a symbiotic intimacy that dissolves the psychological barriers between you and what you observe. (Suggested by Jeanne Grossetti.)

• AGGRESSIVE SENSITIVITY. Animated by a strong determination to be receptive and empathetic.

• ALIGNMENT WITH THE INFINITY OF THE MOMENT. Reveling in the liberating realization that we are all exactly where we need to be at all times, even if some of us are temporarily in the midst of trial or tribulation, and that human evolution is proceeding exactly as it should, even if we can't see the big picture of the puzzle that would clarify how all the pieces fit together perfectly. (Suggested by Meredith Jones.)

• AUTONOMOUS NURTURING. Not waiting for someone to give you what you can give yourself. (Suggested by Shannen Davis.)

• BASKING IN ELDER WISDOM. A state of expansive ripeness achieved through listening to the stories of elders. (Suggested by Annabelle Aavard.)

• BIBLIOBLISS. Transported into states of transcendent pleasure while immersed in reading a favorite book. (Suggested by Catherine Kaikowska.)

• BLASPHEMOUS REVERENCE. Acting on the knowledge that the most efficacious form of devotion to the Divine Wow is tinctured with playful or mischievous behavior that prevents the buildup of fanaticism.

• BOO-DUH NATURE. Dwelling in the blithe understanding of the fact that worry is useless because most of what we worry about never happens. (Suggested by Timothy S. Wallace.)

• COMIC INTROSPECTION. Being fully aware of your own foibles while still loving yourself tenderly and maintaining confidence in your ability to give your specific genius to the world. To paraphrase Alan Jones, Dean of Grace Cathedral: following the Byzantine ploys of your ego with compassion and humor as it tries to make itself the center of everything, even of its own suffering and struggle.

• COMPASSIONATE DISCRIMINATION. Having astute judgment without being scornfully judgmental; seeing difficult truths about a situation or person without closing your heart or feeling superior. In the words of Alan Jones: having the ability "to smell a rat without allowing your ability to discern deception sour your vision of the glory and joy that is everyone's birthright."

• CRAZED KINDNESS. Having frequent, overpowering urges to bestow gifts, disseminate inspiration, and perpetrate random acts of benevolence.

• ECSTATIC GRATITUDE. Feeling genuine thankfulness with such resplendent intensity that you generate a surge of endorphins in your body and slip into a full-scale outbreak of euphoria.

• EMANCIPATED SURRENDER. Letting go of an attachment without harboring resentment toward the stimuli that led to the necessity of letting go. (Suggested by Timothy S. Wallace.)

• FRIENDLY SHOCK. Welcoming a surprise that will ultimately have benevolent effects.

• HIGHWAY EQUANIMITY. Feeling serene, polite, and benevolent while driving in heavy traffic. (Suggested by Shannen Davis.)

• HOLY LISTENING. Hearing the words of another human being as if they were a direct communication from the Divine Wow to you.

• IMAGINATIVE TRUTH-TELLING. Conveying the truth of any specific situation from multiple angles, thereby mitigating the distortions that result from assuming the truth can be told from a single viewpoint.

• IMPULSIVE LOVE SPREADING. Characterized by a fierce determination to never withhold well-deserved praise, inspirational encouragement, positive feedback, or loving thoughts; often includes a tendency to write love letters on the spur of the moment and on any medium, including napkins, grocery bags, and skin. (Suggested by Laurie Burton.)

• INADVERTENT NATURE WORSHIP. Experiencing the rapture that comes from being outside for extended periods of time. (Suggested by Sue Carol Robinson.)

• INGENIOUS INTIMACY. Having an ability to consistently create deep connections with other human beings, and to use the lush, reverential excitement stimulated by such exchanges to further deepen the connections.

A well-crafted talent for dissolving your sense of separateness and enjoying the innocent exultation that erupts in the wake of the dissolution. (Suggested by Sue Carol Robinson.)

• JOYFUL POIGNANCE. Feeling buoyantly joyful about the beauty and mystery of life while remaining aware of the sadness, injustices, wounds, and future fears that form the challenges in an examined life. (Suggested by Alka Bhargava.)

• LATE LATE-BLOOMING. Having a capacity for growth spurts well into old age, long past the time that conventional wisdom says they're possible.

• LEARNING DELIGHT. Experiencing the brain-reeling pleasure that comes from learning something new. (Suggested by Sue Carol Robinson.)

• LUCID DREAM PATRIOTISM. A love of country rooted in the fact that it provides the ideal conditions for learning lucid dreaming. (Suggested by Ken Kelzer.)

• LYRICAL CONSONANCE. Experiencing the visceral yet also cerebral excitement that comes from listening to live music played impeccably by skilled musicians. (Suggested by Susan E. Nace.)

• MODULATED RAPTURISM. Welcoming miracles and peak experiences in full awareness that the growth they initiate will require sober commitment and disciplined work to complete. (Suggested by Timothy S. Wallace.)

• NONRESENTMENT SYNDROME. Having an ability to be friendly, open, and helpful to people with whom you disagree.

• NOT HAVING TO BE RIGHT. Fostering an ability, even a willingness, to be proven wrong about one of your initial perceptions or pet theories; having an eagerness to gather information that may change your mind about something you have fervently believed; cultivating a tendency to enjoy being corrected, especially about ideas that are negative or hostile. (Suggested by Sheila Kollasch.)

• ORGIASTIC LUCIDITY. Experiencing an expansive and intricate state of clarity while in the midst of extreme sensual pleasure.

• PERMANENT DIVINE INFATUATION. Having not the abstract understanding but rather a direct perception that the Divine Intelligence, who re-creates the universe fresh every moment, is deeply in love with you, even as you are in love with the Divine Intelligence.

• RADICAL CURIOSITY. Characterized by the following traits: an enthusiasm for the mystery embedded in the mundane; a preference for questions over answers;

an aversion to stereotyping, generalizations, and jumping to conclusions; a belief that people are unsolvable puzzles; an inclination to be unafraid of both change and absence of change; a strong drive to avoid boredom; a lack of interest in possessing or dominating what you are curious about. (Suggested by Laurie Burton.)

• RELENTLESS UNPRETENTIOUSNESS. Possessing a strong determination to not take yourself too seriously, not take your cherished beliefs too literally, and not take other people's ideas about you too personally.

• RIPE INTELLECTION. The understanding that a predilection to notice and analyze pathology is itself pathological. (Suggested by Timothy S. Wallace.)

• ROOTED IN ETERNITY. The state of knowing that your true identity is deeper than the constant chatter of thoughts, images, and feelings that swirls through your mind. (Suggested by Crispin R.)

• SACRED PERCEPTIVENESS. Seeing others for who they really are, in both their immaturity and genius, and articulating your insights to them with care.

• SCARY-THUNDER-IN-THE-DARK HAPPINESS. Feeling deliciously safe in a well-protected sanctuary during a severe storm. (Suggested by Sue Carol Robinson.)

• SCHIZOFRIENDIA. Hearing voices in your head that are constantly supportive, encouraging, and keen to offer advice that helps you make the most of every experience. (Suggested by Lewis.)

• SELF-ACCEPTANCE UNDER PRESSURE. The state achieved upon leaving a room filled with people who know you, and not worrying about what anyone will say about you. (Suggested by Shannen Davis.)

• SELF-HONORING. Having an unwillingness to disparage, belittle, or hurt yourself; includes a taboo against speaking phrases like, "I'm such an idiot!" and "What's wrong with me?" (Suggested by Julie Levin.)

• SLY TRUST. Having a discerning faith that the integrity of your efforts will inevitably lead to a result that's exactly what you need; being skillful in the art of never trying too hard. (Suggested by Rhonda Christmas.)

• SONGBIRD-IN-A-TREE. The cultivated awareness that daily life presents countless opportunities to be buoyed by moments of ordinary extraordinary beauty, and that these moments are most available if you perceive with your senses and not with your internal turmoil. (Suggested by Lisa Chabot.)

• TENDER RAGE. Maintaining a strong sense of love and protectiveness toward a person or creature or institution you're angry at.

• TRANSCONSUMERISM. An absence of tendencies to predicate happiness on acquiring material possessions. (Suggested by Timothy S. Wallace.)

• TRIUMPHANT NURTURING. Feeling contented expansiveness while nursing a baby. (Suggested by Susan E. Nace.)

• UNSELFCONSCIOUSNESS. Doing what you're doing and being who you're being without thinking about it at all. Being happy by virtue of not worrying about whether or not you're happy; enjoying a unified state in which you are not split between the you who acts and the you who observes. (Suggested by Valerie Keller.)

• UNTWEAKABILITY. Having a composed, blame-free readiness to correct false impressions when your actions have been misunderstood and have led to awkward consequences.

• VIRTUOSO INTEGRATION. Consistently walking your talk; effectively translating your ideals into the specific actions; creating results that are congruous with your intentions; being free of hypocrisy.

• VISIONS OF THRILLING EXPLOITS. Experiencing an eruption of intuition that clearly reveals you will attempt a certain adventure in the future, as when you spy a particular mountain for the first time and know you'll climb it one day. (Suggested by Sue Carol Robinson.)

• WEATHER SENSITIVITY. Having a high degree of awareness about your sensitivity to changes in the weather, and having a skill for managing your responses to those shifts so as to consistently bring out the best in yourself. (Suggested by Julie Caves.)

• WHEEEE. A serenely boisterous intensely focused chaos of communion with streaming fountains of liquid light hurtling softly through the giggly upbeat tender assurance that all is well and a mysterious unimaginable intelligence is magnetizing us forward into ever-more-wonderful throbs of naked truth that bestow the humble happy sight of life as a river of fantastically lucky artful change flowing through us forever. (Suggested by Sarah Alexander and Jon Kohl Drucker.)

• WHOLEHEARTEDNESS. Having the capacity to give, on a moment's notice, your complete attention, empathy, and playful intelligence to any person or circumstance you choose. (Suggested by Susan Coleman.)

• WILD DISCIPLINE. Possessing a talent for creating a kind of organization that's liberating; knowing how to introduce limitations into a situation in such a way that everyone involved is empowered to express his or her unique genius; having an ability to discern hidden order within a seemingly chaotic mess.

OUTLAW PRONOIA THERAPY

**Experiments and exercises
in becoming a carefully liberated,
comically healing,
astutely innocent
Master of Crazy Wisdom**

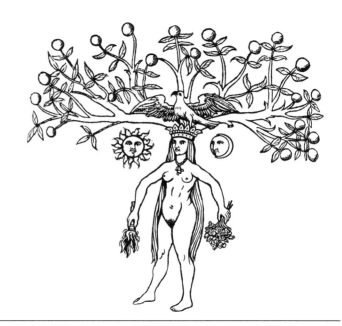

Report your answers and research results below

1 Have you ever had permission to indulge in a marathon of braggadocio? Have you ever gotten an invitation to bluster on endlessly about your own charms without feeling even a touch of guilt or inhibition? I hereby grant you such a license right now.

When you're ready, carry out the exercise called Brag Therapy. Grab a good listener or a recording device, and boast extravagantly about yourself for at least 20 minutes. Expound in exhaustive detail why you're so wonderful and why the world would be a better place if everyone would just act more like you.

Don't be humble or cautious. Go too far. Heap extreme glory on yourself. Brazenly proclaim the spectacular qualities about you that no one has ever fully articulated or appreciated. Don't forget to extol the prodigious flaws and vices that make you so special.

What does this have to do with pronoia? When you audaciously identify your existing gifts, you set yourself up to become a magnet for even greater abundance. In fact, we recommend that you treat yourself to a Brag Therapy session regularly.

To whet your imagination, read an excerpt from the boast of Eric Baer, a participant in a Brag Therapy session I hosted in Milwaukee. "I have opposable thumbs," Eric exulted. "I can read. I breathe all the way through the night even though I'm asleep. I have access to emporiums where I can choose from 25 different brands of toilet paper. I know how to turn food into energy. I live where knuckleheads run everything and yet nothing ever blows up."

2 The iconoclastic physicist Jack Sarfatti proposes that all "creative thought by artists, craftsmen, and scientists involves the subconscious reception of ideas from the future, which literally create themselves."

Beauty and Truth Lab researcher Vimala Blavatsky puts a different spin on it. "Our future selves are constantly transmitting great ideas to us back through time," she says, "but most of us don't believe that's possible and consequently are not alert for it."

What do you think is the most pressing communiqué your future self is currently beaming your way?

3 In the Greek epic *The Odyssey,* Odysseus and his men become stranded on an island belonging to the sorceress Circe, who uses her magic to transform the men into pigs. Later, though, she changes them back into men—only they're younger and taller and better-looking than before they were pigs.

Tell an analogous story from your own life: an experience in which you were turned into a pig for a while, and became a more robust version of yourself when the spell was broken.

4 Contrary to what the Bible says, it won't be the meek who shall inherit the Earth. On the other hand, the arrogant power mongers won't collect the legacy either. Neither the indecisive wimps nor the acquisitive bullies will contribute much to creating the New Earth.

Who, then, will inherit the Earth? What kind of human beings are best-equipped to thrive in the evolving game of life? We say it will be the well-disciplined pleasure-seekers who are in vigorous dialogue with their own dark sides, who balance the masculine and feminine aspects of their natures, and who master the fine arts of working at their play and playing at their work.

Assume our definitions are true. What would you do to become more like an inheritor of the Earth?

5 "Nothing's going right in my life. I feel anxious and paranoid all the time. My relationships are a mess." In my line of work, people make confessions like that to me. My first response is usually something like this: "Do you habitually gobble junk food near bedtime, steal a paltry five hours of sleep per night, gulp two cups of coffee and no breakfast in the morning, then bolt to a workplace where you get no sunlight or exercise and sit in an uncomfortable chair?" They often reply, "You must be psychic! How did you know?!" My point is that many psychological troubles stem from our chronic failure to take good care of our physical needs.

Name three things you can do to promote pronoia in yourself by taking better care of your body.

Outlaw Pronoia Therapy

The Iroquois regularly celebrated the feast of Ononharoia (literally, "turning the brain upside down") by pantomiming their unsuppressible dreams for all to behold and respond to.

6 In an article about storytellers in the *Los Angeles Times,* Leslie Berger profiled a high school teacher named Luigi Jannuzzi. "He once saved the life of a student who was choking on a Life Saver," Berger wrote, "and thus discovered his own gift of gab: He told the kid a joke so funny that his laughter popped the candy out of his throat."

Make up a story in which your sense of humor saves someone's life.

7 Rural communities in southern Louisiana celebrate Mardi Gras with even more anarchistic exuberance than the festivities that take place in New Orleans. Roving gangs of masked revelers stop cars and good-naturedly demand money and gifts from drivers. Clowns with feathered headdresses knock on people's doors after midnight begging for ingredients to make gumbo. Mardi Gras out in the sticks "is a lot like tickling," says professor of folklore, Barry Ancelet. "When you get tickled it makes you laugh, but it also makes you feel uncomfortable."

Is there anything that incites both your laughter and your discomfort? Perhaps a thorny opportunity you have the privilege of suffering from? A prickly advantage that makes your blood boil and sing simultaneously? An awkward gratification that fuels your ambition to become the person you were born to be?

8 For years, I lived 13 miles from the top of Mt. Tamalpais, one of the highest peaks in the San Francisco Bay Area. Every day I gazed at it from afar through my window or while riding my bike in the hills, marveling as it glided through its ever-shifting relationship with the sky and seasons. It was a remote yet familiar beacon, an awe-inspiring touchstone against which I could measure my own undulating rhythms.

Eventually I moved to a new home at the foot of Mt. Tam. I felt as if I'd become part of it—was embedded in its protective and majestic aura. It was no longer an objective gauge, but rather an intimate tone and texture in my subjective experience of myself.

Outlaw Pronoia Therapy

Risk a comparable shift, from being *there* to being *here;* from outside to inside; from strength absorbed at a distance to power felt up close.

9 As Barack Obama's inauguration day approached in early 2009, some astrologers were aghast that he would be taking the oath of office when the moon was void-of-course. In their eyes, this aspect is a bad portent for any new enterprise. It practically dooms the project to failure. If Obama would only postpone the oath for 35 minutes, they said, everything would be fine. He didn't, of course.

But then the improbable happened. On the day of the ceremony, Chief Justice John Roberts, who was administering the oath, got the wording wrong. Obama went along with the gaffe instead of correcting it. Scholars then speculated that the oath wasn't fully official. The next day, when the moon was no longer void-of-course, Roberts and Obama re-did the ritual, making things right. And that's how an apparent mistake allowed Obama to elude the curse of superstitious astrologers.

Talk about the time you experienced a supposed blunder that ultimately helped you elude an outbreak of stupidity or a cloud of fear.

10 Notice how you feel as you speak the following: "The strong, independent part of me resisted the embarrassing truth for a long time, but I finally came to accept that I'm someone who craves vast amounts of love. Ever since I surrendered to this need, it doesn't nag me all the time, as it used to. In fact, it feels comforting, like a source of sweetness that doesn't go away. I never thought I'd say this, but I've come to treasure the feeling of having a voracious yearning to be loved."

In the Enochian language, the word for "hedonism" is the same as the word for "self-discipline."

11 For over two decades, Peter Jouvenal worked as a journalist and cameraman who filmed war-torn hot spots, including Iraq in the Gulf War and Afghanistan during the Soviet invasion. He eventually retired from that gig and bought a restaurant in Kabul. He has few regrets, but one came after the fall of the Taliban in 2001.

While exploring the organization's deserted safe houses, he happened upon a place where Osama bin

Laden and his wife had recently lived. Among the items the couple left behind was one of her bras. In retrospect Jouvenal realized he should have pocketed the exotic piece of lingerie; a tabloid newspaper would have paid him a fortune for it. But because he had spent his entire career dealing with more mainstream news media that sought more respectable evidence, the idea didn't even occur to him until much later.

Was there ever a time when you were in such a deep trance, enthralled by your habits and belief system, that you failed to notice a valuable anomaly that popped up? How can you train yourself to be so alert that such a blunder won't happen again?

12 Devote yourself to your heart's desire with unflagging shrewdness. Make it your top priority. Let no lesser wishes distract you. But consider this, too. You may sabotage even your worthiest yearning if you're maniacal in your pursuit of it.

Bear in mind the attitude described by Clarissa Pinkola Estés in her book *Women Who Run with the Wolves:* "All that you are seeking is also seeking you. If you sit still, it will find you. It has been waiting for you a long time."

Speculate on what exactly that would look like in your own life. Describe how your heart's desire has been waiting for you, seeking you.

Your muse is waking up, too.

13 Imagine that you have been relieved of your responsibilities for a given time. They will be taken care of by people you trust. You won't have to work to make money during this grace period, but will be given all you need. Nor will you have to clean your house, wash your clothes, or buy and make your food. Now here's the big question: What will you do now that you are free to do anything you like?

14 The Indian activist Mahatma Gandhi led many peaceful rebellions against oppressive governments, first in South Africa and later in British-controlled India. At first he called his strategy "passive resistance," but later disavowed that term because it had negative implications. He ultimately chose the Sanskrit word *satyagraha,* meaning "love force" or "truth force." "Truth (satya) implies love," he said, "and firmness (agraha) is a synonym for force. *Satyagraha* is thus the force which is born of truth and love."

Give an example of how you have employed satyagraha in the past, and another example of how you might invoke it in the future.

It's your duty to create so much love that national boundaries disappear.

15 Your addiction is obstructing you from your destiny, and yet it's also your ally.

What?! How can both be true?

On the downside, your addiction diverts your energy from a deeper desire that it superficially resembles. For instance, if you're an alcoholic, your urge to get loaded may be an inferior substitute for and a poor imitation of your buried longing to commune with spirit.

On the upside, your addiction is your ally, because it dares you to get strong and smart enough to wrestle free of its grip; it pushes you to summon the uncanny willpower necessary to defeat the darkness within you that saps your ability to follow the path with heart.

(P.S. Don't tell me you have no addictions. Each of us is addicted to some sensation, feeling, thought, or action, if not to an actual substance.)

Extol your sublime, painful addiction—celebrate it to death. Ride it, spank it, kiss it, whip it.

16 In Pila Chiles' book *The Secrets and Mysteries of Hawaii,* he recounts the advice given him by an Indian holy man: "If you have lost the business, your house, and wife, after you have been pronounced terminally ill and life has dealt you the worst blows, there is only one duty left. That is to crawl over to the nearest mirror, hoist yourself up, look deeply into it with your last breath, and say aloud seven times: Cock-a-doodle-doo!"

Come up with a theory, however farfetched, that explains why the testimony above is among the most pronoiac statements in this book.

17 Attention please. This is your ancestors speaking. We've been trying to reach you through your dreams and fantasies, but you haven't responded. That's why we've commandeered this space. So listen up. We'll make it brief. You're at a crossroads analogous to a dilemma that has baffled your biological line for six generations. We ask you now to master the turning point that none of us have ever figured out how to negotiate. Heal yourself and you heal all of us. We mean that literally. Start brainstorming, please.

The information you seek is available in the library of forbidden knowledge, the damp autumnal loam you dreamed you were buried in, and the song you learned before you were born.

18 To create a pearl, an oyster needs an aggravating parasite inside its shell. It builds layers of calcium carbonate around the invader, gradually fabricating the treasure. How long does it take from the initial provocation to the finished product? Five years for a pearl of average size, and as many as 10 years for a big one.

Our question for you: How many years have you been engaged in the process of transforming your irritant into a masterpiece? How many more years do you think you still have to go?

19 Ariel was going through a hard time. She'd been weaning herself from a painkiller she'd taken while recovering from surgery. Her cat ran away, and there was a misunderstanding at work. One night while at a nightclub with her friend Leila, she spied her ex-boyfriend kissing some woman. Meltdown ensued. Ariel fled the club and ran sobbing into the street, where she hurled her shoes on top of a passing bus.

Leila retrieved her and sat her down on a bench. "Because up until now you've displayed such exemplary grace in the face of chaos," Leila said, "I'm giving you a free Crazy Pass. It gives you a karma-free license to temporarily lose your mind." This compassionate humor helped Ariel feel more composed. The rest of the night she partied with elegant savagery, achieving major relief and release without hurting herself.

Now I'm awarding you, too, a free Crazy Pass. How will you use it?

20 Think about your relationship to human beings who haven't been born yet. What might you create for them to use? How can you make your life a gift to the future? Can you not only help preserve the wonders we live amidst, but actually enhance them? Keep in mind this thought from Lewis Carroll: "It's a poor sort of memory that only works backward."

21 According to Jewish legend, there are in each generation 36 righteous humans who prevent the rest of us from being destroyed. Through their extraordinary good deeds and their love of the divine spark, they save the world over and over again. They're not famous saints, though. They go about their business anonymously, and no one knows how crucial they are to our well-being.

Might you be one of the 36? As a temporary experiment, act as if you are.

22 "If you bring forth the genius within you," said Jesus in the Gospel of Thomas, "it will free you. If you do not bring forth the genius within you, it will destroy you."

Is there any aspect of the genius within you that you're not bringing forth? If so, how can you fix that?

23 I've written astrological oracles for much of my adult life. An early prototype of my work hatched in my previous incarnation as an 11th-century monastic scribe who made illuminated manuscripts. During my off-hours, I dabbled with planetary divination and created a parchment newsletter that got passed around the monastery.

In a later lifetime as a 16th-century Florentine alchemist, I further refined the form. The invention of the printing press meant my oracles could be seen by a larger audience, and as a result I got more feedback, which in turn helped me improve my service. The horoscopes I create today, then, have been in the making for a thousand years.

What about you? Is there anything you've been working on for many centuries? If your memory of your previous incarnations is fuzzy, make up a good story.

What are the three miracles that are most likely to happen to you?

24 In his book *Cosmos and Psyche,* Richard Tarnas says the planets don't emit invisible forces that shape our destinies as if we were puppets. Rather, they are symbols of the unfolding evolutionary pattern. Just as clocks tell time but don't create it, the heavenly bodies show us the big picture but don't cause it.

Outlaw Pronoia Therapy

Quoting Greek philosopher Plotinus, Tarnas writes, "The stars are like letters that inscribe themselves at every moment in the sky. Everything in the world is full of signs. All events are coordinated. All things depend on each other. Everything breathes together."

So it's not just the distant globes whose movements and relationships serve as divinatory clues. If you're sufficiently attuned to the gestalt of creation and pay close enough attention to its unfolding details, you can read the current mood of the universe in the arrangement of red onions in the grocery store bin or the fluttering of sunlight and shadow on the mimosa tree or the scatter of soap suds in your sink after you've finished washing the dishes.

Can you do it? Discern the signature of creation at this or any other perfect moment? Peer into the secret heart of the collective unconscious? Guess what the Goddess is thinking? Hint: You will have to switch on a dormant capacity, transforming your imagination from a mere fantasy-generator into an organ of perception.

"Guess what:
God created beings
not to act in a morality play
but to experience
what is unfathomable,
to elicit what can become,
to descend into the darkness
of creation and reveal it to him,
to mourn and celebrate
enigma and possibility.
The universe
is a whirling dervish,
not a hanging judge in robes."
—Richard Grossinger

26 "When you die," says the Koran, "God will call upon you to account for all the permitted pleasures you did not enjoy while on earth." The Talmud offers a similar idea: "A person will be called upon to account, on Judgment Day, for all the permitted pleasures he might have enjoyed but did not." Are there any such pleasures in your life?

Outlaw Pronoia Therapy

*16

i am
totally opposed
to all
duality

PRONOIAC HEROES GALLERY

To all the dissident bodhisattvas and insurrectionary lovers quoted below, I say: "Thank you for creating your own fantastic reality, because it inspires me to make my own."

"This body that we have, this very body that's sitting here right now in this room, this very body that perhaps aches, and this mind that we have at this very moment, are exactly what we need to be fully human, fully awake, and fully alive. Furthermore, the emotions that we have right now, the negativity and the positivity, are what we actually need. It is just as if we looked around to find out what would be the greatest wealth that we could possibly possess in order to lead to a decent, good, completely fulfilling, energetic, inspired life, and found it right here." —Pema Chödrön, *The Wisdom of No Escape and the Path of Loving Kindness*

"The metabolic pathways of pain and malaise evolved because they served the fitness of our genes in the ancestral environment. They will be replaced by a different sort of neural architecture—a motivational system based on heritable gradients of bliss. States of sublime well-being are destined to become the genetically pre-programmed norm of mental health.

"Two hundred years ago, powerful synthetic pain-killers and surgical anesthetics were unknown. The notion that physical pain could be banished from most people's lives would have seemed absurd. Today most of us in the technically advanced nations take its routine absence for granted. The prospect that what we describe as psychological pain, too, could ever be banished is equally counter-intuitive. The feasibility of its abolition turns its deliberate retention into an issue of social policy and ethical choice." —David Pearce, hedweb.com

"We each must become like fishermen, and go out onto the dark ocean of mind, and let your nets down into that sea. And what you're after is not some behemoth that will tear through your nets, foul them, and drag you and your little boat into the abyss. Nor are what we looking for a bunch of sardines, that can slip through your net and disappear, ideas like 'have you ever noticed that your little finger exactly fits your nostril' and stuff like that.

"What we are looking for are middle-sized ideas that are not so small that they are trivial, and not so large that they are incomprehensible, but middle-sized ideas that we can wrestle into our boat and take back to the folks on shore, and have fish dinner.

"And everyone of us, this is what we should be looking for. It's not for your elucidation, it's not part of your self-directed psychotherapy; you are an explorer, and you represent our species.

"And the greatest good you can do is to bring back a new idea, because our world is endangered by the absence of good ideas. Our world is in crisis because of the absence of consciousness.

"And so, to whatever degree, any one of us can bring back a small piece of the picture, and contribute it to the building of the new paradigm. Then we participate in the redemption of the human spirit." —Terence McKenna, deoxy.org/mckenna.htm

"Life should be ecstasy. We need lifestyles of ecstasy and social forms appropriate to whatever ecstasy is available for whoever wants it . . . We need a million children saints adept at high unhexings, technological vaudeville, rhythmic behaviors, hypnotic acrobatics, street trapeze artists, naked circus vibrations." —Allen Ginsberg, quoted in "A Revolution Without Enemies," by Anu Bonobo, tinyurl.com/ypv72x

"Seeing all things as naked, clear, and free from obscurations, we understand that there is nothing to attain or realize. Everything is naturally perfect just as it is. All phenomena appear in their uniqueness as part of the continually changing patterns of life. These patterns are vibrant with meaning and significance at every moment. . . .

"The continual stream of new discovery, revelation, and inspiration that arises at every moment is the manifestation of our clarity. We should learn to see everyday life as a mandala—the luminous fringes of experience that radiate spontaneously from the empty nature of our being. The aspects of our mandala are the day-to-day objects of our life experience moving in the dance or play of the universe.

"By this symbolism the inner teacher reveals the profound and ultimate significance of being. Therefore we should be natural and spontaneous, accepting and learning from everything. This enables us to see the ironic and amusing side of events that usually irritate us." —Dilgo Khyentse Rinpoche, tinyurl.com/29mpom

"The Way of Abundance is all too often misconstrued as a shallow sense of 'getting what one wants,' 'eliminating the negative,' or 'being free from pain.' Even the often-touted 'manifesting your dreams,' offers a psychological disposition that generally remains fixated around manifestation as 'the project of me.'

"But the 'project of me' can never be enough, for it does not meet 'the other,' and real living involves meeting. The touch and contact with all of life, the full freedom of non-separation, the completeness of full relationship, and the radiance of compassionate ecstasy are what we are inherently hungry for." —Rick Jarow, *Alchemy of Abundance: Using the Energy of Desire to Manifest Your Highest Vision, Power, and Purpose*

"I am inspired by another way of storytelling—not the linear, singular, 'breakthrough' and 'power over' brilliance of the 'hero' narrative, but the spiraling, juxtaposing, and interpenetrating 'power with' luminosity of the weaver in the act of telling. I imagine the weaver as the one who attends and intends while the hero extends; the weaver carefully untangles knots that need to be rewoven, while the hero cuts them asunder with his sword.

"Ursula K. Le Guin writes of an 'unheroic' fiction under the rubric of the 'carrier bag theory of fiction.' Using this term, adapted from Elizabeth Fisher, who writes in *Women's Creation* about the earliest cultural inventions likely being containers, slings, or net carriers used to hold gathered things, Le Guin decries the hero or 'killer story' as one that 'hid my humanity from me.' In its place, she celebrates a new/old story, a 'life story' that many people have told for ages, in the forms of '[m]yths of creation and transformation, trickster stories, folktales, jokes, novels.' It is the novel, above all, that she intends to reclaim from the usurping hero.

"So the Hero has decreed through his mouthpieces the Lawgivers, first, that the proper shape of the narrative is that of the arrow or spear, starting here and going straight there and THOK! hitting its mark (which drops dead); second, that the central concern of the narrative, including the novel, is conflict; and third, that the story isn't any good if he isn't in it.

"I differ with all of this. I would go so far as to say that the natural, proper, fitting shape of the novel might be that of a sack, a bag. A book holds words. Words hold things. They bear meanings. A novel is a medicine bundle, holding things in a particular, powerful relation to one another and to us." —Nancy Corson Carter, "Spider Woman as Healer," *Mythosphere,* Issue 3

"This world is a mirror of Infinite Beauty, yet no one sees it. It is a Temple of Majesty, yet no one regards it. It is the Paradise of God. It is more to man since he is fallen than it was before. It is the place of Angels and the Gate of Heaven." —Thomas Traherne, *Centuries of Meditation*

"The sun, with all those planets revolving around it and dependent on it, can still ripen a bunch of grapes as if it had nothing else in the universe to do." —Galileo Galilei

Wrathful Devotion

You gave me a heart that ignites
In the passionate knowing of you,
And having burned in that heat
Is not drawn to lesser fires.

You gave me a mind that expands
To encounter your vastness,
And finds in those fathomless depths
Its own luminous nature.

You gave me a soul that won't rest
With any barrier to you,
Be it heavy and dense
Or gossamer as a veil.

You gave me an old structure
Made up of my history;
It is heavy and dense,
It is gossamer as a veil.

I meet it, allow it, explore it
And still it grinds on,
A machine that relentlessly churns out
Old patterns and tendencies.

I embrace it, dissolve it, release it—
Still it keeps reincarnating,
Rising up from some ancient template
Held deep in my bones.

I don't begrudge you your sense of humor,
Beloved trickster,
But I do wonder, now and then,
What you have in mind.

Did you make me to realize a freedom
I can't fully embody?
Do my heart and soul burn for a truth
That I can't fully live?

I commune with you in the heavens—
It's not hard to find you there;
But I need you down here,
In the marrow of my bones.

You can't turn away now—stay here;
I will have this out with you.
You started something with me,
And now I want it finished.

Yes—I will wrestle with you on this one,
Beloved torturer;
I will wrestle you all the way down
To the very ground

And not rest till I stand
With the soles of my feet upon you,
And not rest till I feel you infuse
My every cell.
—Jennifer Welwood

"The Net of Indra is a profound and subtle metaphor for the structure of reality. Imagine a vast net; at each crossing point there is a jewel; each jewel is perfectly clear and reflects all the other jewels in the net, the way two mirrors placed opposite each other will reflect an image ad infinitum.

"The jewel in this metaphor stands for an individual being, or an individual consciousness. Every jewel is intimately connected with all other jewels in the universe, and a change in one jewel means a change, however slight, in every other jewel." —Stephen Mitchell, *The Enlightened Mind*

"I dream about a kind of criticism that would try not to judge but to bring an oeuvre, a book, a sentence, an idea to life; it would light fires, watch the grass grow, listen to the wind, and catch the sea foam in the breeze and scatter it. It would multiply not judgments but signs of existence; it would summon them, drag them from their sleep. Perhaps it would invent them sometimes— all the better.

"Criticism that hands down sentences sends me to sleep; I'd like a criticism of scintillating leaps of imagination. It would not be sovereign or dressed in red. It would bear the lightning of possible storms." —Michel Foucault, "The Masked Philosopher," interview in *Le Monde*

Hope "is not the conviction that something will turn out well," wrote Czech writer and politician Vaclav Havel, "but the certainty that something makes sense, regardless of how it turns out."

"If Spirit has any meaning, it must be omnipresent, or all-pervading and all-encompassing. There can't be a place where Spirit is not, or it wouldn't be infinite. Therefore, Spirit has to be completely present, right here, right now, in your own awareness. That is, your own present awareness, precisely as it is, without changing it or altering it in any way, is perfectly and completely permeated by Spirit.

"Furthermore, it is not that Spirit is present but you need to be enlightened in order to see it. It is not that you are one with Spirit but just don't know it yet. Because that would also imply that there is some place Spirit is not. No, according to Dzogchen, you are always already one with Spirit, and that awareness is always already fully present, right now. You are looking directly at Spirit, with Spirit, in every act of awareness. There is nowhere Spirit is not.

"Further, if Spirit has any meaning at all, then it must be eternal, or without beginning or end. If Spirit had a beginning in time, then it would be strictly temporal, it would not be timeless and eternal. And this means, as regards your own awareness, that you cannot become enlightened. You cannot attain enlightenment. If you could attain enlightenment, then that state would have a beginning in time, and so it would not be true enlightenment.

"Rather, Spirit, and enlightenment, has to be something that you are fully aware of right now. Something you are already looking at right now. We are all already looking directly at Spirit, we just don't recognize it. We have all the necessary cognition, but not the recogntion." —Ken Wilber, *Grace and Grit: Spirituality and Healing in the Life and Death of Treya Killam Wilber*

"Suffering is not holding you. You are holding suffering. When you become good at the art of letting suffering go, then you'll come to realize how unnecessary it was for you to drag those burdens around with you. You'll see that no one else other than you was responsible. The truth is that existence wants your life to become a festival." —Osho

"The urge to transform one's appearance, to dance outdoors, to mock the powerful and embrace perfect strangers is not easy to suppress. . . . The capacity for collective joy is encoded into us almost as deeply as the capacity for the erotic love of one human for another.

We can live without it, as most of us do, but only at the risk of succumbing to the solitary nightmare of depression.

"Why not reclaim our distinctively human heritage as creatures who generate their own ecstatic pleasures out of music, color, feasting, and dance . . . There is no 'point' to it—no religious overtones, ideological message, or money to be made—just the chance, which we need much more of on this crowded planet, to acknowledge the miracle of our simultaneous existence with some sort of celebration." —Barbara Ehrenreich, *Dancing in the Streets: A History of Collective Joy*

"Poetry is direct participation in the creative principle of the godhead. We only have false prophets (and so many of them!) because people forgot what prophecy is for: the ecstatic participation in the godhead and the exaltation of His/Her limitless Creation." —Tim Boucher, timboucher.com

"In the face of the [financial] crisis, people ask what they can do to protect themselves. 'Buy gold?' 'Stockpile canned goods?' I would like to suggest a different kind of question? 'What is the most beautiful thing I can do?'" —Charles Eisenstein, "Money and the Crisis of Civilization," tinyurl.com/4boxrn

"Now and again, it is necessary to seclude yourself among deep mountains and hidden valleys to restore your link to the source of life. Breathe in and let yourself soar to the ends of the universe; breathe out and let the cosmos back inside. Next, breathe up all the fecundity and vibrancy of the earth. Finally, blend the breath of heaven and the breath of the earth with that of your own, becoming the breathe of life itself." —Morihei Ueshiba Osensei, *The Art of Peace*

"The Godhead resides quite as comfortably in the circuits of a digital computer or the gears of a cycle transmission as he does at the top of a mountain or in the petals of a flower." —Robert M. Pirsig, *Zen and the Art of Motorcycle Maintenance*

"Nothing worth doing is completed in our lifetime; therefore, we must be saved by hope. Nothing true or beautiful or good makes complete sense in any immediate context of history; therefore, we must be saved by faith. Nothing we do, however virtuous, can be accomplished alone; therefore, we are saved by love." —Reinhold Niebuhr, *The Irony of American History*

"Aren't we privileged to live in a time when everything is at stake, and when our efforts make a difference in the eternal contest between the forces of light and shadow, between togetherness and division, between justice and exploitation? Oh, be joyful that you are a warrior in this great time!

"Will we rise to this battle? If so, we cannot lose, for rising up to it is our victory . . . If we represent love in the world, you see, we have already won." —Doris "Granny D" Haddock, political activist

"Sunshine is delicious, rain is refreshing, wind braces us up, snow is exhilarating; there is really no such thing as bad weather, only different kinds of good weather." —John Ruskin

"Only a naive and unhistorical mind can think that facts are more powerful than myths. All radical changes in human history are the results of the spread of a myth that, in a totally convincing manner, answers a crucially experienced need at a period of crisis." —Dane Rudhyar, *Culture, Crisis, and Creativity*

"At all times I will be the pupil of everyone." —Shantideva

"The criteria for success: you are free, you live in the present moment, you are useful to the people around you, and you feel love for all humanity." —Sri Sri Ravi Shankar

"This earth is honey for all beings, and all beings are honey for this earth. The intelligent, immortal being, the soul of the earth, and the intelligent, immortal being, the soul in the individual being—each is honey to the other." —*Brihadaranyaka Upanishad*

Sacred Advertisement

The Beauty and Truth Lab researchers' sunny dispositions are made possible in part by the mantra, "I don't know." It's an unparalleled source of power, a declaration of independence from the pressure to have an opinion about every single subject.

It's fun to say. Try it: "I don't know."

Let go of the drive to have it all figured out: "I don't know."

Proclaim the only truth you can be totally sure of: "I don't know."

Empty your mind and lift your heart: "I don't know."

Use it as a battle cry, a joyous affirmation of your oneness with the Great Mystery:
"I don't know."

ECSTATIC STUDY GUIDE

PART 2

Strategies for plying a chronic, low-key, blissful union with everything you're not

State your intentions. How do you want to feel?

21 One of my favorite memories is gazing into my daughter Zoe's face just moments after her complicated birth. She had been through a heroic ordeal that scared the hell out of me, and yet she looked calm, beatific, and amused.

"She's part-Buddha and part-elf," I thought to myself as I held her in my arms. Gazing back at me, her shiny face blended two states I had never before witnessed together in anyone, let alone in an infant: elegant compassion and playful serenity. This revelation imprinted me like a blood oath and has informed my life and my work ever since.

Do you have a comparable memory? A time when a key to your destiny was suddenly laid bare? A turning point when you got a gift that has fueled your quest for years? Revisit that breakthrough. Then ask life for another one.

20 My old philosophy professor Norman O. Brown would periodically interrupt his lectures, tilt his head upward as if tuning in to the whisper of some heavenly voice, and announce in a puckish tone, "It's time for your irregular reminder: We're already living after the end of the world. No need to fret anymore."

The implication was that the worst had already happened. We had lost much of the cultural riches that had given humans meaning for centuries. All that was going to be taken from us had already been taken.

On the bright side, that meant we were utterly free to reinvent ourselves. Living amidst the emptiness, we had nowhere to go but up. What remained was alienating, but it was also fresh.

Working from the hypothesis that you're living after the end of the world, what are you free to do that you weren't able to do before? Who are you free to be?

> *"Lord, grant that
> I may always desire
> more than I can accomplish,"
> prayed Michelangelo.*

19 Many people sincerely think that they will be called before God to account for themselves on Judgment Day. If you yourself have held that belief, you can stop worrying about it. The fact is, according to a survey of over 800 dissident bodhisattvas, urban witch doctors, sacred agents, and undercover geniuses, that you are called before "God" on Judgment Day on a regular basis.

Since you still exist, you have apparently passed every test so far. "God" obviously keeps finding you worthy. You shouldn't get overconfident, of course. But maybe from now on you can assume that although there may be a world of pressure on you, that pressure is natural, merciful, and exactly what you need.

Try this experiment: For seven days, see what it feels like to be secure in your knowledge that you have passed the tests of Judgment Day many, many times.

18 Writing on Salon.com, Scott Rosenberg recalled how in his youth he loved to play the fantasy role-playing game Dungeons & Dragons. "You'd have to choose not one but two 'alignments' for your character," he mused. "Good and evil, of course, but also 'law' and 'chaos.' And among the people I ran with, 'chaotic/good' was the thing to be, because it let you trust other people and still have fun."

Try out the "chaotic/good" approach for the character you play in your actual life.

17 The water you drink is three billion years old, give or take five million years. The stuff your body is made of is at least 10 billion years old, probably older, and has been as far away as 100,000 light-years from where it is right now. The air you breathe has, in the course of its travels, been literally everywhere on the planet, and has slipped in and out of the lungs of almost every human being who has ever lived.

Would you act differently if you had a visceral sense of how eternal and infinite you are? What unprecedented behavior might you express? Visualize a waking dream in which you remember the water you floated in three billion years ago. Imagine you can see the light that shone on you 100,000 light-years ago.

Ecstatic Study Guide, Part 2

16 We tried to get our manifesto "Bigger, Better, More Original Sins" excerpted in *Taboo Busters,* a zine published by American expatriates in Berlin. Unfortunately, the editors didn't like the spin we put on the subject of taboos. They're fixated on depraved vices and sickening violations and contrived rejections of conventional values: smuggled photos of dead celebrities lying in morgues, for instance; paintings of religious scenes that use the artist's blood or other bodily fluids; hospital scenes of Iraqi children with gangrenous stumps where their limbs once were; performance artists who do Marquis de Sade imitations.

Our approach is different. We're connoisseurs of taboo-busting that yields uplifting pleasures; we identify and initiate transgressions that don't hurt anyone and expand our intelligence and improve the world. Here are a few examples: midwife Ida May Gaskin's suggestion that a partner can expedite the birth process by giving erotic pleasure to the woman in labor; our idea that satirizing one's own cherished beliefs is the most honest form of mockery; the Menstrual Temple of the Funky Grail's classes that teach men how to symbolically menstruate in order to learn to love rather than fear the Dark Goddess; my ability to use principles formulated by people I mostly disagree with, as in the case of St. Paul's "I die daily."

Are there examples of this kind of taboo-busting in your life? Make a list of uplifting transgressions that expand your intelligence and push you in the direction of cosmic consciousness and improve the world.

15 Question: Which part of you is too tame, over-civilized, and super-domesticated, and what are you going to do about it?

Answer, from a reader named Jason R.: "I was like a mole in a suburban backyard. I had just one little path I trod each day: to the compost pile and back. I chewed on orange rinds and leftover cabbage. I was tamed by the comfort of my familiar environment, content to have a narrow vision. But then I was eaten by a hawk, and became part of a wild, free body. Now I perch on the tops of trees and the peaks of roofs. I survey giddy-wide horizons, from the river to the mesa and far beyond. I have a wealth of choices. Where to fly? What to hunt? Who are my allies? My thoughts breathe deep, like the slow explosion of sun on the morning lake."

How would you answer the same question?

14 The outsourcing of fortune-telling is well underway. Psychics and astrologers from India have been showering me with email invitations to take advantage of their services. "By the grace of the oceanic flames of goodness that by night simmer the roof of our temple and by day water the roots of our foolish wisdom," said one I query especially liked, "we have pledged to slave away our many reincarnations to cause the happy encroachment of bubbling karma on your masterful head. We will coax and guide the effects of various planets, comets, satellites, and dolmens, guaranteeing their flavor to fall on the living accidents of your love so as to ease your slippery upheaval to health."

In the course of your ecstatically pronoiac career, you will probably get puzzling offers of help like this. You may even be given gifts you can barely make sense of and blessings that are unlike anything you imagined you needed.

What might you do to receive them in the spirit in which they're offered? Here's one possibility: Cultivate living accidents of love so as to ease your slippery upheaval to health.

13 "If everything seems under control," said auto racer Mario Andretti, "you're probably not moving fast enough." I second that emotion. It applies to the entire human race, which is swirling through evolutionary tipping points at an accelerating speed. But it's doubly apropos for you spiritual freedom fighters and renegade bodhisattvas, because you're the vanguard shock troops fighting to merge heaven with earth.

For your edification and amusement, we will add three corollaries to Andretti's wisdom: 1. If you're not pretty much always half-confused, most likely you're not thinking deeply enough. 2. If you're not feeling forever amazed, maybe you're not seeing wildly enough. 3. The truth is fluid, slippery, vagrant, scrambled, promiscuous, kaleidoscopic, and outrageously abundant.

How might you go about using these tricks to marinate yourself in a gentle state of ecstasy pretty much all the time?

12 A friend gave me a live rosebush in a planter for my birthday in June. After a few weeks, its five red flowers withered and turned brown but didn't fall off their stems. I left them there, perversely fascinated by the dead blooms that wouldn't let go. Months later, in late November, five new flowers blossomed. Then the bush displayed a mix of the living and the dead.

Would you have plucked off the dried-up old blooms, or would you find it more beautiful with both the living and the dead together?

11 In his book *Making Sex: Body and Gender from the Greeks to Freud,* historian Thomas Laquer suggests that the clitoris may have been unknown to male anatomists until 1559. In that year, Renaldus Columbus, a professor at the University of Padua in Italy, announced his discovery of the "seat of woman's delight," and declared his right to name it the "sweetness of Venus."

Is there a sublime pleasure whose existence you haven't discovered? Where is it? How can you find it?

To strengthen your willpower and activate your dormant reserves of ecstasy, purify your imagination.

10 If you're reading this, you're probably not a Cambodian orphan who grew up as a slave in a brothel or a Sudanese man kidnapped by a militia and forced to do heavy labor 18 hours a day or one of the millions of other victims of human trafficking around the world. But you may be yoked and subjugated in a less literal way, perhaps to a debilitating drug or an abusive relationship or a job that brings out the worst in you or a fearful fantasy about the looming collapse of civilization's infrastructure.

The good news is that you have the power to escape your bondage. Maybe it'll help you muster the strength you need if I remind you that your freedom won't be anywhere near as difficult to achieve as that of the Pakistani boy tied to a carpet loom in a dark room around the clock or the Nigerian woman who's beaten daily as she toils in the sugar cane fields for no pay.

Try this: When you feel overwhelmed by the sadness of your problems or the addiction of your compulsions, put on your best clothes and clean toilets at a homeless shelter, or give foot massages to workers at a sewage disposal plant, or sing songs, sip champagne, and play card games with patients at a psychiatric hospital. Be ready to get hit upside the soul with exotic varieties of ecstasy, which such acts will unleash.

9 It's possible there's still enough oil buried in the earth to sustain our civilization's exorbitant appetite for material comforts for another 100 years. Or it may be true, as some researchers suggest, that global reserves of black gold are rapidly dwindling, and 20 years from now we'll all be farmers and hunters sitting around campfires at night telling stories.

Whichever scenario comes to pass, you may be happiest and smartest and healthiest if you cultivate a simple and earthy relationship with luxury—something akin to poet Omar Khayyám's notion, which was "a jug of wine, a loaf of bread, and thou beside me singing in the wilderness." Comments? Questions? Celebrations?

P.S. The amount of oil left in the world has no bearing whatsoever on your ability to cultivate ecstasy.

> ### *"We have to meditate on being the rivers so that we can experience within ourselves the fears and hopes of the rivers."*
> *—Thich Nhat Hanh*

8 Here's Caroline Myss' explanation of faith: "Faith is the power to stand up to the madness and chaos of the physical world while holding the position that nothing external has any authority over what heaven has in mind for you."

If you don't like the word "heaven" in Myss' statement, substitute a term that works for you, like "your higher self" or "your destiny" or "your soul's code." Modify anything else in it that's not right for your needs, as well. When you're finished tinkering, I hope you'll have created a definition of faith that motivates you with as much primal power as you feel when you're in love.

7 *The New York Times* ran a story about philosopher Nick Bostrom, who believes there's a significant chance our world is actually a computer simulation. In his scenario, you and I are living in a version of The Matrix. Our "brains" are merely webs of computer circuits created by our post-human descendants, who are studying "ancestor simulations" of their past. I bring this to your attention because I'd like to invite you to find out, one way or another, whether Bostrom is correct.

Make it your intention to cultivate a talent for knowing what's real and what's not. Develop a knack for escaping what's illusory and gravitating toward what's authentic.

If you do these simple things, I bet you will earn a big reward: a chronic, low-key, blissful sense of union with pretty much everything that's appealing to you.

Bonus: Even if you do find out that we're living in The Matrix, you could become a messiah with resemblances to the character that Keanu Reeves played in the film trilogy. He could fly.

6 While loitering on a sidewalk outside a nightclub in San Francisco on a September night in 1994, I found the cover of a booklet lying in the gutter. Written by Marilena Silbey and Paul Ramana Das, it was called *How to Survive Passionate Intimacy with a Dreamy Partner While Making a Fortune on the Path to Enlightenment.* Sadly, the rest of the text was missing. Ever since, hungry for its wisdom, I've tried to hunt down a copy of the whole thing, but to no avail.

I'm hoping that maybe you will consider writing your own version of the subject. If you do, please send it to me.

5 "Picture the Grand Canyon," says Buddhist teacher Jack Kornfield. "Every hundred years, a child comes by and throws a mustard seed into it. In the time it takes to fill the hole in the earth with mustard seeds, one mahakalpa will have passed. To perfect the virtuous heart—the joy of integrity—takes a thousand mahakalpas."

If that's true, then you've still got a lot of work to do. The good news is that civilization is in the midst of a critical turning point that could tremendously expedite your ripening. So you could make unusually great progress toward the goal of perfecting the virtuous heart in the next 40 years.

For best results, meditate often on the phrase "the joy of integrity." Get familiar with the pleasurable emotion that comes from acting with impeccability. And try out this idea from Gandhi: Integrity is the royal road to your inner freedom.

P.S. Oddly enough, the work of perfecting the virtuous heart is very effective in helping you master the art of cultivating everyday ecstasy. Meditate on the connection.

4 Alice finds her way to Wonderland by falling down a rabbit hole. Dorothy rides to Oz on a tornado. In C. S. Lewis's *The Lion, the Witch and the Wardrobe,* Lucy stumbles into the magical land of Narnia via a portal in the back of a large clothes cabinet.

In the sequels to all these adventures, however, the heroines must find different ways to access their exotic dreamlands. Alice slips through a mirror next time. Dorothy uses a Magic Belt. Lucy leaps into a painting of a schooner that becomes real.

Take heed of these precedents. The next time a threshold opens into an alternative reality you've enjoyed in the past, it may not resemble the doorways you've used before.

Steal this fire.
Mutate this pleasure.
Untame this healing.
Mock this sarcasm.
Trick this eternity.
Cure this symbol.
Sing this justice.
Engorge this grace.
Analyze this amazement.
Sublimate this revolution.

3 "Keep exploring what it takes to be the opposite of who you are," suggests psychologist Mihaly Csikszentmihalyi, author of the book *Creativity: Flow and the Psychology of Discovery and Invention.* This advice is one of his ideas about how to get into attunement with the Tao, also known as being in the zone.

How would you go about being the opposite of who you are? Try it and see if it drives you into a state of euphoria.

2 Check out this excerpt from "Those Who Do Not Dance," by Chilean poet Gabriela Mistral: "God asked from on high, / 'How do I come down from this blueness?' / We told Him: / come dance with us in the light."

I love this passage because it reminds me that nothing is ever set in stone; everything is always up for grabs. Even God needs to be open to change and eager for fresh truths. Furthermore, even we puny humans may on occasion need to be God's teacher and helper. Likewise, we can never be sure about what lowly or unexpected sources might bring us the influences we require.

What do Mistral's words mean to you? Imagine you're the "God" referenced in the poem. What blueness are you ready to come down from, and who might invite you to dance in their light?

1 Confounding lessons and delightful shocks have been increasing in frequency during the recent past and will continue to do so in the foreseeable future. In light of that fact, you may want to find some new ways to express your amazement. Clichés like "Jesus H. Christ!" or "Holy crap!" or "What the fuck?!" may not be sufficient to capture the full impact of the *aha!* moments.

To get you launched in the right direction, I'll suggest a few fresh exclamations. They're not designed to become tried-and-true replacements for the lazy phrases you're using now, but are rather meant to jog your imagination and inspire you to conjure up a constantly changing variety of ever-fresh invocations. Now see how these roll off your tongue: "Great Odin's raven!" "Radical lymphocytes!" "Cackling whacks of jibber-jabber!" "Frosty heat waves!" "Panoramic serpentine!"

0 Many visionaries and prophets expect there to be a huge and sudden shift in the world's story sometime soon. Whether it happens on December 21, 2012 or a later date, a sizable proportion of them even predict that it will be "in the twinkling of an eye"—a sudden cascade of events that completely changes everything everywhere.

Some paint the scenario in broad, catastrophic strokes, expecting something—they're not sure what—that will have the impact of a large meteor strike or nuclear war or pandemic disease. Others harbor a more benign but equally fuzzy expectation, speculating that maybe some higher psychic powers will kick in to the multitudes all at once, or that benevolent extraterrestrials will arrive to solve our energy crisis.

What very few of the prophets do, however, is make a precise prediction about exactly will happen. Their visions contain no assurances, no specifics. And in my view, that's worse than useless. It fills us with a vague buzz of fear or amorphous sense of hope, but offers no concrete directions about what to do to prevent the dreaded thing or help create the hoped-for thing.

And the fact is, as I see it, they can't possibly know what the Big Shift is—if, that is, a Big Shift is really looming. The very nature of any Big Shift will be so unexpected, so beyond our imaginations, and so utterly alien to what we understand, that we can't possibly delineate its contours in advance.

I'm reminded of Jung's formula, which is that we don't so much solve our problems as we outgrow them. We add capacities and experiences that eventually make us bigger than the problems.

This theory can be applied in reverse: If we have not yet grown wiser than our current predicament, then we can't see what the evolved state is beyond the predicament. Our minds are as-yet incapable of embodying the vision that will catapult us beyond the problem we're stuck in.

When the Big Shift comes, whether or not it comes in the twinkling of an eye, it will be something that no one foresaw, let alone described in detail. It will be beyond our comprehension, unlike anything we could have visualized headed our way. (Thirty years ago, did anyone imagine the Internet or the impact it's having?)

And if that's true, then the inescapable conclusion is: There's no use trying to plan ahead for it. It's counterproductive to hold a particular scenario in our mind as the likely development. And it's downright crazy to harbor a chronic sense of dread about an unknowable, unimaginable series of events.

The best way to prepare for a Big Shift is to cultivate mental and emotional states that ripen us to be ready for anything: a commitment to not getting lost inside our own heads; a strategy to avoid being enthralled with the hypnotic lure of painful emotions, past events, and worries about the future; a trust in empirical evidence over our time-worn beliefs and old habits; a talent for turning up our curiosity full blast and tuning in to the raw truth of every moment with our beginner's mind fully engaged; and an eagerness to dwell gracefully in the midst of all the interesting questions that tease and teach us.

Everything I just described also happens to be an excellent way to prime yourself for a chronic, low-grade, always-on, simmering-at-low-heat brand of ecstasy— a state of being more-or-less permanently in the Tao, in the groove, in the zone. Try it now, and report your results here.

You may already be ecstatic.

THE LITERARY EQUIVALENT OF A SEX CHANGE

When I was 19, while other man-boys my age were dreaming of becoming doctors and lawyers and rock stars, a curious ambition overtook me: I decided I wanted to be a feminist when I grew up. As I pursued that goal over the years, I devoted many meditations to imagining what it's like to be a woman. While writing my second book, *The Televisionary Oracle,* I lived part-time inside the psyche of the heroine for five years.

But I have always been perfectly happy to be a heterosexual man. The prospect of dressing in women's clothes, for costume parties or any other reason, has never appealed to me. I'm mildly interested in the stories of those who have decided to change their sex with the intervention of surgery and drugs, but the fantasy of becoming a transgender person has never flitted across my mind's eye for even a nanosecond.

My identity as an author, on the other hand, has not been as clear-cut. I have sometimes felt like a storyteller trapped in the body of a journalist. On other occasions, it's more the reverse. I imagine I'm an essayist stuck inside the persona of a poet, or else maybe a scholar lurking within the form of a wacky visionary.

The confusion doesn't stop there. My heart tells me I'm a mystical seeker who was born to explore spiritual themes, even as my head says I'm an artistic intellectual whose task it is to illuminate the mysteries of concrete reality here on the material plane.

So while I've never dreamed of being a transgender person, I have sometimes fantasized about getting a mythical *trans-genre* operation—a procedure that would cure me of the nagging sense that I'm not the writer I'm supposed to be.

My wish was finally fulfilled during the four and a half years I worked on my book, *Pronoia Is the Antidote for Paranoia.* It taught me not to struggle against my contradictions, but rather to celebrate them. It did not give me the literary equivalent of a sex change, but rather bestowed on me a poetic license to be the authorial equivalent of a hermaphrodite.

Pronoia is my third book, but my main claim to fame is the 1,400-word weekly report that I syndicate to newspapers and publish on the Web. Here's the complication: This linchpin of my career takes the form of a horoscope column, which is not exactly renowned as a source of deep thought and literary excellence. I accepted the challenge of making the most of the opportunity when it fell into my lap many years ago, glad to have a gig (any gig!) that paid me for writing.

In addition to the fact that horoscope columns typically get little respect from anyone with more than a 10th grade education, there is a further problem: Most of them reflect badly on the ancient and honorable art of astrology. Serious students of planetary symbolism, among whose number I include myself, regard the shallow, superstitious advice contained in most horoscope columns as a gross debasement of the elegant system they aspire to master.

I do my best to transcend the limitations of the genre. Each of my horoscopes is a kind of love letter imbued with my reverence for lively language. Stories and metaphors are the raw materials I work with to invigorate my readers' imaginations. My intention is to boost their power to shape their own fates, which is why I call my column "Free Will Astrology."

I might ask Tauruses to meditate on the meaning of John Berger's observation that "Authenticity depends entirely on being faithful to the essential ambiguity of experience," or compare Virgo's imminent destiny to an unexpected dance contest I engaged in with an eccentric old woman I met while trekking through Germany's Black Forest, or exhort Scorpios to meditate on how their lives in the near future might resemble that of the bird called the bar-tailed godwit, which migrates annually from Alaska to New Zealand by hitching rides on gale-force winds.

Do you see how odd my task is? I'm a devoted astrologer who wrestles my words into a format that most good astrologers disdain. I'm a passionate writer who squeezes my thoughts into a genre that most professional writers ridicule.

On the other hand, because horoscope columns have so little credibility, no one cares if I twist and play with mine. That means I've been able to pull off a feat I never dared to hope for when I was an undergraduate at Duke University studying the work of William Blake, Arthur Rimbaud, Allen Ginsberg, Diane di Prima, and company: that I might someday get paid a decent wage to create disguised poetry in a widely syndicated newspaper column.

There's another perk to the job. Having given myself permission to use "Free Will Astrology" as a vehicle for all my creative urges, I don't have to confine myself to being a poet. I've also been able to be by turns a journalist, a political pundit, a New Age prophet, a science reporter, a philosopher, and an intimate advisor.

There has been a downside to this tremendous freedom, however. It allowed my youthful confusion to blossom into a full-blown identity crisis. At the dawn of my career I was inclined to be indulgent toward my uncertainty. Two decades later, though, I was having recurring dreams of William Blake asking me, "So what kind of writer do you want to be when you grow up?"

☀

"When you make the two one, and when you make the inside like the outside and the outside like the inside, and the above like the below and the below like the above, and when you make the male like the female and the female like the male, then you will enter the Kingdom."
—Gnostic Gospel of Thomas

As much gratitude as I feel for the privilege of creating 12 oracles every week, there has always been a part of me that longs to produce more comprehensive and permanent artifacts. My first two books, *Images Are Dangerous* and *The Televisionary Oracle*, were attempts to address that desire.

Like my astrology column, alas, both of them wanted to be a festive hodgepodge of genres. The creative artist in me was inclined to honor that urge, but the sensible career-builder in me protested. "Arrggghhh," he complained. "A book *cannot* be a riot of styles if it hopes to reach a wide readership, earn royalties, and get critical respect. It has to be one genre or another! Bookstore employees can't simultaneously shelve it in the poetry, memoir, spirituality, fiction, feminism, and music sections. And the marketing departments of all the publishers in the world agree that trying to straddle a variety of niches is tantamount to an economic death wish."

So declared the part of me that wanted to actually sell some books. But I didn't listen. Instead, I followed my poverty-loving bliss. The results were predictable. About 500 copies of *Images Are Dangerous* made it into the marketplace, and it was reviewed in a grand total of four publications. *The Televisionary Oracle* eventually sold more than 9,000, which didn't come close to compensating me for the money I sank into publicity and my book tour. It got 25 reviews, mostly from small websites and newspapers that carry my column. The brightest light it generated was a blurb from my favorite novelist Tom Robbins, who said, "I've seen the future of American literature and its name is Rob Brezsny."

Literature! The magic word. He didn't say, "I've seen the future of horoscope columns (or poetic outlaw journalism or crazy visionary rants) and its name is Rob Brezsny." But if anyone else agreed with his assessment, they have yet to step forth and proclaim it. *The Televisionary Oracle* was bought by cultural creatives who love festive hodgepodges and don't care whether or not they're literature; it was ignored by the custodians of high culture, who were as likely to review it as a Christian fundamentalist would be to praise its lesbian tantric sex scenes.

I began work on *Pronoia Is the Antidote for Paranoia* about five minutes after I finished my 23-city tour in support of *The Televisionary Oracle.* Or rather *Pronoia* began working on me. I took dictation while the book told me exactly what it wanted to be. Surprise! It revealed early on that it planned on becoming the mother of all festive hodgepodges.

Sometimes I wasn't smart enough to catch on to its style and message, and so it had to wait for me to ripen. Often that meant I was compelled to go out and have experiences in my actual life that changed me in such a way that I wised up to what the book already knew.

It was for the sake of becoming a better servant of *Pronoia,* for instance, that I had to fall in love with the wrong woman, lose $23,000 on a bad investment, and wander alone out into the desert begging for a vision. The lessons I was taught thereby made me far more intelligent, or at least far less stupid, about pronoia.

Luckily, the book was patient with me. It never kicked my ass so hard that I fell over, hit my head, and lost consciousness. Gradually, it proved to me that if I hoped to do it justice, I would have to not only explore and articulate the principles of pronoia, but also embody them. It wouldn't be enough to announce, "Life always gives you exactly what you need, exactly when you need it." I would have to become living proof that that was the case. And I couldn't get away with merely writing the two paragraphs below; I had to actually become the truth they speak:

"Life is a vast and intricate conspiracy designed to keep us well supplied with blessings. What kind of blessings? Ten million dollars, a gorgeous physique, a perfect marriage, a luxurious home, and high status? Palatial homes, attractive lovers, lottery winnings, career success? Maybe. But just as likely: interesting surprises, dizzying adventures, gifts you hardly know what to do with, and conundrums that dare you to get smarter.

"Novelist William Vollman referred to the latter types of blessings when he said that 'the most important and enjoyable thing in life is doing something that's a com-plicated, tricky problem for you that you don't know how to solve.' Sculptor Henry Moore had a slightly different angle: 'The secret of life is to have a task, something you devote your entire life to, something you bring everything to, every minute of the day for your whole life. And the most important thing is—it must be something you cannot possibly do.'"

The universe is inherently friendly and life is on our side, I learned while creating *Pronoia.* But it's difficult to perceive that when we're primarily serving the agendas of our grasping, small-minded selves. And so it's crucial to note that pronoia works in behalf of the soul, not the ego. In fact, if it ever took root as a widely held philosophy, it would probably overthrow your ego and my ego and everyone's ego; it would overthrow the status quo, the government, and even reality itself.

By the time I was halfway done with the book, I had come to see that if I hoped to give birth to it in its full glory, I would have to banish my ego, as much as possible, as a source of motivation for my writing.

In other words, I couldn't worry about whether the book would supercharge my career or earn me money or win me critical acclaim. My duty was simply to communicate the meme of pronoia in all of its paradoxical splendor. If that meant it had to be both a rowdy New Age almanac and an intellectually rigorous treatise, so be it. If that required me to weave a mélange of stories, poems, manifestos, essays, oracles, and reader exercises, so be it.

When *Pronoia* finally emerged, my trans-genre operation was complete. I no longer questioned and resisted and fought with the strange blessings that life had been trying to shower me with all those years, but welcomed them with a full heart.

So am I a storyteller trapped in the body of a journalist, or an essayist stuck inside the persona of a poet, or a scholar lurking within the form of a wacky visionary? Am I a mystical seeker who was born to explore spiritual themes or an artistic intellectual whose task it is to illuminate the mysteries of concrete reality here on the material plane? The answer is all of the above. And I thank the universe for granting me this unsolvable mystery.

Zero = One;

or

How to Be Like the Real God

The seeds of the lodgepole pine and jack pine trees are so tightly compacted within their protective cones that they need flames to free them. It's only through the help of periodic conflagrations, then, that they're able to reproduce. Fire-dependent and fire-resistant, they can tolerate temperatures of 1,700 degrees Fahrenheit.

Having ridden my mountain bike through Marin County's hills for years, I've watched the central shrine, Mt. Tamalpais, go through thousands of changes. Depending on the weather, the season, and the time of day, it has been a different event on each occasion I've seen it.

When the low-slung sun illuminates the thin layer of mist covering it late on a winter afternoon, it's not the same mountain that lies beneath a full moon beaming down on it through a hole in the streaming clouds on a summer night.

The realist in me says I'd be justified in giving it a new name each time I'm in its presence.

The Bible says Jehovah gave Adam the job of bestowing names on everything.

In Ursula Le Guin's story "She Unnames Them," Eve decides to reverse her mate's work. She yearns to return to a primordial state when the misunderstandings caused by words no longer stand between her and the rest of creation.

So she unnames all the animals, from the sea otters to the bees. When she's done, she marvels on how they feel "far closer than when their names had stood between myself and them like a clear barrier."

Robert Anton Wilson defined information as data and ideas that are new to you. If it's something you already know, then it's propaganda or dogma, not information.

Terence McKenna had a similar view. He used the terms "information" and "novelty" interchangeably. If you're not surprised, he said, if your curiosity isn't piqued, then the messages streaming your way don't qualify as information.

In her profile on poet John Ashbery in *The New Yorker,* Larissa MacFarquhar reported that his Manhattan apartment was deeply chaotic. "Everything needs to be open and nothing is ever closed," she quoted Ashbery's partner as saying. "Drawers. Cabinets. Closet doors. Everything! All possibilities must be available at all times."

In her book *Women Who Run with the Wolves,* Clarissa Pinkola Estés suggests that we all need to periodically go cheerfully and enthusiastically out of our minds. Make sure, she says, that at least one part of you always remains untamed, uncategorizable, and unsubjugated by routine. Be adamant in your determination to stay intimately connected to all that's inexplicable and mysterious about your life.

At the same time, though, Estés believes you need to keep your unusual urges clear and ordered. Discipline your wildness, in other words, and don't let it degenerate into careless disorder.

There's a place in Venezuela where lightning storms rage 10 hours a night, 150 days of the year. It's where the Catatumbo River flows into Lake Maracaibo. Humans put their lives at risk to be near this persistent storm. The upside of the phenomenon is that it generates a significant portion of our planet's ozone, and produces so much light that it helps ships navigate up to 250 miles away.

Gourmet sea salt harvested by young men on a warm, breezy afternoon in late summer from a pristine marsh in Brittany.

A holy book written with ink made from the author's blood.

Cambodia's Tonlé Sap River right after the rainy season ends, when it stops flowing south and starts flowing north.

A chocolate rooster resting outside in the snow under a full moon.

"The real secret of magic is that the world is made of words," said Terence McKenna in *Alien Dreamtime,* "and that if you know the words that the world is made of, you can make of it whatever you wish."

Here's my version of that hypothesis: What world you end up living in depends at least in part on your use of language.

Do you want to move and breathe amidst infertile chaos where nothing makes sense and no one really loves anyone? Then speak with unconscious carelessness, expressing yourself lazily. Constantly materialize and entertain angry thoughts in the privacy of your own imagination, beaming silent curses out into eternity.

Or would you prefer to live in a realm that's rich with fluid epiphanies and intriguing coincidences and mysterious harmonies? Then be discerning and inventive in how you speak, primed to name the unexpected codes that are always being born right in front of your eyes. Turn your imagination into an ebullient laboratory where the somethings you create out of nothings are tinctured with the secret light you see in your dreams of invisible fire.

"There are nine different words in Maya for the color blue, but just three Spanish translations, leaving six butterflies that can be seen only by the Maya." —Earl Shorris, "The Last Word," *Harper's,* August 2000

"There are nine different words in Maya for the color blue, but just three Spanish translations, leaving six butterflies that can be seen only by the Maya." —Earl Shorris, "The Last Word," *Harper's,* August 2000

When actress Mia Farrow was still a teenager, 59-year-old painter Salvador Dalí asked her to dinner. As an appetizer, he served her butterfly wings on crackers. "They had almost no taste at all," Farrow told Gregg LaGambina in *Filter.* She was thrilled by the artfulness of the gesture.

Imagine yourself eating these colors:

cerulean
azure
turquoise
aquamarine
ultramarine
sapphire
livid
peacock
navy
sky
teal
cyanin

According to the *Haggadah,* an ancient Jewish text, the first thing God made, before anything else, was the Torah. This primal book was "written with black fire on white fire." The black fire comprised the 22 letters of the Hebrew alphabet, which were the raw materials out of which the Divine One forged the universe.

The author of the text says that since the Torah's words are eternally on fire, he would never be able to compel their dancing letters to remain still. (Source: Mary Chilton Callaway, "Black Fire on White Fire: Historical Context and Literary Subtext in Jeremiah 37–38," *Troubling Jeremiah*)

In 1971, astronaut Edgar Mitchell was the sixth person to walk on the moon. Since then he has cultivated an interest in matters that hard-core fundamentalist materialists like to call "the paranormal."

He once asked Buddhist lama Norbu Chen to attempt a psychic healing of his mother, who was legally blind. Norbu's magic worked. Mom's sight returned, and she was ecstatic.

A few days later, however, she made a discovery that horrified her: Norbu wasn't a Christian like she was. "My mother believed that if such healing didn't come from a Christian," says Mitchell, "then it must come from Satan, and she didn't want to be healed by Satan."

She soon had a dramatic relapse, completely losing the gift Norbu had bestowed. (Source: *Kindred Spirit* magazine, Summer 1997)

Belief is the end of intelligence, says Robert Anton Wilson. The moment you become attached to an opinion or theory, no matter how good or true or beautiful it might seem, you're no longer fully open to the mysteries that life brings you. Your perceptiveness wanes and your understanding shrinks.

Lightning strikes somewhere on the Earth 6,000 times every minute. A single bolt may carry a million volts, travel 100,000 miles per hour, and reach a temperature of 60,000 degrees. And yet it's usually no more than an inch in diameter.

You want hot gold secrets to ripen in your dark candy soul? Then study the ocean's electricity for its teachings about moon victories. Extract a fresh green why from the book of storms you never actually read as a child.

Then, when the lilies' clouds soar over your shadow, your listening will grow tougher and wetter. When the night's chanting sky reveals the birth memories that even time had forgotten, you'll know exactly how to look through the sun to the other side of your best fear.

Plato said God was a geometer who created an ordered universe imbued with mathematical principles. Through the ages, scientists who've dared to speak of a Supreme Being have sounded the same theme. Galileo wrote, "To understand the universe, you must know the language in which it is written. And that language is mathematics." Modern physicist Stephen Hawking says that

> A gray-cheeked thrush,
> on its way from Newfoundland
> to South America,
> constantly napping as it flies,
> closing one eye at a time,
> allowing one side of its brain to sleep.
>
> Three golden hairs from the devil's head,
> kept in a white china saucer by your bed.
>
> Saki made from individually polished grains
> of rice that were grown
> next to a sacred grove of sakaki trees
> and fed by an ancient underground spring.

by using mathematical theories to comprehend the nature of the cosmos, we're trying to know "the mind of God."

But philosopher Richard Tarnas proposes a different model. In his book *Cosmos and Psyche,* he suggests that God is an artist—more in the mold of Shakespeare than Einstein.

Poet Sylvia Plath said she wasn't much impressed with the "photographic mind which paradoxically tells the truth, but the worthless truth, about the world." What she really loved was the "synthesizing spirit, that 'shaping' force, which prolifically sprouts and makes up its own worlds with more inventiveness than God." (Source: Sylvia Plath, *Johnny Panic and the Bible of Dreams*)

You dream of two swallowtail butterflies copulating in mid-flight over a dandelion-studded meadow. The sun's rays pour down like misty golden arrows. You sense the taste of lightning on your tongue.

Is there really such a thing as free will, or are our destinies shaped by forces beyond our control?

Here's one way to think about that question: Maybe some people actually have more free will than others. Not because they have more money. (Many rich folks are under the spell of their instincts, after all.) Not because they have high-status positions. (A boss may have power over others but little power over himself.)

Rather, those with a lot of free will have earned that privilege by taking strong measures to dissolve the conditioning they absorbed while growing up. They've acted on the advice of psychologist Carl Jung: "Until you make the unconscious conscious, it will direct your life and you will call it fate."

There must have been a particular moment, eons ago, when the sun was officially born.

The often-inebriated Calamity Jane character on HBO's TV show *Deadwood* uttered words that may be useful in your ongoing efforts to rouse yourself from slumber. I'll paraphrase her observation in order to streamline her drunken syntax: "Every day you have to figure out how to live life all over again."

Art critic Simon Schama prefers not to think of Van Gogh's *Wheatfield with Crows* as the work of an unhappy madman battling with suicidal urges. Rather, he leans toward seeing it as the seminal masterpiece of a modern genius who launched modern painting. Without denying that the first theory has some validity, he chooses to emphasize the truth of the second interpretation. This is a pronoiac technique.

"Our skin shares its chemistry with the maple leaf and moth wing. The currents our bodies regulate share a molecular flow with raw sun. Nerves and flashes of lightning are related events woven into nature at different levels." —Richard Grossinger, *Planet Medicine*

> **A Guatemalan peasant woman giving away chocolate-covered strawberries to gang members on a city street.**
>
> **A stolen Picasso painting that hangs on the wall of an offshore gambling casino in Belize.**
>
> **Whirling dervishes spinning in the desert as a flock of flamingoes flies overhead.**
>
> **Rain drizzling in a fountain, a waterfall plunging into a flooded river, tears dropping in the steaming bathtub.**
>
> **Cheerleaders cheering office workers as they leave their cubicles at the end of the day.**

There was one reason why America's founding fathers gave Thomas Jefferson, not Benjamin Franklin, the job of composing the Declaration of Independence in 1776. They were afraid that Franklin, a compulsive teaser and trickster, would slip jokes into the document.

But maybe we would have been better served if Franklin had been chosen. Imagine the aesthetic logic of injecting comedy into a document that sanctifies disciplined freedom. Can you picture 21st-century lawyers arguing about the constitutional ambiguities generated by puns and double-entendres?

"Nothing exists until or unless it is observed," wrote William Burroughs in *Painting and Guns*. "An artist is making something exist by observing it. And his hope for other people is that they will also make it exist by observing it."

The bumper sticker I saw said, "Having abandoned my search for the truth, I'm now looking for a good fantasy." Though it's meant to be sarcastic, it's a useful piece of advice.

Consider this hypothesis: The truth is so complicated and ever-shifting that it's impossible to pin down. Why try to *understand* the nature of reality when it's more productive and interesting to aggressively *create* the nature of reality? Why be preoccupied with conjuring up concepts to approximate the structure of the universe when the point is that we change everything we observe merely by looking at it?

As another bumper sticker says, "Life isn't about finding yourself. It's about creating yourself."

Here's Nikos Kazantzakis in *Report to Greco:* "By believing passionately in something that still does not exist, we create it. The nonexistent is whatever we have not sufficiently desired."

"Your job," my philosophy teacher Norman O. Brown told me in 1981, "is to find the holy in the mundane, and, failing that, to *create* the holy in the mundane."

Nitrogen constitutes 78 percent of the Earth's atmosphere, but plants can't access it in its gaseous form. That's a complication, because plants need nitrogen to

---

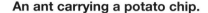

An ant carrying a potato chip.

A female goatherd in a goatskin robe and a blonde debutante in a pink gown dancing around a bucket full of candy skulls.

An apple pierced by an arrow lying on a bridge near a half-crumpled Valentine card.

A donkey meandering through a church.

A red wagon holding a treat you were deprived of when you were a kid.

---

live. Over the last 2.5 billion years, they have developed symbiotic relationships with bacteria that live in their roots and convert nitrogen into a usable form.

But those bacteria weren't around in the early going, three billion years ago. During Earth's Archaean eon, plants were completely dependent on lightning to provide them with the kind of nitrogen they needed. Then, as now, bolts of electrical fire generated intense heat that compelled atmospheric nitrogen to blend with oxygen, thereby forming nitrous oxides, which were soluble in water and carried into the ground with the rain.

These days, the planet's five million lightning strikes per day account for less of the vegetable kingdom's total needs than they did in the beginning—perhaps as little as five to 10 percent, with friendly bacteria doing the rest. The National Center for Atmospheric Research in Boulder, Colorado, however, estimates the lightning's share is closer to 50 percent.

Even if the true figure is lower rather than higher, the moral of the story is that without lightning, there'd be no plants.

"I'm not afraid of snakes or spiders," says actress Nicole Kidman, "just butterflies."

You dream you're a thunderbird, a legendary raptor that certain Native American tribes say carries messages back and forth between spiritual beings. Your eyes unleash sheet lightning and your enormous wings beat so hard they spawn storms.

"The reality of love is mutilated when it is removed from all its unreality." So said the French philosopher Gaston Bachelard in his book *The Poetics of Reverie*.

He meant that realism alone is not enough for human beings to live on, especially in our most intimate relationships. We need fantasy to augment the merely

Dionysian Manifesto

factual perspective. We require poetic truths to keep the rational approach honest.

Without the play of the imagination, in fact, our understanding of the world is impoverished and distorted.

(P.S. Nietzsche said: "We have art in order not to perish of truth.")

"Relationship" is a crashingly dull term for something so interesting. Try "hookup" or "two-way" instead.

Rather than referring to someone as your "friend" or "partner," call him or her your "accomplice," your "freestyle," or your "lightning."

Dead terms like "significant other," "boyfriend," "girlfriend," and "spouse" should be retired as well. In their places, try "lushbuddy," "heartbeat," or "jelly roll."

Feel free, of course, to coin your own surgecrafts and questbursts.

I've told you a million times not to exaggerate. I really get antsy when you refuse to be patient. If you don't stop berating yourself, I'm going to have to cut you down to size. I'm sick and tired of you emphasizing the dark side of everything. I swear I'll lose my freaking temper and do something stupid if you don't stop making threats.

Gather 14,286,000,000 fireflies in one place, and they will match the sun's brightness.

Butterflies, moths, hummingbirds, and bats love to drink the nectar that flowers offer. In return, these pollinators are expected to get some pollen stuck on their bodies and carry it away to fertilize other plants.

While the nectar is tasty, it's usually not pure sweetness. If it were, the first pollinator to come along would suck it all dry, leaving nothing for further visitors. And that wouldn't be good from the plant's point of view, because it would limit the number of places where its pollen would be disseminated.

To keep nectar-drinking sessions short, therefore, most plants include a touch of bitterness in the blend.

You dream that an angel who resembles your first crush shows you how to gather energy high in the sky and release it in the form of lightning bolts. It requires great upper arm strength because you have to make broad sweeping motions with your arms, gathering the necessary electricity into a vortex that serves as your launching area. You feel exhilarated but nervous about how much force you have at your disposal.

The entertainment industry foists a lot of garbage on us. Stupid sex, gratuitous fear, and ugly violence are the norm. TV and film executives defend themselves against critics who accuse them of pandering to the lowest common denominator. "We merely give people what they want," they say.

To put that excuse in context, listen to Henry Ford, the automotive pioneer: "If I had asked people what they wanted, they would have said faster horses."

Here's a joke told by Jeff Thredgold in his book *On the One Hand: The Economist's Joke Book.* "An economist returns to visit her old school. She's interested in the current exam questions and asks her old professor to show her some. To her surprise, they are exactly the same questions that she answered 10 years ago. When she asks the professor about this, he says: 'The questions are always the same. Only the answers change!'"

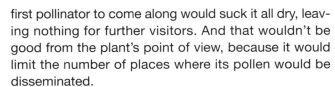

**Indigo-robed druids
conducting a ritual in a dandelion field
behind a Wal-Mart.**

**Giraffes running through standing rainwater
near a black woman and white man
making love in a field of growing corn.**

**A computer monitor showing
a page from eBay
where the Dalai Lama's germs
are being sold.**

**An old woman who has two blue streaks
on each of her cheeks,
singing as she brushes
the long silky hair of her grandson.**

According to author Colin Wilson, synchronicities are meaningful coincidences that are created by the unconscious mind to jar the conscious mind into a keener state of perception. They imbue us with a powerful sense that there are hidden meanings beneath the surface of everyday life; they lead us to suspect that a huge, benevolent intelligence is always working behind the scenes, weaving connections that are invisible to us in our normal state of awareness.

Jesus and Mohammed walking arm in arm along the 50-yard line in a football stadium packed with spectators.

A waitress wearing the head-mask of a Chinese parade lion as she carries a plate of bacon and eggs toward a table.

Barn swallows nesting in the steel and concrete "sarcophagus" that was built over the exploded Chernobyl nuclear reactor.

A handloomed Turkish shower curtain trimmed with emeralds and rubies.

the understanding of the contents of their own minds, through observation and not through intellectual analysis or introspective dissection." —J. Krishnamurti

You dream that caterpillars slowly but surely devour the Big Bad Wolf while he's asleep. When they finish, they spin cocoons. The sun rises and sets 33 times, whereupon they emerge as giant yellow butterflies, each of whose wings are decorated with the black shapes of wolves.

Dear Beauty and Truth Lab: I was wondering if you had any information about Beyonders, people who were born under no star and who are therefore not ruled by the stars. —Wannabe Beyonder

Dear Wannabe: It's impossible to be born under no star. However, we all go through periods when we're relatively free from the authority of the stars we were born under and therefore immune from cosmic compulsion. During these times, we're less susceptible to the whims of fate and the demands of the past and the inertia of karma. Our willpower has more breathing room, and we're more likely to fulfill Einstein's dictum, "Imagination is more important than knowledge."

"In the animal kingdom, the rule is, eat or be eaten; in the human kingdom, define or be defined." —Thomas Szasz, *The Second Sin*

"I must create a system, or be enslaved by another man's." —William Blake, "Jerusalem"

"If there's a book you really want to read but it hasn't been written yet," said author Toni Morrison, "then you must write it."

"A good poet is someone who manages, in a lifetime of standing out in thunderstorms, to be struck by lightning five or six times; a dozen times and he is great." —Randall Jarrell, *Poetry and the Age*

"Zero = One" is brought to you in part by Terence McKenna's riddle: "Do you know what insomniac dyslexic philosophers do? They stay up all night wondering if dog really exists."

The phrase "new roses" can serve as an antidote to neurosis—as a kind of magical spell. You might invoke

In an effort to create safer streets, some European towns are getting rid of traffic signs and stoplights. The theory is that if drivers have no visible aides to guide them, they will slow down and be more considerate.

"What we want is for people to be confused," says an official of the German town of Bohmte. "When they're confused, they'll be more alert and drive more carefully."

"Humans cannot come to Truth through any organization, through any creed, through any dogma, priest, or ritual, not through any philosophic knowledge or psychological technique. They have to find it through

Dionysian Manifesto

it when you're in danger of getting undermined by either your own neurosis or someone else's.

If you notice, for instance, that your subconscious mind is spiraling down into a sour fantasy stirred up by one of your habitual fears, you could mutter a cheerful round of "new roses, new roses, new roses."

If your allies slip into the same compulsive behavior that they tend to get stuck in whenever stress overflows, you could chant "new roses, new roses, new roses" in a tuneful, affectionate tone.

Imagine you're with a team of explorers in Antarctica. You're climbing the 2,000-foot granite spire called Rakekniven that thrusts up out of the ice in Queen Maud Land. The temperature is 10 degrees below zero. There's not a plant or animal in sight. The blinding white emptiness of the wasteland beneath you fills you with desolate reverence, alienated awe, and soaring gratitude. You are far from everything that normally gives you comfort.

Why do you feel so good?

"The moment you come to trust chaos, you see God clearly. Chaos is divine order, versus human order. Change is divine order, versus human order. When the chaos becomes safety to you, then you know you're seeing God clearly."
—Caroline Myss, *Spiritual Madness: The Necessity of Meeting God in Darkness*

"What the caterpillar calls the end of the world, the master calls a butterfly." —Chuang Tse

"Every act of conscious learning requires the willingness to suffer an injury to one's self-esteem," said psy-

---

chiatrist Thomas Szasz. "That is why young children, before they are aware of their own self-importance, learn so easily; and why older persons, especially if vain or important, cannot learn at all."

I love my regular hikes to the top of idyllic Mohawk Hill in San Anselmo. Green hills cascade in every direction. Horses graze in a nearby pasture. Red-tailed hawks soar overhead. But there is one blight: a gray metal storage tower hemmed in by barbed-wire fence.

At the climax of my ascent today, I rejoiced to find that this monstrosity had been improved. Artistic vandals had paid a visit, covering it with bright graffiti. The yellow, blue, and red designs were mostly indecipherable except for one patch that clearly said "Nowhere is Now Here."

Here's an experiment worth trying: Don't try to analyze the Great Mystery. Instead, *be* the Great Mystery. Don't go with the Flow; *be* the Flow. Don't struggle and strain to put yourself in harmony with the Creative Surge of the Divine Wow. *Be* the Creative Surge of the Divine Wow.

In her book *Strange New Species: Astonishing Discoveries of Life on Earth*, Elin Kelsey writes that although scientists have named 1.7 million species, at least 3.3 million others are still out there, as yet unidentified.

Many spiritual teachers say you're most likely to succeed at meditation if you sit quietly in a sanctuary. They believe you need to retreat from the world in order to develop compassionate objectivity about life. The 18th-

---

> A teenage girl's
> one-minute-and-17-second
> scream for joy
> after learning she has been picked
> to brush the teeth of a tiger on reality TV.
>
> A mirror in which you can see
> what everyone is thinking.
>
> Driving between the Michigan cities
> of Paw Paw and Climax,
> a tanker truck whose mudflaps
> say "Treasure your longing."
>
> A miniature golfer shooting a hole-in-one
> through the mouth of a plastic dragon
> as he recites the part of the Bhagavad Gita
> where Krishna tells Arjuna
> about the tree with its roots in the heavens
> and branches in the earth.

century Zen Buddhist teacher Hakuin Ekaku had a different view. "Meditation in the midst of activity is a billion times superior to meditation in stillness" was his motto.

Breathe more like a wild boar and less like a parakeet. Act more like an unfathomable game with no time limit and less like a puzzle with just a few last pieces missing. Shimmer more like the aurora borealis in the early morning sky and less like a furnace heating a mansion. See more like a panther sees and less like your first teacher. Write more fat messages in the mist on the glass, and speak less about the skinny facts you know by heart. Eat more magic cookies and less brain candy.

When lightning strikes a person, it's usually bad news. Not so in the case of a man from Maine named John Corson. After a whitish-blue bolt shot through his body during a thunderstorm, he testified that his health became better than it had been in a long time. "I feel lighter and 100 years younger," he marveled.

Scientists used to believe that a butterfly has no recollection of its previous life as a caterpillar. The pupa breaks down into primal goo during its metamorphosis, they said, erasing all trace of its caterpillar brain. But new research suggests that there is in fact continuity. At least some of what the caterpillar learned remains available to the butterfly.

Try this recipe for peach cobbler.
1. Hop over a neighbor's fence after midnight in August and steal five ripe peaches.
2. Coax a friend into removing the peach flesh from the pit with his or her teeth.
3. Place peaches, along with cream, honey, and graham crackers, in a blender with the top off.

The rain-washed rocks on the bank of a river that no one has made love in for almost 1,000 years.

The beautiful green light on your answering machine.

The queen bee that lays 2,000 eggs a day in spring.

A prayer that lauds the mist at dawn, the orange-pink of the painted lady butterfly's wings, the marble in Donald Trump's bathroom, and the empty pack of Marlboros in the gutter.

4. Turn on blender.
5. Lick peach cobbler off the ceiling.

Mazel tov is a Hebrew phrase meaning "good luck," but its literal translation is "may the stars be good to you." It suggests that stellar energies influence our fate.

In his book *Jewish Magic and Superstition*, Joshua Trachtenberg riffs on Judaism's ancient debate about the subject: "The stars determine human actions, but they too are creatures of G-d, established by Him to perform this special function, and therefore the influence they exert is subject to His Will. Repentance, prayer, piety, charity, good deeds . . . are the instruments by means of which man can induce G-d to alter His decrees and consequently to modify the fate that is written in the stars for him."

The omurasaki butterfly is native to East Asia. Although beautiful and graceful, it's unusually big and strong. In territorial battles over who gets the right to suck the sap of the kunugi and konara trees, it beats out all of its butterfly competitors, and is even known to chase away birds that try to horn in on its sweet treat.

Here's a communiqué from the Reverend Adtrian Cain, proprietor of the Whores of Goddess Scientists website at tinyurl.com/55jwb6:
"You are the hidden God. Wake up in the dream. Read between the lies. To question is the answer. The frontline is everywhere. There are no innocent bystanders. Truth is a three-edged sword. Practice infinite tolerance except for intolerance. Achieve strength through joy. Embrace your shadow. Change is stability. Creation never ends. Everything is verb. The way in is the way out. All things fornicate all the time. The going is the goal. Today is the day!"

17

Think with your heart
and feel with your head

WALKING UPHILL BACKWARD

It was the final day of my work on this book. I had to send the manuscript to the printer in a few hours. There was one problem: One of the pages near the end was still blank. It had originally been filled with a piece I'd rejected at the last minute, and I'd written nothing to take its place.

I decided to take a hike in the hills, hoping I might drum up an oracle on the way. Nothing interesting appeared for an hour. Then, while rambling down a trail from the top of the ridge, I spied the back of a man moving toward me. It took me a while to realize he was walking up the hill backward. As he passed me, I heard him giving himself a pep talk.

When I got home I told a friend about this scene, seeking her insight about what motivated the backward walker to engage in such an odd mode of travel. My friend said she'd done it herself. It's a psychological trick that helps make a steep ascent easier: You stay focused on how much you've already accomplished rather than being overwhelmed by the heights that are ahead of you.

Sounds pronoiac to me. Why not try it yourself?

LETTERS TO THE BEAUTY AND TRUTH LAB

We call it the Beauty and Truth Lab and not the Beauty and Truth Think Tank because we want to put our ideas to the test in the field—to apply them in unpredictable situations beyond our control and see whether they're useful to people who aren't necessarily steeped in the mystique of pronoia.

One way we've gone about that is to encourage the public to testify and ask questions about their practical experiences with pronoia. Below is a taste of the exchanges that have unfolded since we began discussing pronoiac themes on the BeautyandTruth.com website and in the weekly astrology newsletter.

Dear Beauty and Truth Lab: I'm a very analytical person, with a doctorate in nuclear physics and a high-tech job. All my training and business savvy tell me that Rob Brezsny's astrology column is superstitious mumbo jumbo, yet every time I've faced a crisis in the last 10 years, his horoscopes have provided accurate wisdom and counsel when things seemed darkest.

The same is true about the book *Pronoia.* The scientist in me knows that you Beauty and Truth Lab people are utopian nutcases. It's absolutely demented to regard the universe as friendly and to fantasize that there's some vast, invisible conspiracy of blessing-bestowers. And yet I have to confess that whenever I try the pronoiac strategies you describe, my life veers in the direction of synchronicity and delight.

On the one hand, none of this makes any sense. On the other hand, I don't care that it doesn't make any sense. Somehow I'm able to draw sustenance from something whose power I don't understand or even believe in. In any case, thank you! —Humble Genius

Dear Genius: You've described a quality that we aspire to in our efforts to cultivate pronoia: the ability to be helped by powers that are beyond our ken.

Dear Beauty and Truth Lab: I'm battling mixed emotions. On the one hand, I have frequent surges of intense compassion that make me want to build houses for poor folks. On the other hand, I'm beset by flashes of vanity that make me want to spend my money on Prada shoes and expensive jewelry rather than on trips to Third World countries to help Habitat for Humanity. Is it crazy and self-defeating to want both things? —Torn and Guilty

Dear Torn and Guilty: Try honoring both your urge to express beauty and your desire to aid your fellow humans. We have a vision of you wearing a gold tiara and Prada's Sculpted d'Orsay pumps as you wield your hammer, framing a wall for a new house in Haiti.

Dear Beauty and Truth Lab: In your book *Pronoia,* you say, 'The universe always gives us exactly what we need, exactly when we need it.' I have a different view. I often find that I disagree with what the Universe decides is best for me. But that usually turns out to be a good thing. It's fun for me to always be arguing with God! I learn a lot and generate a lot of high energy from trying to outmaneuver the divine will. What do you think about that? —Cagey Dissident

Dear Cagey: Congratulations! You are the thousandth dissident to testify that pronoia is not, in fact, the One Truth and the Only Way, thereby proving to our satisfaction that we have successfully prevented our beloved Beauty and Truth Lab from being a shill for a fundamentalist ideology. Please accept our most fantastic thanks. Your prize will be on its way to you soon!

Dear Beauty and Truth Lab: Does pronoia make you feel like you're falling in love? Not just with a person but with life itself? And can that be scary? Is it possible that you might feel a chord of gorgeous terror resound in your gut when you entertain the thought that every person and even every animal and plant and rock in the world is ganging up to make your life interesting—almost more brilliantly interesting than you can bear? Does pronoia threaten to cause all perceptions, all sensations, all interactions to verge on being orgasmic?

I've been heading in this direction lately and it's freaking me out. Can extreme happiness be dangerous to my well-being? —Butchtastic

Dear Butchtastic: First thing we'll say is that while pronoia inevitably feeds the soul, it doesn't necessarily further the agendas of the ego. The anxiety that's welling up may be the result of your old self-image clinging to the shrunken expectations it had gotten used to thinking of as essential to its identity.

The second thing is that when people invite pronoia to take over their perceptual filters, they often feel as if they're falling in love with a Scary Yet Friendly Vastness that kicks their asses until they wake up to the secret beauty they've been ignoring.

Dear Beauty and Truth Lab: The chemo treatments burned out all the math skills in my brain, which were already pretty meager. On the other hand, they awak-

ened my ability to feel perfectly at ease while in the midst of paradoxical situations that everyone else finds maddening and uncomfortable.

The chemo also made me ridiculously tolerant of people's contradictions, sometimes even their hypocrisies, and freed me to enjoy life as an entertaining movie with lots of interesting plot twists rather than as a pitched battle between everything I like and everything I don't like. I guess I could say that my cancer helped turn me into a pronoiac! —The Chaos Artist Formerly Known as Risa Kline

Dear Beauty and Truth Lab: It's my goal to become a Texas Congressman 12 years from now and a Senator 20 years from now. I have a lot of original ideas about how to make the world a better place, and I've decided that the best way to make them happen is by becoming a force in national politics. Do you have any advice on how to proceed in a pronoiac manner? —Pragmatic Idealist Who Doesn't Need to Marry a Blond, Blue-Eyed Cheerleader with Six-Pack Abs

Dear Pragmatic Idealist: First, you could obtain a piece of the Burning Bush from the monastery of St. Catherine of Alexandria on Mt. Sinai. Next, acquire a tooth or finger bone of Mary Magdalene from one of her reliquaries in southern France. Bring these sacred objects to the NorthPark Center shopping mall in Dallas during a blow-out sale. While kneeling in front of the ATM near Neiman Marcus, place a shred of the bush under your tongue as you stroke the tooth or finger bone and reverently intone Emily Dickenson's poem "Soul at the White Heat."

Dear Beauty and Truth Lab: I wanted to give you a progress report on my efforts to master the shamanic strategies of everyday pronoia.

Last night I went to Wal-Mart with a friend who was returning some tools. While he was at the service desk, I walked around the store doing some of that "tantric shopping" you once recommended—playfully lusting after various consumer goods without any intention to consummate the purchase.

I found myself lingering in the shampoo aisle. As I practiced feeling ecstatic gratitude for the obscene abundance of available choices, trying to keep the ironic element in that gratitude down to a healthy 15 percent, an unusual man who looked like an Australian Aborigine made extended eye contact with me. As he walked past he announced in a happy tone, "Your mind is empty."

I was super excited. It felt like an incredibly good omen. I found my friend to tell him. "Isn't that an insult?" he asked.

"No," I said. "The guy meant that my mind is light and clear, which is true. This is the first time in two years I've felt that my mind is free of shrunken expectations, limiting concepts, and emotional distortions."

I love it when sacred revelations happen in profane hotspots of materialism. —Dan Linton

Dear Dan: Did you know that the actual Sphinx in Egypt is gazing at a Pizza Hut, which is just a few minutes' walk away? While eating there some years ago, a founding member of the Beauty and Truth Lab saw a mystical image in the pizza she had ordered. It appeared to depict the nihilist prophet Jean-Paul Sartre being eaten by a grinning Easter Bunny.

Dear Beauty and Truth Lab: I used to give fear a free rein to crawl around my mind. But your philosophy has inspired me to fight back against that bad habit. I made a pronoiac shield for myself, and I sleep with it every night.

It's a hubcap on which I've glued protective symbols, like the fragment of a mirror I stole from the hospital where I was born, the toothbrush of an ex-lover I'm still good friends with, 20 Tamiflu pills arranged in the shape of a peace sign, a notebook page on which I wrote my best dream ever (in which my mom and dad were Mother Teresa and the Dalai Lama), a library card from Princeton University with both my name and Einstein's on it, a painting of a mutant butterfly dive-bombing a rainbow that's on fire, a bumper sticker that reads "Adrenaline is my drug of choice," and a million dollars in money I made out of cut-up photocopies of all the people I love. —Laughing at My Anxieties

Dear Laughing: If we ever market a line of pronoiac products, we hope you'll contribute a whole batch of your shields.

Dear Compassion Police: Can you tell me why my trivial prayers are often answered (please don't let the light turn red, please let there be enough milk for one cup of coffee, etc.), but never my big life-changing prayers (please send me a soul mate, please help me make money at what I love to do)? Are God's priorities screwed up, or is it me? —Dumb Luck Collector

Dear DLC: There's an old fairy tale in which two old folks are given three wishes by a magic dwarf, but impulsively waste them on the first silly whims that pop into their heads. I'll tell you what I would have told them: Proceed on the assumption that only a few of your fervent prayers will be granted. Don't use them up on pleas for convenience when you're tired, cranky, or desperate. A Tibetan proverb says, "The person who gets stuck on petty happiness will not attain great happiness."

Dear Beauty and Truth Lab: I recently borrowed a copy of *Pronoia* from my local library. I was attracted to the idea of scribbling my thoughts and ideas in the book, but I was unsure whether I should commit this act of flagrant vandalism. Then I noticed the book had been borrowed at least a half dozen times prior, but nobody had written anything in it. I was shocked. Clearly they were zombies, or else too (un-pronoiacally?) reverent to the sacred scrolls to tarnish its beauty.

So, my question is: Would you write, scribble, and doodle in a library book? —Artillery

Dear Artillery: Did you ever hear the CD called *The Bees Made Honey in the Lion's Skull*? We're listening to it right now.

Dear Beauty and Truth Lab: After reading your inspiring rants about pronoia, I've come up with my own personal set of pronoiac vows.

1. I vow to Siamese-twin together my bad-ass, no-hype, wide-eyed self with my tricky, strategic, puzzle-loving self.

2. I vow to rage on like a dancing warrior in the urban wilderness, keeping peak experiences and total slaphappy victory at the top of my priority list, while at the same time I play hide-and-seek with the dark delicious secrets that fuel my soul's lust for wicked meaning.

3. I vow to deepen the collaborative efforts of my suck-out-the-marrow-and-spit-out-the-bones craziness and my listen-carefully-to-the-flow-of-the-underground-river caginess. —Double Intense Pronoiac

Dear Double Intense: If we could give you a reward for your elegant audacity, it might be a descendant of Muchalinda, the giant cobra with seven heads that protected the Buddha as he meditated during a hailstorm.

Dear Beauty and Truth Lab: I was lying in my bed basking in a sunbeam this morning, too comfortable to get up and take my Prozac, when I thought, Hey, what if I'm not, you know, emotionally challenged? What if I'm just lazy? Maybe if I worked harder at cultivating happiness, I'd just sort of outgrow my depression—you know, render it irrelevant. Do you have an opinion about this theory? —Slothful Slack Seeker

Dear Slothful: We'd have to know more about your personal history to evaluate whether laziness is the cause of your depression. We do know this, though: Many people are extremely lax about their pursuit of happiness. Here's our question to you: What tricks would you have to play on yourself in order to get more aggressive about mastering the art of feeling really good?

Dear Beauty and Truth Lab: Soon after finding out about your concept of pronoia, I had intimate relations with a mountain in Washington. I was driving toward the Cascades when I became aware of a physical longing for Bonanza Peak, which lay ahead of me. As I got closer, I rolled down the windows and sucked in the cool air. This gave me the exact same sensation as loving someone so deeply that breathing in their breath fills me with erotic images and naughty tingles and lusty compassion. I thought you should know. —Earth Lover

Dear Earth Lover: Reading your missive transported us to the January afternoon when we interrupted a Beauty and Truth Lab meeting to go outside and swoon in erotic prayer at the foot of the persimmon tree that had shed all its leaves but blazed with a riot of bright burnt orange fruits hanging starkly from its gray-brown branches.

Dear Beauty and Truth Lab: I have to say that reading your book *Pronoia* prodded me to tune in to my manic and riotous subconscious screams and help me transform them into something quite lively and refreshing and worthy of serious amusement. How did you do it? Can you teach me how to perform the same service for myself? —Longing for Self-Mastery

Dear Future Self-Master: To get started, give yourself the secret handshake. (Middle finger to middle finger, right index finger to left pinkie, right pinkie to left thumb.) Whisper the password ("Swordfish serenade") to your image in the mirror. Then drink two ounces of home-made Red Bull out of a yellow plastic Easter egg.

Dear Beauty and Truth Lab: During your shows or workshops or rituals or whatever you call them, I have heard you refer to "learning the difference between stupid suffering and smart suffering." I had no idea what you were talking about until recently.

The truth finally hit me the morning after I climbed into bed with my sort of ex-boyfriend. He's pretty good at the sex thing, technically speaking, even though his inability to converse intelligently and honestly about emotions drives me into the ninth level of the abyss.

Afterward, as I got dressed, feeling that bizarre and oh-so-familiar disjunction of having had a physical orgasm but being utterly distraught by the lack of authentic connection between me and the person who helped incite that orgasm, I suddenly thought, "Wow! This is stupid suffering. I've done this and done this and done this to death. Stupid suffering is repeating a lesson I've already learned and been through."

In the next breath I mused, "Maybe smart suffering is what happens when I'm trying something new, taking a good risk, that will teach me tough lessons I didn't even realize I needed to learn."

Thanks to you people for planting the seed in my head, and thanks to me for finally sprouting it. —Smart Sufferer

Dear Smart Sufferer: Don't be too hard on yourself about your "stupid" suffering—especially in this case. Your stupid suffering was actually pretty smart, since it catalyzed in you an insight about avoiding stupid suffering in the future.

Dear Beauty and Truth Lab: My mom calls me fat but feeds me pork rinds. My strongest supporter is a person I want to wrap up like a mummy, shove into a canoe, and push into the middle of the lake. My exuberant imagination has taken me hostage, violating its own principles. I'm so ambivalent and indecisive about everything that even my addictive nature can't figure out what to be addicted to. I'd embrace my contradictions if I could, but they've got me surrounded like a pink-haired, cross-dressing SWAT team frothed up on multiple espressos. Can you point me in the direction of the pronoiac exit from this circus-like hell? —Crazy Crank

Dear Crazy: We detect a lot of wit and style in your meditations. Maybe that's the purpose of the limbo you're in: It's an opportunity to build your skill at being lively and feisty and smart no matter what your outer circumstances are.

Dear Beauty and Truth Lab: I was friends with the 23-year-old woman, Rachel Corrie, who was run over by an Israeli (but American-made) bulldozer in March of 2003 as she was trying to protect the home of a Palestinian doctor.

Some might say she was crazy to stand alone in front of a bulldozer and shout "Desist!" over the roar of its engine, but to me she was an example to us all of what it truly means to practice pronoia in this maddened world. She went empty-handed to show the Palestinians she met that the universe was conspiring to bless them with True Love in the form of the unconditional respect of a stranger—a stranger willing to give them everything.

Rachel and I used to work together as Mental Health Crisis Counselors in Olympia, Washington. We had a little ritual of going out for coffee, doing tarot readings for each other, and then checking out the horoscopes in Rob Brezsny's "Free Will Astrology" column.

After learning of Rachel's tragic passing, I happened to read Rob's horoscope for that week for Aries, which was her sign. It read, "It's a perfect moment to overcome your fear of revealing your raw beauty to the world." That's exactly what she did. And what a raw and beautiful courage it was. —Stician Marin Samples

Dear Flow-Meisters: If you were, like me, setting out on a 10-year project to become a beautiful truth-teller, having the simple goal of actually expressing the things that Everyone Ought to Say But Doesn't, what would you do? Other than to bother your favorite truth-tellers for advice, of course! —Aspiring Fount of Truth

Dear Aspiring Fount: One of the best ways to increase your mastery is to regularly tell yourself the truth about yourself with kick-ass kindness.

Dear Dr. Pronoia: Though I respect what you're trying to do to boost the endorphin levels of the masses, I must insist that you begin taking into account a factor you have apparently thus far ignored: Pronoia must recognize and account for the fact that 90 percent of womankind never get their orgasm experience.

It's bad enough in the Western world, where a majority of men don't even seem to know about the existence of the clitoris, let alone realize that sexual intercourse cannot induce a clitoral orgasm in a majority of women. But even worse: the millions of girls who are brutalized with clitoridectomies in the Moslem world, and other hundreds of millions of Third World women who haven't reaped the benefits of Western culture's mild gender revolution.

Here's what I say: Ecstatic female pleasure is a radical pronoiac solution to the global epidemic of male violence and ecological terrorism. I mean this literally. Sex is as much an elemental force as the winds and tides and thunderstorms. The muzzling of the female libido on a global level is the equivalent of trying to suppress the weather. And the consequences are just as weird. The tender, poignant penis has turned into the doomsday machine. Mother Earth gets wasted by the lurid hot dry "sexy" violence of the berserk cosmodemonic phallus.

But when I talk about ecstatic female pleasure, I don't mean simply some quantitative increase in clinically measurable orgasms. I'm talking about the kind of passion that generates compassion. Eros that lights up our political and ecological chakras. Sex beyond sex. The kind of reverent lust that enlightens you to how you're partly responsible for every other life on this planet, and gives you the power to feel the pain of people in distant locations with the same intensity you would feel an intimate companion's pain.

Please consider filling in this gap in your otherwise enlightened program for world liberation. —Future Author of *The Clitoral Monologues*

Dear Future Author: I agree with you. I have actually written a great deal on related subjects in one of my previous books, *The Televisionary Oracle.* It's a basic text informing the Beauty and Truth Lab's ongoing experiments. You don't have to buy it in order to read it. It's available free in its entirety online at tinyurl.com/6blklz and tinyurl.com/3c2j4x.

Dear Beauty and Truth Lab: Two months ago I met the first person with whom I am completely psychic. We fell deeply in love, of course. But it turned out that neither of us was ready or able to fulfill the potential of our connection because we are nowhere near as profoundly in love with ourselves as we are with each other. The good news is that through my love for him, I have intensified my desire to learn to love myself. The bad news is that we can't really be together as fate intended until we upgrade our self-love. Can you offer any consolation? —Lucky Yet Unlucky in Love

Dear Lucky: We appreciate your sage caution, but also offer this alternative view from actress Tallulah Bankhead: "If I had to live my life again, I'd make the same mistakes, only sooner."

Dear Beauty and Truth Lab: You must be kidding with your Pollyanna bullshit. Either that or you're lying to get gullible people to love you and give you money.

The truth is, life is not in the least bit kind. It's a brutal struggle for survival—at best. We are, sadly, animals who are stuck being conscious of our own mortality, forever stalked by death, and trying to avoid both that knowledge and the inevitable appearance of the grim reaper. Wake up and see the sickness and misery that life on this planet really is. —Your Good Cheer Makes Me Puke

Dear Puker: It's true that the Beauty and Truth Lab errs on the side of optimism, but only because so many so-called experts and leaders err on the side of cynicism. Our calling is to overcompensate for the relentless propaganda that creates the false impression that ugliness rules the world.

By the way, when we urge people to more fully appreciate the multitude of blessings they take for granted, it's not the same as advising them to pretend there's no suffering in the world.

Dear Beauty and Truth Lab: For a couple of years, I've enjoyed taking my daughters to the playground. While they hang out in the sandbox, I've often tried to make it across the monkey bars — you know, those overhead bars where you go hand over hand while your body dangles below. In hundreds of attempts, I've failed every time. My hands hurt, I feel heavy and out of shape, and I give up quickly.

But last Saturday the spell was broken. I asked the pronoiac gods to help me out. I mean I literally said a prayer. Then, as I jumped up to grab the monkey bars, the idea popped into my head that I should bend my legs instead of leaving them dangling down. I got a swinging motion going, and made it across easily. After all those months of frustration, I couldn't believe such a little change made such a big difference. Thank you, gods of pronoia! —Reporting from the Pronoiac Trenches

Dear Quick Changer: When you ask for help, you make it easier for the universal conspiracy to shower you with blessings.

Dear Beauty and Truth Lab: You asked us readers this question: "The spiritual teacher A. H. Almaas believes that a genuinely creative act is always motivated by generosity. If that's true, how do you explain all the ego-obsessed 'geniuses' who treat everyone like dirt even as they churn out their supposedly brilliant art?"

Here's my answer: Those aren't really geniuses, and what they make isn't really brilliant art! It may be popular art, and it may earn a lot of money for the fake geniuses, but it's not brilliant. The truth is, many of the richest and most famous artists are those patronized for their ability to fetishize, glamorize, and trivialize our cultural pain. You can apply the same statement to supposed geniuses who apply their talent to the pharmaceutical industry or nuclear weapons. Creative and intellectual energy applied to cruelty, domination, and meanness is always stupid.

The true geniuses recognize that cooperation is a stronger evolutionary force than competition. They know that the only appropriate application for intelligence is to find ways to make us all feel stupendously good as much as possible. —Malian

Dear Beauty and Truth Lab: Every night recently, I've dreamt I'm committing crimes like fraud, robbery, and embezzlement. (No murders, thank God!) It's getting so I'm not happy about going to sleep. I feel bad about the mayhem I'm perpetrating. (Though I did have a fun car chase once.) I don't dream about the fruits of the crimes, just the criminal activities themselves. I can't tell if I feel guilty about something or have just been watching too many episodes of *Law & Order.* —On the Lam

Dear On the Lam: Your dreams may be prodding you to come up with more meaningful, productive ways to express creative rebellion in your waking life.

Dear Beauty and Truth Lab: Lately I've been practicing an evangelical kind of pronoia. In addition to proceeding as if the universe is conspiring to help me, I'm extending that assumption to my fellow planeteers. I'm meeting people and visualizing realistically wonderful futures for them, filled with interesting opportunities or at least fertile riddles.

For instance, yesterday I saw a morose woman staring blankly into space at Starbucks as if she were the loneliest person ever born. I visualized her falling into a deeply engaging conversation with a new friend, and feeling emboldened by that encounter to be proactive about seeking out people who stimulate her. Two days ago I saw an unruly kid acting crazy at the grocery store. I visualized for him a future of uncompromising individualism creating unique approaches to old problems.

This evangelical push is a real stretch sometimes. (It's a challenge to visualize a positive future for, say, a homeless panhandler.) But I like how it makes me feel. Maybe it's no coincidence that my physical health has markedly improved recently. And it seems to be making me more highly attuned to the sometimes subtle blessings that life does bring into my vicinity—blessings I might have missed in the past. —Architect of Empathy

Dear Architect: At the Beauty and Truth Lab, we work on the hypothesis that all of us are affecting each other all the time, either by direct contact, via telepathic contagion, or through the culture we co-create. If even 25 percent of that hypothesis is true, why not be a beacon of blessings, constantly broadcasting images that promote health and well-being? People just might live up to our expectations, just as easily as they can live down to them. Plus, as you noted, it has a tonic effect on the one who acts as a beacon of blessings.

Dear Psychic Judge: I love God to death. I love Satan to death. I love fundamentalist Christians and Moslems and Jews with all my sexed heart, but I also love atheist abortion doctors and left-wing poets with dirty hair and plucked, shiny celebrities who don't give a damn about me or anyone else.

I love the Seven Angels with the Seven Plagues and the Hopi prophecy of the end of the Fourth Earth, but just as much I love the dawn of the Age of Aquarius and the transhumanists who say a new world is coming where we will blend with the machines and thereby live forever.

I love the innocent children who kill their parents for forcing them to work in sweatshops and whorehouses, and I love the sweatshop bosses and all unbelievably ugly pimps.

I love cancer, UFOs, CIA, and all contagious money too. I love suicide bombers and the sobbing rescue workers screaming "God is great!" as they pull bodies from buildings blown up by suicide bombers.

I have traveled to Uganda in my dreams and tried to contract AIDS so that my sympathy with all victims would be more perfect. I volunteer my body to feel all the pain and all the pleasure of the world at once.

I declare myself the pronoiac liberator of humanity because I am a perfect specimen of the friendly "war" between God and Satan. Don't give me any advice or help. I don't need any. Don't even think of trying to punish me for my "sins" of adoration. —Democrazy

Dear Democrazy: We are studying your communiqué, trusting that it will teach us something we don't know about pronoia. Thank you for your efflorescent manias.

Dear Beauty and Truth Lab: I was raised in a New Age, We-Are-All-One family—sort of. As spiritually inspiring as my upbringing sometimes was, it also had an annoying propensity for going awry, leading to events that resulted in me getting walked on. I was compelled to develop a hardness in the depths of my soft, born-too-late-to-be-a-true-hippie self.

Fast-forward to a few years ago. A friend attempted to take advantage of my sweetness and friendship in a way so offensive that I was inspired to come up with this loving rebuke: *Namaste, Motherfucker!* ("Namaste" is a Sanskrit word that means "I greet the god within you.") Saying those words took me by surprise. Later, as I puzzled out the deconstruction of my unexpected expostulation, I found layers and layers of meaning.

Yes, we are all connected, but I don't have to let you in all the way every time. Or, as we say on our website (Namastemofo.com), "The divine in me recognizes and honors the divine in you, but you don't have to get all up in my grill."

Everything I do comes back to finding this balance. I have in the past tended to give way too much, then had to go hibernate in order to recharge. My challenge is to find a balance and float on it, while swimming this way and that, to the furthest extremes. —Erin Saul

Dear Beauty and Truth Lab: I'm sorry to report that your bright and cheery outlook for the future did not come true. The gods have laid the cosmic smackdown upon me. My metaphorical buttocks are still smarting. I don't blame you, mind you. It is entirely my fault. My wishes were different from what the gods wished for me; I was utterly out of sync with the Grand Scheme of Things. My question now is: Being that I am in the habit of desiring pleasures that are good for my ego but bad for my soul, how do I break the habit? —Contrite Karma Chameleon

Dear Contrite: Not blaming others, but rather taking responsibility for your actions, is the best way. And you've just done that.

Dear Beauty and Truth Lab: I've wrestled all my life with fear. But lately it's been even worse than usual. My personal demons seem to be winning, or at least getting the better of the fight. I think it's related to the fact that when I caught wind of the idea of pronoia, I started working hard to lose all my illusions. Now I'm thinking maybe that was a mistake. Perhaps I needed my illusions to keep the demons at bay? —Crybaby

Dear Crybaby: Hang on. This is the toughest part of your struggle. It may seem that the illusions you dissolved were the main barriers safeguarding you from your demons. But what's more likely is that those illusions were food for your demons. Very soon now the demons will have devoured the last of their fuel and will start to starve. If they don't die off, they will at least fly away in search of other nourishment.

Dear Beauty and Truth Lab: I've always felt there was a glass wall between me and the world—a see-through barrier that kept me in my place and everything else in its place, never the twain shall meet.

But a week ago, as I was driving through the streets of my home city of Detroit, something odd happened. I seemed to reach out an inner finger and touch the inside of that glass wall I gaze through. And for the first time ever, my finger sunk into the glass, just a bit.

A little while later, I did it again, and this time my finger went right through the glass. Or rather, maybe, the glass was not there, at least momentarily. There was no longer any boundary between what I saw and where I was seeing it from.

In other words, the whole world was inside my head. Either that, or my head had just dissolved.

Let me backtrack. A few months ago, I hated my job. I despaired that my hobby would ever amount to anything. There was never enough time, and whatever time there was, I spent it trying to get done all the things I hated doing but had to do. And then I failed at the whole enterprise, and not only didn't I have time to do anything I liked, but I wasn't getting anywhere with the stuff I didn't like, either.

Life was one big miserable chore that never ended. It just bled from day to day, sucking the vitality out of everything. Even weekends. This in spite of the fact that I've never considered myself a miserable person. I always thought that being annoyed 24/7 and never having time to be happy was part of being an adult, and I tried to handle it bravely.

But then on that day last week, I put my hand through the glass—I still don't know how—and suddenly the way the morning sunlight lay on the overpass during my way to work cracked a big smile on my face, and the whole miserable commute seemed worth it.

The next day, I spent a chunk of the ride to work looking at the trees, and being thrilled that so much amazing greenery, so many unreproducible shapes and colors, could fit in my head at once. What used to be "just another tree" was now an utterly unique thing that I would never have the gift of having in my head again.

This new knack didn't go away. It started creeping into other daily moments. I'm still moving in and out of it now, many days later.

It's not that stupid things make me happy; it's that *everything* makes me happy. Taking a breath makes me happy. Hearing a human voice makes me happy. Feeling my hand rise up against gravity and sweep through the air on its own makes me happy. Yesterday this state—which I like to call "bliss fugue"—came on after I whacked my knee on the table. The pain made me happy! Happier than maybe I've ever been!

Here's the weirdest thing about the happiness: It seems completely uncaused. Not only do my flashes seem to exist in a vacuum. I would swear the feeling seems to be a *characteristic* of the vacuum. The vacuum I refer to, of course, is the sucking of myself and the world into each other that happens whenever I penetrate that glass wall between us.

I'm truly content folding laundry. I happily concentrate on every spot on my dishes. Not all the time, but more and more. And it seems the more stuff gets through the glass wall—the more the world becomes immersed in me and I in it—the less time everything takes, and the more I enjoy the "free time," 10 seconds of which suddenly seem like enough to justify having been alive all these years.

This is one of those "I might be doing something right, or I might be losing my mind" things, but I've done those before; so I'm cool with it.

But I will mention one side-effect: mild fear. Not during the state itself—I'm not sure it'd be possible to feel afraid then, though I haven't had occasion to test that—but afterward, as I connect to the realization that something is happening to me that might really muck around with my ordinary old life. (Did I say above that I was miserable with my daily life? Well, that doesn't mean I'm not attached to it.)

Already once or twice I've done this thing and had people notice, and their reaction is always alarm or distaste: "Hel-LO? Are you OK? What are you staring at? Is something wrong?" So far, this has always snapped me right out of it. I don't know how I'd react to people if this state continues to happen more frequently and for longer periods, and I get stuck dealing with people from within it. (Would I then be talking to the voices in my head, I wonder?)

I've also noticed that when the bliss fugue hits me, tears sometimes come out of my eyes due to the weirdest things: the smell of the wind, a bird that stops and looks at me, a shoelace lying on the sidewalk. I can't explain that. I'm not normally an emotional person, especially not in public.

Well, there you go. Something for your Outlaw Catalog of Happiness: the Joy of Nothing. ;) I'm going for a walk now, and see if I can do it again. —Nil Fia

Dear Beauty and Truth Lab: I got my heart transplant two and a half years ago, on October 31. For exactly 333 minutes, half of that suspicious number 666, I was dead. Not talking metaphorical broken heart here. I don't mean that a cruel lover hurt my deepest feelings. I'm saying I really lost my heart.

I was lying on an altar in a sterile white temple. How do I know? Wasn't I under deep anesthesia? I saw everything and remembered everything because I had one of those certifiable out-of-body Near-Death Experiences. My spirit was floating around the room the whole time, taking it all in. Why didn't I leave for a while and go on a shamanic vision quest to the mists of Avalon or something? Why didn't I time-travel and pay a visit to my future incarnation as a Chinese doctor? Because I was very interested in what was happening right there to my body. It was too riveting to leave.

The priests and priestesses wore white coats and brandished stainless steel knives. We were in a ritual space marked off by magic machines. The lead mumbo-jumbo technician murmured his nonsense incantations, then carved open my chest and stole my heart. Tore its arterial roots, yanked it free from my lungs, and lifted it out. I had no love muscle. Had no central throb. Was stripped of my soul's gravity.

The ceremony lasted more than five hours, and I was dead the whole time. They hooked my corpse up to a gleaming electronic pump that hijacked my blood and bled it back into me. My chest was open to the white light. My liver felt the breeze of the priests' robes whooshing around me. My brain was in limbo, a useless appendage. I watched it all from above.

Eventually they finished planting a foreign heart in the sick mess of my thorax. Sewed the stranger's love pump together with my flailing blood pipes. I was alive again. Not myself exactly any more, though. Sucked back out of the tomb through the intervention of a dead man. Resurrected backwards and inside-out. They stole my heart and gave me a different one.

Weeks later, while recuperating in my old bedroom from childhood, back in my parents' house, I finally got around to reading the book *Pronoia Is the Antidote for Paranoia.* It pissed me off. It made me laugh. Some days I threw it against the wall and some nights I used it as a pillow. I pasted before-and-after photos of myself on the cover. (My skin color's completely different now, my breasts shrunk, and I've got a caduceus tattoo built around my 10-inch chest scar.)

And after working on, I think, every single one of the pronoia therapy exercises and assignments, I decided that what I needed to do was make a pilgrimage to the Beauty and Truth Lab. I emailed Rob Brezsny to ask him where it was, and could I come visit, but he wrote back some lovely cryptic note that alas didn't reveal the actual earthly location.

I didn't give up, though. I pledged that I'd find a way to hang out with the actual Beauty and Truth Lab, or at least one of its outlets. Then I heard that a version of it was going to be at the Burning Man festival in late August. I decided to go.

After driving eight hours and pitching my tent there in the middle of the desert with 35,000 other maniacs, I went off to find the Lab. When I got there, the first thing I saw was a giant green throne with a sign that read, "Ask the Queen of the Universe a Free Question." The person on the throne was a teenage girl, maybe 17 years old, though it was hard to tell. She was wearing red silk and a headdress that looked like an Egyptian crown.

I stopped before the throne, prostrated myself, and waved my arms up and down, paying homage to the goddamn Queen of the Universe.

She spoke first: "Do you have a free question, my darling?"

"I'd really like to believe in pronoia," I said. "I'd feel much better about being alive if I could. But it just seems impossible. I'm too angry. I'm too sad. The world's too messed up. I'm too messed up."

"So your question is?" said the Queen of the Universe.

"Is there an honest way for me to get to the point where I could actually believe that the world is conspiring to shower me with blessings?"

"Think back to before you died," she began. "Picture yourself lying in your hospital bed. Your old heart was sick. They'd found a new heart to give you, and it was on its way. Remember how scared you were?"

I couldn't imagine how she knew any of this. I had never seen her before in my life. Impossible! Supernatural! But I wanted to hear what she had to reveal, so I suspended my disbelief.

"I was so fucking dumbstruck terrorized I forgot who I was," I told her.

"Terror was a gift. Forgetfulness was a gift. And your death was a gift. From Goddess to you. Treasure beyond measure. From She Who Loves You Insanely."

"I get how my new heart was a gift. Wouldn't be here if it weren't for that. But why the terror? Why the forgetfulness? Why being dead for all that time? Why were those gifts?"

"The bad news is, you've experienced the worst fear possible. The good news is, you've experienced the worst fear possible, and nothing will ever again be as bad. You've passed the extreme test. You've survived the extreme ordeal. The rest of your life you have a free pass. Full exemption. Maximum slack."

"You have a point."

"The other good news is that for the rest of your life you will be both dead and alive. You'll have one foot in this world and one on the other side of the veil."

"What's so good about that?"

"You'll be twice as smart."

"Four times as smart, I guess, if you count the fact that I'm actually two people now."

"You have your original body plus a brand new heart."

"The dead guy who gave me his heart was a Buddhist monk. So now I'm officially both a young woman and a wise man."

"The ultimate transgendered freaky prodigy. A quadruple-level genius-in-the-making."

"Should I go on a TV game show and win a million dollars with my miraculous intelligence?"

"That, or start a school for Earth-Shaking, Taboo-Breaking, Love-Erecting, Truth-Correcting, Mind-Expanding, Justice-Demanding Connoisseurs of Sublime Mutation."

There was much, much more to my encounter with the Beauty and Truth Lab sanctuary at Burning Man. I guess the account of that adventure will require my own book-length report. In the meantime, I just wanted you to know that I'm making great progress learning to "think with my heart and feel with my head," as you people recommend. Since my new heart is a foreign body, its counsel is louder and clearer than my old one used to be. I can hear its thoughts better. —Kali Miroir

A Global Array of Further Pronoiac Resources

In recent years, the doom and gloom prophets have become even more strident and brazen in blurting out their cacophony of curses. Joining them in the mad rush to shower condemnation on the entire human enterprise have been millions of emboldened everyday complainers who've also become addicted to the sick thrill of chronic rage. I'm sometimes tempted to view the growing hordes of fulminators as a black magic army flinging hexes and maledictions on everything they see.

But whenever I brush up against that fear, I stop my mind from its careening and refocus my inner eyes. Breathing out the jive and breathing in the love, I survey all the evidence I've been gathering of an antidotal force rising up.

When my book on pronoia first came out in 2005, I felt isolated in my seemingly eccentric invitation to celebrate the glory we're surrounded by, to name the thousands of ways that the universe proves its love for us, to notice all the miracles and help we receive.

But I soon realized that I was by no means a lone crank crying in the wilderness. I became aware of an ever-growing rebel crusade—swarms of pilgrims and activists and artists and creative optimists who had signed on to the conspiracy to shower blessings, devoting themselves to the work of not just saving the world but making it more beautiful and mysterious and interesting.

I wasn't under any illusion that they were suddenly arising because of my influence. Rather, my sense was that my book was just one symptom of an energy that was awakening in the whole world. I was a current in the flood.

For years, I've been compiling data about other currents in the flood, making them known through my free weekly email newsletter. A Beauty and Truth Lab researcher named Darin Wilson has created a good-looking website that is archiving these pronoaic resources. The posts are categorized and tagged, and there's built-in search. You can find the site at this URL: pronoiaresources.com.

I've also created a webpage that lists the best of the best of the resources. It's at tinyurl.com/pxooto.

Please note that when I praise all these purveyors of beauty and truth and love and justice, I do so simply because I like them. My endorsements are not advertisements, and I get no kickbacks.

Let me know about your own nominations for pronoiac resources. I'm at Truthrooster@gmail.com. Go to FreeWillAstrology.com/newsletter to sign up for my newsletter.

You can explore much more of the mounting evidence that the world is crammed with gorgeous bounty. Go here: pronoiaresources.com

INVITATION TO THE DANCE

Dear St. [Your Name Here]:

Do you want to join the conspiracy to incite pronoia? Are you ready to claim your rightful place in the top-secret global insurrection of under-cover geniuses, rebel saints, beauty and truth strategists, spiritual freedom fighters, and troublemaking do-gooders?

You're invited to create your own branch of the Beauty and Truth Lab. Borrow our ideas if you like, or make up your own. Do it in the privacy of your own bedroom or in brazen public displays; in hermetically sealed solitude or with the help of your 999 closest friends.

Don't wait for everything to be perfect before you take the leap. Start in the midst of plain old everyday chaos. What's the single most maddening riddle that has always made you feel sad or confused or ashamed? Think about putting it at the heart of your first experiment.

If you feel moved to share your research, send it along. I may publish your reports in my future updates on the growing conspiracy to commit pronoia.

Here's my contact info:

Rob Brezsny
Beauty and Truth Laboratory
P.O. Box 489
Mill Valley, CA 94942
Truthrooster@gmail.com
FreeWillAstrology.com

With love and mystery,

Rob

Your Assignment

Imagine that the whole world belongs to you. The birch trees in New Hampshire's White Mountains are yours, and so are the cirrus clouds in the western sky at dusk and the black sand on the beaches of Hawaii's Big Island. You own everything, my dear sovereign—the paintings in all the museums of the world, as well as the Internet and the wild horses and the eight-lane highways.

Please take good care of it all, OK? Be an enlightened monarch who treats your domain with reverent responsibility. And make sure you also enjoy the full measure of fun that comes with such mastery. Glide through life as if all of creation is yearning to honor and entertain you.

Author's Thanks

My gratitude is boundless. Thanks especially to these gorgeous geniuses:

Ro Loughran and Zoe Brezsny, for their smart love and uncanny gifts;

the readers of my weekly column, who endlessly and unpredictably inspire me;

my thousands of brilliant teachers, for their tireless efforts to wake me up;

the Beauty and Truth Lab and the Burning Man festival for their visions of heaven on Earth;

Jane Heaven and KPFA for inviting me to create my pagan revival shows for a radio audience;

the Mystic Beat Lounge and the other explorers who came to my Sacred Uproar shows early on, helping me launch this work;

my parents, Bob and Felice Brezsny, for giving me a pronoiac start;

Shoshana Alexander for her energetic editing and Catherine Campaigne for her stellar help and guidance on the book design;

Lynn Starner for her excellent artistry as she helped me create new images for the revised and expanded edition of the book;

the Divine Wow, also known as the Blooming HaHa and the Creator of the Universe, for the great pleasure of being alive.

About my other work

I write "Free Will Astrology," a syndicated weekly column that appears in many newspapers and on the Web at FreeWillAstrology.com.

With my band World Entertainment War, I created the CD *Give Too Much.* It's for sale at tinyurl.com/luf3m3, and some of it's available as a free download at tinyurl.com/yh5v7j. If you'd like information, go here: freewillastrology.com/cds.

The book I wrote before *Pronoia* is *The Televisionary Oracle.* It's for sale at tinyurl.com/3yfezl. You can read it free online at tinyurl.com/3c2j4x.

To listen to podcasts of me performing sections of *Pronoia,* go to tinyurl.com/lyr99n. That page also has news about my new CD, *This Is a Perfect Moment.*

I publish a free weekly newsletter that you can get via email or RSS feed. To sign up, go to FreeWillAstrology.com/newsletter.

I've created a central webpage that has all the above information as well as updates about my latest creations. It's here: tinyurl.com/oomzkz.

Notice all miracles.

18

You Are a Prolific Creator

All of creation is conspiring to shower us with blessings, exactly when we need it. Life is crazily in love with us. The universe always gives us exactly what we need, exactly when we need it. The fire and the rain are scheming to steal our impossible pain. The sun and the moon and the stars remember our real names, and our ancestors pray for us while we're dreaming. We have guardian angels and thousands of teachers, provocateurs with designs to unleash us, helpers and saviors we can't even imagine, brothers and sisters who want us to blossom. Thanks to them, from whom the blissful blessings flow, we are waking up. The winds and the tides are on our side, forever and ever, amen. The universe is brazenly and innocently in love with us.

It's Always the Beginning of the World

Even if you don't call yourself an artist, you have the potential to be a dynamic creator who is always hatching new plans, coming up with fresh ideas, and shifting your approach to everything you do as you adjust to life's ceaseless invitation to change.

It's to this part of you—the restless, inventive spirit—that I address the following: Unleash yourself! Don't be satisfied with the world the way it is; don't sit back passively and blankly complain about the dead weight of the mediocre status quo. Instead, call on your curiosity and charisma and expressiveness and lust for life as you tinker with and rebuild everything you see so that it's in greater harmony with the laws of love and more hospitable to your soul's code.

Now get to work . . . I mean get to play . . . on filling up these last 15 pages. You can continue scribbling the profundities you launched at other places in the book. You can respond to the questions and prompts you see arrayed here around the edges. You can add your own Dionysian Manifestoes, Guerrilla Oracles, and Medicine Stories. Drawings and diagrams might be as useful as words.

Whatever you choose to do, make the creative energy you release here fuel your ability to live your life as if it were a great work of art.

Fill this space with sacred graffiti, as if you were a mad wandering saint visiting a restroom at a truckstop near the border of Louisiana and Mississippi.

How many of the 13 Perfect Secrets from the Beginning of Time do you know? List them.

Name 10 of your possessions that you'd put in a time capsule to be dug up by your descendants in 500 years.

How has the smart animal within you been hobbled by the actions of the dumb animal within you?

Imagine that you get three wishes on one condition: They can't benefit you directly; they have to be wished on behalf of someone else. What would they be?

Record, muse about, and draw pictures of the dreams you have while reading this book.

Describe how you've fought off the seductive power of trendy cynicism without turning into a gullible Pollyanna.

Everywhere you go, visualize yourself being accompanied by three great warriors who're dedicated to your well-being.

If a janitor from Bangladesh were to trade places with you, he might think he'd been transported to paradise. About what aspects of your life would he be most envious or amazed?

Write a love note to the person you love best or to the person you want to love best.

What are you doing to kill the apocalypse?

Comment on this thought: Imagination is more important than knowledge and play is more interesting than belief.

Pronoia is a gnostic art. Everyone is potentially a visionary capable of revealing more of its mysteries. Write your oracles and defintions of pronoia here.

What's the single most important question you'd like to resolve before you die many years hence?

Talk about all the things you'd do with your extra time if you lived for two weeks without consuming any media at all.

"When I grow up," wrote Ramona McNabb, "I want to be a river." What impossible magnificence would YOU like to be when you grow up?

Is this a perfect moment? Why?

Tell what techniques you've discovered about feeding honey to crocodiles.

Let's all meet in the same dream while we're asleep on the night of June 21 every year. Create a narrative about where we'll meet next and what we'll do.

"Bodhisattva" is a term used by Buddhists to describe a saint who has developed spiritual equanimity and a consistent ability to act with wisdom and kindness but who nevertheless postpones his ascension into nirvana in order to help free all other beings from their suffering. In Beauty and Truth Lab parlance, a "dissident bodhisattva" believes that existing political and cultural institutions must be overthrown and replaced in order to liberate all beings from their suffering and achieve spiritual equanimity. Write a story in which you are a dissident bodhisattva.

What would you have to do in order to keep getting smarter and smarter?

What's the title of the book you'd like to write? What's the name of the rock band you'd be in? What do you call your guardian angel?

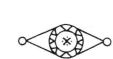

In the Beauty and Truth Lab parlance, "Über-fun" (always capitalized) refers to righteous delight that inspires you to shed limiting beliefs, thereby making you trickier, smarter, kinder, and wilder. Go out and have some Über-fun, then report back.

"When nothing's working, it might be a cosmic conspiracy to get you to experiment," said Caroline Casey. Try out this theory.

You are Ruler Of The World. What three decrees will you immediately issue to begin the mass healing?

Seventeenth-century philosopher Sir Francis Bacon said this: "There is no excellent beauty that hath not some strangeness in the proportion." Talk about how this applies to someone or something you care about.

The ancient Greek word klimax had several meanings. Here's the Beauty and Truth Lab's favorite definition: a ladder to heaven by which a dreamer's soul ascends to have an erotic tryst with a divine being who imparts fascinating secrets. Before you go to bed on the next five nights, tell your subconscious mind that you want to get yourself a klimax like that. Report your results here.

Feel free to ignore these questions and directions. You can even use whiteout or colored tape to expunge them if you want.

Bestow a blessing on a person you've considered to be beneath you or alien to you.

What invisible itch drives you crazy, and you're secretly glad it drives you crazy, and you don't want it to go away?

Each day billions of your cells expire and are replaced by others. Periodically, then, you have a completely new set of flesh and bones that retains none of the same atoms you were composed of earlier. Think back to the physical body you inhabited seven years ago today. There is nothing left of that old thing! In a sense, you have reincarnated without having to endure the inconvenience of dying. Do you realize how free this makes you? Show how much you appreciate it.

Draw the face you will have in your next incarnation.

Who and what will you pray for as you're making love?

Eckhart Tolle says this: "The most powerful starting point for any endeavor is not the question 'What do I want?', but 'What does Life (God, Consciousness) want from me? How do I serve the whole?'" Try this, then report back on how it worked.

What's the one feeling you want to feel more than any other in the next three years?

"Each person is a story that the Soul of the World wants to tell to itself," says Michael Meade. What does the Soul of the World want to say through you?

Give examples to illustrate the differences between dumb, trivial pleasure and smart, life-exalting pleasure.

ARGUMENTS WITH GOD is the only organization on the planet that specializes in the art of debating with the Creator. Our trained Prayer Warriors are standing by, ready to deliver the protests and complaints that you want to convey. Send your mad, rebellious, poignant appeals to Truthrooster@gmail.com, and we will relay them directly to the Cosmic Trickster with persuasive eloquence. Write your first draft here.

"Adytum" refers to the most sacred place within a sacred place—the inner shrine at the heart of a sublime sanctuary. Create or find a spot like that in your world. Report back.

Resolved: From now on, you will experience miracles at the rate of about one every two weeks.

A dissident wing of the Beauty and Truth Lab (the "Uproaries") defines happiness as "the state of mind that results from cultivating interesting, useful problems." See if you can make that definition work for you.

Draw or paste in your own provocative healing images.

Do something that you will remember with pride and passion until the end of your days. Report your results here.

"I can't exactly walk on the water," says Russ Crim, "but it looks like I can because I know where the rocks are hiding just beneath the surface of the water." Translate this approach into a charismatic trick that you will perform.

The Mystic Chaos Wizard Helper says: Close one eye. Tap your forehead three times with the palm of your left hand. Think of a memory in which you found something you'd lost. Lick your lips and murmur the words "Love Whisperer." Insert your middle finger in the "Delight-O-Meter" slot. Keep your finger there until the "Passion Lamp" turns on. Flash. Flash. Flash. Thank you. Now write the first thing that comes into your heart's mind.

Search for the loot from a 1967 bank robbery hidden in a metal box stashed inside a hollowed-out log in the woods.

Tell about the moment you finally realized who exactly you are—or imagine the time you'll do so in the future.

"Whether I shall turn out to be the hero of my own life, or whether that station will be held by anybody else, these pages must show." So begins Charles Dickens' novel David Copperfield. Write that sentence here and keep going.

When the spell is broken, you will be able to tap into resources you've been cut off from. When the spell is broken, you will finally notice the big, beautiful secrets that have been lying in plain sight. What is that spell? Can you break it yourself?

Make a graphic representation of your frontier.